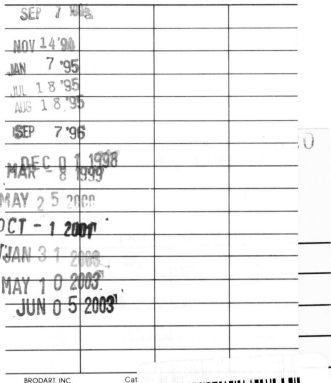

Westad, Kim.
    The God-sent child : the bitter adoption of baby
David / Kim Westad. -- Toronto : Viking, 1994.
    xi, 426 p. : ill.

07455526   ISBN:0670856207

1. Sawan, Teena. 2. Indians of North America - Alberta.
3. Interracial adoption - Alberta. 4. Adoption - Law and
legislation - Canada. 5. Cree Indians - Biography. I.
Title

3242   94OCT18   06/he   1-00635419

"For the Lord seeth not as man seeth: for man looketh on the outward appearance, but the Lord looketh on the heart."

Samuel 16:7

THE GOD-SENT CHILD

THE BITTER ADOPTION
OF BABY DAVID

❖ ❖ ❖

Kim Westad

VIKING

VIKING
Published by the Penguin Group
Penguin Books Canada Ltd, 10 Alcorn Avenue, Toronto,
Ontario, Canada M4V 3B2
Penguin Books Ltd, 27 Wrights Lane, London W8 5TZ, England
Penguin Books USA Inc., 375 Hudson Street, New York,
New York 10014, U.S.A.
Penguin Books Australia Ltd, Ringwood, Victoria, Australia
Penguin Books (NZ) Ltd, 182-190 Wairau Road, Auckland 10,
New Zealand

Penguin Books Ltd, Registered Offices: Harmondsworth,
Middlesex, England

First published, 1994

1 3 5 7 9 10 8 6 4 2

Copyright © Kim Westad

Printed and bound in Canada on acid free paper ♾

Canadian Cataloguing in Publication Data

Westad, Kim
The God-sent child
ISBN 0-670-85620-7

1. Sawan, Teena.   2. Indians of North America - Alberta.   3.
Interracial adoption - Alberta.   4. Adoption - Law and legislation -
Canada.   5. Cree Indians - Biography.   I. Title.

HV 875.7.C22A53 1994   362.7'34'097123   C94-931424-2

Copyright acknowledgments on page 426.

To my parents, Margaret and Dennis Westad

Acknowledgments

While many tasks are accomplished single-handedly, writing a book is not one of them.

Research took me to the small towns of northern Alberta. Many people in Manning, Fairview, Grimshaw, Peace River, Cadotte Lake and Little Buffalo were helpful in providing me with information and memories, as well as explaining the rhythms of life in the north. I am grateful for their time and reflections, and would like to extend personal thanks to Betty and Wolf Rautenstrauch of Grande Prairie for their generosity.

I would like to thank those in the extended social work system—foster parents and support workers—some of whom are identified in the manuscript, others who would speak only on the condition of anonymity.

Last Stand of the Lubicon Cree by John Goddard (Vancouver: Douglas & McIntyre, 1991) brings to life the history of the northern Alberta Cree, and was an enormous help in my research.

The lawyers involved—Jean Morgan, Trudi Brown, Brian Young, John Jordan and Carol Boire—offered valuable insights into an emotional and trying case. I would like to extend my appreciation to Justice Allen Melvin, for his cooperation, as well as to Lex Reynolds and Bernd Walter.

The writing of this book would not have been possible without the support of the management at the Victoria *Times-Colonist* newspaper. Sincere thanks to publisher Paul Willcocks, managing editor John Wells, and city editor Jody Paterson, who together granted a leave of absence on three days' notice without batting an eye, and were understanding of the time needed to complete such a project. My gratitude as well to the photographers at the *Times-Colonist*, whose work graces the jacket and much of the photo section.

Thanks to Paula Finch, Steve Kelliher, Dawn Leroy, Barbara Lewis, Dale Marshall, Gail Patterson, Clark Purves, Claire Tollefson, Claudia Turner and Lorna Veregin, who showed up one morning to find out they had a new part-time office mate. They were gracious in accepting something they were given absolutely no choice in, and provided a much appreciated camaraderie and link to the world beyond my computer.

I would like to offer a special thank you to Adrian Brooks, who found enthusiasm that surprised us both, and whose support and patience I counted on far more than he realizes.

To all at Penguin Books Canada—who have the ability to make their difficult jobs seem effortless—many thanks. I am particularly grateful to Jackie Kaiser, whose astute editing and guidance were essential in making this book a reality. Special thanks also to Catherine Marjoribanks, Tania Craan, Renée Cuthbertson, Lisa Hilderley and Lori Ledingham.

For the record, no one interviewed for this book was paid or promised any special treatment. I spoke with Teena Sawan and Miles Schoendorfer at many points throughout this project and interviewed Jim and Faye Tearoe extensively during the court process. I talked with Jim periodically throughout the writing of this book, but Faye's initial enthusiasm about the project waned when she learned that I could not, for reasons of journalistic integrity, pay her or allow her to view the manuscript prior to publication.

Writing about the tangled web that defines emotions and intentions is never easy. Those intrinsically human elements are not easy to comprehend at the best of times, and perhaps least of all when a child's future is at stake. I have tried to be as factual, truthful and understanding as I can about the human frailties and strengths recounted here. This document is not intended as an advocacy book for any party involved. The aim is to present a difficult situation, with its complexities intact. I hope readers can find in it whatever answers they deem important.

Introduction

With a child on one hip and a hastily packed overnight bag over her shoulder, the harried woman looked much like any other mom hurrying to catch the ferry to Vancouver for the weekend. But Faye Tearoe was running for another reason: she felt certain a police cruiser would speed into the crowded Vancouver Island ferry terminal at any moment, its siren blaring, knowing she had something the law said didn't belong to her.

That something was David James Tearoe, a handsome child with a mischievous grin who eagerly pointed to the seagulls flying overhead and greeted strangers with a wave. Faye prayed passersby wouldn't recognize them from the nightly newscasts. She avoided eye contact as she quickly walked along the crowded passageway to the ferry, and stopped only once to stare back through the swarm of people saying goodbye to loved ones. What she saw broke her heart. Her husband stood in the warm afternoon sun, staring at the water, one hand jammed in the pocket of his pants pressed that morning. The other arm held their daughter tightly to his side. She could just make out Heidi's hands, clutching Jim's jacket. It might be the last she saw of her family.

Faye couldn't bear any more. She quickly walked the last few steps on board and found a relatively quiet spot on the tourist-laden ferry. The nineteen-month-old child in her arms gradually fell asleep, part of a cookie giraffe mashed in his chubby hand.

At 3:00 p.m., when she was supposed to be handing the child she had raised since he was two months old to his birth-mother, Faye stared out at the Gulf Islands as the boat lazily drifted past. As of 3:01 p.m., she was in contravention of a B.C. Supreme Court order.

"Lord, what have you done?" Faye Tearoe questioned over and over again in her mind. The child she had prayed fourteen years to her God for breathed heavily against her chest. "I have given you everything. How can you take my precious son?"

At the same moment, outside the Tearoes' yellow, vinyl-sided split-level home, another woman, almost three decades younger, was waiting. There was no sign of the Tearoes. Where were they? Teena Sawan again pressed the doorbell of their immaculately kept home, but only the barking of their cocker spaniel in the back yard answered. A small plaque screwed into the door announced, "In all thy ways acknowledge Him, and He will lead thy path."

The tiny Cree woman was waiting for her son, Jordan Michael Sawan, to be returned to her. The court battles couldn't be undone by something as simple as the Tearoes just not showing up, thought the worried woman, who barely looked old enough to have a driver's licence, let alone a child.

The dog soon became used to the strangers in the front yard and went back to sleep by the neatly stacked woodpile. Country music wafted out the open balcony door of a neighbour's home.

By 5:00 p.m., there was still no sign of the Tearoes. They were two hours late.

It was time to call the police.

The disparate universes of Jim and Faye Tearoe and Teena Sawan are the last anyone would expect to collide. They are as different as race, culture, economics, age and life experience could conceivably make them. Yet the lives of a middle-aged, middle-class, devoutly religious white couple are inextricably linked to that of a single, twenty-year-old native woman struggling to improve a life burdened with problems of alcohol, abuse and poor education. It is a collision that drove an utterly law-abiding Christian couple to break the law, and inspired a young Cree woman to change her life. Their battle was over a child, their battleground the courts, the press and public perception.

Justice—legal, social and moral—is a high-wire balancing act. Decisions are made based on a one-dimensional face put forward for public consumption, and so it was with the Tearoe-Sawan case.

The case focused a public spotlight on the politics of adoption, particularly one that cuts across economics and culture. It began as intensely personal for each. But by the end, nine months later, the Tearoes and Teena Sawan were each symbols of changing social times and issues that cut to the core.

Into the emotional cauldron of adoption was hurled the question of aboriginal rights. Thousands of native babies were exported to white families in Manitoba twenty years ago, many of whom grew up to have no sense of who they were. Would this happen to little David, as he grew up in a white, middle-class world defined by Jim and Faye Tearoe? Would the little boy suffer the identity problems many adoptive children do, wondering why his birth-mother gave him away? Or would he be glad he had an upbringing in a city with all of the advantages and security life in the middle class provides?

But the question everyone wanted the quick, easy answer to was: who *should* get the child? The wording of the question is loaded, as if one must have something in order to be deserving of a baby.

Chapter One

❖❖ ❖❖ ❖❖

G OD played matchmaker for Jim and Faye Tearoe. Wearing bathing suits with sweatshirts pulled overtop to ward off the brisk November night air, the two wondered if they were crazy as they jumped out of the car and ran towards the water. The beach was smooth and cool on their bare feet and plumes of sand scattered behind them as they raced across it.

Laughing and not quite believing what they were about to do, Jim Tearoe and Faye Broughton headed straight towards the still grey water. The evening tide on November 17, 1978, was a long way out. Crowded with tourists in the summer-time, the White Rock beach was deserted at ten o'clock on a near-winter night. A thick fog was rolling in. It was far from ideal as a spot for a baptism.

Jim and Faye had spent the evening at the home of David DiCamilis, who, just weeks before, had been baptized. Throughout dinner, David had regaled them with talk of how wonderful it was to be saved. By the end of dinner, the two looked at each other across the table. "Why not?" they ventured.

David was adamant the baptism take place that night, and

Faye and Jim sat on the couch as he called several pastors, trying unsuccessfully to find someone available on a half-hour's notice on a Saturday evening. Faye and Jim exchanged glances. Well, it would either happen that night or it wouldn't, and they were content to let it be. But David wasn't put off by the lack of a pastor. They could do it themselves. The beach was just a short drive away. He gathered up bathing suits and they were off.

Jim Tearoe is the eldest of four sons in a close-knit family. He grew up in a comfortable home in West Vancouver, British Columbia, where his building contractor father, Clifford, built many of the area supermarkets, and his mother, Connie, was a kindergarten teacher. With four children in eight years, the Tearoes were not wealthy by any means, but they worked hard to provide a pleasant lifestyle for their family. Like his brothers, Jim had a morning paper route, and the frugality he learned as a child is still with him today.

After graduating from high school, Jim worked for a while at Williams Colour, a camera and photo-finishing shop in Vancouver, where he repaired cameras, took studio photographs and printed and developed pictures. Jim had a passion for photography and threw himself into his job with great determination. He liked the methodical process, where certain steps produced certain results, and he could spend hours in the dark-room. After a few years, however, Jim decided to make photography a hobby and enrolled in the B.C. Institute of Technology's forestry program. Forestry represented an ideal way to mix his love of the outdoors with work. Jim had found his niche.

By the time Jim was in his mid-twenties, he was looking forward to marrying and starting a family. He had known from a young age that children were definitely something he wanted in his life. But just as he was leaving Vancouver for a job in the B.C. interior, he suffered one of life's big disappointments: his relationship with a woman with whom he had shared his deep desire for a family—specifically for a boy he had already named David James Tearoe—had come to an end.

He left the city in 1973 with no romantic strings, but he kept in touch with several friends. One of those was Faye Merelie Broughton, whom he had first met in 1965 as a fellow employee at Williams Colour.

"I remember thinking that whoever got Jim was getting a bargain," Faye recollects. "I never thought it would be me!"

Faye has large, deep-set eyes and a small, bow-shaped mouth. Her eyebrows are slightly downturned, giving her a perpetually worried look. But her manner is anything but gloomy. She was personable and chatty to everyone in the store, her conversation peppered with "Oh my goodness!" and accompanied by an easy laugh. Indeed, she sometimes gave the impression of vivacious ditziness. "Charming and kind of kooky," remembered one customer fondly.

She and Jim hit it off from the start. Thin, and wiry as a whippet, Jim had a broad face and well-defined features. He seemed like a solid, straight-ahead guy who, unlike most men, loved to talk. He was quite extroverted and became as excited as a child when talking about seemingly ordinary things that intrigued him. Faye thought of herself as a chatterer, and long before they became romantically involved, she felt she had met her match in Jim.

The duo's friendship continued via letter when Jim left in 1973 for a mountain-climbing trip, followed by work in the B.C. interior. Possessed of an independent spirit, Faye too moved on, heading to the northern B.C. town of Cassiar, near the Yukon border. She worked two jobs, at an office in the daytime and at a lab at night, saving money for a down payment on a house in the Vancouver suburb of Surrey. "I had big thoughts," she says now, laughing.

A few months after moving north, a freak accident placed Faye in the hospital for a month and tested her mettle for considerably longer. She was rooming on the top floor of a women's dormitory and one night fell ten feet from a trap door, left open for the house cat, to the cement floor below. Her tailbone was shattered and she suffered a concussion. After a month, Faye thought she had fully recovered. But a further two months later, she began experiencing debilitating headaches. The twenty-nine-year-old woman moved back in with her parents in Surrey. The cause of the pain was a mystery, until she went to a bone specialist who told her she had decaying disks in the middle of her back. "He said he'd have to operate and take bones from my legs and put them in the back of my neck, and I'd never walk again. It was the end of the world."

Though the headaches continued, Faye refused the operation and spent much of her time flat on her back. The pain left her bedridden in a dark room. Her life seemed over. One afternoon, a nun came to visit her. "She was a dear little old lady and she prayed for me, that I would be healed. I thought, 'That's nice' and went back to bed." The next morning, the headache hit again. "I cried and said, 'Oh, God, if you're real, please heal me.'"

The prayer was followed by a strange sensation. Faye sat on the edge of her bed, feet dangling to the floor. It was as though hot oil was pouring through her body, from the top of her head to her tailbone. Within weeks, she was out of bed and back to normal.

Meanwhile, in the B.C. interior, Jim was finding himself drawn to the ardent ways of the Pentecostal Church. "It felt meaningful. They were more serious. I read the Bible and my eyes were opened to a lot of things." In mid-1978, Jim talked Faye into attending a Christian businessmen's convention in Edmonton. There, he joined a group of people who went forward to have their ills healed. Jim had never been able to see the colour red. If placed directly in front of him, and very bright, he could distinguish it, but as soon as it was more than an arm's length away, it faded to an indistinct grey. At the front of the packed auditorium, Jim kneeled with his glasses by his side, his hands pressed tightly over his eyes. The prayer swelled around him, and when he removed his palms, all was blurry. He made his way back to his seat beside Faye and a miracle happened. "I looked at this great big enormous room with a big banner across the front, saying, 'His banner over us is love.' It was in bright-red letters."

Faye and Jim had both been inching towards a full-fledged commitment to the Lord, and needed only their friend David's push to make it. But as they stood numbed to their calves in the water off the White Rock beach, the duo fought back a healthy dose of scepticism. David had told them the Holy Spirit might make His presence known in their body by speaking in tongues during the baptism. "I didn't really know much about it, and I was a little afraid of it, too," recalled Jim of that November night. "I didn't quite know exactly what it was, if it was some kind of spiritual kind of thing that was 'way out.' I didn't know if it was something that was really Christian or if it was something that was not."

Faye's teeth chattered as the trio moved up to their thighs in the gently lapping water. This was crazy. She grabbed Jim's hand, looked skyward and said, "'Lord, if you're in this, I need to know that. Let us know by warming us up because I'm sooooo cold.' And it was as if hot water poured over us! We warmed up like summertime."

That prompted Jim and Faye to dunk under the water, and what happened as they came up removed any doubts they might have had about the Lord's power. As they rose, water streaming from their faces, they were both speaking in tongues. "I was like a brand new person," recalls Faye, her voice hushed at the memory.

Jim was more surprised than anyone, perhaps because his mind tended to favour mathematics and certainties. "It was THE turning point in my life," he said.

It was the beginning of what Jim and Faye call their "walk with the Lord," and also the beginning of romantic feelings for one another. Religion and love combined. Faye recalls looking at Jim afterwards and realizing that the Lord wanted them to marry.

Jim recalls their shift from friendship to romance in a more pragmatic manner, commenting on shared interests in photography and the outdoors more than on their spiritual discovery. He liked Faye's "country girl" background. Faye was born in Thunder Bay, Ontario, but had moved west at the age of twelve when her parents bought a hotel and ranch near

Merritt. It was something of a dude ranch, where city people came to see what B.C.'s version of the west was like. "We were sharing our faith together. We realized that each of us was a good option for the other," Jim says. Marriage seemed the next logical step, and they set the date.

But before they married, there was something Faye had to tell Jim. She could not have children.

"You have no idea what it is like to be a born mother and not be able to bear children. I'm barren. The word of God says that the Lord will cause a barren woman to keep house and be joyful of her children. Why couldn't I have children? Because the Lord promised me that. So, did the Lord fail me in that area? No. He gave me something special.... If you've ever been a mother that doesn't have children, you always feel there's something missing. You always feel you missed out. I've cried buckets over that. The Lord stores them up in a bottle. He fulfils our greatest desires. He says, 'Delight thyself in the Lord. Trust also in Him and He will bring it to pass.' So the Lord will bring it to pass."

Faye's admission caused Jim to have second thoughts about their future. "I wanted to have children.... I had a lot of thinking to do. How I was going to handle that, and whether I wanted to accept that as part of my potential future. Eventually, I decided that I loved Faye and it was more important to be with her than worry about whether children came or not."

Jim's reaction made Faye love him all the more. But she still tried to remedy the infertility in a series of operations, all to no avail. They married as planned on June 14, 1980, in a small ceremony in Prince George. Faye was thirty-six, Jim thirty-five.

The doctors had failed Faye Tearoe, but the Lord wouldn't. Every prayer she and Jim said included a blessing for Anne Merelie Tearoe and David James Tearoe, the children they knew the Lord would some day provide. Each night as they said their dinner prayer, Faye and Jim reached to the empty chairs on each side of them. Their children would one day fill these places. Jim quoted from Psalm 128: "Happy are all who fear the Lord, who live according to his will. You shall eat the fruit of your own labours, you shall be happy and you shall prosper. Your wife shall be like a fruitful vine in the heart of your house; your sons shall be like olive-shoots round about your table. This is the blessing in store for the man who fears the Lord."

Faye explains that what Christians do is keep giving thanks to the Lord for something. "We just said, 'We're gonna thank the Lord for our children. He'll give us children.'"

Their prayers became very detailed, right down to the physical description for a girl. "We understand we're supposed to pray specifically. So we said, 'What do we want? A boy or a girl first?' We decided we wanted our little girl. We wanted her to be tall, and we wanted her to have the Broughton eyes," recalled Faye.

The Tearoes had applied to adopt a child through the B.C. Ministry of Social Services as soon as they were married. A social worker came to their home and did a home-study in advance. After their chat, Faye saw her scrawl, "THESE PEO-PLE ARE VERY RELIGIOUS" across the bottom of the file and underline it. Faye cried after she left. "We've either blown it or the Lord's on our side."

In June 1984, the Tearoes were notified that a baby girl was available for adoption. She had been born to a single mother in Quesnel, a logging and pulp mill town. The birth mother had requested a religious adoptive family. Faye and Jim were so excited that they drove to Quesnel a day early and slept in the parking lot of the hospital. The sound of the rushing Fraser River to the west of the hospital accompanied the thankful prayers said that morning before they walked through the hospital doors to receive their daughter and the realization of their dreams.

The little girl exceeded their prayers. "We did not pray for beauty, but she was beautiful too," said Faye, who was instantly smitten.

The only thing wrong was the name. For years, they had prayed for Anne Merelie, but it didn't seem quite right when they looked into their baby's eyes. Jim had a vision of the name Heidi and it seemed to fit; the little girl's mother was of German descent, according to the Social Services file. But they needed a sign from the Lord that this was the right name. "I woke up in the middle of the night and I said, 'Lord, are you there? I need a name!'" Faye recalled.

At seven o'clock the next morning, a friend telephoned and said breathlessly that the Lord had woken her in the night and said Faye and Jim's baby was to be named Heidi Marie. Faye received a second call saying the same thing. "Okay Lord," said Faye, as she stood doing the dishes a few mornings later. "You'll have to confirm this."

A baby shower was held the next night, and in the middle of it, Jim turned to his wife, a wide smile on his face. "Honey, the Lord just told me the name is to be Heidi Marie!"

Their wishes confirmed, the baby girl was named Heidi Marie.

In 1985, the Tearoes were living in Port McNeill, a small town on Vancouver Island. Their prayers for a baby son had not ended, even though they had been told by B.C. Social Services that they could not adopt through the government. Although they had the major prerequisite called for in the B.C. Adoption Act, namely that they were married, they were disqualified by something they had no control over— age. Faye was forty-one and Jim forty. They were too old. The cut-off age for adopting an infant was forty.

Well, that's just fine, Faye thought, pushing away feelings of anger at a regulation she thought ridiculous. She redoubled her prayers to the Lord, and backed those up by putting the word out in their tight church network. Pastors often knew of young women in trouble. Their unshakeable faith that a child would come their way surprised some, and caused a few raised eyebrows.

Little Heidi joined in the nightly prayers as soon as she could speak. The name David was one of the first words she learned, and she too asked the Lord for David James Tearoe.

The Tearoes thought their prayer had been answered one

afternoon when they received a telephone call from a church contact about a baby boy in Vancouver. But just as they were heading out the door to go pick up the infant, they received another call. The birth-mother had changed her mind.

In 1988, the Tearoes moved from Port McNeill to Victoria, where they bought, with the help of Faye's parents, a newly built house in Colwood, a suburb west of the city. Ever since then, Jim has worked in the valuation branch of the ministry of forests, where he has an office job looking after the waste left behind after logging is completed on crown land. Jim's office, on the crowded second floor of a downtown Victoria building, is one of a row of cubicles. The bulletin boards beside his computer are adorned with outdoor scenes, each with an inspirational biblical quotation. Pictures of Faye and Heidi are on the bookshelf, which is crowded with technical textbooks, and an anti-abortion pin asking "What freedom of choice do the unborn have?" is jammed beside a pile of memos. Jim is thought of as pleasant and a good worker in his office—he is a stickler for detail—but he eats his packed lunch alone at his desk most days, reading his well-thumbed Bible, often telephoning Faye at home with a verse of scripture he finds particularly inspiring or interesting.

The Tearoes believe that if you pray long and hard enough for something, the Lord will provide. "Everything I've ever desired or prayed for, I've got," Faye said. "I guess I'm like a dog with a bone. I won't give up. I could have given up. I had major surgery to see what they could do so I could have children. I lost all my strength. I'm a farm girl. I'm used to being strong. Then I realized I should have just trusted the Lord instead of doing my own thing. So I just continued to thank the Lord for our children.... First you ask the Lord if you can have such and such, and then, after you've asked him, you thank him. He's gonna do a miracle to do this thing you've asked him to do. He's not gonna leave you hanging dry."

It was early 1992, and Jim and Faye Tearoe's twelve years of prayer were about to be answered.

Chapter 2

Prairie sunshine beat down on the Alberta landscape, slowly unthawing after months of winter's siege. The harsh light shone through the window of Teena's second-floor bedroom, warming her cheek and highlighting the pamphlets scattered across the blue chenille bedspread.

The opened booklets covered a book of *Calvin and Hobbes* cartoons. Teena would much rather have been reading it. Leaning against the wall, the pillow bunched up behind her, the teenager felt sick, unsure whether it was nerves, the remnants of a particularly wicked and long-lasting hangover, or morning sickness inflicting itself in the mid-afternoon. Whatever its source, she could have done without it. Through the wall she could hear the radio in the next bedroom, this month occupied by Tracy, a fourteen-year-old girl who kept running away from her foster parents. Teena reached a thin arm over and tuned her radio to the same station so she could hear the song—a cover by one of her favourite singers of Otis Redding's "Sittin' on the Dock of the Bay." Yeah, that would be a great place to be. Any place but right here, right now.

The group home workers had borrowed a book on pregnancy from the Grimshaw library for her. It showed a picture of a blonde woman with her hand resting on her swollen belly, smiling dreamily off into the distance. It was a pretty, well-thumbed book. Teena held it close to her face and squinted at the picture to see if a wedding ring graced the woman's finger. She imagined it did. That's what she had always planned for herself, whenever she thought about the future. First "a good relationship." Then marriage at about twenty-two and a baby at age twenty-three. It had all seemed a long way away. Instead, she was unmarried and pregnant at seventeen, and going to have a baby at eighteen—if she had the baby.

When she'd got to the group home that spring, she'd confided in a couple of friends that she had skipped her period, and the rumour that she had been "knocked up" spread quickly through the group home circuit. Her pregnancy had been verified just the day before, after a trip to the public health clinic. Accompanied by one of the group home workers, Teena had slumped in an orange plastic chair, waiting for her name to be called. Next to her sat a woman whose face was vaguely familiar from junior high school. Teena had stared at the linoleum and opened a magazine on her lap to cover the still-warm urine sample the doctor was to test.

Although Teena had been 99 percent sure she was pregnant, the doctor's confirmation left her dizzy. She didn't want it to be true. She wasn't ready. And she had been drinking heavily for months, including the night before the pregnancy test.

"This cannot be happening," she recited internally, matching each word with a footstep as she walked back to the home. Teena stayed in her bedroom the remainder of the afternoon and evening, not coming out until the next day, when she was silently handed the books on pregnancy and the abortion pamphlets. She retreated to her room.

Teena lay still on her bed in the sun that spring afternoon in 1991, her fingers splayed across her belly. Twenty-four hours ago, it had been rumour. Now, beneath the jeans and thin layer of flesh was a baby the size of a thumb. In a little over six months, it would be born, as big as a yellow-haired doll she remembered playing with years ago, when she lived with her mother. She would have a son or daughter by Christmas.

The book might show the different stages a pregnant mother could expect to go through, but the pamphlets offered a different story. They talked about abortion—something Teena had never thought she would consider. She loved kids and had always hoped to have them, although not exactly like this. But the more she looked at the drawings of perfectly formed creatures in the womb, the more she realized she could never abort her baby. She'd have to go through with the pregnancy, and figure out what to do along the way. It was a decision that came not from her mind really, but from somewhere else—her heart, she guessed. Whatever was inside her was already a person. That was it.

If only her mother were still alive. She would have been able to help, to tell Teena what to expect, to tell her she was doing the right thing. She wondered how her mom had felt when she was pregnant. Had she been happy or afraid or both or neither? Six children, and she'd still been there for Teena—most of the time, anyway. Memories of being with her mother gave the teenager comfort. It was the only time she could remember feeling completely loved. She curled up on the bed, the radio patter in her ears, and dreamed of her mother, Maryann Clara Sawan, a full-blooded Cree, the woman Teena cried for then and dreams of today.

Maryann Sawan lived, off and on, in several of the small farming and forestry towns dusted across northern Alberta. But she came from the native communities of Cadotte Lake and Little Buffalo. Numerous native settlements are clustered on the shores of tiny lakes dotting the northern Alberta interior, their names culled from the buffalo and fish that were once plentiful in the region.

In her teens, Maryann ricocheted between the native communities and the predominantly white settlements of Manning, Grimshaw, Fairview and Peace River. The several-hour trip west into the towns on a muddy, narrow road was a journey into another galaxy: most houses had running water and indoor toilets, and there were bars, a liquor store and shops to look in. It seemed almost luxurious compared to the relative isolation and lack of amenities at Cadotte Lake and Little Buffalo.

But most of the significant events in Maryann's life continued to centre around her home and family in the native communities. She returned for the birth of several of her children, including her first in 1967. Maryann was seventeen years old when Christine Amanda was born. The four-pound infant was delivered by Maryann's mother, Annie, with the help of Annie's older sister, Josephine.

Annie Sawan, who spoke only Cree, provided much of the care for the infant Christine while Maryann continued her nomadic existence. Her life straddled two cultures. She conversed in Cree to her family and to some of the native friends she made in Manning; she spoke English with a heavy Cree accent to the white people she met, usually at the small-town parties and bars she attended. Like her mother, Annie, Maryann was a binge drinker, and her usual loving nature evaporated when she was drunk.

Maryann had a second baby, Colin Noah, thirteen months after giving birth to Christine, and in 1973 she was pregnant with her third child. She again returned to Cadotte Lake. On May 28, in her mother's eighteen-by-twenty-foot cabin, kitty-corner to a postcard-pretty brown-steepled Catholic church and across the road from a small store originally built by Oblate priests, Maryann gave birth to Cecilia Augustine. Annie delivered the baby, her second granddaughter. Although Maryann drank heavily throughout the pregnancy, Cecilia—promptly nicknamed Teena by her mother—appeared strong and healthy. The baby inherited her mother's light complexion, the colour of clear tea. A mop of glossy, brown, poker-straight hair shot straight up from her head.

On Teena's birth certificate, a firm pen line is stroked through the section on father; no information, not even the name is provided. Maryann had little involvement with the fathers of any of her first four children. It would be seventeen years before Teena finally met the man who identified himself as her father, Albert John Auger, a tall, quiet man from the Big Stone Cree, a central Alberta band.

Annie was pleased at having another grandchild, and not at all dismayed that there was no man around to help with the new baby. She had not been married to Maryann's father, either, and she thought that she had made out okay. She had received help from her large extended family, spread throughout the Lesser Slave interior. Teena would take her mother's last name, Sawan, as Maryann and all her children had before her.

As a young child, Teena was with her mother and siblings, and their life was split between Manning, where they more or less lived, and Little Buffalo and Cadotte Lake. Maryann Sawan made the pilgrimage to the native communities every couple of weeks, with her young children piled in the front of the pick-up borrowed from Bluford Gardiner, a Metis some thirty years her senior. Maryann was back and forth so often—visiting with aunts and uncles so numerous Teena has difficulty now remembering all their names and exactly how they are related to her—that the mother tongue of her children was Cree.

Teena remembers sitting on her mother's lap and hearing stories in Cree about the tea dance, a spring and fall tradition that sounded magical to the little girl. Maryann told her of the daylight hours draping poles with canvas and moose hides to make a tenthouse that looked like several teepees joined together. At sundown, the community gathered for a festivity that lasted until sunrise. Offerings were given to past generations, and the spirit of those gone was called upon to guide the living. As the sun set, four fires—one for each season—were lit inside. Singing, praying, feasting and dancing around the glowing fires filled the night.

But for Teena, those happy memories of close times with her mother are interspersed with memories of fear and confusion. There were times when the young girl came home after an afternoon of play with cousins to find her mother and grandmother loud and angry, for no apparent reason. When this happened at Little Buffalo, Teena stayed outside, seeking refuge in the scrubby brush. Through the cabin window she could see the women, silhouetted at the kitchen table. Sometimes their heads were thrown back and they laughed; other times there was just shouting and the sound of bottles clinking.

The same thing sometimes happened in Manning. Weeks or months of relative stability were interrupted by Maryann's drinking bouts. It was at "the zoo," a faded hotel bar with low ceilings and tabletops covered in terry cloth, the lighting focused over the green felt of the pool tables in the centre of the room, that Maryann often spent time. Townspeople remember young Teena sitting in the smoky lobby of the two-storey hotel, built at the edge of the Mackenzie Highway in hopes of attracting drivers too tired to make it to the next spot to sleep. The little girl waited patiently for her mother to come out of the bar. Her short hair was combed flat, and she wore pants with a bright pattern of Popeye faces on them—Teena's favourite article of clothing at the time.

Maryann had formed a steady relationship with Bluford Gardiner, a pensioner and trapper whose figure was easy to spot around town, with his stilted gait, braying laugh and a cowboy hat chronically roosting on his head. When they were in Manning Maryann and her kids lived with Bluford in a bungalow a few houses off the highway. He eventually fathered two of Maryann's children, Grace and Peter, and Teena called him Dad, though she knew he wasn't really her father. For weeks at time, and sometimes months, Maryann was dry, living with Bluford, tending house and looking after her kids. Maryann is remembered by Manning townspeople as a big-hearted woman who loved her kids, but also loved drinking. "I liked her when she was sober," is a common refrain in Manning, a small town with a vivid memory.

"I remember we were taken care of really good," says Teena, whose faith in her mother is complete and unwavering. "She made sure we had clean clothes and food. I remember I used to think my mom was everything to me. People tell me that I did everything with her, that wherever she went, I went. 'You always helped your mom do the dishes, or sweep the floor,' they say, and that makes me feel really good. I remember going on walks to the park with her. We used to do a lot of things together and I really enjoyed it. At Christmas and our birthdays, we got presents. She tried to make us as happy as she could. If she had the money, she would try to buy us the things we wanted."

But some nights, Teena woke to loud music and voices blaring, and lay in bed praying everyone would leave. When she went out to the living room, Maryann didn't seem to want her there. Confused, Teena returned to her bedroom and cried. "It scared me sometimes because I didn't know if she would be happy or sad, or why she was mad. It just seemed like she didn't want us around when she drank. We'd be pushed to the side. There would be times when there wasn't anyone in the house sober enough to look after us. I just didn't want Mom to drink because then she would get upset."

Sometimes Maryann went on a tear and was gone for days at a time, ending up in a neighbouring small town. The children were left with Bluford, who, at almost sixty-five, often found several young children too much to handle.

The Alberta Department of Family and Social Services stepped in when Teena was about four years old. Maryann needed a break, she had too many kids to take care of, the social workers gently told the kids. The older children, Christine, Colin and Teena, were packed up and driven back to Little Buffalo, where their grandmother and aunt looked after them full-time. John and Grace stayed with Maryann in Manning. Things would get better, the social worker said, after Maryann had some time. While sad to leave her mother, Teena was content to be back at Cadotte Lake and Little Buffalo, living with relatives and playing with her cousins. Then, after a couple of months, their mother showed up. "I remember one day after school this truck pulling up to the house and I went running because I thought it was my mom and here it was! She took us home that day."

The family tried trial weekend reconciliations, but they gradually petered. Soon John was placed in foster care, and Maryann drove to Little Buffalo with Grace, a toddler, and Peter, a newborn, to leave her two youngest children with relatives as well.

The flip-flopping back and forth between their mother and relatives—usually Annie Sawan—continued. Christine, who is now twenty-six, remembers Social Services being concerned about the kids all staying with their grandmother, who could not read or write and communicated in Cree. She also drank a lot. What if the kids had to go to the hospital, or to a doctor? How would Annie Sawan be able to deal with it, knowing little English? A neighbour had also expressed concern about Annie's care of the rambunctious children.

It was then, when Teena was about five years old, that a series of several short placements in foster homes, all of them parented by white couples, began. Sometimes Teena was with one or two of her siblings, sometimes not. One of the first foster homes was in Dixonville, a hamlet just outside Manning, where Teena was registered in kindergarten. Teena's teacher grew frustrated with her new pupil when she couldn't understand the little girl's mix of Cree and heavily accented English. The same happened at the first foster homes, where Teena remembers being taught her A-B-Cs in English. She soon forgot her native tongue.

The series of short-term foster placements took its toll on Teena and her siblings. "As soon as we were put in a foster home, we'd have to be transferred again. We figured that no one cared for us because we were always being thrown back and forth," Christine says now, thinking back on what are for her difficult memories. The feeling of abandonment is obvious in her voice, which is thick and ragged, with a slight Cree accent. "We were bounced back and forth. All of us kids were separated from being a family. We knew we had brothers and sisters, but we didn't know exactly where they were. All we wanted was for us kids to grow up together in one home and be as a family. We didn't have our mother and fathers around, so we wanted each other to be our family."

Finally, when Teena was about eight, she was transferred to a home in Fairview, to the same home that cared for Christine and Colin, in an effort by long-time social worker Rick Biggs, a gentle giant of a man, to bring the siblings together. The three Sawan children joined the family of Ted and Fern Gardecki, a couple then in their late twenties who also had two children of their own, Ben and Ryan, one and two years younger than Teena.

It was Teena's first taste of security and belonging since leaving her mother, some four years earlier. Teena attached herself to the Gardeckis, a loving couple with Christian beliefs practised at the Seventh Day Adventist Church. They welcomed the foster children into their home as family members. Ted Gardecki was an assistant administrator with the Fairview Hospital, while Fern, a round-faced woman with a quick laugh and yards of patience, ran a home bake shop out of their home, a few miles north of the town of Fairview.

Teena was enrolled in grade two at Oliver Elementary School, where she was a favourite in gym class, often the most cruel testing ground for new kids. But her love of activity didn't translate to neatness.

"You gotta look after yourself," Christine would tell Teena, as she held her little sister still between her knees methodically brushing her thick hair and securing it at the sides with butterfly-shaped barrettes. "You have to stay clean, keep yourself up. People won't want you if you're not clean."

Although Teena felt loved by the Gardeckis, indeed thought of their relatives as hers, and went to Bible camps in the summer and on holidays with the family, her mother was never far from her mind. Some nights, as Teena and Christine lay in bed, they would talk about Maryann, and the younger sister would try to figure out what made their mother tick.

"Do you think she hates us? Is that why we're here?" Teena asked, lying on her side in the single bed, dark eyes wide open. "Is it because we were so bad, is that why Mom didn't want us?" Christine had no answers.

The visits with Maryann were conducted at an office in the provincial government building in Peace River. They usually started with the kids somewhat bashful and Maryann asking them questions about school and what they were learning. By the end of the visit, the shyness abated and Teena snaked her thin arms around Maryann's neck and stroked her hair. To this day, Teena vividly recalls the last visit with her mother, when she was about ten years old. "The social worker said the time was up, that it was time to go and I don't know why, I just didn't want to go. My mom told me not to worry, that we'd have another visit, but I cried a lot and I wouldn't get into the car with my foster parents. And then my mom came out of the door and I tried to jump into her vehicle. I didn't want to let her go. I shouldn't have to this day because that was the last visit I remember having with her."

Social workers later told Teena that Maryann had been given a choice after that visit: stop drinking, or the children would be taken permanently. "They told me that she chose drinking. It was something I never forgot, ever. I always figured, well, one day I'll find out the truth about why our visits were cut off, because I'm sure my mom tried to sober up and get her life straightened out and get her kids back. I'm sure she wouldn't have just said, 'Well, I don't want them anymore.' She wouldn't have chose to keep drinking over us."

Teena became, for all intents and purposes, a white girl, living in a white family. Being native was not something she thought about, and contact with relatives at the reserve was almost non-existent. "Growing up, I always considered myself white. People always said, 'You don't look like a native,' when I told them I was. I didn't really feel like a native, even at the reserve. I always knew I was native, I just didn't feel native, because I was brought up with white people."

Teena's hair was dark brown, her skin light, with a few tiny, dark freckles scattered across her narrow, straight nose.

Her eyes were slightly almond-shaped, clear and brown, and her teeth grew white and straight. Like all the women in her family, she was smaller than average, but not alarmingly so. Class photographs show a pretty child, neatly dressed in colour-co-ordinated outfits.

After Teena had been at the Gardeckis' for two years, her youngest siblings, Grace and Peter, also came to the home. (No one was quite sure where John was at that point.) Teena was ecstatic. She had gone through a bad time for a while, because Christine and Colin, then in their teens, had begun to fight with the Gardeckis, not listening and wanting to be doing their own thing, which included drinking and partying with their teenage friends. Christine ran away several times, and when she was fifteen, did so permanently, hitch-hiking around Alberta with a girlfriend. Colin soon followed suit. Having Grace and Peter at the home was a life-saver for Teena, who to this day says she needs to have at least one of her siblings nearby and involved in her life to feel whole and experience some measure of security.

It was clear something was up. Sitting around the kitchen table were a couple twelve-year-old Teena hadn't seen before, an angular man, a small woman beside him. They weren't friends of the Gardeckis that Teena, Grace or Peter could recall meeting before, and when they were called into the room to meet them, Teena's antennae went up.

After introductions, the kids sat at the table and self-consciously visited. The couple asked questions, and the kids stared at their laps. The couple seemed nice to Teena, although she later said bitterly to Grace, "I bet these people are here to foster us. They'll be our new foster parents for a while and then we'll be shipped off somewhere else." The last thing Teena wanted to do was leave the Gardeckis', especially if it turned into the usual cycle of staying at one place for a while before being told they had to move to another. Although Teena had been at the Gardeckis' for several years, she still remembered the terrible feeling of being transplanted.

After seeing the couple a few times at the Gardeckis', the trio of kids went to their farm for a weekend visit, and things went relatively smoothly, although Teena later said she had an "eerie feeling" about them. She considered telling Social Services she didn't want to go with the new couple, but it seemed pointless. They were going to have to go somewhere. At least Grace and Peter would be with her.

Teena was hurt and angry at Ted and Fern, whom she had considered "Mom and Dad," when they told her she would be moving. She wondered what she had done wrong to make them not want her any more. Hadn't they all got along okay, at least as well as most families? It wasn't until several years later that she understood that the Gardeckis had been going through personal problems of their own and feared they might split up, which they eventually did. The Gardeckis wanted Teena, Grace and Peter to have a stable, permanent home; they thought they were doing the best thing they could for the kids they cared deeply for.

Change was coming, Teena knew, and she wasn't happy about it. It hit her even harder when she learned that they were going to move to a small town in Saskatchewan.

The day of the move to the new home came quickly. The Gardeckis kept to the usual Sunday ritual, rising and going to church. Fern tried to keep cheerful, making lunch for the family and doing the dishes. But when it came time to say goodbye, her control fled. Teena, too, was unable to keep from crying, especially when she saw the tears on Fern's cherubic face. "It's okay, Teena. We still love you," the foster mother said to the girl she had raised for four years. "We'll write you letters and you can come and visit. It will all work out." The Gardeckis' children were sobbing as Teena, Grace and Peter got in the vehicle and drove off with their new parents. Teena hunkered down in the seat and gazed through swollen eyes at the passing fields, wondering why no one seemed to want her for long.

A picture in Teena's photo album shows a plain-looking couple and a seasoned Saskatchewan farmhouse. In front are

Grace and Peter, and standing a foot or so away is Teena, legs like pipe-cleaners supporting her skinny frame. It is a family photograph of a sort, of the Sawans' new home and parents.

To Teena, the new couple now seemed much colder than they had during the trial visits. Rules were firmly laid down, and breaking them was punished with a spanking. At times, Teena hit back. She missed her school and friends, but she especially missed the Gardeckis, with whom she had felt loved. She often cried herself to sleep at night.

School became a refuge. She stayed late, offering to do whatever extra class activities had to be done for her teacher Mrs. Mitchell, a thirtyish woman with cat's-eye glasses and hair teased fashionably on top. Teena dreamed of turning sixteen; then she'd be able to leave any home she was put in, find her mother and live with her. No one could keep Teena away from her forever.

It was when Teena's new mother left for her Women's Aglow meetings at the church that Teena grew most afraid. She lay in her bed upstairs, stomach in a knot so tight she thought she would vomit, listening to Grace's even breathing in the bed across the room. The creaking stairs signalled that her new father was on his way. Teena turned her face to the wall as his bulk settled onto the side of the single bed. Teena held the bedcovers tightly wrapped under her chin but his weight pulled them taut around her neck, like a cloth noose. He slipped his hands under the thick covers and rolled her body towards him, placing Teena's hand on his penis. Teena held her breath, closed her eyes and prayed her little sister would not wake up.

After a time, he would leave, slipping quietly down the stairs. Sometimes when Teena awoke in the morning, she found she had wet the bed.

An October 27, 1985, accident, twelve miles north of Grimshaw during one of the season's first cold snaps, evoked outrage in the small northern communities. Killed was a twenty-two-year-old woman who was the area's figure-skating professional, a bright and outgoing woman who was the centrepiece during annual ice carnivals, and who taught young girls the art of twirling gracefully until their puffy homemade skirts billowed. Her untimely death shocked and saddened those in the area. But there was little mention of Gary Gardiner, the eldest son of Manning old-timer Bluford Gardiner, or of Maryann Sawan, mother of six, the people who had been killed in the second vehicle, the people who had been drinking.

Teena heard of her mother's death from her new parents. Though she rarely loses control of her emotions, to this day Teena cries when she mentions her mother's death and speaks bitterly of her new parents' way of dealing with it. "He gave us a tape of Christian music and told us to go upstairs and listen to it, that it would make us feel better."

With her mother gone, there was no place to go. Twelve-year-old Teena often looked out her bedroom window at the tree limbs brushing against the pane. She dreamed of getting a thick piece of rope, fastening it to a limb and hanging herself. The children were not returned to attend Maryann's funeral at the Chapel of Memories, at Cadotte Lake. The thirty-five-year-old woman was buried at Little Buffalo on October 31, 1985, in a small graveyard where tall brown grass hides the graves. Many of the sites are unmarked. Teena says if she ever gets some money saved, she will make sure a marker is at the site, to remember her mother.

It was Mrs. Mitchell, her grade five teacher, who ultimately helped Teena. She saw her former "teacher's pet" becoming increasingly truculent and rebellious. The girl's mother had been killed, she knew, but she felt certain the behaviour problems had started before that.

"Is there anything you want to tell me about?" the teacher asked Teena one day after school. No, nothing, the girl responded. The teacher persisted, asking again, telling the young girl that there wasn't anything she couldn't tell her. Finally, Teena started to cry. "I cried and I cried and I cried and I told her I knew it was all my fault, that I was a bad person and I asked for it."

Teena told of the sexual touching, and the teacher told her firmly that it was not her fault and that she did not have to continue living there. The police were called and went with Teena that afternoon to pick up her clothes from the house. She was put in a group home for a few weeks. Teena said she heard later through social workers that the man first denied having done anything improper, but then later admitted to it. His wife said Teena was a liar. The man, as far as Teena knows, was never charged but did receive several months of counselling.

Teena, Grace and Peter were returned to Fairview, Alberta, where Social Services arranged for Teena to see a counsellor to talk about her mother's death and the sexual abuse. That counselling would continue off and on for several years. But there was little counsellors could do for Teena's shaken faith in the system, specifically in Social Services.

"They were the ones that put us in that home. They thought it was such a good home to be in and look what happened. Social Services are always saying, 'Well, these are good people. We've screened them. They don't drink, smoke and they go to church.' So what? Do those things make them good people? I've never trusted Social Services since. They lost my trust entirely."

Chapter 3

Bolting full speed down the court, the basketball bounding up at her side like rain slapping a shallow puddle, the forward looked taller than her five feet. But perhaps more importantly, she felt taller, with the pebbly ball hitting her reddened palms and shouts of "Go Teena! Go Number Five!" seeming to ring out from all sides. In reality, the cheers came from a rather haphazard group of parents, some still struggling to get their coats and scarves off. The gym seemed like a cavernous sauna after hurrying in from the sub-zero temperature outside.

Teena felt like a character in a movie, the hero who cascades across the floor to make the basket that takes the underdog to the championship. She did make the basket, but instead of being a crucial tie-breaker, it just added to her team's already substantial lead over the Grimshaw squad in one of the opening games of a round robin tournament. Still, it was exciting to hear the cheers, have her teammates pat her on the back, tell her she had done a good job. In grade eight, Teena was one of the youngest players on the Fairview team, and the fact that she got to play as often as she did was another feather in her athletic cap.

It was easy to bury herself in sports now that she was back
in Fairview and enrolled in junior high school. Finding a
niche with her new family wasn't quite as easy, however,
even though her new foster parents were trying hard to
make her feel at home and alleviate the fears that had travelled with her from Saskatchewan.

Upon their return to Alberta, Teena, Grace and Peter had
been placed in a temporary receiving home for two months,
until the home with Bob and Sherry Ayres was found. The
Ayres' home, next door to the church where Bob was pastor,
was in Heinz Creek, a few miles south of Fairview, back in
the familiar territory the Sawan children had left before
going to Saskatchewan.

Teena was quite happy with the Ayers, was doing okay in
school and enjoyed being on the basketball team. But after
about a year, she began to chafe under the relatively strict
house rules which forbade such things as dancing, for religious reasons. "I don't know what happened in grade nine. I
was about fourteen and something just clicked and I wanted
to be with my friends, and do the things they were doing,"
Teena recalls now. Some of those friends were out partying,
staying out late and drinking beer.

Teenage rebellion, perhaps combined with a permanently
scarred sense of trust, led Teena to take matters into her own
hands. If the Ayres wouldn't let her go out, she'd just find a
way to do it on her own. She began running away, like her
sister and brother had done before her. Sometimes she'd
return in the morning and promptly be grounded. Then
she'd turn around and run away again for a few days. The
process repeated itself, like a stuck record. No one was going
to tell Teena what she could and couldn't do. She began to
drink more and more beer when she ran away. It made her
feel good, powerful in fact, something she hadn't felt before,
and after a few drinks she didn't care about anybody or anything. Comments made about her in the past, especially from
her Saskatchewan days—that she was stupid, that she was
ugly and would never amount to anything—bleached into
nothing.

"What do you want to do?" the Ayres implored. "We want this to work out." Teena had no ready answers. She knew the Ayres' hearts were in the right place and that the couple wanted to make up for the kids' rough childhood, but Teena wanted to do what she wanted to do.

By the middle of grade nine, Teena was missing school on a regular basis, running away consistently. The girl in the school picture—wearing a pink dress and spice-coloured nylons, hair neatly curled around her shoulders—quickly grew up. She chopped her hair short and experimented with dying the top blonde. One evening she sat down with a photograph album, pair of scissors and a ballpoint pen, methodically cutting herself out of pictures with various foster families and scribbling out faces of others.

Teena quit school sports teams. Stopped in the hall by one of the coaches, she simply shrugged when asked why she wasn't playing and said people should leave her alone. Teena spent more time "lipping off" teachers than listening to anything they had to say. She just didn't care any more. She often thought of her mother, and having a drink helped when depression led to suicide fantasies.

A social worker at the end of her rope suggested that Teena be put in "YAC," the youth assessment centre, basically a detention home of sorts for hard-to-handle kids. Although the Ayres were dispirited, that seemed like too much of a dead-end for a teenager they knew was intelligent and caring underneath her cape of indifference. But the running away continued, and her behaviour eventually became too much for them.

In early 1989, social workers asked Teena where she wanted to go. "Little Buffalo," she said, more a knee-jerk response than a well-considered answer. Teena hadn't really thought about what it would be like to move back to the community she had had little involvement with for years.

Teena Sawan's ancestry is intricately linked to the area she was returning to. Moise Sawan and Nora Adams, Teena's great-grandparents, met at the Whitefish Lake settlement, south of Little Buffalo, in the early 1900s. Moise was an adept trapper, and his family's lifestyle reflected that of the time and culture of the Cree of the northern Alberta interior. The Woodland Cree were nomadic within the Lesser Slave interior, a sweep of lightly wooded and lake-filled land marked by the Peace River to the west, the Athabasca River to the east and Slave Lake to the south. Their lives followed the seasons and the natural habitats of the animals they sought. They travelled with a group of families from one settlement in the winter to another in the spring and summer.

Moise and Nora had four children together, Josephine, Joe, Peter and Annie. While there were some log cabins in the area during the 1930s, tents and teepees were common, and Teena's grandmother, Annie, born in 1930 at Bison Lake, lived in a teepee for much of her early life. Formal education was provided at residential schools run by Oblate priests at Grouard and an Anglican Church school at Whitefish Lake. Annie never went: attendance required students to leave their families for ten months of the year, as parents returned to the northern lakes to hunt and trap.

Annie learned a love of liquor from her father and mother, both of whom drank periodically. As a teenager, she lived off and on with her parents at Bison Lake and a few other settlements, staying with them for a time after she had each of her children, Maryann in 1950, when she was twenty years old, followed by Peter and Eddie.

When Annie's children reached school age, Moise built a cabin at Cadotte Lake, where there was a school. Moise wanted his grandchildren to have the education that neither he, Nora nor any of their children had. Here, Annie's children learned English, although they still spoke Cree to their mother.

It was in this cabin, hand-built by her grandfather, that Teena Sawan was born.

Nearing Little Buffalo, Teena Sawan stared anxiously out the car window at each house they passed. Was this where she would live? she thought as the car bumped along, passing a few tiny houses that Teena thought looked like shacks. Though the foster homes she had lived in had not been grand, none had rusty old cars littering the front yard, and she felt distinctly turned off by the idea of living in such a place now. She hoped her Aunt Esther lived in one of the bigger houses that looked like the places in town. She also hoped her aunt would be happy to see her. Teena had only fuzzy memories of Esther Auger, who was actually her cousin but whom she called her aunt. "She wanted to be with family, so I offered my home," Esther Auger explains matter-of-factly, bemused that something as fundamental as taking in a relative in need would require explanation. Many of the families at Little Buffalo and surrounding communities are large, and kids moving fluidly from one relative to another was, and is, commonplace.

Esther was used to the lack of modern conveniences but wondered how her new charge would adjust. Teena found the airy outdoor privy "gross," but she quickly grew used to the morning races out to the biffy.

Fitting in with her peers proved the more difficult adjustment. Although Little Buffalo was not a reserve—in fact, it was and is a municipal hamlet and cannot legally be designated a reserve—it was a reserve in Teena's eyes because the people living there were native. With Teena's light skin and naturally dark hair bleached reddish-blonde, she did not look particularly native. But language was the biggest barrier. Standing outside her aunt's house one afternoon shortly after arriving at the tiny community, Teena overheard kids referring to her as the "white princess." The remark drew a double-edged reaction—while it hurt, at least she understood what they were saying. Although most of the younger residents of Little Buffalo spoke English, comments made about her were usually expressed in Cree, the language she no longer understood or spoke. Sitting at the kitchen table in her Aunt Esther's house, some of her cousins vainly tried to teach her a few Cree words. She self-consciously attempted the lyrical pronunciations but gave up when people laughed. Teena knew virtually nothing of her culture. When her Aunt

Esther talked of drying moose meat, selling the hide, making moccasins, setting traplines, it was like someone talking about the distant past, activities done hundreds of years ago, not today or just a decade earlier by her mother, of all people.

Within a couple of months, Teena began to feel a bit more at home. Grace and Peter came for her sixteenth birthday and met relatives they barely recalled. But Teena began to feel restrained by her Aunt Esther's rules, and when not allowed to do something, she heeded the advice of new-found friends to sneak out. Teena decided to move in with another aunt, where the rules were a little more free and easy and she was allowed to set her own agenda. Now she saw a different side of the community, one her Aunt Esther had sheltered her from. "There was a lot of drinking at Little Buffalo, and when people drink, they went nuts. There were people going after each other with guns, shooting them at each other and stuff. It was bizarre," recalls Teena. Some attributed the behaviour to an increasing sense of social malaise caused by spiralling unemployment in the area and the demoralizing battle to obtain land promised decades before.

Teena eventually forged an identity with a beer in her hand. But when she drank her usual easygoing nature vanished, replaced by fury. Fistfights with other girls were not uncommon, and Teena's thin arms and long fingers hit and slapped with far more power than her five-foot, ninety-five-pound frame might have indicated. "Looking back on it now, I think I did that stuff because I had a lot of pain inside and I didn't know how to deal with it, so I lashed out at whoever was around me when I was drunk," Teena said.

It didn't take long for word of Teena's activities to get back to Social Services. Walking a tad unsteadily down the gravel road one afternoon, Teena recognized the vehicle driven by her social worker. The sixteen-year-old had been drinking—was on the verge of being quite drunk—and ran into the bushes when she saw the van. Damn, damn, damn—she did not want to be caught drunk and did not want to be sent somewhere else. Her hiding spot was soon found, and she was taken back to Grimshaw, screaming and swearing through much of the two-hour drive. "Why are you taking me from my family?" she yelled.

The Fairview group home she was taken to was used to dealing with kids like Teena—teens who some said were uncontrollable. The first thing they did was spell out the clear and unequivocal rules that were to be followed. For those who complied, privileges were granted. Teena spent most of the first two weeks in her bedroom, sometimes angry at Social Services, sometimes crying because she wanted to be back at Little Buffalo. She made friends with some of the others, with one friendship cemented by the teenagers carving their initials and a cross on their lower left forearms with a pin. The drawings were filled in with midnight-blue India ink, creating a crude tattoo. After a while, Teena earned TV privileges and began going on outings with the other kids in the group home. Some days, it seemed as close to home as she could imagine.

"Let's go drinking," Colin said, swinging up a case of beer he had resting at his cowboy-booted feet.

"Sure." Teena glanced over her shoulder only briefly before boldly walking out the front door of the home that she wasn't supposed to leave after 10:00 p.m. on weeknights. It was something to do, and somewhere to go.

She and her brother Colin, four years older and living on his own with a friend a few blocks away, had started to drink together. She often snuck out a window, or sometimes walked brazenly through the front door after curfew, and they'd go to his apartment and drink beer, or Teena's favourite, Alberta Premium Rye and Coke. Sometimes she and Colin talked about their upbringing and compared notes on where each had been. Colin now had a steady girlfriend and was trying to make that work. Their younger siblings, Grace and Peter, were in a foster home in Fairview, but neither was sure where John was. Their older sister, Christine, was somewhere in Alberta, they thought Edmonton. Christine, six years older than Teena, had spent much of her teens hitch-hiking here and there, following whims. At age sixteen she'd tracked down their mother, Maryann, and lived with her and Bluford Gardiner for a while. "I tried to be a good person to my mom when I was there, tried to stay out of her way," recalls Christine, whose feelings towards her mother are far more uncertain than Teena's. "But my mom always seemed more interested in her boyfriend than me."

Christine became pregnant around that time and went to a home for unwed mothers in Edmonton. There, she received counselling for alcohol abuse, as well as emotional support both during her pregnancy and after the birth. Maryann came to visit Christine and loved her little grandson to bits. During those visits, Christine gained some longed-for insight into the woman who had given birth to her.

"She used to tell me that she never wanted us kids to drink at an early age like she did, and that's why she gave us up. She didn't want us to learn that kind of thing from her," says Christine, who is still battling an alcohol problem.

Although Christine stopped drinking for a while after having the baby, she started up again at age eighteen, the same year her mother died. "When I feel bad, I like to drink. Drinking is a powerful thing when you got problems," she says. Christine shared custody of her son with his father. One weekend, the little boy wandered from the father's house to the Safeway across the street, where Christine used to grocery-shop. The police picked up the two-year-old and placed him in a foster home. Christine had weekend visitation rights. "I told them how I grew up, how I didn't like my mom when she was drinking, and I didn't want that little boy to hate me for doing that to him."

One weekend, when the boy said he wanted to stay with her and not return to the foster home, Christine gathered up his clothes and ran away with him. She was arrested. "I was going to be charged with kidnapping," she recalls. "They didn't charge me, but they told me I couldn't see him again because of what I did. If I hadn't run away with him, I'd have been able to see him on weekends, but I screwed that up good.... He's adopted now. He's ten years old."

Teena's grades, previously good, began to plummet, largely because of non-attendance. There was little doubt that she was bright, just as there was also little doubt that she was "a handful," as one of her junior high school teachers put it.

From the group home, she went to another foster home, where she was happily reunited with her younger brother and sister. But within a week, her running away and refusal to listen to anyone prompted the foster parents to ask her to leave. From there, she went to a receiving home until she was eventually placed at a home outside of Whitelaw, a tiny hamlet northeast of Fairview. Teena stayed at Dave and Sharon Bloom's home for almost a year and wishes to this day she had never left.

The teenager that showed up at Dave and Sharon Bloom's door in the early summer of 1990 came with an extensive warning label: "suicidal, drinking, rebellious ..." Sharon Bloom was used to such tags. She and her husband, four years her junior at thirty-four and almost a foot taller, had been foster parents for five years, and Sharon helps train other foster parents in the Peace River region. Before that, the couple worked for the solicitor-general's department, running an open-custody home for young offenders. The couple take things in stride, relying on their religious faith to guide them.

Teena exhibited a common trait of foster kids, a belief that their biological parents can do absolutely no wrong. "It's very common with children who are in care that their parents are the shining princes or princesses that can redeem them or save them, with all these heroic acts," said Sharon Bloom.

Foster kids have another alarming similarity that Sharon Bloom imparts matter-of-factly. "We expect that any child that comes into our home has been sexually abused, because, with kids in care, over 90 percent of them have been. Unless we are told they have not been, we assume they have been. So, being that Teena is female and had been in the system for quite a while, I assumed that she had been abused."

Foster kids were left with no ambiguities about their role

in the Bloom household—they were part of the family, and that meant they were to follow the same rules and have the same privileges everyone else did. There was no drinking or smoking, household duties were set out for each person, and kids were expected to take part in the home schooling that Sharon provided.

"Sharon Bloom said to me, 'If you're going to run away, do it now. I'll point the way,'" recalls Teena, who loved living at the Blooms' and, ironically enough, blossomed under their rules. The relative isolation of the Blooms' home seemed to be just what she needed. The running away stopped, as did Teena's drinking and smoking.

Teena speaks fondly of her time with the Blooms, as the couple does of her. She sounds nothing at all like the Teena Sawan who lived at the group home. "She was a delight to have in the home," recalls Sharon Bloom. "She took on the role of big sister quite easily. She was really close with our younger children and they really cared for her."

Sharon proudly remembers Teena calling her and Dave Mom and Dad. "I think Teena's difficulties arose from the fact that she never really had anybody that she could say she belonged to. That was the part that I seemed to get from her when she was here—that she wanted to be somebody that belonged somewhere, and I think that she just didn't have a sense of identity. She had very low self-esteem, and a very poor outlook on life, as if there was no hope.... For us, the biggest hurdle was getting Teena to believe in and love herself."

Sharon is critical of Social Services for not making more of an effort to keep children of larger families together. "I felt [the Sawan kids] were far too separated from each other.... I think that it is a very poor system for keeping kids in extended families together." Efforts have been made since in the social care system to keep larger families together, she said.

But perhaps most surprising to Sharon Bloom was the fact that Teena knew virtually nothing about being native. "I don't think that she had enough of her cultural background to give her any sense of real belonging in the native community. She was very much more white than she was native," she says, echoing a comment Teena Sawan often makes of herself.

It was Sharon Bloom who first made inquiries into Teena's native status, sending to Ottawa for the appropriate forms so Teena could be registered as a status Indian under the Indian Act. In her view, it was something that should have been done long before. "Somewhere along the line, someone should have been making sure this child's roots were somewhat intact. My husband and I are very strong on the fact that kids need to have their roots, they need to know where they have come from, what the family traditions are, where they belong, who they belong to. Particularly more so for the kids in the system, because they get lost in the shuffle."

The Blooms have learned through experience. They have three natural children and three adopted children. "Our oldest daughter is seventeen and was adopted under a system that is very much like the one that Teena was under, in that there was little contact with extended family. We went through a tremendous amount of heartache and problems, because she wanted very much to know her extended family and it caused a lot of difficulty for her, understanding why she hadn't been able to see and know them as a child. It has just been recently that we have managed to contact her extended family—her grandparents on her dad's side and her grandmother on her mom's side—and she is now living with her biological grandfather, which is something that she always wanted."

The Blooms' two other adopted children have a very open relationship with their biological mother and extended family, and have chosen to live with the Blooms. "We wanted to keep on with it being open...should they ever choose to go back, that option would be available to them," Sharon explains. The Social Services department has taken steps in the right direction in the past few years, she said, including a "real push for children to be matched with homes based on culture, religion and those sort of things. There are a lot more native foster homes now, a lot more people that are skilled in it and that are native that are taking children in care."

One winter day, a telephone message was left for Teena. "Do you know who Albert Auger is?" Sharon asked, when Teena came in that afternoon. "He said he's your father, from Wabasca."

A call to Teena's aunt confirmed that Albert John Auger was the name that should have gone on her birth certificate. Teena talked on the telephone with the man a few times, and plans were made to meet at an upcoming native gathering at Lac St. Anne, near Edmonton. Teena had no idea what to expect, or look for. Wandering around the campgrounds, Teena and her Aunt Angie looked hopefully at short men that passed by. She was short, Teena reasoned, so perhaps her dad was too. It was something to go on, anyway.

"This is starting to seem like a bust," Teena thought, as she and Angie stood outside a flat-roofed building where charred hamburgers and hot dogs were served, peering at men who passed by. Teena felt a tap on her right shoulder and turned to see a man standing behind her, one hand in his blue-jeaned pocket, the other at his side.

"Cecily?" he asked.

"Are you looking for Cecilia?" she asked, giving him her birth name, still used by some of her relatives.

He said, "Yeah," and told her he was her dad.

Teena saw a tall, skinny man, his hair long and inky-black over his ears. So this was her father. He asked her about school, what she was doing with her life. Teena nervously answered, often lapsing into silence. She wasn't sure what to say to this man in whom she saw nothing of herself. "Is this really my dad, or is he just claiming to be my dad?" she couldn't help wondering. After a while—they spent some four hours together—Teena asked him about his relationship with her mother. He was candid about his reaction to finding out he was going to be a father. "I was too young, so I left."

At the end of the afternoon, the two promised to keep in touch, although that continuing contact did not materialize.

Teena said she recently tried to track him down through the Big Stone Cree, a reserve in Wabasca. But there were about twenty Albert Augers. "It's kind of like John Smith there." Teena takes comfort in the knowledge that she has a father. "I'm still glad to this day that I met him."

Near Valentine's Day, 1991, Teena decided to move out with another teenager. She could set her own hours, answer only to herself, have a place that was truly hers to call home. She was seventeen.

Her roommate was Louanne Gullion, who had also been living at the Blooms'. Gullion had turned eighteen, and so there was no longer a place for her in the foster parent system. Sharon Bloom still questions whether Teena moved out because she wanted to, or because she felt that was what Social Services expected her to do, since she was turning eighteen in the spring. (Indeed, a study released in 1993 after eighteen months of research by Alberta Children's Advocate Bernd Walter indicates a significant pressure to get adolescents "off the system." One of the findings of Walter's 321-page report is that children are bearing the brunt of government pressures to cut budgets, and the pressure to get adolescents off the system is being "pushed down" to include children as young as thirteen or fourteen.) The Blooms kept their misgivings to themselves. "We stayed out of the decision-making, because we thought it was something she should decide on her own. But looking back in retrospect now, we think we should have told her how we felt, that we didn't think that she was ready for it and that she should stay with us a little longer," Sharon said.

Teena and Louanne Gullion rented a two-bedroom house in Bluesky, a hamlet of about 250 people a few miles away from the Blooms'. A neighbour, Greg Walker, helped them move, and then helped with the rent. The former truck driver turned farmhand was twenty-five years older than Teena. Nevertheless, he often spent weekends at the Bluesky house, and eventually began "horsing around," to use his own words, first with Teena and then with Louanne.

Within a couple of weeks of moving, Teena and Louanne had a housewarming party. It was to be the first of a series of ongoing parties, and Teena fell back to downing beer, and whatever other alcohol was brought over, as well as smoking marijuana when it was occasionally passed around.

Some weekends, Greg brought with him his eldest son, Arlen, who, at fifteen, cut an attractive figure with his bright blond hair and blue-green eyes. The young teenager had the short, stocky build of a hockey player. The Walker marriage had broken up when Arlen was a youngster. Arlen was eventually put in care and lived at several foster and group homes. While at a Fairview group home in 1991, he spent some weekends with his father, who was helping his own father tend the family farm outside Fairview. One weekend at Teena and Louanne's, Greg Walker hemmed and hawed about what to do with his son; he had cows to check back at the farm. One of the stipulations of the weekend visits was that Greg would keep his eye on the teen the entire time. But Greg was in a hurry—the cows wouldn't wait—and there didn't seem to be any harm in leaving the boy with Louanne and Teena. The teenagers wanted to go skating in the morning. "I said, seeing as you guys aren't going nowheres tonight, you got no wheels, it seemed okay to me," Greg Walker recalled. The last thing he said as he walked out the door was, "I don't want no horsing around between any of you."

Moments after Walker roared off, friends of Louanne and Teena's dropped by, packing a case of beer, which the group sat around and drank. "We got pickled," Louanne recalls bluntly. Teena and Arlen ended up in the bedroom. The same thing happened the following weekend. It was "just something that happened," said Teena, who dislikes the thought of appearing "sleazy." "It's not something I'm very proud of."

Soon after, Teena and Louanne moved back to Fairview. Neither had a vehicle, and Bluesky felt awfully isolated. By that time, Teena was pregnant, although she wasn't to have it confirmed by a pregnancy test until several weeks later.

In the meantime, the drinking and partying continued at a ferocious pace. "It turned out to be a disaster," Teena said later, "because drinking just led to more drinking. I had friends popping over with alcohol and it just kept growing. I feel really bad to this day. I should never have left the Blooms."

Louanne Gullion saw sides of Teena that left her baffled. There was the drinking, smoking, partying Teena, who sometimes yelled at her when Louanne told her to take it easy; there was the Teena who, when sober, could be a good friend; there was the Teena who took correspondence school courses and did well; there was the Teena who cried for her mother. Louanne couldn't figure her friend out.

Teena often talked to Louanne about getting her life together. Then the drinking carried on, and Louanne became discouraged. On one occasion, Louanne took Teena to the hospital with what she thought was alcohol poisoning. After that scare, Louanne told her things were getting out of hand. Teena promised her friend she was going to clean up her act. She returned to the group home in Grimshaw. It was time to deal with the facts of life. And that included the fact that she was pregnant.

Chapter 4

The word was out on the group home grapevine: Arlen Walker had got Teena Sawan pregnant. Although Arlen had moved to another group home—somewhere in Winnipeg, Teena thought—he had apparently been one of the people doing the bragging. She sent him a letter, care of his mother, as Teena wasn't sure exactly where the fifteen-year-old father was, confirming the rumour. The note went unanswered, and Teena left it at that. If Arlen wanted something to do with her or the baby, he knew how to find her. Pursuing it any further seemed a sure-fire way to court rejection.

That the father of her baby seemed to want no involvement did not faze Teena. Although in her dreams a child came with both a mother and father, she knew reality didn't necessarily provide this: her mother and grandmother had both raised their children alone. So would she.

Workers at the group home had more immediate concerns. "The drinking has to stop," said more than one worker after Teena's decision against an abortion. "I know. I know," Teena replied. She remembered the ease with which she had stopped drinking while living with the Blooms, and knew she could do it again, especially if there were supportive people around her, which the group home workers definitely were. They often sat at the kitchen table with her after supper, telling of their pregnancies and childbirth experiences. "I can do this," Teena thought hopefully, pulling her sweater flat against the barely perceptible swell of her belly, staring at it in her bedroom mirror for long minutes on end.

Pangs of insecurity about whether she could handle the responsibility for another life were overwhelmed by a sense of wonder, especially given the thrilled reaction of her younger brother and sister. Peter wanted to name the baby Michael Jordan, after his favourite basketball player, and Grace favoured Brianne for a girl. Teena loved the idea of having "somebody to be with me all the time, to love and to hold and to grow up with. It kind of reminded me of my mom a bit, I don't know why. I thought, 'Mom would be really proud of me, she'd be proud of her grandchildren.' Just the fact that I was having a baby—I was having a baby! It was pretty amazing."

The actual baby seemed a long way away, but it became a lot easier to imagine when she wandered through the Saan Store, looking at the miniature clothing. Teena bought a tiny sleeper. She thought boys should wear blue, girls pink; yellow seemed a safe bet.

Her eighteenth birthday, on May 28, 1991, was marked by a family celebration. Her brother Colin and his girlfriend Suzanne, who was also pregnant, came to the group home, as did Grace and Peter and Christine. A picture of the "Sawan women" was taken in front of the home, and Teena is smiling broadly. "It was the best birthday I can remember, having family with me." But the birthday meant Teena was no longer a Social Services ward. She had to move out, although the group home workers said she could still count on them for moral support. Colin and Suzanne lived a few blocks away and invited Teena to live with them, but the living arrangement didn't last long. Colin was drinking a fair bit, and he and his girlfriend often fought. After only a few weeks, Teena tried to figure out a place to go where life would be on an even keel. She kept a mental list of people who had been kind to her, and one night she sat down and wrote a letter to Ralph and Bea Cowie, a Manning couple who had provided "escort service" for foster kids years before. The couple had driven the Sawan kids from their foster home to visit Maryann. Teena had liked them, and knew they had lots of kids. Maybe they wouldn't mind having one more.

The letter caught Ralph Cowie by surprise. He hadn't seen the Sawan children in years. Sitting at the post office in the driver's seat of his mud-spattered pick-up truck, he easily remembered the kids' barely contained excitement to see their mother, whom Ralph knew from her drinking days in Manning. The Cowies had to turn down Teena's request to live with them and go to school in Manning; neither was home that much because of work, and they didn't think they could be home enough to take responsibility for a teenager. Ralph Cowie wonders to this day how different Teena's life might have been had they taken her in when she asked.

Bob and Sherry Ayres, the couple with whom Teena had lived in her early teens, opened their home to Teena in the summer of 1991. During the abbreviated, hot summer typical of northern Alberta, the pregnancy began to show, and there were nights when, lying in bed, the sweat slick on her nose and clammy on her back, the reality of the responsibility soon to be hers began to take shape.

She stared at the ceiling and wondered how you bathed a baby. She knew you had to support the head, but how did you make sure the baby didn't wriggle out of your hands? When people saw her tiny frame swollen with pregnancy, some tentatively asked her, "What are you going to do?" Sometimes it made Teena angry. "I'm going to have a baby," she curtly told one woman at a downtown store. In her heart, she knew she wanted to keep her baby, and to be a mother to him or her, but over time, the comments and doubting looks sharpened deeply ingrained insecurities.

The Ayres said they would support Teena in any decision she made about what to do with the baby, but pointed out that it would not be easy to be a single mother. Teena decided to talk with a family support worker, but the focus of the few counselling sessions seemed, to Teena, to promote adoption. Raising a child on her own would not be an easy task, the counsellor said, especially as Teena was on welfare, with little education and no job. The counsellor urged Teena to think of the child, and the advantages he or she could have with two people to provide a stable, loving home. Teena had her whole life ahead of her.

After one of the visits, Teena was left with the profiles of several couples hoping to adopt. She took them home with her and read about the people who so much wanted the baby inside of her, and all the things they could offer. They were all married, had homes—some of them paid for—and good jobs. The words attached to Teena, on the other hand, were teenager, single mother, alcohol problem, uneducated, welfare—they made a steady drumbeat that would haunt Teena Sawan for a long time to come.

At about the seventh month of her pregnancy, after two months at the Ayres', Teena was on the move again. Louanne Gullion called, and the former roommates decided to move to Manning, just ten miles north of the farm home where Grace and Peter lived. In October 1991, Teena and Louanne rented a one-bedroom apartment in a large, grey house one block from the high school her sister attended, and Grace often visited Teena after school. Louanne and Teena made a deal: Louanne would cook if Teena would clean. Teena signed up for prenatal classes, with Louanne as her coach. The two attended five of the seven classes, the capper being the class where a film of childbirth was shown. It didn't look that bad, Teena thought to herself.

She often lay on her side, hands wrapped underneath her stomach, and remembered sitting curled against her mother, Maryann's black hair soft against her cheek. Teena imagined giving her own child that comfort. Other days, she woke up depressed and drained, looking at her sparsely furnished apartment and digging through her purse in hopes of finding stray bills to buy groceries, and imagined the child being adopted by a family who could provide far better than she could. Of one thing she was certain—if the baby was adopted, it would be done privately. Teena wanted as little as possible to do with the Alberta Department of Family and Social Services. The way she saw it, the government agency had controlled her entire life and had messed up badly. She certainly didn't trust it to find a home good enough for her baby.

In November 1991, one month before her baby was due, Teena went so far as to call a licensed private adoption agency called Adoption Options. She told the woman who answered that she might place her child for private adoption. The Adoptions Options counsellor called the Social Services adoptions worker for the Peace River area, Erin Harris, and told her of Teena's call. Harris called Teena, and the two discussed the different types of adoption—ward, which was essentially through the ministry, or private—and left it with the teenager. By the end of November, Teena had changed her mind and called Harris back—she was going to keep her child. The baby was due December 3, and Teena changed her mind almost every day.

At 8:00 a.m. on December 1, Teena went to the Manning General Hospital so her doctor, Daniel Bester, could try to induce labour. Bester was leaving for a holiday in the Bahamas that night. But all efforts to encourage the baby were unsuccessful. Teena thanked the doctor, with whom she felt she had a good relationship, and went home to wait. Dr. Bester was one person who didn't give Teena advice on what to do once the baby was born. "He told me everything seemed to be going fine. He was concerned about health, getting exercise and eating properly."

Nature took its course. Teena woke about 11:30 p.m. on December 2 to find herself in a pool of water. "Either I wet the bed or my water broke," said an embarrassed Teena to the admitting nurse. Dr. Bester was already gone, so a female obstetrician, Dr. Hallinen, looked after the delivery. The labour was difficult for both mother and coach. It was primarily back labour, and Louanne, who said all the right things, bore the brunt of Teena's complaints.

At 8:15 a.m. on December 3, Teena Sawan gave birth to a six-pound, eight-ounce baby, whom she named Jordan Michael Sawan. Teena couldn't quite bring herself to name him Michael Jordan, the name suggested by Peter. But she liked the names transposed, and the Michael had special meaning—it was also her young brother's middle name. With the cleaned newborn at her side, pride Teena had never felt before washed over her. That this perfect being actually came from her was amazing. After counting all his fingers and toes, inhaling his baby fragrance and marvelling at his flawlessness, Teena fell into an exhausted sleep.

She woke up four hours later to see Peter sitting in a chair in the corner of the hospital room and heard Grace talking with nurses down the hall. "How long have you been there?" she asked, surprised and groggy. "Since Jordan was born!" Thirteen-year-old Peter was thrilled to have a nephew. As he held the baby not yet one day old in his arms, Peter told the infant how he was going to teach him to ride a bicycle. "Take it easy," Teena replied, "He has to learn to walk first!"

Peter and Grace's foster mother, Iris Land, listened to their excitement with a sense of gloom. She prayed Teena's antics would not give Grace or Peter any glorified ideas about single parenthood. A child came with the union of a man and woman in marriage, not from a drunken teenager fooling around with a boy who would probably be bragging in the bars about bedding her.

Teena had thought that the hard part ended with labour. She was wrong. An unnerving despair settled in on her about a day after the birth. Dr. Hallinen gently told the young mother she was suffering from post-partum depression, something relatively common for new mothers. Teena could barely stand to be in the same room with the baby she had first been so excited about.

Sitting in her room, Teena cried and stared out the window at the riverfront park across the street. The doctor wanted Teena to stay in the hospital longer, so she could keep an eye on her.

"What if he starts to cry and I don't know what to do with him? What happens if I drop him?" Teena thought. "I was really unsure of whether I would make a good mother or not. I wanted to. I wanted to give Jordan whatever he wanted, to give my son the best of everything. But I just didn't know if I was capable enough to do it, strong enough to do it."

Two days after Jordan's birth, while still in the hospital, Teena telephoned Sharon Bloom. She had talked to Sharon during her pregnancy, asking for her advice. Sharon had suggested that Teena think about adoption, and emphasized that if she chose that route, open adoption was the way to go. That way, Sharon said, Teena could keep in contact with her child and still be able to carry on with improving her life. But that day on the telephone, Teena didn't ask about adoption. She asked Sharon if she could move back with her and Dave on their farm.

"What did you have in mind about caring for Jordan?" Sharon asked.

Teena had it all figured out. Sharon could look after Jordan while Teena went to school.

Even though Teena meant a lot to Sharon, she had to decline. "We have six children that we home school, and I told Teena I just couldn't home school these six kids and look after her baby at the same time. For me, it just wasn't possible to do that." She also told the teenager that she had to take responsibility for her actions.

Teena hung up the phone, upset and somewhat angry. There didn't seem to be anyone to turn to. On December 9, Teena called Erin Harris, the adoption worker who she had spoken with in November. The women again talked about the different forms of adoption, and at the end of the conversation, Teena still wasn't sure. She lay back in the hospital bed and her head pounded.

After eight days in the hospital, Teena was going snaky. She had to get out. She couldn't breathe, she couldn't think properly. Dr. Hallinen suggested leaving Jordan in hospital for a few more days, to give Teena time to get herself together and figure out what it was she wanted to do. Teena agreed.

On December 13, two days after she was released from the hospital, Teena called Erin Harris once again. She had made up her mind—she was going to keep the baby. She felt a rush of resolve, sure she could care for the child she had loved in her body and had loved the second he had been laid at her side.

Teena called the hospital and told them she would be coming by later that day to pick up her child, but the nurse said the doctor wanted to see her first. Sitting in an office, Dr. Hallinen told the teenager she thought it would be best if Teena gave the baby up for adoption. Teena was so young, the doctor said, she had her whole life ahead of her, a life where she could try to further herself. She could have babies later, the doctor pointed out. Despite the doctor's words, Teena refused to change her mind. "No, I want to take my son home," she said flatly, staring down at her hands. The two women sat in silence for a minute or so before the doctor stood up, signalling that the meeting was over.

Teena walked to the nursery, where Jordan was asleep. The nurse wrapped him up tightly in a hospital blanket and handed him to the young mother. "Good luck," she whispered as she put the baby in Teena's arms. The nurse watched the tiny woman walk down the hall alone and couldn't help but worry. A child with a child.

Teena left the hospital with her newborn son in one arm and a plastic bag with a few diapers, a baby sleeper and two stuffed animals the hospital staff had given Jordan in the other.

Dr. Hallinen wasn't the only one who wondered how Teena was going to care for a baby while on welfare and alone. How could she provide for the child? How could she buy him diapers, clothes, food? How was she going to buy him toys or provide an education for him? And didn't a child have the right to a father, the stability two parents offered?

To the eighteen-year-old, the comments seemed to come from everywhere—the doctor, friends of friends, people she barely knew. She was not the person who could give her baby a future, although she had given him life.

Teena had perfected a blank response that some people found frustrating. While her face registered nothing and her voice remained nonchalant, each new mention of her inadequacies sliced a little deeper, until there were times when all Teena could see was what she lacked. The meagre faith she had in herself was gradually eroded. Maybe they were right—she could never be a good mother to this child, she was a drunken welfare mom, an Indian who had never been anywhere and would never go anywhere. She was nothing.

That night, like several before, Jordan cried and cried. After hours of walking him around the small apartment, rocking him at her side, rubbing his back, Teena was at her wits' end. "What is it? What is wrong?" she asked the tiny baby, whose red teary face stared up at her, lips stretched back from his pink-gummed mouth. It was terrifying. His arms waved around, fists balled and punching the air. Why didn't she know what to do to make her baby stop crying? "Please stop, please stop, please stop," she thought wearily. She couldn't take much more of this. She felt as if she had walked the confines of the apartment a thousand times. At moments like this, all Teena wanted was her mother, who she was sure would have known exactly what to do. Finally, worn out, Jordan did stop crying, his whimpering petering out to little sputters. He seemed exhausted, occasionally letting out tiny hiccups as he dozed somewhat awkwardly near her armpit.

Teena rested her head against the wall and slid to the floor, staring out the small window at the Christmas lights on the outside window frame. The lights were almost the best thing about Christmas. A few sockets were bare, smashed out by wind or kids throwing rocks, but the remaining bulbs of red, blue, green and yellow threw a steady stream of colour across the crusted snow and inside the apartment. Finally, Teena too fell asleep, the rainbow of lights reflecting smudged tears on the faces of both mother and child.

One night, when the colicky baby refused to stop crying, Teena asked Judy Waldo to come and help. She had met Judy through Louanne and quickly grew close to the mother of three. "Just take your time," Judy told her, "you're doing fine." But some nights, the pressure was too much, and Teena yanked on her pink ski jacket and took off to meet friends, leaving Jordan with Louanne.

The next day, Teena held her child close to her on the bed and traced the outline of his arched eyebrows and the ears she thought were a replica of her own. Though their colouring was as different as it could be, Teena thought the baby had her lips, and his chin was small and pointed, just like hers. Sometimes she lay and stared at him for long minutes on end, his round, blue eyes staring back into her dark brown ones. *What am I going to do, baby Jordan, what on earth am I going to do?*

It was Pastor Kelly Taylor's first Christmas Eve service at the Manning General Hospital, and he was enjoying it immensely. The young pastor's first impression—that Manning was a town he and his family could stay in awhile—had deepened in the six months they had been there. With a population of almost 1,200, Taylor thought Manning had "the spirit of the north." The interdenominational service was meant to lift the spirits of those kept in the hospital over the holiday season, especially children, and Pastor Taylor helped lead rousing versions of hymns and carols, followed by prayer for all and sundry.

On Christmas Eve 1991, the attention of the thirty-two-year-old pastor was drawn to a baby, held by a wan-looking girl slumped in a couch waiting to see a doctor. Some of the parishioners talked to the girl, who didn't look to be much older than a teenager, and asked about the baby lying beside her. One woman said she thought the child belonged to Teena Sawan. All that was known for certain was that the girl with the baby was not his mother. Well, where was the mother? they asked among themselves.

The mother was in the hamlet of Deadwood, spending Christmas Eve and Christmas morning with her brother and sister at their foster parents' house. Teena said that some of the kids at Iris and Ellis Land's house had been ill with the flu, and she didn't want Jordan to catch it. Louanne volunteered to care for Jordan while Teena headed out for the night to see her siblings. But Louanne ended up with a bad case of the flu herself, so sick she carted Jordan with her to the hospital to get some medicine.

Driving home that night, Kelly Taylor's thoughts returned to the infant. The young pastor had a soft spot for children. His son, Joel, would soon be six years old. He stamped the snow off his shoes on the mat outside the side door of his 4th Street East home and met a gust of warm air as he entered the house. The cat mewed about his feet and followed him into the kitchen, where his wife, Esther, was sitting at the table. When he told her about the young woman and the baby, Esther—described by her husband as "the one with a heart as big as Texas"—immediately wanted to help.

Over the next couple of weeks, both Esther and Kelly Taylor did some discreet asking around, not that much was required in the small town, where information bled. Iris Land discussed her concerns about Teena and the child with the Taylors and told them that Teena wasn't sure what to do about the future. The Taylors listened intently.

As people made preparations to ring out 1991 and welcome 1992, Teena piled her belongings in a friend's pick-up truck. Louanne had moved out. She understood that Teena was depressed and anxious about her baby's future, but she was tired of bearing the brunt of her friend's moods. Teena had then decided to return to Fairview. She rented a three-bedroom house over the telephone and was going to share it with a couple of people she knew from town.

"I wanted to get away so I just up and left. It was a last minute decision, not thought out. I didn't know who I'd see as a doctor, or who would support me and Jordan. It was just, 'I want to leave and I'm leaving.' People were always saying to me, 'You're too young. You can't look after a baby.' I was sick to death of it. I just couldn't deal with it any more."

Teena quickly fell back into the old Fairview habits, partying with teenagers who didn't question her about her mothering capabilities. The small, peach-coloured house on 104th Street became known as the place to go for parties, and Teena acquired a sense of self-worth by hosting these events. She could go to the liquor store and buy beer and booze for her fourteen- and fifteen-year-old friends, who skipped school and hung out for the day at her house, cooing over the doll-sized baby. But even as she drank, a voice in Teena told her not to. And she put Jordan in her bedroom when there was a party. She felt too guilty when he was in the thick of things. It made her feel like a bad mother.

She missed Louanne, she missed her younger brother and sister, she missed Judy Waldo—all the people who had been at least somewhat supportive of her ability to be a mom. It seemed everything was falling in on her in Fairview, and she berated herself for making the hasty move.

On January 5, 1992, she telephoned the Alberta Department of Family and Social Services and asked if they could arrange for Jordan to be looked after for a little while. She needed to clear her head. It was just so difficult to make the right decision, especially when she had all these people around, and she didn't seem to be able to find the strength within herself to say no to them. The next day, Teena spent an hour with social worker Lynne Smith, confiding in her that she didn't know what to do when Jordan cried in the night and that she wanted him to have things she could not provide. Smith, who had found Jordan clean and well cared for, reminded Teena that things would get better, that she would learn what Jordan wanted and he would eventually sleep through the night.

Teena signed a temporary custody order that afternoon, which put Jordan in the care of Social Services at an approved foster home for thirty days. She would get her life straightened out in that time and bring Jordan home again. It was noted on the form that the order was at Teena's request. She could visit the child anytime she wanted, and she could terminate the placement at any point. Lynne Smith emphasized that a long-term decision had to be made soon. Teena knew that too.

Kelly and Esther Taylor had met Jim and Faye Tearoe in the mid-1980s, when both couples were living in Port McNeill, B.C. Esther Taylor had spent many of her growing-up years in the fishing, mining and forestry-based town of some ten thousand people at the northern end of Vancouver Island's east coast. Kelly Taylor had interned there at a small church after their marriage, and it was in that capacity that the two couples met. They had kept up casual contact in the years after both moved away, and one thing remained clear— despite the years, the Tearoes still very much wanted to adopt a second child, and had their hearts set on a boy.

Kelly Taylor liked the Tearoes but did think of them as a tad eccentric, "in the sense that they were both extremely intelligent, but have slightly different ways of viewing things." The young pastor was referring to the Tearoes' abiding belief, in spite of the rules observed by Social Services which deemed the couple too old to adopt, that they would receive a sibling for Heidi.

Remembering what doting parents the Tearoes were for Heidi, Esther soon thought of them when they learned from Iris Land that the baby boy seen at the hospital Christmas Eve might be available for adoption. Late on the evening of January 6, 1992, the Taylors called Jim and Faye at their suburban home just west of Victoria. Would they like to be considered as prospective parents for this child, should the mother decide to proceed to adoption?

Jim and Faye were thrilled and eagerly said yes. The Taylors passed the news to Iris Land, who told Teena that the Taylors knew of a couple who would very much like Jordan and would make wonderful parents. It seemed almost too good to be true to Iris, who had prayed long and hard for some good to come of the situation.

The Tearoes began to include Teena Sawan and her child in their evening prayers. They would wait for the Lord's will to be done.

For Teena a sense of freedom arrived after Jordan was placed in temporary care. She no longer felt guilty when people at her house drank, smoked or blasted the music. She wasn't waiting for the cry of a baby to indicate something was needed. But the nights were tough. She missed his small body in the bed with her and sometimes woke up, thinking there was something she had to do, before realizing Jordan was gone.

"On days when I didn't drink, I thought about Jordan a lot and thought, 'I want my son to come home and be with me, and take care of him and love him and see him go to school and see him take his first step and speak his first words.' But when I was drinking, it didn't matter. That was just terrible. I hated those kind of feelings and I hated myself for having them. I wanted him back so bad and yet I wasn't doing anything to do it."

The social workers who knew Teena made a couple of impromptu visits. Erin Harris dropped by Teena's home unannounced on January 13, a week after Jordan was put in the temporary care home. But as she stood on the front step, she heard music blaring and people inside singing loudly. It didn't seem the best time to talk about adoption, and she left without seeing Teena. Three days later, Lynne Smith made a surprise "home visit" to Teena, but the teen was not home, so she left a message. Teena called Smith and was adamant about wanting to keep Jordan. She missed and loved her little boy, she said, and thought about him a lot. The social worker asked her why, if she was sure she wanted Jordan back, she hadn't called Smith earlier and told her that. Teena said she was trying to get together a crib and other baby things, a comment that sounded to Smith like an excuse. The social worker said Teena knew to call Social Services for extra money for such things.

When Smith called Teena on January 22, the teenager was

again undecided about what to do with Jordan. She had talked with Esther Taylor about the Victoria couple who so wanted to adopt her boy. Teena had listened closely to Esther's kind words about the couple and had carefully written down their name and telephone number. She visited Jordan twice at the foster home, some two blocks from her house. Once, she brought along two girlfriends, and they fussed with the baby. Teena thought he seemed happy to see her and it made her feel more confused than ever.

One afternoon in late January, when she was home alone, she sat down in her bedroom. "I have to make a decision. This cannot continue," she thought, as she rocked back and forth on the bed with her head in her hands. By herself in the quiet room, it was easier to push the long list of her inadequacies out of her mind. All that was left was a desire to have her son with her. When she let her feelings settle it, the decision was easy. She loved her baby. She wanted Jordan.

On January 29, Smith visited Teena, and the teen said she definitely wanted Jordan back. Teena had borrowed a crib and had also made arrangements for Jordan to be cared for at the foster home during the day while she returned to school. She wanted to finish her grade ten and had gone to the high school to see about enrolling (a fact that Smith confirmed with the principal). Teena and Lynne talked about Social Services providing some parenting support for her when Jordan returned. On January 31, Teena picked up her son from the temporary foster home.

The Tearoes had talked of little else since receiving the phone call from Kelly and Esther Taylor. They were overjoyed to think that the answer to their prayers could be so near. When they hadn't heard anything by January 22, they called the Taylors to see if the couple had heard anything about how the mother was doing. The Taylors weren't aware of any decision having yet been made but told the anxious couple that the teenager had taken their telephone number. The Taylors promised to look into it. They called Jim and Faye back the next day and said they hadn't found out anything specific, but would let them know if they did. They also promised to alert the local social worker that the Tearoes were interested in adopting the child.

Not content to leave the matter be, the Tearoes called Alberta Social Services on January 26 and January 29. On January 30, they received a call from a woman they believed to be named Gail from the ministry. She told them of Teena Sawan's decision to keep her child but added that if, for some reason, she changed her mind again, the Tearoes would likely be the ones to receive the boy.

Faye Tearoe hung up the telephone and felt oddly optimistic. Faye "just had a feeling." It felt as if the Lord had told her, "This child is yours."

For the first two days after Jordan's return, things seemed to work out. Teena attended high school while Jordan was babysat by the woman who provided temporary foster care. But people didn't stop using Teena's house as a drinking spot, and Teena found herself enmeshed in it, despite her best intentions.

As her friends partied in the living room, the eighteen-year-old mother stood in the kitchen looking at the telephone number scrawled in the back of the telephone book. The name Tearoe was written beside it, along with "love God and children." Religion was important to Teena. Although she no longer attended church on a regular basis, the values she considered Christian—kindness, forgiveness and acceptance—were the ones she wanted instilled in her child.

The next day, Teena called Jim and Faye Tearoe. In her hand was a sheet, given to her before Jordan's birth, when she had first contemplated adoption. It suggested questions mothers should ask prospective adoptive parents, such as their interests and hobbies. Teena had kept the questionnaire in her brown suitcase, with other belongings she considered important.

The call went well—she talked to both Jim and Faye, and they sounded thrilled to hear from her. Faye had a lively voice and described herself as a full-time mom, while Jim worked for the government. They liked hiking and the outdoors and had family outings planned each weekend. Teena ended up having to ask very few questions—the Tearoes were very chatty and quick to tell her about themselves. They loved their little daughter, they said, and would dearly love another child. The Lord was also very important to them. They loved Him as one of their family.

For the Tearoes, the call seemed like a way of God keeping in contact with them. Each day, they included Teena and her little boy in their prayers, and they still prayed nightly for David James Tearoe. They asked the Lord to carry out His will. Faye could not forget the optimistic feeling she had, even after initially being told that Teena had decided against adoption. Here was the proof that the Lord did not disappoint those who served Him.

For the next two days, the conversation stayed in the back of Teena's mind. The Tearoes sounded stable, as if their life was on an even keel all the time. They could probably give Jordan a lot of things—things Teena knew, at that point, were far beyond her. With the Tearoes, her baby could have a life that everyone thought he should have, with two parents and a nice home. On February 4, 1992, she telephoned the couple again. She had made up her mind, she told them. They seemed like good people. If they wanted her son, they should come and get him.

"Praise the Lord," the ecstatic couple said, telling the young mother they would be there in two days.

Little did Teena know that they would soon be involved in a battle that was decidedly unChristian.

Chapter 5

❖ ❖ ❖

Less than twenty-four hours after receiving Teena's phone call, the Tearoes were buckled into their brown VW Rabbit, an empty car-seat in the back beside Heidi, and on the highway to catch the first ferry off Vancouver Island.

Receiving a baby boy seemed like a gift from God, a cement for their marriage, which had gone through a rough patch. Bound together by their twin beliefs in family and the Lord, Jim and Faye's marriage seemed solid. But their relationship had grown strained after 1984, as Jim spent more and more time studying to become a registered professional forester. Once Jim's courses were over, they began to go to weekly sessions with a marriage counsellor, which got the couple talking again. "It's like the Lord put our marriage back together, and then he blessed us with David. It was just like cream!" said Faye.

The thousand-mile trip to Fairview, Alberta, was carefully plotted out on the map before they left the house. If they drove steadily, they could be there within two days. The family made good time in their little car, eating a lunch packed by Faye the night before and stopping only for restroom breaks and to gas up. Jim wasn't his usual cautious self and exceeded the speed limit steadily the first day en route to Prince George, a mid-size pulp and forestry city in the B.C. interior. This was their midway point, and they stopped there for the night at the home of long-time friends.

They made one unscheduled stop on the lightning-quick trip up, in Quesnel, a town sixty-five miles south of Prince George, so Heidi could see the hospital where she'd been born on June 13, 1984. The Tearoes had made a point of telling Heidi she was adopted as soon as she could understand, explaining to her that although she came from another woman's tummy, the Lord had given her to Jim and Faye Tearoe, and they were her mommy and daddy. And that they were all members of a much larger family—that belonging to the Lord. Soon, they said, that miraculous event would happen again with another child.

Jordan lay on the bed with Teena on one side of him and a flat foam pillow on the other, though Teena knew that, at only two months old, it wasn't likely he was going to roll anywhere. Jordan had slept in the double bed with her that night, likely the last she would ever spend with her child.

Later that February 5 morning, Teena answered the phone to hear Lynne Smith's voice. The social worker said she was following up on a telephone call received the day before. "It was from someone concerned about young people partying at your house, Teena," Smith said, adding that there were reports of excessive alcohol and that Teena might be charged for providing liquor to some of her under-age friends.

Teena ignored her comments; she didn't want to deal with them, and there was little to say in her own defence. Instead, she tersely told the social worker that Jordan was going to be adopted and that the people she had chosen as parents for him were on their way up.

"I think it would be a good idea for Jordan to go to Carolyn Grayson's for the night," Smith said, naming the woman who had provided temporary care for Jordan in January. Teena was silent for several seconds and then agreed. It would probably be easier for everyone that way, she thought. She'd take him over to Carolyn's that afternoon.

There wasn't a lot to pack, but Teena folded the few baby sleepers and diapers neatly, placing them in a bag as Jordan lay on the bed. She wrapped him up tightly, picked up the bag and walked the two blocks to Carolyn Grayson's sky-blue and white frame house. Rounding the corner by a tidy Anglican church, Teena had only one more block to walk with her son, who, lodged against her skinny hip, seemed contented out in the brisk air. She imagined this would be the last time she would hold him, or ever walk anywhere with him. Teena quickened her pace, knowing the sooner Jordan was gone from her arms, the better it would be for everyone. She didn't want to change her mind again.

Lynne Smith made inquiries about procedures and documentation and called Teena back later on that afternoon. There were forms that had to be completed and signed within thirty days, she told the teenager, adding that once the forms were signed, Teena would have ten days in which she could change her mind and have the baby back, no questions asked—provided the ministry received notice of that change of heart in writing within the prescribed time limit.

The extent of Social Services' involvement in what was a private adoption surprised Teena. She had not intended to make any contact with the ministry, had planned simply to give the baby to his new parents, with provisions that she be kept up to date on his progress. Lynne Smith was well aware that Teena wanted the department involved as little as possible. Still, someone had to give her the necessary forms and explain the policy and procedures.

The Tearoes' estimate that they would be in Fairview by mid-afternoon on February 6 was on the mark. By three o'clock, they were walking up the sidewalk to the small, peach-coloured house, Heidi at their side. The differences between birth-mother and prospective adoptive parents became quickly apparent. Faye, who likes gospel and classical music, was immediately put off by the "loud rock music" bursting from the house. Teena glanced out the window and saw a couple she thought of as looking "old" walking towards the front door and wondered who they could be. In a community where mothers often start their families young, someone who was pushing fifty was more likely a grandparent than a parent. It never occurred to the eighteen-year-old that these people could be her son's new parents.

The Tearoes were expecting a young woman, but Teena, with her hair straight and short, looked even younger than eighteen, and they were not expecting Teena's friends, whom Faye described as "non-Christian. Oh, they were definitely not a Christian crowd. They were not wholesome-looking." Though Faye acknowledged that no one was drinking at the time, she described them as looking "like drinkers, just not a good bunch for a Christian girl to be with. You can tell a good person, and they were just not that crowd." The other teenagers at the house were not well versed in the social niceties and simply drifted out of the room to let Teena and the Tearoes have privacy rather than waiting around for introductions or chat.

Fighting an innate shyness, Teena told the couple and their daughter that Jordan was at Carolyn Grayson's, and that a social worker would be there shortly so they could sign the papers. Faye was obviously excited and animatedly asked questions about the baby: When and where was he born? What is his background? Who is his father? Teena did not name the father but said he was a white man with blond hair, short like herself.

Jim asked Teena what her plans for the future were: they had heard she wanted to finish her schooling. How was that going? A high school diploma followed by some sort of training was the route to employment, Jim said.

The group was in the difficult position of trying to form some sort of connection, or at least to pass the time amicably as they waited for the social worker. Lags in the conversation were filled with Jim and Faye's repeated thanks to Teena for choosing them as her son's new parents. Teena asked them about their religious beliefs, and they quickly assured her that the boy would get a good, Christian upbringing, just like Heidi. The trio also discussed ongoing contact. Would Teena be able to see how Jordan was growing and getting along? The Tearoes were enthusiastic about the idea and promised letters and photographs. She should feel free to write as often as she wanted, and they would do the same. Teena was also more than welcome to come and visit when she could, Faye added. Perhaps she could even attend school in Victoria, and their church, too? Christianity and education went a long way in life, the older woman advised.

Teena's attention often returned to Jim, whose air of calm seemed superficial. He checked his watch, wondering aloud why the social worker was late. After about an hour, when all conversation seemed to have run out, Teena suggested that perhaps they could go to Carolyn Grayson's home, pick up Jordan and bring him back to Teena's to wait. Jim stood and pulled his coat on. He would drive Teena the two blocks over, so she didn't have to walk back alone with the baby. Faye and Heidi waited at Teena's for the social workers.

Carolyn Grayson is relaxed in the hubbub that often engulfs her comfortable Fairview home. Located at the corner of Fairview's main street and a residential area, the frame house could use a coat of paint, and in the backyard a children's sandbox strewn with toys sits beside a teenager's bicycle, while a scruffy dog peers out through the slats of a white fence and barks haphazardly at passersby.

A divorced mother of four, Grayson, forty-eight, is a friendly woman with long curly hair and kind brown eyes. Her home is open to anyone who needs a place, and for the past three years it has been an approved receiving home for foster children. She provides care for up to sixty days, until a permanent-care home can be found for the children, or the child is able to go back to his or her family. Her involvement with the foster care system came about more or less by happenstance. One afternoon, a two-year-old child was found wandering the streets; the mother was apparently at home, passed out. Someone found the child and took it to the hospital, not knowing who the toddler belonged to. A hospital employee recognized the tot as a child that Grayson's daughter had babysat in the past, so the child was dropped off at the Graysons'.

"I was flabbergasted that a child would just be dropped with a family that they didn't even know. I thought, if Social Services are so short of foster care that there was no place for this little child to go, I've got to help out."

The Grayson home is jampacked—piles of books and magazines line one side of the small dining alcove, a sewing machine and computer sit on the other, with plants and knick-knacks in between. "I have a very high tolerance for mess," she laughs. There is a hominess about the place. Grayson's kitchen is often a gathering spot for her two teenager daughters, their friends or resident foster kids.

On that day, Grayson had just turned on the overhead kitchen light and was gazing out the window while peeling potatoes for supper when there was a knock on the door. A slice of cold air swept in as she opened the door and saw a man she didn't know holding open her screen door, with Teena Sawan standing in front of him.

"I'm here for Jordan," Teena said quickly. Jim said at almost the same time, "I'm here to pick up the baby."

Grayson was a bit taken aback. Although the foster care mother had heard talk from a social worker a few days earlier that Teena was going to give her child for adoption, she had not been formally notified that the adoption was proceeding. There was no way she was going to simply hand over a child in her care to a stranger. And Teena seemed uncertain of what to do. "She just stood there and looked helpless, that's the only way to describe it," Grayson recalled. She had seen Teena only twice or three times previously at her home, when Teena came to visit Jordan while Grayson was caring for him in January. The first visit, Teena brought two of her girlfriends with her, and it seemed like a "show and tell," said Grayson. Jordan was held by the girls, and although there was little opportunity for "quality time" between mother and child, he seemed happy with the attention. "He was a gregarious little boy," Grayson said.

The foster mother was somewhat surprised that Teena did

not come to visit him more often. "I had told Teena from the start, please feel free to come and visit him. Maybe it was too painful for her. I have no way of knowing. I didn't really know Teena at all. This whole thing just seemed overwhelming."

When Jim Tearoe again said that he was there to pick up the child, Grayson said, politely but adamantly, "No, I'm afraid you're not." The fact that neither Jim nor Teena had cast a glance towards Jordan, who was in a baby-swing by the fridge some six feet away, confirmed in Grayson's mind her initial uneasiness. She thought it odd that Jim Tearoe, who would ostensibly within hours welcome this child into his heart and life forever, didn't even look in his direction now. She assumed Teena felt too uncomfortable with the situation to do much more than stand there, shoulders slightly hunched, fingers playing with the zipper on her jacket.

In the three weeks Jordan was at her home in January, Grayson had grown close to the boy, probably too close for her own good, she later said. "Of all the babies I've had here, he's my favourite. We really hit if off. He was the perfect little baby." She said it took a few tries to find the right formula for him—he was picky about that—but otherwise, he seemed a healthy baby with a cheery disposition.

Grayson decided she had best call Lynne Smith and ask her what to do. While Teena and Jim Tearoe stood in the kitchen, Grayson got in touch with the social worker, who was in her van with a colleague heading in the opposite direction from Fairview. "I got it across to Lynne that I was uncomfortable with this man by one-word answers," recalls Grayson. "She said, 'Is there a problem?' and I said yes. She said, 'Would you like me to come down?' and I said yes."

Teena and Jim left, returning to Teena's house two blocks away, to wait for the social workers. Carolyn Grayson forgot about making supper and sat down at the kitchen table with a cup of coffee, holding Jordan.

Within an hour, Lynne Smith and a second social worker Teena and the Tearoes remember only as Ray knocked on the door of Teena's home. Inside, they found an amicable conversation going on between Teena and the Tearoes. Smith first talked to Teena alone, retiring to Teena's bedroom for privacy. She outlined the papers that would need signing and asked Teena if she was comfortable with the adoption. Teena said she was.

The Tearoes joined the social worker and Teena in the bedroom, sitting on the side of the bed and on chairs in the neat room. After further explaining the documents, Lynne Smith told Jim Tearoe of Carolyn Grayson's concerns that he had appeared aggressive and almost intimidating at the foster home, and that she was concerned that Teena was being coerced into leaving the child with him. Jim explained that he had felt uncomfortable at the Graysons' because of the "physical standard" of the home, and that he was used to a home where everything was in its place, not a home that was "untidy and cluttered." As for seeming indifferent to the child, Jim said it was the exact opposite. He was very excited about the "little man," he said, and could hardly wait to be a father to the boy. Faye Tearoe echoed the comments about the entire family being excited about the little man and impressed Lynne Smith with her obvious excitement about becoming Jordan's mother.

Although Faye had initially been put off by Teena's small house with its minimal furniture, the quiet bedroom calmed her. The wall over the bed was covered with cut-outs from magazines, pictures of gorgeous young models with gleaming white smiles and flowing hair. Some wore black leather, a look Teena considered sophisticated. Her sister and some friends were interested in modelling, and they all liked to look at the pictures and fantasize about the lives the women led. But Faye's eyes were focused on the table by Teena's neatly made bed. The Bible she saw there impressed her.

Lynne Smith had several documents in her bag and explained the legalese to the group assembled around her. The signing of a consent by guardian to adoption allowed the prospective adoptive parents to take the child; however, further legal proceedings would be needed before the child was legally adopted. The same document carries with it the proviso under Alberta legislation that should the birth-mother change her mind about the adoption, she has ten days to notify Social Services in writing. With that written revocation, the child is returned, no questions asked. Smith went through the papers twice with Teena as the Tearoes looked on. There was no doubt that Teena Sawan clearly understood the ten-day provision, as did the Tearoes.

The Tearoes and Ray left for Carolyn Grayson's while Lynne and Teena stayed behind. Smith wanted to make sure the young mother was doing what she wanted to do.

"Are you comfortable with this?" she asked when they were alone again. "Yes," said Teena. "I can't keep going back and forth. I don't want that for Jordan."

"It's a big decision to make," Smith said. "If you want to say no, I will help you do so, even at this stage." Teena said she was sure.

There was further discussion of the forms: the consent to adoption form, and a notice of placement of a child for adoption. Smith also left a social family history form, which has information necessary for finalizing the legal adoption. Smith asked Teena to complete that herself and discuss it further with Erin Harris, the official adoption worker for the area. Smith also told Teena that within thirty days she would have to complete a statutory declaration, which includes such information as the name of the birth-father, where Teena got the Tearoes' name, that no money or gift had been exchanged, that it was a willing placement and that it was a termination of Teena's parental rights. Teena would be notified when the actual legal adoption went through, which wouldn't be for months.

After some forty minutes of talking, the two went over to Carolyn Grayson's, where the Tearoes were getting acquainted with Jordan, who had been woken from his nap to meet his new parents. As Teena and Lynne Smith walked into the house, Jordan was sitting on Faye's lap, gazing around at the new faces, while Heidi sat beside him. "I wanted to grab him from her," recalls Teena. "I just had to swallow hard and look happy on the outside. I wanted to cry,

'What am I doing?'"

Carolyn Grayson's initial impression of Jim Tearoe didn't change, but Faye Tearoe immediately impressed her as warm and absolutely enthralled with Jordan. The Tearoes had several questions about Jordan's schedule, what formula he was on, when he slept, all of which Grayson answered, providing them with a written list. They also asked about Jordan's colouring, if she thought his hair would turn black later. "The question seemed to me to insinuate did I think he would begin to look native. I told them I thought his hair would stay blond."

A space was cleared at the cluttered dining-room table so the documents allowing the Tearoes to take the little boy could be signed. Jim Tearoe pulled a pen from his shirt pocket and nodded quickly as Smith went over the papers one more time, while Faye smiled at little Jordan. Teena sat in a chair off to the side, staring at her hands clasped in her lap. Grayson leaned against the counter and watched a scene that seemed other-worldly to her. With signatures on a dotted line, one family would end and another begin. As soon as Smith finished her explanation, Jim uncapped his pen and signed his name with his characteristic large, flourishing capital letters and looked up, smiling. "Oh, I hope you know what you're doing," Grayson thought as the pen was passed to Teena, who slowly signed her full name.

The documents signed, there was a moment of awkward silence as the pen was handed back to Jim and everyone waited for the next step. The sky outside the kitchen window was dark, and Grayson could already make out a few low stars in the prairie sky. The social workers suggested the Tearoes spend the night and get an early start the next day. "No, no, we want to leave tonight," said Jim, who stood up and put on his coat. He had a final request, though, to take a photograph of their little man's birth-mother. Teena agreed. Jim ran to the car outside and grabbed his camera.

Faye handed Jordan back to Teena, who took off her ski jacket and sat on a naugahyde dining-room chair. Teena held her son on her knee for the last time. Wearing a blue terry cloth jumper, his hair neatly combed after waking from a nap, Jordan stared out at the camera wide-eyed. Teena supported his back and head with one hand while Jordan clenched his tiny hand around the index finger on her right hand, which was holding his side. The young mother rubbed her thumb back and forth across the top of his polished hand, marvelling at its sleekness. "I'm smiling, you know, but it's not really a smile. That's someone trying to look happy," she recalled later.

Two years later, Carolyn Grayson can't recall the scene without feeling torn up inside. "Here was this young girl giving up her baby, and the people wanted it captured forever in a photograph. It was a very sad moment. She sat there with her son on her lap with a smile pasted on her face. It really was tragic." The social workers also took two pictures.

The papers signed and instructions given, all that was left to do was say goodbye in the crowded kitchen. Teena held Jordan close to her one last time. As she hugged him, she whispered "I love you, Jordan," in his right ear and kissed the soft spot near his temple where a blue vein pulsed. Teena had to leave or she would break down and she didn't want to do that in front of these strangers. She couldn't look at Jordan again; she worried she wouldn't be able to leave if she did.

Faye stood and hugged Teena before she left. "Thank you Teena. Thank you. God bless you." Faye didn't know if the young mother could ever understand the magnitude of the gift she had given.

Teena left with Ray. Lynne Smith would later write in her notes that Teena "did not appear overly emotional or upset— more bewildered." Smith stayed behind as the baby began to fuss and cry. Carolyn Grayson started to get teary as soon as the Tearoes packed up Jordan's belongings in preparation for leaving. Smith walked the Tearoes to their car, where they buckled the baby into the car-seat and arranged his bag of belongings in the back-seat, including some of the toys Teena had sent with him.

From inside the house, Carolyn Grayson watched a crying Jordan being taken away. She knew she shouldn't be so upset, but she couldn't help it. After everyone was gone, she sat down at her dining table and cried. She would have to relive the whole day as soon as her daughters came home expecting to see Jordan. The way Jim Tearoe's eyes had lit up the minute he signed on the dotted line made it seem like a business deal had just been completed. Grayson wondered if Teena Sawan had known what she was doing or whether she fully understood giving up a child. Two blocks away, Teena Sawan was wondering the same things.

The Tearoes drove past the queue of grain elevators, crossing the railroad tracks en route to the ribbon of highway that slices through the delicately hilled farmland. By the time they reached the B.C. border late that night, the infant in the backseat was no longer Jordan Michael Sawan. The baby born to a confused Cree mother in a small northern Alberta town had become David James Tearoe, named after a biblical king, the heart's desire of a middle-aged couple whose prayers for a boy child to complete their family were answered by the ultimate Father of all.

Chapter 6

❖ ❖ ❖

The modern white building of the Colwood Pentecostal Church is on the right as one drives west from Victoria, just past a bend on a well-travelled stretch of road called the Island Highway. Underneath the illuminated sign for the church are different axioms, spelled out each week in black block letters, much like a movie marquee. On the weekend after the Tearoes returned with their precious cargo, the sign welcomed David James Tearoe to his new home.

The child was obviously cherished by the doting parents, who proudly showed him off to their fellow worshippers. "This is our son, David James Tearoe," they said to everyone they met. Faye and Jim took turns holding the baby. Although it had been almost eight years since they'd had daily dealings with an infant, the proper way to hold a baby and the cradling motions came back in an instant.

After more than a decade of loving their David, they finally had a face to put to the dream. And what a face it was, with crystalline skin, clearly defined petal-pink lips and a small, narrow nose. With his fuzzy blond hair and blue eyes, he looked as if he could be Jim's natural child, a fact that had not escaped Jim when he saw the baby in Fairview. The white-painted wooden crib that had been Heidi's was brought out from storage.

"Was Heidi always this special?" they asked one another. "There's just something about him that's so special. Every little thing he does. He's our special little man."

They were filled with the best intentions towards the child's mother. "You know, honey," Faye had said to Jim, as they drove back to Victoria, "if we can help this girl welcome the Lord into her heart, let's do that." Both Faye and Jim believe in bringing as many people to a Christian way of life as possible. "As a Christian, Teena's my sister and I'd better take responsibility for her. If she just had the Lord in her heart," Faye said later. Concern about Teena's Christianity was natural for Jim—whenever he met someone, he wondered how he could bring that person to the Lord. "It *matters* whether people are saved or not. When I meet people or see them on the street, I wonder, are they going to Heaven or Hell?"

Jim had the name David James Tearoe added to his medical plan and inquired about the Canadian Scholarship Trust Foundation. They began thinking of an addition to their house that would include a separate bedroom for their son and a family room.

A series of telephone calls were made by the Tearoes to Social Services in Alberta in the few days after they arrived home. The couple wanted to know more about David's father so that they could determine the boy's ethnic status and find out if there were any potential medical problems. Social Services said they had heard the father was one of two people. Determined to find the answer, Jim Tearoe put in a call to Dr. Hallinen, who had delivered the baby, and asked if she could tell him about the infant's paternity. The doctor said she was not at liberty to give out any information about the baby until he was legally adopted by the Tearoes. Well, that was fine, Jim and Faye thought. They had no doubts that the adoption of David would go smoothly, much like their earlier adoption of Heidi. The legalities would be completed and their family would be complete.

Teena sat on the edge of her bed, waiting to feel better and trying to comprehend that she no longer had a baby. She had left Carolyn Grayson's a few hours earlier and felt sick inside. Her friend Christy came in and sat on the bed, putting an arm around Teena and asking if she was okay. Teena nodded and refused her offer of company. If Christy stayed much longer, Teena knew she would break down, and she didn't want to do that; she didn't know how to explain the swells of hopelessness and helplessness to anyone. She had done what was for the best, she kept telling herself, what was right for her child, what would ensure he had all the advantages. But deep in her core, she knew she had done something terribly wrong. Why did she always do what other people thought was best? Why couldn't she listen to what she wanted? Why was she so weak?

That night, she finally fell asleep, only to wake up midway through the night, expecting to hear little Jordan's cry. The sheet stretched out empty beside her, and sleep didn't come the rest of the night.

When Teena told Grace and Peter that Jordan was gone, their reactions added to her upset. "That's my little nephew. Don't you care?" Peter demanded. Teena listened to the crying voices of her younger brother and sister and knew she would never find the words to explain. She tried to talk of something else.

Iris Land thought the best thing had happened for everybody: now, Grace and Peter would not get any ideas in their head about having children out of wedlock, Teena could get on with improving her life, and the child was with stable Christian parents.

"There was so much hurt and so many families crying and praying night and day since the baby was born. Peter and Grace have no idea how many tears and how many hours I spent pondering and hurting for this baby, and wanting the best for him," Iris Land said later. "They want this little guy to play with. They have no idea of what it's like to have a baby screaming night and day. I work at the health unit and I see girls who have husbands, and they are still tearing their hair out. Without support.... I can't imagine what it's like to do it on their own."

But for Teena, the feeling that she had done something that went against the flow of her heart was at least as difficult to live with as the doubts about her ability to cope. Her feelings of loss intensified. Two days after walking out the door of Carolyn Grayson's home, Teena Sawan knew she wanted her son back.

While the Tearoes were unpacking the baby crib, Teena Sawan sat in her bedroom and penned a note in her characteristic round, curlicued handwriting.

To Whom It May Concern,   Feb. 8, 1992
    I Cecilia A. Sawan am revoking my consent of adoption of my Son Jordan Michael Sawan. I would appreciate it if you would contact Jim and Faye Tearoe to return my son to my custody as soon as possible.
Sincerely,
Cecilia A. Sawan

Teena asked her roommate if she had a stamp, but she didn't. Perhaps that was best anyway, Teena later recalled thinking. She was a little concerned about how Lynne Smith would react to the news, since they didn't have an altogether friendly relationship. Teena carefully folded the letter and put it in her brown suitcase. She would call Social Services first and let them know of her change of heart, before mailing the all-important revocation letter. It was two days since she had said goodbye to her baby, and she had eight more days to get him back.

The first of several phone calls between Teena Sawan and the Social Services office in Peace River sixty miles east of Fairview occurred on February 12, six days after Teena gave her child to the Tearoes. She had four days left in which to revoke her consent. The events that followed in this short time span would later be minutely dissected and would decide the future of a little boy.

Peace River enjoys the minor distinction of being the centre of government for the Peace region, and it is in this town, the largest in the area, that the Alberta Department of Family and Social Services has its main office, on the second floor of a flat-topped building on 100th Street. At mid-morning on February 12, 1992, Teena talked to Erin Harris. "I want Jordan back," she told the surprised adoptions worker. "I love my son. He's a part of me and I really miss him." Teena also told Harris that she realized she had wanted to drink more than she had wanted Jordan, and that she wanted to go to AADAC (Alberta Alcohol and Drug Abuse Commission) to get counselling to help her stop.

"You're within your rights to revoke the consent," Harris said slowly, "but it has to be in writing." Teena had until February 16, a Sunday. "What address do I send the letter to?" Teena asked. Harris gave her the Peace River address. Teena said she was going to mail the letter that day. It was also up to Teena, Harris said, to telephone the Tearoes and make arrangements to have Jordan returned, as it had been a private placement.

In the same conversation, Harris asked Teena if she wanted to complete the statutory declaration, the document Lynne Smith had told Teena about on February 6, and which was required by the court in Alberta before an adoption could be finalized. It seemed somewhat strange to ask a mother about such a document when she had just called to say that she wanted her child back. Teena refused to complete it.

Teena's telephone call set off a small storm of action in the Peace River ministry office. After placing the receiver back in its cradle, Erin Harris let the person responsible for distributing the mail know the office would be receiving correspondence from Teena Sawan. When it came, the mail clerk was to keep the envelope. The legislation says the birth-parent who has consented to the adoption of a child may, not later than ten days after the date of the consent, revoke the consent by providing written notice. As long as the postmark was within ten days, the revocation would be acceptable.

Harris talked to Lynne Smith, who, in turn, discussed the situation with her casework supervisor.

Although Teena's right to change her mind was acknowledged, Smith had some concerns and scepticism about Teena's ability to sustain a change in lifestyle, concerns that were documented in her "contact notes," which detail a social worker's involvement in cases. In compressed handwriting on the lined, legal-length paper, Smith wrote, "Teena's ability to make rational decisions and ability to care for Jordan questioned." She did not indicate what these comments were based on. Smith called Gail Friesen, who had provided some counselling to Teena during her pregnancy, but was unable to reach her.

The next morning, February 13, 1992, Gail Friesen returned Lynne Smith's call and, according to Smith's notes, said she was very much opposed to Teena getting her child back. Of the conversation with Gail Friesen, Smith wrote: "Tina [sic] changes mind all the time. Is very irresponsible. Gail not prepared to encourage this. Role is not to say, get your act together. Yet at this point may be what needs to be said. No commitment. Does not follow through when decisions are made. Every decision made with Gail, Tina overturned every decision on impulse."

Lynne Smith and Teena talked on the telephone in the afternoon of February 13, exactly a week after Teena gave up Jordan. Their recollections of that conversation differ slightly, but they agree on one thing—it was clear from the conversation that Teena wanted Jordan returned, as was her right under Alberta legislation. Smith recalls reminding Teena that she needed the revocation notice in writing and into the office and Teena saying that it had been mailed the previous day, after talking to Erin Harris. Teena's recollection is that the letter was sent after the conversation with Smith, because she wanted to tell Lynne about her change of heart before mailing the letter.

Whether the all-important letter was mailed on February 12 or February 13 was relatively insignificant in the long run. Either day would have shown it was done within the ten-day time period. What was to become of some significance, at least to those who later doubted that the letter was ever sent, was that Teena said she mailed a photocopy of the letter, not the original. To Teena, the reasons for keeping the original were obvious. It was clear in her mind that if she had the original, there would be no way anyone could doubt that she had written the letter. "I thought Social Services might try to say something about it, might try to screw me around, so I thought I better keep the original," she recalled. Teena said she photocopied the letter at the Fairview Provincial Building and mailed it in a white envelope with blue inside, around the same time she mailed her financial benefit cards.

The remainder of Teena and Smith's February 13 conversation centred on ideas for follow-up care of Jordan upon his return to Teena. Smith told Teena about the Carritas Centre, a residence where single mothers can learn parenting skills. And she thought the department would need to be involved when Jordan came back, "that Teena was not going to make it alone." Teena agreed that she had to deal with her drinking, and that it was perhaps best that Jordan, when returned, be cared for in a foster home while she sought help. She did not object to Social Services providing that help. Smith told Teena that it was the Tearoes' responsibility to bring the baby back and asked when Teena wanted Jordan returned. Smith said the response she received left her "doubtful of [Teena's] decision to have Jordan back." Smith contends that Teena said she wanted Jordan back "after the weekend," as she was busy. Teena does not recall saying that.

All that remained was to telephone the Tearoes and tell them of her change of heart. Teena made that call the morning of February 14, eight days after the Tearoes had left with Jordan, and still within the legally prescribed ten-day limit she had to change her mind.

The mornings were especially busy for Faye Tearoe, a time when the demands of getting an eight-year-old girl ready for school, her husband out the door to his office job, feeding the family dog and readying herself for household tasks made her feel her life was complete. With the arrival of David, things grew more hectic, but it was a commotion the family relished. Jim raced out at the last minute, as did Heidi, leaving Faye with the newest family member. This was the Lord's plan for her, being a wife and mother. She was having a moment to herself, taking her first sips of coffee brewed from freshly ground beans, when the call that turned her life inside-out came.

In her slightly singsong voice, Faye answered the ringing phone, sitting on the ledge that divided the white and mahogany kitchen and adjacent family room. She expected another congratulatory call on the addition to the family, or perhaps her parents, checking to see how their grandson was doing.

"Hi, is this Faye Tearoe?" the voice on the other end of the line asked.

"Yes, it is."

"It's Teena...Sawan calling," the teenager said, not sure how far she had to go to identify herself.

"Teena, how are you?" asked Faye, an undertone of anxiety mixed in with the friendliness.

"I'm okay," replied Teena, leaning against the counter in the small kitchen of the Fairview house, her fingers entwined in the telephone cord. She didn't know how else to ask for Jordan back other than to say it bluntly. "I'm calling because I want Jordan back. I'm supposed to phone you about getting him brought back."

Faye's eyes darted around the room frantically, and she grasped the receiver with both hands. She filled her fear with words, her voice arching towards hysteria.

"Oh no, Teena, you don't want to do that. Teena, the baby is happy here. You can come down and see him if you want to and spend a couple of weeks with him. Or a couple months. You could catch the bus down. You could go to school down here, you know, we have the same schools as they do up there, you could continue your schooling and stay here with us and see how happy he is. He's very happy, praise the Lord."

When Faye stopped for a breath, Teena quickly and shortly said, "No, I don't want to do that. I want my son back."

Faye asked her several times if she wanted to talk to Jim, answering the question herself, yes, Teena should talk to Jim about this, to which the teenager again said no.

After hanging up the phone, Teena walked the three blocks along the snow-packed streets to Fairview's main street, hands jammed in the empty pockets of her ski jacket. The outside air was sharp and bright, and she felt clear-headed, better than she had in a long time. Finally, she was doing what her heart told her to. She knew she had to clean up her life, that there was no way she could continue to live the way she had been and be able to give Jordan the kind of home she wanted to, or that Social Services would approve of. She would get away from the Fairview friends she couldn't say no to and clean up her life. She wanted to rent a nice apartment, or maybe even a house, take high school upgrading, be near Grace and Peter, and have her son with her. She wanted to be with people she loved, and who loved her in return. That afternoon, it all seemed possible. Gazing in the windows of the Co-op, Teena saw a little sweatsuit bearing the insignia of her favourite hockey team, the Calgary Flames. It would be perfect for Jordan. When she got her Social Services cheque, she'd go buy it for him, a welcome home gift.

Faye Tearoe tried to keep the terror of loss at bay. As soon as she hung up the phone, she quickly punched in the number to Jim's office, but her fingers shook so badly she had to try it twice. Her voice feverish, she relayed Teena's message to Jim. "Oh no, dear Lord, no," he said, holding the phone with one hand and his forehead with the other. The thought of losing the little boy who seemed already to have a special cache of smiles for his dad was too much for Jim. Faye soothed her husband by detailing her suggestion that Teena come and stay with them and see the home David was living in.

"This just can't be. She can't want the little man back," Jim said. After a few minutes, the couple decided they had best call Lynne Smith.

Months later, when relating her conversation with Smith, Faye Tearoe says that she would have, albeit unwillingly and against her better judgment, returned the child if the social worker had told her she had to. Smith's contact notes indicate a subtly different scenario. According to Smith's notes, Faye was adamant that Teena had said she was coming to B.C. to see them and the child, something Teena is equally resolute she never agreed to. Faye was going to help the teenager with her life and introduce her to a "good crowd," she told the social worker. Smith had talked to Teena shortly after the teenager's conversation with Faye and as far as she knew, Teena had been clear with Faye that she wanted Jordan back and had never indicated she was going to stay with the Tearoes.

"We love him, we want to keep the little guy," Faye told the social worker. The baby had travelled well on the return to Victoria, was contented and happy, Faye said. She had never had a more peaceful child, although she complained "our little baby just reeked of smoke" after they left the foster home with him. At one point, Faye asked Lynne Smith, "How can we get this baby back? Teena wanted a Christian home—she has one." Faye also inquired about the money they had already spent—who would pay for their trip and Jim's time off work?

Lynne told the obviously upset woman that, by rights, they had to return the child immediately. But, Smith added, Teena had indicated she was busy on the weekend, and Monday was a statutory holiday in Alberta called Family Day. Would the Tearoes mind caring for the baby until Tuesday? That was no problem, Faye said, David was "so precious."

After hanging up, Faye went to the bassinet where David lay sleeping. "Dear Lord, show us the way," she said, rocking the bed slowly.

Smith talked with her supervisor and was directed to contact the Tearoes again. In their second conversation Feb. 14, she told Faye that until Teena's written revocation of consent was received by the department, there was no need to return the baby. Faye listened intently as Smith explained to her that Teena said she had mailed the letter, but that it had yet to arrive. The next mail would be in the Social Services office on Tuesday afternoon, February 18. Essentially, the Tearoes could rest easy until Teena's revocation letter was received. It was a glimmer of hope for the Victoria family.

Jim and Faye turned to prayer that weekend, reciting scriptures to fight fear. Faye believes that doubts and worry are Satan's work, and that "Satan can whisper in your ear to worry, but he has to leave if you put the word of God out there." Amid their weekend prayers and recitations, they also called their lawyer. They told John Jordan about the situation and asked him to find out what he could.

Faye finally found her answer to the all-encompassing fear of loss in the biblical story of Abraham, who was told by the Lord to sacrifice his only and much-beloved son Isaac on a mountain-top pyre. Isaac had been God's gift to one-hundred-year-old Abraham and his wife Sarah, whose infertility was cured by the Lord. As the father and son trekked up the designated mountain, Isaac asked his father where the animal was for sacrifice. "God will see to it, my son," the father replied. The two built the altar and laid the wood. Abraham bound his son and laid him on the pyre. Just as he was about to plunge his knife into his son's chest, the Angel of God shouted to the father from Heaven, telling him to stop. The angel said it was clear God was first in Abraham's life. Just then, a ram was caught by its horns in a nearby bush and replaced Isaac as the offering. The Angel of God called again to Abraham from Heaven, telling him that because he had obeyed the Lord and did not withhold even his precious son, he would have incredible blessings, and the Lord would multiply his descendants into countless thousands and millions, like the stars above and the sands along the seashore. The descendants would conquer their enemies and be a blessing to all the nations on earth.

"You know how Jim and I weigh it up?" Faye says. "When

Teena first phoned, I was really upset. The child we've so desired and prayed for for fourteen years, you know, we'd just always thank the Lord for David James Tearoe, and I said to the Lord—it took me two days to do this—I said to the Lord, 'Lord, I'm putting David on the altar, just like Abraham did.'... I said to myself, I have to do this. I have to put my son on the altar, and say, 'Father, he's not mine at all. He's yours. You do with him as you want. He's not mine. He's your child.' And when I could take my hand back and say, 'Father, he's in your hands, if you want me to take him back to Teena, I will,' the Lord gave me such peace about it! And then Teena never bothered phoning back or doing anything about it, so David really was ours. He really was ours."

On the morning of Tuesday, February 18, John Jordan called Lynne Smith. Jordan, himself the father of two, told the social worker he had been contacted by the Tearoes and asked if the birth-mother was still of the same mind. Smith said she assumed so, although the written revocation had not yet been received. What about the cost so far to his clients, Jordan asked, and what were they to do if the revocation of consent was received that day? Lynne said she would be in touch after the day's mail was received.

No revocation of consent from Teena Sawan was received that day, although the Social Services office did receive another piece of correspondence from her. In a blue envelope, the kind used for birthday or greeting cards, was Teena Sawan's social allowance card accompanied by a handwritten note to her financial benefit worker apologizing for mistakes made on the cards. The postmark showed it had been mailed February 14, 1992, from Fairview. Smith called Faye to tell her the news. Teena's time was almost out.

After the mail was delivered on February 19, Lynne Smith called Faye again. "There is still no letter," she told the anxious woman. Faye left the conversation with her fears assuaged. Her clear impression was that Teena's time was up. "Lynne said, 'Look, as far as we're concerned at this point you can go ahead and adopt him,'" Faye Tearoe would later explain of the February 19 conversation. The women talked about shots the baby needed. Later that same day, the Tearoes contacted their lawyer and told him it appeared that they could proceed with the legalities of the adoption. No letter had been received and the ten days were up. The black-and-white rules had not been followed. Without the written word, the baby was theirs.

While Faye's view that Teena did nothing further to get her child back undoubtedly gave her much solace, the comments were not in fact correct. The young mother called Social Services again on February 19. "Did you get my letter yet?" she asked Lynne Smith. It was Teena's fourth call about her son. No, they hadn't, Smith told her. But it had been mailed the previous Wednesday, said Teena, who Smith later described as "sounding puzzled."

"I'm sorry, Teena, we don't have it."

Smith suggested Teena contact Canada Post to see if the letter had gone missing. The social worker also recommended that Teena talk to a lawyer. The ten-day revocation period was over. If the teenager wanted to take it any farther, it would be a legal battle.

All that stood between Teena Sawan and her child was a slip of paper, one she said had been mailed. With that piece of paper, the baby had to be returned to the young mother. Without it, he would stay where he was, despite the fact that Lynne Smith, Erin Harris, their supervisor, Jim and Faye Tearoe and their lawyer all knew within the ten-day time period that the teenager had changed her mind.

Two days later, on February 21, Smith's supervisor contacted the family law department of the Social Services ministry in Edmonton to ask their opinion on the Tearoe-Sawan matter. A lawyer with the department advised that, even though the department had received verbal revocation, the original consent signed by Teena Sawan on February 6, 1992, was still valid, because they had not received the revocation of consent in writing, as is stated in the regulations.

On February 24, Lynne Smith sent a letter to Teena Sawan, outlining the ministry's position.

February 24, 1992

Cecilia A. Sawan
General Delivery
Fairview, AB
T0H 1L0

Dear Tina [sic]:
RE:PRIVATE ADOPTION OF JORDAN MICHAEL SAWAN
It is important to make clear the present situation regarding
Jordan. In order to do so it is necessary to summarize the
events of the past few weeks.

On January 6, 1992, a Custody Agreement was signed
between yourself and the Department in relation to Jordan,
and he was placed in a foster home. This was done because
you felt unable to care for Jordan while you made arrangements for his Private Adoption. During the next few weeks
you expressed doubts about Jordan being adopted and eventually decided to keep him.

On Monday, February 4, 1992, you contacted Jim and Faye
Tearoe of Victoria, British Columbia and arranged to place
Jordan with them for the purpose of Adoption. I was advised
of your plans when I called you about another matter. Jim and
Faye travelled to Fairview and met with you on Thursday,
February 6, 1992. I was also involved in this meeting.

You decided to place Jordan with this couple, and after they
had gone to meet Jordan, who was by then back in his foster
home, we discussed some of the legal aspects of the situation.

You signed two forms in my presence. One was the Consent
to Adoption form, the other was a Notice of Placement of a
Child for Adoption. We talked about the effects of an
Adoption Order and you seemed to understand the permanency of such an order.

I explained to you that should you change your mind about the adoption, you were required to notify the Department in writing within ten days and that Jordan would then be returned to you.

On Wednesday, February 12, 1992, you contacted the Department by telephone and advised that you had changed your mind, and wished to have Jordan returned. You were again advised of your requirement to give this information in writing. You called again on February 13, 1992 to say you had mailed the letter the previous day.

Since that date, no written statement has been received from your [sic] regarding this matter, although the mail on February 18, 1992, contained some correspondence between yourself and your social allowance worker.

Even though we were advised verbally, we did not receive the required notice in writing, so we are taking the position that no revocation of your consent to the adoption of Jordan has been received. Thus the Department is not in a position to assist you with Jordan's return. If you are still wishing to pursue this, you need to consult with a lawyer.

If would be helpful if you would confirm in writing that your understanding of the situation is as I have outlined. I would also ask you to inform the Department of what your intention is, do you wish to proceed with the placement, or will you be seeking legal advice?

A copy of this letter has been sent to Jim and Faye Tearoe.

Yours sincerely,
Lynne Smith
Social Worker

Teena rarely checked her general delivery mail in Fairview and did not see the letter from Lynne Smith. The Tearoes received their copy on March 1 or 2. Teena had had plenty of time, in their eyes, to figure out what she wanted to do with the child, and had made a choice. She had "signed her baby" over to them. "How much does she want her baby back when she didn't even get her little note in within the ten days?" Faye later said.

Whether or not the all-important revocation letter was written when Teena said it was would become a significant and perplexing question in the months to come. There would be some who suggested the letter was penned months later, not on February 8 as Teena Sawan said.

Would Teena lie about sending the letter, then call Lynne Smith to specifically inquire whether it had arrived and sound puzzled that it had not been received? It would have been much easier to mail the letter. Could the blame be with Canada Post? Could the letter have been received by Social Services but inadvertently—or even purposely—misplaced? No evidence has come to light to support any one of these scenarios.

Smith's contact notes make it clear that Social Services had strong reservations about Teena Sawan's abilities to mother. On the one hand, they show social workers concerned about a young mother's ability to cope. On the other, they show a marshalling of offences against that same young mother. Teena was described by Gail Friesen as given to changing her mind quickly and repeatedly. Did Teena's decision to revoke her consent simply seem like more waffling? The social workers had witnessed Teena changing her mind numerous times, during her pregnancy and in the months following, about what to do with her baby. Perhaps they questioned the wisdom of moving a child when they didn't expect that Teena was going to follow through on her decision. There was no doubt from anyone, Teena Sawan included, that she had been a handful for Social Services during her teenage years, refusing to follow rules, running away from homes found for her. What role did her past play in how she was dealt with by the government agency that had control of her life from the time she was four years old? Against Teena's

history with the ministry, how compelled would social workers be to help return the child? Did they think Teena Sawan
would just go away?

Chapter 7

❖❖ ❖❖ ❖❖

The suggestion that she check with Canada Post and get a
lawyer left Teena Sawan upset and bewildered. In her
mind, she had done what she was supposed to. She had written a letter telling Social Services she wanted her son back,
called Social Services and let them know, notified Jim and
Faye Tearoe of the same, and then called again to see if her
letter had arrived. None of it had worked.

Teena didn't know who to talk to about her situation. Her
mother was dead, she didn't know where her father was, her
older brother and sister were having difficulties in their own
lives, and she couldn't see what help her younger siblings
would be in a situation like this. What family she knew of
back at Little Buffalo did not have money. She thought of
calling Louanne, but the two had not parted on good terms.
Teena's sense of isolation was complete.

Teena would later say she wasn't sure how to get a lawyer,
much less how to pay for one. Her impression of the profession came from television, movies and gossip, and at all levels, one thing was clear—lawyers were expensive. Her
welfare cheque covered the essentials of life but didn't leave
much for extras. She wasn't even sure if there were lawyers

in Fairview. They were probably all in Peace River, an hour's drive east.

One thing Teena did know was that she had to clean up her life. But saying it and doing it were entirely different matters. She stayed in Fairview for a couple of weeks after the February 19 conversation with Lynne Smith, and her lifestyle didn't change. The small house was still home to many a party, and anyone packing a case of beer was welcome. Teena got in trouble with the law, writing a bad cheque for groceries at the Fairview IGA. She blames herself and the easy influence her friends had on her. "They said, 'Come on, come on, don't be a wimp,' and I was stupid and listened to them. It was a very stupid thing to do."

She was easy to catch up with—she had signed the cheque—and she was soon charged with fraud. She appeared without a lawyer at the Fairview courthouse and pleaded guilty. The judge gave her a $300 fine and a short lecture. The court appearance was the final straw. She had to get out of Fairview. Teena Sawan was at the proverbial fork in the road, one she herself recognized. "My life could either continue on like it was in Fairview, or I could try and change it." She packed up her meagre belongings and left.

Bundled in the back of a friend's four-door Pontiac Parisienne car, Teena's thoughts were on what she hoped would be another fresh start. It was the beginning of March 1992, and she was moving back to Manning, near to Peter and Grace. Piled up around her were clothes, blankets, a set of mismatched dishes and two photograph albums filled with pictures of her younger brother and sister, some of herself with various foster families, her relatives at Little Buffalo and her only picture of her mother, Maryann, standing behind a snowmobile on Bluford's trapline.

There is little mystery in Manning, a town of just over one thousand nestled in a valley on the banks of the Notikewin River and surrounded by golden fields in the summer. It takes only a whispered "Who's that?" to find out at least a few of the details behind a strange face. Most everyone knows each other's family tree, and many families date back to the first settlers in the area. Those who stayed learned a lesson common to people in small northern settlements—be neighbourly because security comes in knowing you are not alone. That spirit of neighbourliness lives on in Manning, an unpretentious town that proudly proclaims itself "Manning—Land of the Mighty Moose." A huge wooden moose welcomes people driving north on the Mackenzie Highway, and while it may be mighty, it is also missing its antlers. A few years ago, pranksters made their way through town, stripping the outdoor moose replicas—and there are more than a few—of their crowning glory.

Newcomers to town who are not obviously part of travelling oil crews, or "rig pigs" as they are locally known, are noted. Locals sitting in the town's main coffee shops—the Manning Motor Inn at the south end of town and Grimm's Truck Stop at the north—can see every vehicle coming through town. The cars and trucks rarely slow down as they zip through; there are no stoplights in the town. Vehicles are more likely to slow to dodge the sandwich-board on the yellow line of the highway, advertising the skating club's Friday night bingo. There is a strong sense of community, and minor hockey leagues, skating clubs and softball teams are a cornerstone. On Sundays, the church parking lots are full of pick-ups. Church-going is an integral part of many people's lives, with the usual mix of devout Christians and Sunday morning socializers. There is little that happens in the morning in Manning that is not known by the end of the day.

It was to this town that Teena Sawan moved back in March 1992, hoping to clean up her life.

When she got to Manning, Teena moved in with Judy Waldo, who had been a big help to Teena and Louanne when Jordan was first out of the hospital. At thirty-six, the mother of three had just left her husband and was coping with challenges of her own. She had also been fined under the Liquor Control and Licensing Act when a friend of hers was caught with open alcohol in her car. To Teena, Judy was both a friend and older sister, someone to whom she could turn for advice.

Life followed a relatively simple course. Teena was on welfare and helped Judy out with her children during the day. She read a bit, slept in, sometimes did needlepoint, went to the arcade or watched television, carefully checking the TV listings and marking on a calendar programs that interested her. Grace and Peter were nearby, and she and her younger siblings, especially Grace, often spent after-school afternoons together.

She began seeing an AADAC counsellor once every couple of weeks to talk about drinking. Teena says now she found it easy to stop drinking at that point, in large part because she had supportive people around her. She is inconsistent about whether or not she considers herself an alcoholic. Sometimes, it seems to her that she has been unfairly termed an alcoholic because she is native. At other times, she says she "used to be an alcoholic but I'm not any more, because I'm not drinking and I don't crave alcohol." Teena understands alcoholism to mean you can't stop once you have one drink, and says that this does not apply to her.

Teena and Judy often sat at the kitchen table talking, and as they grew closer, Teena opened up about missing Jordan and wanting him back. Judy encouraged her to talk about her feelings, realizing her young friend found that difficult to do.

One afternoon in mid-April, Teena arrived at the home she shared with Judy to find a large, brown envelope waiting for her. It had been sent to Teena in Fairview and forwarded to Manning. The postmark indicated that it was from Victoria. Teena sat down with a cigarette at the kitchen table and used a fingernail to carefully open the sealed flap. Inside was a letter on pristine-white paper. It didn't take long to comprehend, and her response was immediate.

"I'm not signing anything," she said to Judy, who was standing across the kitchen. "What do they think they're doing, anyway?"

John E. Jordan
April 8, 1992

Ms. Augustine Cecelia Sawan
General Delivery
Fairview, Alberta
T0H 1L0

Dear. Ms. Sawan,
Re: *Jordan Michael Sawan - Adoption - James and Faye Tearoe*

This letter is to advise that the writer has been engaged to act as solicitor on behalf of James and Faye Tearoe with regard to the adoption of Jordan Michael Sawan.

I am writing to you to ask that you consent in writing to the proposed adoption of Jordan Michael Sawan to James and Faye Tearoe. I would ask that you write to me informing me of the fact that you will consent to the proposed adoption.

In addition, our Superintendent of Family and Child Adoption, here in British Columbia, will require an interview to be made with you and I anticipate that they will be contacting you shortly in this regard. In order to facilitate this interview, would you be kind enough to provide us with your phone number so that both the Superintendent's office and the writer may contact you directly.

I look forward to hearing from you as soon as possible.

Yours truly
John E. Jordan
cc: Mr. and Mrs. Tearoe

Teena ripped the letter in half and threw it in the garbage. A few days later, on April 22, she telephoned the Alberta Family and Social Services office in Peace River. She talked to Erin Harris and told the woman again that she wanted her son back. It was Teena's fourth telephone call to Social Services in this regard, her second directly to Erin Harris.

"Wants to get Jordan Back—revoke her consent," Harris wrote in her notes of the brief conversation. "Advised her we received no letter & she needs to contact Legal Aid to get a lawyer & try & get her consent revoked."

Erin Harris would later say she gave Teena Sawan the telephone number for legal aid and that she thought Sawan knew a legal aid representative was in Manning on court days, information Teena Sawan does not recall being given. The adoption worker asked Teena if she had received the letter sent by Lynne Smith in February and Teena said she hadn't. Harris promised to mail that to her, along with two photographs of Teena and Jordan taken the day the Tearoes left with the baby. She added that if Teena changed her mind about the revocation, there were some forms that still needed signing. As she had the first time Harris asked her about signing the forms she had mentioned two months earlier, Teena said no.

A few days later, Erin Harris's letter arrived, in which she again advised Teena that she should get legal help if she intended to continue with the revocation. As for the photographs, Teena carefully fit one into her wallet, alongside her son's birth announcement, cut from the Manning *Banner-Post*. The second photograph she gave to Grace.

The legal machinations behind the Tearoes' adoption proceedings had begun weeks before Teena Sawan's April 22 call to Social Services. As soon as the department told the Tearoes the consents were, in their view, valid, the Tearoes had instructed their lawyer to move ahead. This was John Jordan's first adoption case, and he researched the B.C. Adoption Act. One of the basic requirements is a home-study of the prospective adoptive parents, to be completed within six months of the child being in the home. Before any formal adoption proceedings can start, the home-study must be done and all the required documents must be in order.

It was with this in mind that B.C. social worker Greta Vanderleeden wrote to the Alberta Family and Social Services office in Peace River.

March 16, 1992

Dear Sir
Re: Augustine Cecilia Sawan
Address: General Delivery, Fairview, Alberta, T0H 1L0

The above-named birth mother placed her baby privately for adoption with a family in British Columbia. I understand that the adoption was facilitated by your agency.

I am writing to request that the above named birth mother be interviewed. Our policy requires that in private placements, a Ministry person or a person from a recognized agency must interview the birth parent to obtain both background information and the circumstances leading to the placement. Information we need is:
1. Did the birth mother understand the meaning of adoption and was she aware of alternatives available?
2. Was the child relinquished voluntarily and without due pressure?
3. A social history.
4. Why did the birth mother relinquish her child?
5. Was the birth father involved in the planning for the child and is background information on him available?

Our Adoption Act regulations also require that the person who places a child or who facilitates the placement must report certain information to the Superintendent of Family and Child Services. I have requested that the adopting parents' lawyer obtain the facilitator's report and it would appear that your agency facilitated the adoption.

Yours truly

Mrs. Greta Vanderleeden
Social Worker
Adoptions/Permanent Planning L32

Greta Vanderleeden received a telephone reply from adoptions worker Erin Harris, who told her that Teena Sawan understood the adoption and was aware of the alternatives. Meanwhile, Vanderleeden was beginning the required home-study on the Tearoe family. Essentially, such studies consist of three or four scheduled visits over a six-month period and are designed to determine the suitability of the prospective couple as adoptive parents.

When Vanderleeden drove up to the Tearoes' home on the afternoon of May 8, a Friday, the social worker was already familiar with the Tearoes, having become acquainted with them during their adoption of Heidi. She considered herself to be somewhat of a friend, although she wasn't concerned about losing her professional objectivity. Vanderleeden was impressed with what she saw that day, a couple living in a spacious home who obviously doted on their children. Jim had a good government job, Faye was a stay-at-home mom, their daughter Heidi a personable and affectionate child. What Vanderleeden saw seemed, to her, to be an ideal home, though there would still have to be two more home visits before her report could be concluded.

The several-hundred-square-foot addition to Jim and Faye Tearoe's home was well underway, and the couple were proud of what was surely going to add to the value of their home and quality of life. And it was all done for baby David. They had refinanced their home to pay for the additions of a bedroom for David and an airy recreation room, for the children to play in and also to provide Faye with a quiet space for prayer.

On a Saturday afternoon in early May, Teena Sawan called the Tearoe home. Jim Tearoe was alone and took the call. He remembers the conversation as fairly short, with Teena wanting to know how Jordan was doing and asking for photographs of the baby so she could see how he was growing. Jim told her the baby was very happy, that he loved listening to the music the rest of the family enjoyed and was even starting to clap along with the lively Bible tunes, just as his mom and dad did. The call left Jim feeling confident that Teena Sawan had given up on her efforts to get the boy back.

She had asked only how he was and had not mentioned the child's return. He did not know that the short phone call had in fact intensified Teena's desperate longing for her child.

A few days after the telephone conversation, Teena Sawan decided to make what she felt at the time was a last attempt to get her son back. Sitting down at the kitchen table, she penned a four-page letter, addressed to Jim and Faye Tearoe.

May 12, 1992

Dear Jim, Faye and Family,

Thought I'd better write to tell you how I've been feeling these past couple months since Jordan has been gone.

When Jordan first left, I couldn't help but think of him all the time. I missed holding him, laying with him, etc. So then I started to think that maybe I'd like to get custody of Jordan again. He's my only child and I wanted so much to raise him, see him go to school, say his first words, walk for the first time. That's when I got in touch with Social Services to get him back.

When I gave Jordan to your family, the day he left I sat and cried all day and I sat up all night thinking of him. Jordan means everything to me and he's even that much more special to me because he was my first child...

I know this letter will come as a shock and I'm not trying to make things harder for your family. Jordan has been with your family for two months and from talking to Jim the other day, things seem to be going well. I'm not sure what else to say. I've always felt a piece of my life missing since Jordan has been away. I have nightmares at night about him.

I wanted to be honest and tell you how I was feeling so you would be able to better understand the reason behind what I'm doing. It's not easy being a first-time mother with no one there to help you out.

But at the same time, it's not easy having your first and only child apart from you. I know I'm not in school and I don't have a job, but that doesn't mean I wouldn't try to provide Jordan with a good home and an education.

When I first had Jordan all I could think of was, this is my son!!! I was a very proud mother, carrying Jordan for nine months, feeling him kick and move. It was exciting for me when he was born. Jordan is a very special baby to both myself and the Lord.

When I first found out that I was pregnant, I wasn't sure if I wanted to be a mother yet. I had contemplated abortion when I was 11 weeks pregnant. But deep down in my heart, I said to myself that this innocent child has every right to see the world and to live. After I decided to have Jordan, that's when my love for him grew.

Looking back now, I ask myself if Jordan was so special and meant so much to me, why did I want him adopted. I was confident I had problems in my life just like everyone else. Jordan was not a problem. I wanted to have him and I wanted so badly to keep him. I needed support and help to raise him in Fairview but had none.

I felt like people were pushing me to give him up saying it was the best for him.

I regret what I did to this day because in all honesty, I wanted to keep him and not give him up. I miss Jordan to this very day, even more now than yesterday.

I hope you can understand how I feel. I'm not trying to upset you and your family, I'm just expressing the way I feel. I'd like Jordan back and I realize you probably would like to keep him.

Yours Truly
Teena Sawan

She mailed it from the Manning post office, a pleasant walk from Judy's in the dawning spring. The only remnants of winter were patches of snow, silver with dirt, lining the roadside. The aspen trees already had green buds, and the crops in the distance turned the fields into sheets of gold. "I thought if they heard from me directly," Teena said later, "they would reconsider and bring Jordan back to me. I thought, 'All I can do is ask them to bring him back, and tell them that I love him and want him back.' I thought they should have the heart to bring him back."

Jim Tearoe received the envelope marked "Personal" at his downtown Victoria office on May 21, 1992. He sat in his swivel chair and stared at the photographs of his family on the desk for a long while that afternoon, the letter in his lap. Later he met with John Jordan and left feeling much calmer. Teena had still not done what was required of her to get her child back. When Jim told Faye about the letter that night, she refused to read it. It was too upsetting.

Jim put it in an accordion file with all the other correspondence relating to David. The Tearoes did not write back.

The second home visit by Greta Vanderleeden, a week later, went as well as the first. The middle-aged, willowy social worker was offered coffee and cookies as she sat in the family room, looking out the sliding glass doors to the Tearoes' fenced, private backyard. Daffodils were in bloom, and scarlet tulips were splashed amid the greenery. White plastic chairs were neatly stacked in a corner of the cement patio. The mood was pleasant as the Tearoes talked to the social worker of their love of their children and the Lord. They told her how little David had enriched their lives, and related anecdote after anecdote of his attachment to them and theirs to him. After about two hours, the visit came to an end. Vanderleeden got into her car and backed out of the Tearoes' driveway, the family standing at the door under the carport, waving goodbye. David was in Jim's arms, Heidi standing by his side, tugging at her dad's arm to hold her little brother, all oblivious to the fact that today was Teena's nineteenth birthday, an occasion she was celebrating with a suicide attempt.

Judy's eight-year-old daughter Brittany sang "Happy Birthday" to Teena the afternoon of May 28. Teena often babysat the girl, and they had formed a friendship. The shyness Teena often felt with adults disappeared when she was with children. That shyness also disappeared when she drank, which she had started to do again. A few days before her birthday, Teena had gone to the arcade and pool hall on Main Street, where she and other teenagers often hung out. A friend of her brother Colin's had offered Teena a drink of her favourite rye, and she knew she should say no. She hadn't been drinking for months and wanted to keep it that way. But what would it hurt? She had been feeling down, fighting off dark feelings of depression.

Teena still hadn't paid the $300 fine she'd been given for writing the bad cheque, and it was supposed to be paid by June. She didn't know what would happen if it wasn't paid. Maybe they'd throw her in jail. But more importantly, there had been no word from the Tearoes about Jordan. If they didn't respond to her letter, that seemed like it was pretty well it. What else could she do, except to continue to refuse to sign any forms? She had four rye and Cokes that night, and more the next. Teena began drinking again for a simple reason—at the beginning of the night, after the first couple of drinks, she felt better.

Teena was not a particularly happy drunk. She thought of the losses in her life—her mother, her son—and cried uncontrollably, wishing she were dead. So on May 28, 1992, she downed a handful of pills, some she had for her ulcer, others for a respiratory infection, along with several beer. An hour later, at about one o'clock on the morning of May 29, she was in the emergency unit of Manning General Hospital, taken there by a friend. Asked by the emergency room nurse why she took the pills, Teena mumbled, "I just want to die."

Teena was kept overnight, and by nine o'clock that morning she seemed to be back to normal. Dr. Hallinen had treated her and realized after talking with Teena that she had not meant to kill herself. But there was no doubt that Teena Sawan was going through personal problems that called for counselling. "It was unclear whether [Teena] in fact was depressed or had a personality disorder. In any case," the doctor wrote in her notes of the incident, "the diagnosis at present is adolescent adjustment reaction. She was encouraged to come to the clinic for further counselling if she felt she needed it. She was also advised to contact me personally if she felt suicidal at any point."

More than a year later, Teena shifts uncomfortably when talking about what was termed a suicide attempt. "I didn't want to die. It was just that things seemed so difficult. The pills and alcohol—it was a stupid thing to do. It seemed like I was never going to see my son again and life just didn't seem to hold out much hope. I think it was my way of trying to get some help, some attention, someone to pat me on the back and tell me it was all going to be okay."

The same day she was discharged from the hospital, John Jordan sent her another letter, along with a copy of the B.C. legal documents that he thought needed to be signed before the Tearoes could legally adopt the boy they thought of as their own. The lawyer had no idea of Teena's suicide attempt.

29 May 1992

Cecilia Augustine Sawan
General Delivery
Manning, Alberta
T0H 2M0

Re: Adoption of Jordan Michael Sawan
Dear Ms. Sawan,

We act as solicitors on behalf of Jim and Faye Tearoe with respect to the proposed adoption of Jordan Michael Sawan who is now in their care and custody here in Victoria.

I am enclosing a copy of my letter of April 8, 1992 addressed to your former address and would ask you to take note of the contents of that letter.

We are enclosing the following documents on the assumption that you have not revoked your consent to the adoption by Mr. and Mrs. Tearoe, as follows:

Consent of Natural Mother
Affidavit of Natural Mother
Affidavit of Witness to its Consent

We therefore ask that you execute the Consent in the presence of a witness and may we suggest in the presence of your
foster mother, Iris Land, who we understand acted as the
facilitators for this adoption and that both the affidavit of
natural mother to be sworn by yourself and the affidavit to
be sworn by the witness to the execution of your consent
(assuming this to be your foster mother, Iris Land) to be done
before a notary public in and for the Province of Alberta. We
have taken the liberty of contacting, by separate cover, Pastor
and Mrs. Taylor as we understand that they were the facilitators of this adoption and advised them of our actions. Should
you have any questions at all, please do not hesitate to contact the writer either by letter or by telephone collect. We
look forward to hearing from you.

Yours truly,
John E. Jordan
cc: Jim and Faye Tearoe

When Teena received the letter and documents a few days
after being released from the hospital, she showed them to
Judy, who asked her what she was going to do. As before,
Teena did not sign them. Without signing them, her son
couldn't be adopted, she told herself. If they wouldn't bring
him back, she would do what she could to make sure they
couldn't keep him.

As pastor of the Manning Calvary Gospel Temple for ten
years, Pastor Henry Langerud had a strong rapport with
many of the people in his congregation. Some parishioners
referred to the narrow, angular man simply as "Pastor
Henry." His church drew a group of about seventy-five each
Sunday, among them Iris and Ellis Land, the foster parents of
Peter and Grace.

In early June 1992, the pastor was asked if he could get Teena Sawan to sign the needed documents. Pastor Henry did not know the couple on whose behalf he was helping procure a child. All he knew was that, according to Iris Land, the Tearoes were "a good couple, a religious couple, Christian and very, very keen on keeping the child." That was enough for him.

He did not know Teena Sawan either, other than to greet her at his church which she occasionally attended. But he had heard about her lifestyle from people in the congregation. "It was an up and down sort of life and that's the reason we didn't feel it was a good place for a child," Langerud said from his home in Wetaskiwin, a small town in central Alberta, where he moved in mid-1993 upon retiring from the ministry. "I heard this from different people that knew her, especially Iris Land. She knew Teena much better than I did and she did not recommend the child come back to Teena. Iris did not want to get personally involved because she had the other two Sawan children, but she was very concerned for the child."

With that information in hand, Langerud agreed to act as a "liaison" to convince Teena Sawan to sign the documents, copies of which had been sent to him to take to her. Langerud telephoned Teena, but she told the pastor she had already received the documents and wasn't going to sign them. Nevertheless, she agreed to let the insistent pastor visit her. Langerud got the impression that Teena had agreed to meet with him to sign the documents, and relayed that to Iris Land, who in turn conveyed it to the Tearoes' lawyer.

On a warm June afternoon, Henry Langerud walked up the sidewalk to visit Teena at Judy Waldo's home. They sat in the dining room, and Pastor Henry did most of the talking, his hands holding the sheaf of unsigned papers that Teena thought protected her from losing her son forever.

Pastor Henry outlined the reasons she should sign the documents, asking how she was ever going to buy food and clothing for a child while living on welfare. "Of course I tried to persuade her to let the child remain with the Tearoes,"

Pastor Henry recalled. "The child was in very good care, I told her. I felt the child was well taken care of. I guess she opposed that."

After some fifteen minutes, the pastor rose to his feet. He would call her in a week and see if she had changed her mind. As he walked down the street, Teena asked Judy why people made her feel so bad. "He made me feel like I could never give Jordan a good home, like I wasn't even worth stepping on," she cried. Judy told Teena they were just words and to ignore them, but Teena was wounded. "I had no faith in myself. You get told something enough times and you start to believe it."

Pastor Henry called Teena Sawan back a week later to see if she had changed her mind. She told him she hadn't. They never talked again.

Teena had yet to pay the fraud fine given her in Fairview. She had little extra money—she received minimal social assistance because she was not paying rent at Judy Waldo's—and the fine was to be paid by mid-June. Her distress over the fine was put to rest with the help of Manning RCMP Constable Robin Haney, who suggested she get a job, and put in a good word for her at the Aurora Hotel. Teena was hired as a chambermaid. She didn't mind the methodical work, where the results were quick and apparent. There was a certain satisfaction in scouring the bathrooms with Comet, watching the blue-green grit slide down the drain with the night's grime. She enjoyed pulling shut the door of another neat room, wheeling her cart of supplies to the next, the smell of disinfectant stinging her nostrils. Life that summer fell into a rhythm of working and going out.

Teena and a girlfriend went to the Aurora bar, "the zoo," the same place Maryann Sawan had spent time fifteen years before. Teena drowned shyness in a few drinks. "After a couple beer, I got courageous," recalls Teena. She and her friend had run out of cigarettes and, on a dare, Teena walked across the smoky, low-ceilinged room and asked the lanky guy leaning against the bar if she could borrow a cigarette.

"It'll cost you ten bucks," he replied, flirting with the cute, dark-haired teenager standing at his side. With her smooth skin, round brown eyes and white smile, she didn't look old enough to be in the bar. What the hell, it wouldn't be the first time under-age people got in the Aurora, Miles Schoendorfer thought, asking the girl her name and telling her his as he offered her a cigarette. Within a few days, the two were a steady item.

Chapter 8

Donna Ominayak, education co-ordinator for the Woodland Cree band, shifted uncomfortably at her desk. It was mid-morning already, and she had made little headway in the heap of work to be done. The telephone ringing was a welcome interruption to the tedium of paperwork, stacked in three piles in front of her.

"Hi Donna, it's Teena," said the young-sounding voice on the other end of the line.

"Hey Teena, how are you doing?"

It was October, and Teena was calling with her first report card marks—all As, with two A-pluses. Recently, she had come to an important decision, one that she hoped would help to make a big change for the better in her life. With moral support from Judy Waldo, she'd decided to register full-time at school again. The Woodland Cree band, which Teena had joined in 1989, while living with her Aunt Esther in Little Buffalo, would help out with a $1,500 per month education subsidy. The only condition was that she keep her marks up. It was up to Teena to make it. In their conversation that October day, Donna asked about the rest of Teena's life. The last time Donna had seen Teena, she had been pregnant.

Donna asked about the baby and Teena filled her in on what had happened, finishing her story with a sigh of resignation.

A fiercely intelligent woman in her mid-thirties who had experienced her own share of hardship, Donna Ominayak was impressed with Teena and thought the teenager was very bright. She wanted her to believe in herself. She had known Teena's mother, and could still remember Maryann Sawan crying as she left her children at Little Buffalo. She'd ask around, she told Teena, and see if she could find out if there was a way to get a lawyer. She occasionally dealt with legal issues through her involvement with other bands.

It was October 14, 1992, eight months and eight days after Teena gave her son Jordan up for adoption, exactly eight months since she had telephoned Jim and Faye Tearoe and asked for him back. It would be another eight months—to the day—before the case to determine the fate of the little boy known as David James to the Tearoes and Jordan to Teena would be heard by the courts.

Teena hung up the telephone and went upstairs to the kitchen, where Bea Cowie was doing dishes, and stood awkwardly in the doorway. She still felt shy around Miles's parents, even though she had lived at their home since September. Miles had just brought her there one day and they had stayed, without really specifically asking Bea, Miles's mother, or Ralph, his stepfather. Neither parent had said anything, and both had simply accepted her. With seven kids between them, Ralph and Bea were used to new faces showing up at their house and took it in stride. Things usually worked themselves out.

Teena trusted Ralph and Bea and remembered the couple from their days shepherding foster kids to visit their parents. They were the first people she'd thought of when she needed a home during her pregnancy, but she never mentioned their not taking her in. Ralph recognized Teena the minute he met her. She still barely looked fourteen.

Teena and Miles were now a steady couple. "I don't remember Miles saying, 'Will you be my girlfriend?' We were just together," Teena recalled. She was flattered by Miles's attention and attracted to his confident manner and appearance. His six-foot, 180-pound frame was usually in tight, thin-legged jeans, a T-shirt or tank-top, hightop running shoes and a black leather or jean jacket. Dark-brown hair varied between swinging past his shoulders with bangs to a shorter cut that curled up over his ears. A cigarette was often between his lips, smoke floating past his moustache, wide-set blue-green eyes and rough skin. If he were walking down a city street at eleven o'clock on a Saturday night, people would peg him as heading to the bar where the rock and roll band was booked. To men who dress in suits, Miles's look might be termed "greasy." Teena thought he looked like Tom Selleck.

Ralph and Bea, both of whom are Manning born and bred, met through their children twenty years ago. "We don't know if it was a fix-up," laughs Ralph, whose kind intelligence is not to be missed behind his baseball cap, flannel shirt covered with silhouettes of moose and green hunting vest. After a few years of dating, Ralph and Bea married and combined their families—Ralph had three children, Bea four. Ralph's first marriage had split up in the early 1970s, as had Bea's. Her first husband, Wolfgang Schoendorfer, had an affair with Bea's younger sister, Alice, and Bea was left on her own with the kids.

Time stitched the wounds, and Bea now works with Alice at Grimm's Truck Stop on the Mackenzie Highway. It is rare in Manning for a person to wear only one job hat, and Ralph and Bea are no different. During the spring and fall hunting seasons, they operate a guiding and outfitting company, and for the past twenty-five summers, Ralph Cowie has organized fire-fighting crews for the forest service. In the winter, he works when he can for oil rigs, doing construction at the oil and natural gas fields that begin thirty miles northwest of Manning. Even with the many jobs, life in the Schoendorfer-Cowie home is lived close to the bone, as it is for many families in the small community.

Bea is an intensely loyal woman, especially to her family, which she feels includes Teena. From the seven children there are already sixteen grandchildren, and Bea can recite each one's birthday and birth-weight without thinking twice about it.

Ralph and Bea are respected in the community as hard-working, church-going people. But several of the Schoendorfer boys have been in trouble with the law over the years, usually for drinking-related offences. As is often the case in small towns, bad reputations take on a life of their own, deserved or not.

Miles is blunt about his problems as a teenager, when he racked up a juvenile record for thefts and break-and-enters. "I did it all. My family didn't have much money and I wanted things, like motorbikes. So I'd go steal them, or steal something to get the money for them," he says in his slightly lispy voice. He ended up in the Youth Detention Centre, and then in a group home in Grimshaw, the same one that Teena was later in. "He understands what I'm talking about when I tell him how I felt there," Teena explains.

Miles attended grade nine while at the group home. "I did really excellent in everything except what I needed for grade ten. I moved back to Manning and took grade nine again and failed with flying colours," he says. It was the end of formal education for Miles, who says dryly that he was one of the few junior high school students who had a driver's licence and shaved.

In many small towns, the lure of labour jobs with good wages is magnetic. What was the point of school when you could quit and try and get on at the sawmill, make money, buy a pick-up? Miles worked sporadically, usually with Ralph on the rigs. But his priority at that time had little to do with work or school.

"I don't drink much now, but I sure used to. I was drunk for five years of my life. I don't think I missed a day there," he says. He has two impaired driving convictions, the last one for driving drunk on a snowmobile. He also has two convictions for driving while his licence was suspended, one for driving a snowmobile and the second for driving a dirt-bike.

Though Miles has had several girlfriends, none of them lasted very long. Teena was different. Miles thought she was one of the "smartest girls" he'd ever gone out with. She liked his down-to-earth attitude that didn't take any guff from anyone. He seemed to know his place in the world. He was full of bluster, but Teena saw a caring heart. Although she rarely spoke with his brothers and sisters and their families when they got together, Teena liked the feeling of family. There was lots of hubbub, with kids running around who took a shine to her, scrambling onto her lap and calling her "Auntie Teena."

Shortly after the two got together, Teena said to her new beau, "I'm native, you know," thinking that with her light skin, he might not have realized.

"Yeah. So?"

"Well, you know, I just thought you should know," said Teena, suddenly feeling awkward.

"What the hell for? So what?" Then he made a joke about her being able to hunt anywhere she wanted, and he'd have to teach her how to shoot a gun so they could go get a moose. That was that. He took the news of her having given her baby up in much the same way, though he initially had to fight off a feeling of jealousy that she'd had a baby by someone else.

On October 14, Teena told Miles that Donna Ominayak was going to see about getting her a lawyer. "Sounds good," he said, not really thinking it through. Later, standing outside the house having a cigarette, the thought of becoming an instant father to a child he'd had nothing to do with creating scared him a little. Then he thought of the family he'd grown up in, how well it had worked out, and about his five half-brothers and -sisters from his father and Auntie Alice. And he loved kids. It made him feel good when they ran to him, happy to see him. He wanted Teena happy, and getting her baby back would definitely go a long way towards that. There were times her moods went on incredible down-swings. When he thought about it, he attributed that to what she had told him about her childhood, and to losing Jordan.

She had shown him the picture of the two of them that she kept in her wallet.

"This is my son, and someday I'm going to get him back," she told him.

"He's a good-looking kid," he said, at a loss for what else to say.

"Yeah, he is. I'm real proud of him," Teena answered.

"What the hell," he thought, "it'll all work out," grinding out the butt of his cigarette under his shoe and heading back into the house.

Between October 14 and November 5, Donna Ominayak made numerous telephone calls to see what could be done to help Teena, and was undeterred by the circular route the calls seemed to take.

Two questions had to be answered: was there anything a lawyer could do for Teena? And if so, how would the lawyer be paid? Donna was used to the tangled web of bureaucracy and worked methodically. She called a child welfare worker at the Registered Bands office to ask if they knew how to help. Donna was told to call Anne in the High Prairie office, which she did several times. Eventually, she was given the name of Susan Grattan, a lawyer in High Prairie, east of Peace River.

Grattan is a sole practitioner with a varied practice of criminal, family and divorce law. For what seemed like the twentieth time, but was more likely the tenth, Donna explained Teena's situation, this time to Grattan. Teena was a member of the Woodland Cree band, she explained, and was sponsored to go to school, but there was little extra money for legal fees. Susan Grattan suggested Donna contact the legal aid office in Peace River.

Donna got in touch with Kim Allen at the Peace River legal aid office and repeated her story. Allen asked Donna to have Teena contact her directly. Donna called Teena at school. "If you want to pursue things further, you should phone Kim Allen," she told Teena, who stood in the cluttered office of the adult learning centre, a former elementary school.

"Really? Do you think they'll give me legal aid?"

"There's only one way to find out," said Donna.

Teena called the legal aid representative and, after explaining her situation and finances, was told she would have to wait and see if her case and situation qualified for funding. Teena tried not to get her hopes up; she didn't want to feel the disappointment if legal aid didn't come through. If that happened, it would mean Jordan was definitely gone. Sitting at school, she found it difficult to keep her mind on *Romeo and Juliet* and business math.

In the first week of December, Kim Allen called Teena: legal aid would fund a lawyer for her. It seemed almost miraculous! For so long, there had seemed to be nobody. Teena called Susan Grattan and arranged to meet the lawyer in Peace River, a midway point between Grattan's office in High Prairie and Teena's home in Manning.

Grattan was a woman in her mid-thirties with blunt-cut blonde hair and a matter-of-fact manner. Teena told her she had written a revocation letter, which Grattan asked to see. Looking over the letter, Grattan said, "A lot of time has gone by, Teena. I don't want you to get your hopes up too high." Teena sat on the other side of the desk and nodded, but she couldn't help the excited stitch in her stomach.

The summer had been a good one for Jim and Faye Tearoe, one of the best in their memory. The fact that they had yet to legally adopt the little boy they proudly introduced as their son was a mere formality. They had absolute faith that it would be done, despite the fact that Teena Sawan had repeatedly refused to sign the documents their lawyer sent to her. Their view on the matter had not changed since February— Teena had signed papers that allowed them to take the child. She had not followed the law, so he was theirs. And Social Services had told them that after ten days, Teena had to put up legal roadblocks to stop the adoption. But most importantly, the Lord would have given them a sign if they were to return David. Instead, the Lord had made the tyke the most dear thing in their lives.

The addition to their home was completed and they were thrilled with it. David was moved into his freshly painted room, next door to Heidi's and just down the hall from Jim and Faye's. Every morning, Faye read Heidi and David a Bible story, followed by playtime. The little boy waved his arms and eventually crawled around, scurrying on his hands and knees after their dog, Natasha, a black-and-white spaniel. By the end of the summer, David's wispy blond hair had thickened and his baby-blue eyes were beginning to turn a light hazel. The little boy loved music, bouncing along to the gospel tunes Jim and Faye played and blowing into a harmonica.

Their lives took on a steady rhythm. Sunday church attendance was a family staple. Faye thought it was pointless to put children in the playroom at the tabernacle. "Then they don't hear the message! We just set out a little blanket at our feet in the church and set down our little man's bottle and some crunchies and he climbs around from mom's lap to dad's and Heidi's and he has a great time." Sunday afternoons were the regular day for hikes, and David seemed to enjoy the scenery of the many trails that Jim took him on, strapped securely in a backpack.

In September, Heidi entered grade three at Lighthouse Christian Academy, a non-denominational, independent school that David too would attend come kindergarten. Housed in a worn church hall, the Lighthouse Academy follows the B.C. curriculum, but with a difference. The school day starts with a fifteen-minute "praise time," a singing and prayer session for the seventy-eight students from kindergarten to grade nine. Core subjects are taught with a strong Christian influence. The Bible is read in English class; science teaches that everything on Earth was created by God.

Heidi, a tall, pretty eight-year-old, did well at school. She was also a big help around the house, scooping up David after he'd finished eating and hustling him upstairs for a bath before her mother had a chance.

One fall afternoon, Heidi complained of a painful stomach ache. Faye quickly sent her to bed, turning down the covers and drawing the curtains so the bedroom was shaded from the glaring afternoon light. When Jim arrived home from work at his customary time of 4:00 p.m., Faye told him of Heidi's pain. He too was concerned, and they walked up the carpeted stairs to their daughter's bedroom. Jim kissed her on the cheek and asked how she was feeling. No better, said Heidi, who lay with her knees pulled to her chest. He asked the girl to straighten her body. Jim knew the cure for this ailment.

He reached forward, placing his long, narrow hands on Heidi's stomach, just beneath her ribs, where she said the pain was centred. Faye joined him, their hands resting on top of the soft brushed cotton of Heidi's pyjamas. The couple closed their eyes and prayed out loud for the Lord to allow His power to heal their little girl, make the hurt go away, for the Lord to pour his strength through Jim and Faye's hands, pressing tight against their daughter's belly. Heidi lay with her eyes closed. As the prayer finished and the room fell still, all three could hear David chattering to himself in his bedroom across the hall.

By dinnertime, Heidi was feeling better and sitting at the table, joining in the evening prayers. Little David chortled and waved his spoon around while sitting in his high-chair, his big sister in her usual spot beside him, her pain cured by the Lord.

Adoption law is set by provincial statute, and so it varies from province to province. Under the B.C. Adoption Act, an adoption cannot be finalized until six months after the Social Services ministry is notified by the prospective adoptive parents that they have a child in their home they wish to adopt. The Tearoes did this on March 6, 1992.

The half-year waiting period gives Social Services time to carry out the three home visits in order to determine the suitability of the parents and the home. Had all the necessary consent documents been in order, the Tearoes could have filed for adoption of the boy on September 6, 1992. Needed in B.C. is the written consent of the natural parent, along with a document called an affidavit of consent. The affidavit, sworn by the natural parent giving up the child, is to establish that the consent was signed freely and voluntarily, and that the parent understood the effect of the consent to the adoption. There must also be an affidavit from a person who witnessed the consent. The witness's affidavit is further proof that the consent was understood and signed freely and voluntarily by the biological parent. If the person who explained the effect of the consent to the person consenting is not a lawyer or social worker, the affidavit must also set out the circumstances and the qualifications of the person who gave the explanation. The final document required is a registration of live birth, obtained from the division of vital statistics.

Once the adoption application is filed, complete with the above documents, the Superintendent of Child Welfare files a report on the prospective adoptive parents, based on the home visits and forwards this report to the court. If all of the documentation is present, the adoption generally goes through without a hitch in a process called a "desk order." It is literally paperwork and never sees the inside of a courtroom. The birth-parent is simply sent a copy of the approved adoption order.

When John Jordan took on the Tearoes' case, he researched the law and decided that the easiest way to go about the adoption was to have Teena Sawan sign the B.C. versions of the Alberta consent forms. He would then file those as a desk order. But it soon became clear that Teena Sawan was not going to sign the B.C. forms, which Jordan had sent to her and which Pastor Henry had also asked her to sign.

So Jordan decided to obtain the Alberta consent forms, sure that those would fulfill the B.C. requirements. But that, too, proved difficult: the lawyer did not physically have in his possession the Alberta forms signed by Teena Sawan on February 6, 1992. He asked the Alberta ministry to send them to him in the summer of 1992 and again in October. But the Alberta ministry had policy hurdles to jump in sending Jordan the forms. Initially, they thought the documents could only be released to a B.C. social worker. That problem was ironed out in a conversation between the B.C. adoption section and Alberta Social Services, and the Alberta department agreed to send the consent to Jordan directly on October 27, 1992. Accompanying the document was a letter from the Alberta Family and Social Services office in Peace River.

October 27, 1992.

McConnan, Bion, O'Connor and Peterson
Barristers and Solicitors
420-880 Douglas Street
Victoria, British Columbia
V8W 2B7

Attention: John E. Jordan
        File Number: 92-24329-J

Dear Mr. Jordan

Re: Adoption of Jordan Michael Sawan

This letter is in response to our telephone call of October 26, 1992. Enclosed is the Consent by Guardian to Adoption that Tina [sic] Sawan signed on February 6, 1992 with a representative of Alberta Family and Social Services. This consent is still considered valid under the Alberta Child Welfare Act because she did not revoke her consent in writing within 10 days after signing the consent.

Information on the child's social history will be forwarded to British Columbia Social Services upon request.

I trust the enclosed document is in order.

Erin Harris, Adoption Worker
Debra Pittman, Casework Supervisor

A week later, a letter signed by Erin Harris and her case-work supervisor, Debra Pittman, was sent to Teena Sawan in Manning.

Dear Tina [sic],

Our office has been contacted by John E. Jordan, the British Columbia lawyer who is representing James and Faye Tearoe in their adoption of Jordan Sawan. He is requesting that we send him the Consent by Guardian to Adoption form that you signed on February 6, 1992, with Lynne Smith. Since we did not receive the required written notice of your revocation within ten days of the signing of the consent, we have no choice but to forward this consent to Mr. Jordan.

We have sent the Consent by Guardian to Adoption form that you completed to Mr. Jordan in Victoria, British Columbia. If you are not in agreement with the adoption we suggest that you contact a lawyer as soon as possible.

Sincerely,
Erin Harris, Adoption Worker
Debra Pittman, Casework Supervisor

The social workers did not know that by this time, Teena had talked to Donna Ominayak and was already working on getting a lawyer.

So, as of November 1992, the Tearoes' lawyer had the initial consent form signed by Teena Sawan in February 1992, along with the affidavit of witness to consent filled out by Lynne Smith that same day. He had also been forwarded the registration of live birth, so he had three of four necessary documents. But the fourth document, the affidavit of consent by the natural parent, was not just slow in coming, it was non-existent. It was one of the documents Teena Sawan had refused to sign after deciding she wanted her baby back.

John Jordan had to decide which route to take in the adoption application in light of the fact that he was missing one of the required pieces of documentation. The Adoption Act and Supreme Court rules did not appear to contemplate situations such as this, and it provided a challenge to the lawyer undertaking his first adoption. Out-of-province consents can be transferred to another province, providing they are carried out correctly and meet the specifications required by both the province in which they were signed and the province to which they are going. Jim and Faye Tearoe were aware that, without the required document, the courts might conceivably think Sawan's consent was not validly executed.

Jordan had to change tactics. He would proceed with the existing Alberta documents, which he believed to be valid in B.C. He'd file for adoption via praecipe, and try to substantiate why the affidavit of the natural mother with respect to her consent was covered by the wording of the Alberta consent form. If an adoption is commenced by praecipe, all required consents are filed and no notice has to be given to any person, not even the birth-mother.

Meanwhile, Greta Vanderleeden was also running into problems, again caused by Teena's passive resistance months before to the adoption of her son. Vanderleeden could not complete her final home-study report, necessary for any adoption, without Teena Sawan's social history form, another document the Cree had refused to complete. In November 1992, Erin Harris completed the social history on Teena's behalf and forwarded it to Vanderleeden. In the typewritten document, the baby's racial origin is described as "Cree Indian/?" and he is described as having brown hair, brown eyes and a fair complexion. Harris says Teena is a treaty Indian and a member of the Woodland Cree band, and her father is Albert Auger. Under a section on Teena Sawan's personality, Harris writes: "Can be stubborn at times and is impulsive. She has low self esteem, but cares deeply for her siblings. Has many friends but is easily led by others. Tina is friendly and eager to please.... Tina is intelligent and does well in school when she applies herself.... Has been hospitalized in the past for breathing problems and headaches. These are believed to be psychosomatic. Teena has suffered from depression in the past. It is believed that Tina did use alcohol in the first trimester until she learned she was pregnant. It is not known how much she used. Tina does have difficulty controlling her alcohol consumption."

At the end of the document, Harris writes: "The Department recommends this adoption proceed as Tina was fully aware of her actions when she placed Jordan for adoption. This social and family history was completed by this worker as Tina Sawan refused to complete the form."

There is nothing in the social history about Teena Sawan's attempts to revoke her consent.

With the social history in hand, Vanderleeden made her third visit to the Tearoe home and continued to be impressed by the care being given the child. She completed her home-study, but had to wait to submit it until there was an actual adoption application filed with the court by the Tearoes. At one point in November, she telephoned John Jordan's office to let the lawyer know she was just waiting for the application to be filed before presenting the report.

But before John Jordan filed any court documents, he received a faxed letter that would change things dramatically. At 9:41 a.m. on December 9, 1992, a two-page letter rolled off the fax machine at McConnan, Bion, O'Connor and Peterson, addressed to Mr. John E. Jordan. The letterhead said "Susan M. C. Grattan," in large, black, capital letters, with "Barrister & Solicitor" in capitals underneath. It was dated December 8, 1992.

Dear Sir:
Re: JORDAN MICHAEL SAWAN

I have been consulted by Cecilia Sawan, the mother of the infant child, Jordan Michael Sawan. Ms. Sawan advises me that on or about February 8, 1992 she sent a written revocation of her consent to her adoption to the director, Alberta Family and Social Services. I am also advised she notified your clients. As I understand it, the director of the Alberta

Family and Social Services has taken the position that they never received written revocation, although they do not deny that Ms. Sawan told them of the written revocation and confirmed her revocation during several conversations.

Since I am unaware of the adoption practise in British Columbia, I thought it advisable to notify you that Ms. Sawan is seeking legal counsel in Alberta, and has revoked her consent to this adoption. I would request that you take no further steps in any proceedings affecting this child's guardianship or custody without reasonable notice to Ms. Sawan. Until counsel is appointed for Ms. Sawan, I will act on her behalf. I do expect to be appointed as her lawyer within the near future.

Although Ms. Sawan is clear about her revocation it strikes me that it might be a service to all parties and particularly the child if an alternative to litigation could be considered. In Alberta we have a mediation service, provided free to litigants in custody disputes. Dr. Kent Taylor would be available to travel to meet with my client. Your clients would likely have to meet with him in Edmonton. I realize this would involve some travel and expense for your client. A highly contested adoption could be expensive in more ways than financial. Ms. Sawan says this was to have been an "open" adoption, with contact between the child and his natural mother. I wonder if some opportunity could be provided for these parties to meet and attempt to establish some workable compromise. In Alberta we have used joint guardianship in situations where a number of parties wish to be involved in the child's welfare. It is always my practise to explore mediation as an alternative to litigation.

Please feel free to contact me.

Yours sincerely,
Susan Grattan Law Office

A letter was also sent to the Alberta Family and Social Services by registered mail. It was marked for the attention of Erin Harris. On the same letterhead, and dated December 7, 1992, the letter read:

Dear Ms. Harris:

Re: Cecilia "Tina" Sawan

Ms. Tina Sawan has consulted me regarding her son, Jordan Michael Sawan. Ms. Sawan advises me that she has on several occasions over the last few months, confirmed that she has revoked her consent to adoption of this child. I enclose a copy of the revocation she said she mailed to your office on February 8, 1992. It is my understanding that the position of your office is that you did not receive this written revocation. Could you please confirm this. I further understand, however, that your office does not dispute that Ms. Sawan has contacted your office several times and spoke with various social workers, confirming that she has revoked. Lastly, I understand a document described as Consent by Guardian has been forwarded to a lawyer acting for the adoptive parents.

This letter will confirm the advice previously given that Ms. Sawan has revoked her consent to this adoption.

I would request that you provide me with a copy of the document you forwarded to Mr. John E. Jordan. I would also request that you notify the adoptions worker in British Columbia of this letter and confirm by return letter to me that you have done so.

Yours sincerely,
Susan Grattan Law Office

On December 22, 1992, less than two weeks after receiving the letter from Sawan's lawyer, an adoption petition was filed in the B.C. Supreme Court at the Victoria court registry by Jim and Faye Tearoe. The petition included affidavits making allegations against Teena. There was no telling that the four-page petition, slipped into the usual registry-issue buff-coloured manila folder by a clerk whose mind was more on Christmas holidays than work, would explode into a national issue.

Chapter 9

Brian Young quickly scanned the file that John Jordan had slid across his desk, looking for advice from an associate more experienced in adoption matters. It was the morning of December 23, 1992, and the law office of McConnan, Bion, O'Connor and Peterson was in Christmas mode. Staff and lawyers were working at less than full speed, and most of the people walking by Young's office were eating chocolates; a raft of them had come in from corporate clients and were stacked in the coffee room.

"It looks pretty straightforward, just a few loose ends to tie up," said Young, flipping the folder closed and sitting back in his chair.

Although Jordan and Young had both gone to the University of Victoria law school within a couple years of one another, experience and circumstance had carved out different skills in each. Young's practice varied from a bit of criminal law to personal injury, but he had also done several adoptions, and was at ease in court if matters went that far. Jordan, on the other hand, preferred to stay out of litigation. A 1983 accident had left John Jordan with only 10 percent hearing in one ear, and it made interactions during lengthy trials difficult.

In Young's opinion, the consent signed by Teena Sawan on February 6, 1992, some ten months earlier, was valid, and her revocation attempts were not. Case closed, thought Young, who personally doubted Sawan's sincerity. "I have to wonder how much she wanted her child back when all she did was telephone two or three times, say she wrote a letter and then do nothing for ten months. She could have tried a lot harder," he said later. "Her efforts just don't cut it—I think that once in a while she wanted him back, but it wasn't consistent."

Jordan had done the right thing, Young said, by filing a petition in the B.C. Supreme Court, asking for an order to grant the adoption. Indeed, Young thought it could have been filed earlier. Had the necessary documents been in Jordan's possession before November 1992, his colleague could have simply applied through the desk order process for the baby to be adopted. Teena would have been notified via a letter when the adoption was complete. "That's not underhanded. That's just the way adoptions are done when the paperwork is in order," Young said.

As with all court documents, those filed by Jordan at the Victoria court registry were wrapped in legalese. What was to essentially become an embittered struggle for the heart and mind of a child was simply court file number 92 4335, "In the Matter of Jordan Michael Sawan."

Jim Tearoe disliked the fact that the boy he thought of as his David James Tearoe had to be referred to as Jordan Michael Sawan in the petition. But legally, that was who the child still was, despite the fact that at almost thirteen months, he responded to the name David and called Jim and Faye Dad and Mom. Jim crossed out the name Jordan Sawan on his copies of the court documents, and replaced it with David James TEAROE, the last name in bold, capital letters.

In the petition, the Tearoes asked that the child's name be legally changed to David James Tearoe, that the adoption be granted and that the consent of Teena Sawan be dispensed with. Since Teena had refused to sign a B.C. consent, in their

view, it was as though no consent at all existed, so they
applied under section 8 (8) of the B.C. Adoption Act, which
stated that the court may dispense with the consent if the
parent has abandoned or deserted the child or has neglected
or refused to contribute to the child's support. There is also a
catch-all phrase allowing the court to dispense with consent
if "in the opinion of the court and in all the circumstances of
the case," the judge deems it appropriate.

Young agreed to take over the case. When he met the
Tearoes later that afternoon, he found the couple to be "very
nice, very religious and very attached to that little boy." The
Tearoes liked John Jordan, who shared strong convictions
about the Lord and who had been recommended to them by
their family doctor. But if he thought Young was more experienced in this type of situation, so be it. Young, a boyishly
handsome man who looks younger than his thirty-two years,
knew how to use his easygoing charm to full advantage. The
Tearoes were soon put at ease by the fact that the lawyer with
the well-cut suit was the father of two children and had been
married for almost a decade to a woman he first met in high
school. They immediately offered their prayers when he told
them at that first meeting of his little girl's recent leukemia
diagnosis.

Young told them he thought the case was relatively
straightforward and would likely cost the Tearoes about
$1,000 to $1,500 in legal fees and disbursements—photocopying, filing fees and the like. (His predictions would prove to
be far off the mark.) Jim carefully noted the cost projections
in a small diary he carried with him. He earned a minimum
of $50,000 per year with the ministry of forests, plus benefits,
but he kept a close eye on their bank account and was always
thinking about the future.

The Tearoes left the meeting with legal jargon that had
already become familiar swirling in their heads. They were
well aware of the difficulties with the adoption—"red tape"
in Jim's eyes—but they pushed negative thoughts out of
their minds. The Lord would not give them a gift of something so precious only to take it away. Several times a day,

the couple said to one another, "The Lord's in charge. The Lord's in charge."

Jean Morgan had dealt with Susan Grattan once before, when the High Prairie lawyer had asked her to act as an agent on another file involving a client from B.C. The lawyers did not know each other personally, but their last association had worked out smoothly, and Morgan had no hesitation in agreeing to act as an agent for Grattan in the Victoria custody case.

Muzak Christmas carols played softly in the outer office, and Morgan shut her door as the Alberta lawyer outlined the circumstances. "When I first heard the facts from Susan Grattan, I was quite shocked at what was going on. I felt it would be very difficult to get Teena's child back because of the amount of time that had gone by, but I was shocked that someone had said and done all of the things Teena Sawan had to try and get her baby back and no one paid attention to this person. I was dismayed. You don't ignore that. This is a mother. This is a child. You are not talking about a car. You are talking a human being," recalled Morgan, a forty-two-year-old family lawyer. "Here is a woman who tells everybody, 'I want my child back.' She tells Social Services, she tells the Tearoes, all within the ten-day time requirement, and who cares? Does anyone do anything to help her? No. The people who have her child refuse to return him. Social Services just sits back. I couldn't believe it. I understand there is a written requirement and one appreciates it, but on the other hand, when you're dealing with a child and adoption, if somebody says 'no,' especially someone who was in Teena Sawan's position, who had changed her mind over and over again about what to do, surely *somebody* would go out there to talk with that person, to get that in writing or to make sure, even to satisfy themselves personally. But there was nothing. Absolutely nothing. And I find that appalling."

Morgan let John Jordan know that she would be acting as an agent for Grattan, which essentially meant that because Grattan was from out of town, Morgan would serve and accept any documents on her behalf. When the Tearoes' adoption petition was filed, a copy was duly delivered to Morgan's office. The lawyer scanned the document and was surprised at a few things.

The petition asked for Sawan's consent to be dispensed with. Morgan understood that the Tearoes and their lawyer had maintained all along that the consent was valid. If it was a valid consent, why did it need to be dispensed with? It made little sense to her.

And Teena Sawan had not been named as a respondent on the petition. In Morgan's view, without being named as a respondent, Teena Sawan had no legal standing in the case. She could not file affidavits in response to allegations made by the Tearoes, nor could she be represented by a lawyer. It was as if she had never existed. Morgan filed a notice anyway, to alert the court of Sawan's interest in the matter.

Within a couple of weeks of becoming an agent for Grattan, it became clear that the case would be heard in Victoria, and Morgan officially took over the file, informing John Jordan of that. He, in turn, told Morgan that Brian Young, with whom Morgan had attended law school, would be handling the case for the Tearoes.

Morgan thought about the case as she left her downtown Victoria office in the light drizzle that misted the December air. She had been in practice since 1989, having come to law later in life, and had focused on family law for a variety of reasons, the main one being that she liked working with people. Already, this case seemed inordinately sad to her, and by the end of her involvement with it, she would call it the saddest she had ever known.

Miles paced back and forth along the sidelines of the Fairview high school gym, a thin caged cat in a black leather jacket. "Go Gracie!" he bellowed, absentmindedly patting his inside jacket pocket to make sure his cigarettes were still there. Grace, embarrassed and pleased by the attention, giggled with the other girls and hid her smile in her hands.

Teena sat in a chair on the sidelines, half-rising out of it when Grace's team was playing well. "Go, girls! Come on girls!" she cheered, at about a quarter the decibel level of her boyfriend.

Teena and Miles tried to go to as many of Grace's high school volleyball games as they could. Grace was doing her share of bench-warming as the youngest player on the senior team, and they were her cheering section. Teena still craved the competition and camaraderie of sports, as did Miles, who often yelled, usually good-naturedly, at the referee. Teena found Miles' ability to say what he wanted and ignore what people thought invigorating. "Fuck 'em if they don't like you," was Miles' advice when she confided that she often worried if new acquaintances liked her. "It's their loss. You know what you are inside and that's what counts."

Teena leaned against Miles's shoulder as they drove back to Manning that night, the dark highway snaking across the snow-drifted prairie. The tapes played, and Miles occasionally sang along to the Steve Miller Band songs that he liked. Teena just wanted to keep driving and driving.

She and Miles had their own apartment, having moved out of Ralph and Bea's house just after Christmas. Miles worked sporadically on the rigs and was gone for a few days or even weeks at a time. Teena attended school at the Manning campus of the Fairview College, taking grade eleven courses and surprising herself by getting top marks. "I never let myself try before in high school, and then I did and I got all As and Bs. I'm pretty proud of myself." English was her favourite subject, largely because it came easiest. She enjoyed reading *Romeo and Juliet*, but couldn't plough through *Hamlet* and watched the video instead. Miles surprised himself by finding it mildly interesting.

Teena somewhat shyly told Ralph and Bea that she had a lawyer who was trying to get Jordan back for her. Family law is complex, and Teena Sawan, like the Tearoes before her, was receiving a crash course. Bea was whole-hearted in her support of Teena getting her child back. The grandkids loved Teena, and it was to the little ones that Teena really seemed to open up.

Ralph was somewhat more careful with his stamp of approval. He thought both Teena and Miles had some growing up to do. Although Ralph loved Miles, had helped raise him since Miles was just a toddler, he also saw that the youngest member of the family was a bit immature. "Miles is twenty-four but his mom has always tied his shoes, so to speak. He needs to assume more responsibility for his actions and he's slowly learning it," he says.

Ralph encouraged Teena to keep on with school. He had a great deal of empathy for the circumstances of her upbringing. "She doesn't trust a lot of people. Whether this is something she has acquired over the years, moving from home to home...I don't know. I think she missed those years of her life, where you develop confidence in other people, and learn to trust." Like others before him, he commented that the teenager seemed to crave a sense of family. In his quiet way, Ralph worked on it. "I tried to talk to her about her dreams, not her problems," says Ralph, an optimistic man whose reading tends towards the *Reader's Digest*, in which every story has a happy ending. "Teena's dreams were to go to school, be self-sufficient, make her way in the world and to have a good home with her family.... It seemed like as long as I could keep her enthusiastic about her dreams, she'd be cheerful," says Ralph.

Teena sat alone in the apartment, wishing Miles was with her. He was working on a rig fifty miles west of Manning, doing construction, and had been gone since the beginning of January. Teena had already flipped through a local TV guide, watched "Who's the Boss?" listened to the radio and cleaned the bathroom, and it was still only suppertime. She hated being alone, when fears of having no one hit her with a vigour she found overwhelming. She remembered the pain of her mother leaving, and everybody else who was gone, including her son.

Sometimes the court petition regarding Jordan didn't seem real to Teena. It was being dealt with by people she had never met in a city she had never seen a thousand miles away. She knew Victoria was supposed to be a nice place, filled with flowers and home to a university. The Tearoes had told her that when they'd picked up Jordan. She wondered what he looked like, if he was walking or talking yet. The Tearoes had not sent her any pictures or updates of her boy; nor had she written them again since her letter in May, asking for Jordan back. So much for an open adoption.

Teena had a difficult time understanding exactly how, when she had asked for Jordan back more than once, the Tearoes chose not to return him. It seemed particularly odd to her in light of the Tearoes' avowed Christian sensibilities. And she was confused and hurt by the comments in the court documents that the Tearoes had filed—insinuations that she was an unfit mother and a drunk. What could they know of her from spending less than half a day with her?

There was no answer at the Lands', and Teena hung up the telephone, unsure of where Grace could be. She would give anything right now for Miles to be home. At times like this, he could often joke her out of her depression, or they would go do something to get her mind off things. Sometimes, Teena was afraid of how upset she got. She didn't know how to stop it. A D and C operation she'd had the week before Christmas still haunted her, and although she knew the much-wanted pregnancy had not been viable—she'd had a blighted ovum—the news had left her in tears. She and Miles wanted to have a child.

Inside the fridge were a few cans of beer and some leftovers. She stretched her arm past the plastic-wrapped bowls and grabbed a beer. As soon as she popped the tab, part of her had second thoughts, but she walked to the bathroom cabinet and took a small bottle of Tylenol and walked back out to the kitchen table.

When two teenagers from next door went to visit Teena later that evening of January 22, 1993, they found her standing in the middle of the small kitchen, making stabbing gestures at her stomach with a steak knife as she stared at them.

"Teena, what are you doing?" they screamed, not sure what to do. One tried to pull the knife from Teena's hands, but her thin fingers were clamped tightly around the wooden handle. They ran and telephoned Judy Waldo, who arrived within minutes. She found Teena sitting motionless at the kitchen table, the knife on a nearby speckled countertop.

"Teena, for God's sake, what are you doing?" Judy yelled, forcing the teenager to stand up and helping her out to the car idling outside. Judy sped to the hospital three blocks away, with a neighbour in the back-seat holding Teena. "Come on Teena, you'll be okay," Judy said soothingly, walking her into the hospital and shaking her head at the teenager whose worries never seemed to go away.

One of the girls who had been with Teena earlier told the admitting nurse that Teena seemed to have had some sort of seizure. The doctor's report of the incident said Sawan "was not responsive at all to painful stimuli. However, she became very agitated when the gastric tube was passed...she has been drinking. Also at 5-6 o'clock this evening she took ? 5-10 Tylenol. Diagnosis: Suicide gesture." Judy stayed with Teena at the hospital.

Teena remembers little of the incident, other than feeling an incredible sense of isolation. Just as she had on May 28, 1992, she claimed that it was not a true suicide attempt. "I never wanted to actually die," she says, struggling to explain. "It just seemed like I was so alone. I think I just wanted someone to say to me, Listen, it'll all be okay. It will all work out."

The next day, Judy let Teena have it. "What do you think Social Services would do if they found out about this?" she asked, trying to shake some sense into Teena. "They'd never let you have Jordan back." The fact that Social Services had nothing, at this point, to do with where the child would live was lost on both women. Teena nodded and appeared to listen to Judy's admonishment, but it didn't stop her downward spiral.

The next weekend she ran into an old friend from the group home. The two hung out at a hockey game for a while, watching the local minor-league team, before he asked Teena if she wanted to drive a car with him to Fairview, so he could pick up his truck. Teena shrugged and said sure. Miles was still working on the rigs and she was sick and tired of being by herself. They started drinking in the car. In Fairview Teena saw Grace and a couple of her friends, there for a game. The girls piled in the car for the trip back. By that time, Teena was feeling drunk, and it showed in her driving.

A few miles outside Manning, Grace became angry with Teena and demanded that she stop the car. When Teena pulled to the side of the road, so did her friend in the pick-up. Grace got out of the car, refusing to drive any further with Teena and began walking home. Teena yelled for her to be careful, but Grace ignored her, walking along the gravel shoulder with one of her friends. Teena pulled the car back out on the road and at the same time, so did her friend in the pick-up. Teena heard a wrenching crunch as she drove into the back of the truck. The hood of the car was dented up in a triangle in front of her and steam was rising. The girls in the back-seat were screaming, but no one was hurt. They too jumped out of the car and Teena drove off, crying. She drove the car with the crumpled front end to Judy's.

Judy was doing laundry when her daughter Brittany, peering out the frosty window, said, "Mom, I see Teena driving up." Judy heard an insistent knocking on her door and opened it to find Teena, sobbing and upset.

"I crashed a car. I crashed a car and it's not mine and I don't even know whose car it is." Outside, steam poured from the smashed front grille and one headlight was gone.

"Calm down, just calm down," said Judy, looking out at the car and wondering how Teena had even driven it to her place. Teena sat on the couch and appeared to Judy to be going into shock. What should she do? Judy wondered, looking at the teenager staring blankly on her couch and Brittany fascinated by the car in the driveway.

A next-door neighbour came over and offered quick advice. Call the cops and an ambulance. If the car wasn't Teena's, they'd better report it. An ambulance took Teena to the hospital, where she could barely move. The nurse noted that she was unresponsive to pain, although her pupils were equal and reacted to light and her reflexes were good.

Judy didn't know what was going on. She knew Teena had an ulcer and mild epilepsy but didn't know if either of those could have anything to do with her condition. It seemed like more than booze. The doctor wanted her to stay overnight, and by later on that evening, Teena had become more alert and regained her orientation. By the next morning, she had no recollection of the previous night's goings-on.

The accident caused a rift in Teena and Miles' relationship. He raced back from the oil rig after hearing of it and ended up getting fired for leaving. He was angry and jealous that Teena had been out with a guy from the group home, even if it was just an acquaintance, and was furious when he learned through the grapevine that the car she had been asked to drive had stolen household goods in the trunk.

Ralph Cowie cared about Teena and thought she had a lot going for her when her life was going well. But news of her recent forays into partying bothered him. As far as Ralph knew, the January 22, 1993 incident had simply been Teena "goofing off"; he did not know it had been termed a suicide attempt. And the accident the following week did nothing to shore up his confidence. He began to wonder if baby Jordan might not be better off with the couple who so keenly wanted to adopt him.

After days of thinking about it as he went about his business, Ralph called Pastor Kelly Taylor, whom he knew through the church, and asked for Jim and Faye Tearoe's telephone number. He called the couple at their home. "Maybe this could all be worked out in a friendly way. I have to be honest—at that particular time, I didn't feel Teena was ready. She was partying and goofing off. I really wasn't on her side, so to speak, at that time. I was thinking of the Tearoes, too. One of the reasons I phoned them was to find out how they felt, how attached they were, were they able to give the baby up, or try to work something out."

After a pleasant conversation with Jim, Ralph knew the Tearoes were not only extremely attached to the baby but would fight their hardest to keep him. He didn't tell Teena he had talked to the Tearoes but he did give her his version of a lecture. "I told her, if she wanted that boy back, she had to clean up her life, she couldn't be drinking or getting sick. I asked her if she thought she was ready for motherhood." But she didn't need Ralph's lecture; the accident had scared her as well. What if they hadn't been so lucky? "I would never have been able to forgive myself if something happened to my sister, never. And what if something had happened to me? What about Jordan? He would never be able to know me. He'd never know that his mom had wanted him back."

Nothing came of the fact that there was stolen property in the back of the car Teena crashed. Teena had had no idea about the goods. And the rift between Teena and Miles gradually healed. They signed up to go to an AADAC counselling session, as Teena had sporadically in the spring and fall of 1992. On February 15, 1993, the two drove to Peace River to buy a dining table for their new apartment and bought an engagement ring instead.

By March, Teena Sawan had still not been added to the Tearoes' petition as a respondent, despite Jean Morgan's numerous requests. So on March 17, 1993, Morgan went to court and made a formal application to have her added. Finally, Sawan would have legal standing in the matter that would directly affect her life. Morgan also decided that it would be a good idea for her client to cross-file her own separate petition for her baby's return.

Because there are no lawyers based in Manning—some lawyers from neighbouring Peace River or High Prairie go to Manning once every couple of weeks, setting up shop for the day at the back of a plumbing store—there was no one locally to act as an agent for Jean Morgan. So Teena and Morgan devised their own method of case preparation. Morgan was vaguely familiar with Manning. She had been through the town a few times in the early 1980s, when the Edmonton-born woman had made several trips to northern Alberta in her work as a researcher for the provincial New Democratic

Party. The routine was that Morgan would mail documents to Stone's Insurance in Manning. After Teena picked up the papers at Stone's, Morgan would call her at the school and explain what the documents meant, and give her legal advice. Teena would write up her reply and take it back to Stone's, where the document could be notarized. Then Teena would send it back to Morgan. And the process started all over again. The women slowly got to know one another, and their numerous telephone conversations in March and April exacerbated Morgan's feelings that what had happened to Teena Sawan and her baby had been profoundly unjust.

"I was talking with a very articulate woman. She was extremely clear in her language, extremely clear about what had gone on. I was surprised at this only in comparison to what had happened to her. She knows what she wants and she says it. What is the difficulty? The tragedy of this case is that all along, everyone knew she wanted her child back and nobody listened. I don't know if they just thought Teena would go away. And time was against Teena. The longer the Tearoes had the child, the better case they had," said Morgan, whose passionate words were tempered by her soft tone.

"Here we have this woman who has almost had her child stolen from her. No one will assist her to get the child back. And then they just leave her alone. I can't say enough about how wrong it is to do that to another human being."

Teena Sawan's counter-petition contains the first reference in court documents to the fact that she is a status Indian and a member of the Woodland Cree band. At that time, Jordan was also on the waiting list to become a band member.

Chapter 10

Every Sunday morning at about ten-thirty, Billy Thomas packs up his string guitar, plunks his baseball cap on top of his thick black head of hair and walks the three hundred yards from his home to the Cadotte Lake Church. Inside, the chief of the Woodland Cree band takes his usual seat on the stool at the front of the tiny sanctuary. On this particularly frosty March morning, only a handful of people are scattered throughout the eight wooden pews. As the minister begins the service, his back stooped and voice monotone, two kids poke at their sister, sleeping in a baby-seat, and smile self-consciously at each other as the adults pray. The sermon is clearly Catholic, and the songs are abundant and lively, led with great vigour by Thomas, whose clear voice rings out with a nasally twang in verses about brotherly love and forgiveness. Thomas is a frustrated country-western singer and plays in a band with his teenage sons.

When Donna Ominayak told Thomas what had happened to Teena and her child, the chief's response was instinctive. "That's her child. He belongs with her." He also thought the child's home was with the band. "He belongs out here. If she gets him back, they'll end up here eventually," says the plain-spoken man. To Thomas, who spent more than a decade living off the reserve before returning to become chief in 1993, it doesn't matter if they return to the reserve tomorrow or a decade from now. "This is her home. It'll always be here," he says with a shrug. "We're not going to leave her. They'll come back when they're ready."

Thomas was only too aware of the generations of native children adopted by white people in past decades—children who became assimilated so far into the white world that there was no Indian left. Thomas remembered Maryann Sawan as a child, speaking Cree with him, knowing her way around a trapline and drying a moose. Maryann's children started their lives with their Cree families, speaking their native tongue. But that was lost as Maryann began to move into the white world, and as her kids were put into white foster homes. Now, Maryann's grandson would have no involvement whatsoever with his heritage. The bond was severed.

The chief hopes to see a resurgence of pride in being Indian at the reserve, and part of that comes from economic self-sufficiency. He has no qualms about working with the white world, welcomes it if that helps the band get on its economic feet. But by doing so, did a person have to give up being an Indian? Thomas didn't think so.

Teena knew little about the tangled history of the 700-member Woodland Cree band formed in July 1991, born out of the painful demise of negotiations between the Lubicon Cree and the federal government.

In the late 1970s and the 1980s, the Lubicon Cree had fought to get a reserve promised them in the 1930s, when white people came into the area and found thriving native communities.

Intense oil exploration in the area had destroyed the rich hunting grounds that had supported generations of the northern Cree. Social assistance claims rose from 10 percent of the workforce in the area to 90 percent between 1979 and 1983.

The Lubicon Cree, to which some of Teena Sawan's family belonged, were desperately trying to get the land promised them, and compensation for devastation of the land so they could create a new economy for their people. After years of trying traditional routes through the courts and attempts to deal with government, the Lubicons took more extreme measures. They called for a boycott of the 1988 Winter Olympic Games in Calgary, followed in the fall by a six-day takeover of a major oil field. Both drew worldwide attention to the isolated area and widespread criticism of the government's actions. Some human rights workers said there could be "genocidal consequences" if a settlement was not reached with the Cree, once a flourishing people. An agreement for land was hammered out with the province in the fall of 1988, but talks with the federal government over compensation broke down, and the government's final offer was rejected. The Lubicons believed it would not be enough to enable them to build a new economy.

The federal government seemed intent on reaching some sort of settlement, and discussions began with a group of natives, some of whom lived in the area but were not on the Lubicon band list, and others who were recruited from throughout northern Alberta, to join a new band called the Woodland Cree. Some observers of the Lubicon struggle saw the formation of the new band and settlement as a crass attempt by the government to weaken the powerful Lubicons by essentially dividing and conquering. If the government could get their numbers down, any potential settlement would be smaller, because reserve size and compensation were based on the number of members.

The Woodland Cree have attracted the criticism of other native groups, who say band members became the "white man's Indian," taking what they viewed as an unsatisfactory settlement. They received a fifty-five-square-mile reserve, with the majority at Cadotte Lake, and two smaller communities at Simon Lake and Marten Lake. Ownership of the two known oil deposits in the area remained with the oil companies. One of the criticisms was that not all of the 700 people that were registered to the band were counted for determining the reserve size. Some $29 million was earmarked for housing and infrastructure, as well as $19 million set aside for economic development.

Numerous Lubicon—estimates suggest about 100—soon joined the Woodland Cree. It seemed the only way they were going to receive anything and have a place to call home. "We were starving," says one mother of five matter-of-factly. Other Woodland Cree band members came from towns and cities throughout Alberta. These people had roots in the area, one of the requirements for initially becoming a band member, through their ancestry. There is a mix of people who have never left their traditions and those who have never known them.

The Sawan family, like many others in the region, are split between the Lubicons and the Woodland Cree. Teena's Aunt Josephine, her grandmother Annie's sister, is married to Edward Laboucan, one of the Lubicon Cree elders and a driving force in the Lubicon movement. Other aunts and uncles are now members of the Woodland Cree.

Conflicts in families over which band to join have started to heal, said Woodland Cree band manager Stella Martin, who grew up in Grouard, a town south of Cadotte Lake and Little Buffalo. Martin, a thirty-five-year-old mother of two, moved to the reserve in 1992, in part because of what seemed like a good job opportunity, in part to discover the roots she came from. She lives in a house trailer with her husband, a white man, and their children, ages nine and two years. "People ask me why I married a white man. Who can tell who you will fall in love with," she laughs.

Like many others, Martin and her family are waiting for their house to be built. There are to be 131 houses by March 31, 1995. Those already completed would fit in well in any city suburb and the community looks much different than it did in 1989, when Teena last lived there. Most are typical two-storey houses, with three bedrooms, kitchen, dining room, living room and bathroom, with a recreation room downstairs.

Some of the reserve has the look of an "instant town," with a few wide secondary roads carved through the bush. They all lead to the main road that has followed the lakeshore for decades. Dirt that has lain undisturbed from time immemorial is overturned and frozen in piles by the roadside to make way for the new sewer and water systems.

There is a waiting list for the new houses, and not all families will get one. Some of the area old-timers don't want to move out of the homes they were born and raised in, where outhouses are a twenty-second sprint from the back door. Their lives are still guided by the seasons, as the lives of their ancestors were. A quick glance out the window, past the steeple of the peak-roofed church towards Cadotte Lake, determines the weather and their plans for the day.

Next door to the church is a tattered-looking aqua building that is the only store. Children racing around on "trikes" (three- or four-wheeled all-terrain vehicles) with dogs barking at their wheels are quick to tell a visitor that although the store is closed on Sundays, it can be opened by heading over to John Cardinal's and telling him what you need. Across the road from the church is the octagon-shaped, modern-looking school, where kindergarten to grade nine are taught. The brown, brick building will be replaced by a new school in September 1995, with home economics and apprenticeship programs, as part of the reserve settlement. The new school will go to grade twelve, and there are hopes that, for the first time, reserve members will be given the opportunity to achieve their high school diplomas, which many had never attained. Beside the school is the adult education centre, where about thirty band members take academic upgrading courses. Many of them had little schooling before. Some had gone a few years at the church-run residential schools in the 1950s and left because of the loneliness of being separated from family.

Cree is spoken fluently by the majority of adults in the community, but, like native languages throughout Canada, it is dying in the younger generation. Many of the adults speak "Crenglish," a mix of English and Cree, and a Cree language course is mandatory at the school. One afternoon shortly after the Martins arrived at the reserve, Stella Martin's nine-year-old son came home crying. Other children were teasing him because he couldn't speak Cree. "You just have to know who you are, that you are native in your soul," she said to the despondent child. Her children are half-white but look like their mother, with her dark, pretty features. There are numerous children on the reserve with mixed blood who are band members. One little boy has light blue eyes and blond hair. "There is no animosity towards him. There is no discrimination in that sense," Martin comments. "I'm sure as he grows up some of the kids will tease him for not looking Indian." She shrugs. "Kids tease other kids for all sorts of reasons." Belonging does not come from the colour of your skin, says Dolly LeTendre, the band social worker. "The kid can have green hair and purple skin and if he's a band member, he's one of us."

Adds Stella Martin, "You don't have to wear the feathers to know that you are native. It's just a sense of knowing where you come from, and being aware of what you come from.... I think culture has a lot to do with identity, who you identify with. What is happening with our younger children now is we're trying to break all the chains that have been put on in the last fifty to one hundred years. What we are trying to do with each new generation that comes up is to get them to break that dependency chain, to make them start thinking of self-sufficiency, to help them realize that they are different, that they have a strong culture that they come from, and that they don't have to copy any other culture. I think that is what has happened—Indians try to assimilate into mainstream society. We are pushed from all sides, you know, 'Come and mingle with us. Be just like us.' With all the things our parents went through, a sense of identity was lost."

Work on the reserve is largely construction, and there are hopes native building crews will bid on outside construction jobs when the reserve building is complete. As well, Martin said there are ongoing discussions with nearby oil and gas companies about job opportunities and training for band members. A small lumber yard and cabinet shop are a sign of the direction the band wants to move in—towards a self-sufficient community.

Dealing with social ills is the difficult part, and not as easy as simply buying equipment and hoping its use will result in viable economics. Drinking was and is an ongoing problem. "On most reserves, especially northern reserves, there will always be an alcohol problem," says Liz Scout, the police co-ordinator for the Woodland Cree reserve. The forty-two-year-old mother of two is in charge of what will, by the spring of 1994, be a three-officer detachment, with an auxiliary. One of the officers, twenty-three-year-old Bill Cardinal, went through RCMP training in Regina, and Cadotte Lake is his first posting. Cardinal's mother is a Woodland Cree, as is he. His father is white, and Cardinal thought little of being native while growing up in Prince George, B.C. That is gradually starting to change, as it is for Sam Laboucan, who grew up in Dawson Creek, Edmonton and Slave Lake. The thirty-year-old returned to Cadotte Lake in 1992, where his grandparents are elders. "The isolation took a bit of getting used to," said Laboucan, who wears a baseball cap with an eagle feather pinned to the side.

Police at the reserve were specifically requested by the elders. The nearest police detachment is in Peace River, and logistics made response time slow. Liz Scout, a heavy-set, talkative woman, is candid about the problems she found on the Woodland Cree reserve upon arriving in early 1992. "When I first started here, there was no law. It used to be just wild on weekends. There were a lot of people drinking, assaults, people doing doughnuts all over the place in their pick-ups." She said the crime was often more of ignorance and poverty than a criminal mind, and the attitude towards criminal offences is still somewhat naive. One weekend, she was about to drive one suspect under arrest into Peace River for court in her Ford Suburban. Her young son sat squirming around in the passenger seat, waiting for his mother to get going. "Boy Mom, your back window sure is clean," he piped up. That was enough to catch Scout's attention. The back window was usually so mud-streaked it was tough to see out of. Looking over her shoulder, Scout saw the entire back window had been popped out, and her suspect was lounging a few yards from the truck. "I just wanted some fresh air," he explained.

There have also been cases of solvent abuse, with several teenagers sniffing gas. Scout said a psychologist visits the reserve three times a week.

"When you live in poverty, as these people lived for years, these are some of the things that happen," said Scout. But things are definitely improving from last year. "People are beginning to feel a sense of pride. They want a good community."

Although legal aid was paying Teena's legal fees, it would not cover travel or accommodation expenses associated with the upcoming hearing in Victoria, set for May 5. So in April Donna drove Teena to the Travellers Motor Hotel, a three-storey building in downtown Peace River, to meet with the band council. Donna thought the councillors might fund Teena's travel costs; it was worth a try.

The councillors were sitting around casually in the double room when Teena came in. She did not know these people at all, although she knew that some of them had known her mother and could remember Teena as a little girl. They pulled up chairs around a small, plastic-topped table, and Donna sat a few feet back, against the wall, leaving Teena at the forefront. The councillors asked her if she could tell them what was going on. "I told them I wanted to have my son returned to me, and I told them the efforts I made to get him back and how they hadn't worked," Teena recalled.

Teena and Donna later went to the motel restaurant for a coffee and a cigarette and awaited the decision. When they were invited back into the meeting, they were told the councillors were impressed with the teenager—the band would pay for her travel expenses, and for those of Donna and Dolly LeTendre, a social worker at the band office, both of whom would accompany Teena to Victoria.

Teena was thrilled and felt a confidence she couldn't remember feeling before. The thought that people believed in her was exhilarating.

A rainy March afternoon spent at the University of Victoria law library turned up several useful nuggets of information for Jean Morgan. She wanted to see if any changes had been made to the Alberta legislation governing adoption in terms of native children. She was aware of the mass exodus of native children adopted to white families from Manitoba in the 1970s. She also knew of the horrifying case of Richard Cardinal, a native teen in Alberta who had hanged himself in the back-yard of his foster parents' home in 1984. He had lived in more than twenty-five foster placements in thirteen years. The case shocked the public and sparked the Alberta government to ask Dr. Ray Thomlison, dean of social work at the University of Calgary, for a review of the child welfare system.

Indeed, there had been changes to the law since Morgan had last studied it. Section 62.1 of the Child Welfare Act, under which adoption regulations fall in Alberta, stipulates that if a director or an officer of a licensed adoption agency has reason to believe a child being placed for adoption is an Indian and a member of a band, and that the guardian surrendering the child lives on reserve, the council chief or the band council must be consulted before the petition for an adoption order is filed. If the director or officer of a licensed adoption agency, or Social Services or whoever is involved with facilitating the adoption, has reason to believe that a child being placed for adoption is an Indian and a member of a band, and that the guardian who is surrendering custody of the child is not living on reserve, they "shall request the guardian who is surrendering custody of the child to consent to a consultation between the director or officer and a chief of the council or the council of the band."

If the guardian consents to such a consultation, the chief of the council or their designate must be consulted before the petition for an adoption order is filed.

One of the documents that is mandatory in filing an adoption petition in Alberta is a statement that section 62 has been complied with. As far as Morgan knew at that point, Alberta Family and Social Services had not complied with this section. It stood to reason, then, that under Alberta legislation, the adoption of Jordan Michael Sawan could not have been completed in the province in which he was born.

As she prepared documents for the May 5, 1993, petition hearing, Morgan found herself harkening back to childhood experience, when she and her family spent time in the summer at a place called Alberta Beach, west of Edmonton. The Glenevis Indian Reserve was nearby and she often played with the native kids that came to the pebbly shore. "When you are a child, you play with people and there is merit in the relationship or there's not, based on basic principles—do I like these kids? Are they fun to play with? Colour of skin played no role whatsoever." But she saw the native kids being treated differently by white adults and children. It offended her sense of fairness even as a child. "When I was a child, it was very clear that Indians had a place in the world, and it was below you. It was absolutely outrageous. I found it despicable when I was younger because I really could not understand it."

Morgan did not come into the case with any background as an advocate for native rights, or any special interest background, other than the "perhaps naive" interest in seeing people treated equally. "I suppose I have a strong interest in seeing or working towards equality for Indian people in Canada because we're still not there. I just think the colour of skin should have no bearing. Period. I don't care if the person is Indian, Chinese, Japanese or whatever—it shouldn't close doors to you. I think we destroy so much from doing that, we really and truly do.... I didn't take this case as a crusade—it wasn't that. I just thought that Teena Sawan had a right to be heard."

Brian Young also had a personal reaction to the case. While it seemed obvious to him that David shouldn't be moved, he had to convince a judge of that. In preparing for the hearing, Brian Young wrote to several people he thought may be able to provide him with information on Teena and the child, and on Social Services' involvement with them before the Tearoes received the boy. One of the main things he was looking for was corroboration of a comment the Tearoes maintained was made to them by Lynne Smith at the time they took custody of baby David—that the child would have been apprehended the next day had the Tearoes not taken him, because of concerns over Teena's ability to parent. To the Tearoes, this alleged comment justified further their belief that David belonged with them.

But Young found himself up against a brick wall in terms of obtaining information from Alberta Family and Social Services. The ministry has a "rule book an inch thick," said one veteran insider who spoke on condition of anonymity. "It's followed within an inch of our lives. No one wants to lose their job, and the way to lose your job is to not follow the rules."

After a little digging, Young learned that the rules of confidentiality prohibit the release of file information to any party other than the guardian, parent or foster parent of the child to whom the information relates or a lawyer representing them. Well, that's fine, thought Young. The Tearoes had parented the child for over a year. Surely they would qualify as guardians or foster parents. He fired off another letter to the Alberta lawyer representing Social Services, and the response left him dumfounded. According to the ministry's lawyer, the Tearoes would qualify as neither. A foster parent is defined as a person approved by a director under the Alberta Child Welfare Act. A guardian is defined as a person appointed under a section of the Domestic Relations Act, or a person made guardian of the child under an agreement or order under the Child Welfare Act.

If Young were to obtain an order from the Alberta Court of Queen's Bench directing information to be provided, the letter from the Social Services ministry's lawyer continued, "my clients would be happy to comply with that order." The lawyer for Social Services added that he had a "certain amount of sympathy" for the situation Young's clients were in.

As Jean Morgan had pointed out in court documents filed on behalf of her client, the Tearoes had done nothing since February 6, 1992, when the initial document was signed, to allow them to legally have the child. Sawan had never agreed to any interim custody agreement with the Tearoes; she had never relinquished her guardianship rights to her son; and the Tearoes had never applied to the court for an order for custody or guardianship in either Alberta or B.C. In effect, without any of the above, and without an adoption order, the Tearoes had the child with no lawful authority. But the longer they had him, the tougher it would be for the birth mother to get him back. Time was definitely on the Tearoes' side.

At the beginning of April, Iris Land wrote the Tearoes, telling the Victoria couple that although she grieved for them and felt that David James should remain in their care, she could not get directly involved in their case. She did not want to do anything to "break the bonding" between her and Grace and Peter. The foster mother noted that Teena was trying hard to get her life back on track, but added that it wasn't fair for the Tearoes to have to give the baby back after so much time had gone by. Land urged the Tearoes to send Teena pictures, as she was grieving for a chance to see her son again, "as any mother would."

One week later and a full fourteen months from the beginning of what was to have been an open adoption, Teena received her first letter from the Tearoes. Glossy photographs slithered out of the envelope, showing her child's new life. The little boy squinting into the sun by a tiny wading pool; a close-up of him and Heidi, her cheeks pink and flushed; the little boy sitting on a piano stool. Captions written on the backs of the photographs referred to "David," but Teena thought of him only as Jordan.

There was also a letter in Jim's neat, slanted handwriting.

April 14, 1993

Dear Teena,

Since your request to get your baby back about 10 days after we got him, we have been reluctant to send any pictures, thinking that seeing him again in the pictures, you would want him back more than ever.

Nevertheless, our intention is not to close the door to you ever seeing your baby again but only to raise him as our adopted son. We have renamed him David James TEAROE; David after King David in the Bible and James after my first name. We call him David and he has been a great delight to us ever since you gave him to us. On February 14th he started to walk and now he is running. We play classical and Christian music which he really likes. He likes to play my harmonica too.

For some reason David bonded to me from the day we got him from you. He shows affection to Mom, Heidi and our cocker spaniel but I'm his favourite! His first word was DAD and he waits eagerly for me to come home each day from work. Then I'm with him til I put him to bed at 7:00 p.m. David is Faye's (mom) pride and joy. She reads him a Bible story each morning and is doing a good job of pottie training him.

Heidi, David's older sister, loves him very much and spends hours playing together with him. She also helps with diaper changing and often they play in the bath together.

How have you been making out, Teena? I hope you are well. Are you going to school or working? We love you, Teena, and are praying for you. We hope and pray that you will start going to a good church and get some nice Christian friends. You will always be very dear to us.

I'm sending you some pictures of our "precious little man." Hope you like them!

Please write to us and tell us how things are going for you in Manning. Is there anything that we can pray for you about?

Take care of yourself, Teena!

With Love,
Jim, Faye, Heidi, David and Natasha (our dog) Tearoe

Teena stared for a long time at the pictures. Her child's hair was still blond, his skin looked smooth and warm and his eyes looked directly at her. She searched for herself and found it in the curve of his lips, the edge of his chin. "My son, my Jordan. I love you, I love you," she thought as she cradled the photographs. She felt both fierce and scared, and as if nothing could stop her.

Chapter 11

The psychological distance between Victoria, B.C., and Manning, Alberta, is as far as the mind can imagine. It's the difference between a capital city that prides itself on being the "City of Gardens" and a tiny northern town that deems itself the "Shangrilah of the North;" between people earning comfortable salaries at varying levels of government bureaucracy and those wearing three or four collars, most of them blue, to make ends meet; it's the difference between Jim and Faye Tearoe and Teena Sawan, and the life the little boy that bound them might lead.

As the May 5 hearing date drew near, the Tearoes and their lawyer began preparing, and while Jim and Faye Tearoe said repeatedly that they left everything about the case in God's hands, they actively sought information to substantiate comments about Teena and her lifestyle that had been passed on to them.

The Tearoes talked on the telephone with various people in Manning who were opposed to Teena Sawan getting her child back. Their comments bolstered the Tearoes' instinctive dislike of Teena's world. The Tearoes thought of the teenager as a "drinker and partier," and certainly not a good

Christian. Jim and Faye could not bear the thought of the boy who was the apple of their eye returning to what they considered a substandard environment.

Iris Land telephoned the couple with allegations that Teena had been assaulted by Miles on April 17, 1993. It fit in nicely with the Tearoes' view of Teena's world. What kind of home was that for a child?

A reputation is a tough thing to live down, especially one earned in a small town. There is none of the insulation that comes from living in a city, no anonymity in numbers. Sunni-Jeanne Walker is blunt about it. Asked how long it would take for Teena Sawan to live down a reputation for drinking and partying, the outspoken deputy mayor answered, "About five years."

When Walker was contacted by Jim Tearoe in the spring of 1993, she didn't want to get involved. All she knew was town gossip. "The Tearoes wanted people to back up their side in the court case, and nobody was going to do it. Being in a small town, it's difficult to get involved in that way. Repercussions come back on you, especially in an issue like this."

Then, says Walker, "One of the Tearoes' emotional pleas got through to me.... They were getting pretty desperate. They needed concerns documented, somebody in a position to come out with an opinion that would help their case to present to the judge. They couldn't understand that while some people in the community didn't want the baby to come back, no one would make an effort on it."

As Iris Land did before her, Walker threw her support behind Jim and Faye Tearoe. Although she had never met the couple, had never seen their home or watched them interact with the child—had, indeed, only spoken to them a couple of times on the telephone—she made up her mind they were the better parents for the boy, based on the power of a middle-class image. Jim's comment that the child would have been apprehended had the Tearoes not taken him helped her make up her mind. She took him at his word.

Walker wrote the following and faxed it to Jim's office one day before the scheduled hearing.

Sunni-Jeanne Walker
Manning Alberta
T0H 2M0

Jim Tearoe
May 4, 1993

I have become quite concerned with the way the child custody hearing has proceeded with the Tearoe family. I also
want to make this quite clear that this will be hearsay since
the people (doctor, receptionist at the health unit and RCMP
officer) who could present information on this matter are
prevented due to their positions. I am in that same position
but I am also tired of society returning the child to the homes
that created the chaos when enough time has not been
allowed for rehabilitation.

The woman in question, Tina [sic], has a history in our
small town of heavy drinking, fighting at parties and travelling with known criminals. In other words an unfit mother at
present. Just a few weeks ago her common-in-law partner
beat her up but charges were not laid.

The present environment offered by Tina would damage
the child while the home already created by the Tearoe family has calmed the child due to its stability.

The reason I am concerned is that the issue of what is best
for the child irregardless of the native element has not been
presented. The Tearoe family has not prevented Tina from
communicating with the child. If Tina cared about this child
then he would be left in the present home and not in the
chaotic environment offered by Tina.

Thank you
Sunni-Jeanne Walker

After sending the letter, Walker thought back to a day in
March when Teena and Miles had come into her accounting
office. Teena had been dressed nicely, Miles in his usual jeans
and T-shirt. Walker chalked up their request for financial

advice as a "scam," something being done to show they had their lives together.

Walker later made a comment that was to become a familiar one as the case progressed. "When I heard the word native, I said, watch out. I pre-warned Jim that if Teena used the native issue, he didn't stand much of a chance. To me, it's not a native issue. It's where the child is best raised. I would personally not automatically agree with the Tearoes. I get nervous with people who are too Christian. I've met quite a few evangelical people living up north. But I'm sure the child will have a very good life, be very loved and have a better chance." She continued, "It started out with Teena saying, 'It's my baby.' Now it's become native. How did it switch so fast? I blame it on the lawyers. But what the heck, the lawyers are out there to win and they chose a very good path."

Then came another criticism of Teena Sawan that would also be repeated during the proceedings. "Teena isn't living native," Walker complained. "If you want to go native, go native. Don't use the native issue unless you're going to perform. I don't see her doing it."

There was no fighting such comments, Teena said later. "People...make up their minds based on gossip.... If I walk by the Aurora, people say, 'Oh, there goes Teena again.' If I sit inside the bar drinking a pop or have one drink or play the lotto machines, people assume I was in there until I couldn't walk any more. I don't know how to fight that, so I just try and ignore it.... People should judge me on who I am now, not who I used to be. Maybe there was a time when people could say, 'She's just a drunken Indian,' and they would be right—I was drunk and I was an Indian. But I should be looked at for who I am today and sure, I've got problems, but who doesn't? And I'm working on making my life better. Maybe even the Tearoes weren't perfect when they were twenty."

Miles, as usual, is more direct, and appears almost hurt when told there are people in the community who doubt his parenting abilities. "These people don't know anything about us. Have they ever been in my home? Tell them to come and live with me for a week and see what I'm like and then they can make all the comments they want. People like that are assholes."

As is standard with such contested court cases, the contents of the affidavits filed began a not-so-subtle form of character assassination.

Reading Jim and Faye Tearoe's separate affidavits, the impression is given that Teena Sawan is usually drunk, living on welfare and with no fixed address. Faye also makes a financial point, stating: "My husband is gainfully employed and has the income to properly support the child. It is our understanding that the natural mother is on welfare." Faye went on to say that she did not wish to limit the birth-mother's access to the boy, but said that a "stable atmosphere is required. When the child is then old enough to make a decision, the child can properly be advised of what has happened in the past. The child will then be able to decide.... We have a wonderful home full of love."

In the spring of 1993, Teena Sawan was living with Miles in a small rented apartment in Manning, going to school and still getting As and Bs. Miles worked on the rigs when he could, sometimes at the tire shop and sometimes not at all. Teena was not on welfare; she was receiving $1,500 a month from the Woodland Cree band as long as she was enrolled in and doing well in school. They still went to the Aurora or the Manning Motor Inn, and played the lotto machines, and Teena occasionally drank on weekends, but it had, she says, calmed considerably. She and Miles had made a pact to support each other in not over-indulging and for the most part, it seemed to be working. Indeed, when Jim Tearoe asked Ralph Cowie to write an affidavit stating his concerns, he refused, saying he thought that Teena had made concerted efforts to clean up her life since the January incidents that had prompted Cowie's call.

In their affidavits, the Tearoes emphasized the bonding between themselves and the child, and pointed out that Teena had known what she was doing when she signed the

February 6, 1992, consents. They also questioned why, if Teena had wanted her baby back, she did not contact a lawyer until the fall. "The result of this long time has done nothing but to bond this child to us," wrote Faye, who also stated that, "Since the time of the adoption, there has been no contact between ourselves and the natural mother. There has been no contact by the natural mother with the child and you would think that if she was so concerned about her child that she would have made efforts to come and see the child. She should have made efforts to contact us. As well it would have been appropriate for the mother to have provided something for the child at Christmas and Birthday times."

Faye's affidavit intentionally or inadvertently ignored Teena's February 14, 1992, telephone call, during which she personally asked Faye for her child back, and her May 1992 letter reiterating her request. Both Jim and Faye seem to have ignored Teena's several phone calls to Social Services stating her desire to have Jordan back, and her passive resistance to the adoption represented by her refusal to sign documents.

Wrote Faye Tearoe in her affidavit: "Prior to our having custody of the child and in particular when the child was with the natural mother, the child was not being well cared for. We have heard recently that there are concerns by people who have contact with the child's mother that her lifestyle is clearly not appropriate for looking after the child. Our sole purpose in mentioning this is to state that the best interests of the child are with us. I believe that the best interests of this child are to remain with us. Clearly he will not have a stable upbringing if he is returned to the atmosphere in which the natural mother lives."

While their affidavits focused on Teena Sawan's perceived parental inadequacies, the Tearoes often wondered privately what motivated Teena to try to get her son back. As Faye rinsed breakfast dishes at the sink and gazed out the window at the thrushes outside, she couldn't imagine giving up the most precious gift God could give, and one that He had chosen not to let her have naturally—a child. Faye thought Teena's desire for her son was, in part, a wish to please her younger brother and sister, who had been against Teena giving up the child. "She wants to prove she is a caring person," Faye said. "The only family Teena really has in the world will come from her womb."

But what really concerned the Tearoes was their conclusion that the Woodland Cree band was a driving force in Teena's bid for her child. "She didn't do anything for ten months. And you know what she did in those ten months?" Faye said later. "She joined the Indian band. And then she got help. And apparently the band is paying for her schooling. Now, what does that say to you?

"Again, there's money involved here and there's also land involved here from the federal government. It says to me that she's been put up to it. Yes, that's what it says to me."

The Tearoes' fear that this was a ploy by the Indians to get more land and money from the government is unfounded. By the time Teena Sawan talked to Donna Ominayak about obtaining a lawyer in October 1992, the reserve was already in place and the addition of one more band member would have had no impact in terms of land or financial settlements. Teena was a member of the band long before she ever talked to Ominayak. She had been put on the band list two years previously by her aunt.

Teena's formal response to the Tearoes' affidavits and petition focused on the fact that she did ask Social Services and the Tearoes for her child back, and that she had neither the funds nor the wherewithal to get a lawyer sooner than she did. "I know I am not a perfect mother, but I am capable of looking after Jordan. I can give Jordan love, stability and knowledge of his culture.... Since the day Jordan left with the respondents, I have wanted him back. I have wanted to be responsible for him and be his mother. In February 1992, I told [the Tearoes] I wanted Jordan back, and I sent the letter to the Department telling them that I no longer agreed to the adoption. I have never stopped loving Jordan; I will not be a perfect mother to Jordan, but I will do my best to give Jordan all that he needs."

Jean Morgan asked Teena about section 62 of the Alberta Child Welfare Act, whether Teena had been asked about counselling with the band. "No, are they supposed to?" Teena asked.

Morgan realized that Teena Sawan knew very little about being a native person. "Is learning about native culture something that interests you?" Morgan asked carefully, not wanting to put words in her client's mouth.

"Yeah, it is," Teena answered. She thought about it later, about how the thought of actually *being* something was new to her, and something she liked. The native people she had met, particularly Donna, made her feel good about herself. When Jean asked if she wanted to include in her affidavit that she would like Jordan to learn about his culture, Teena's response was immediate. "I'd like him to know what I never did."

Just as the Tearoes found the circumstances frustrating, so did Jean Morgan on Teena's behalf. "It constantly astounds me that Teena Sawan is blamed when she did what she could, in her limited world, to get the child back. Teena was eighteen years old and living on her own, on welfare. She had no mother or father to turn to, no family who could help her in this situation to find a lawyer. She had turned to Social Services first, and they were of no help to her other than to tell her to get a lawyer. I think of myself at that age, and I was far more sophisticated and I had two wonderful parents who loved and cared for me, and if someone told me to contact legal aid, I don't know that I would have known what to do. Who do I call? Who will pay for it? I think that, as best as Teena Sawan could, she pursued it. She talks to Social Services again in April, telling them she wants her son back. She writes the Tearoes. She has their friends coming in trying to pursue this adoption. She does everything in her own little way to stop this adoption. She refuses to sign the documents. She stands her ground, and it may seem like nothing to us but I think that takes a great deal of courage for someone with Teena's experiences."

Morgan found suggestions that Sawan should have couriered the letter or faxed it especially vexing. "This is not a fifty-year-old woman who lives in a city. This is a teenager with no money living in a northern Alberta town with no family support who has already turned to the people that have had control of her entire life for help, Social Services, and received none."

Morgan privately noted some of the slight differences between what was stated in the Tearoes' affidavits and what she read in the contact notes she had received from the Alberta Social Services department.

In Lynne Smith's contact notes, Faye is quoted as describing the baby as "peaceful and happy," "never seen a more contented baby." By the time court documents were filed, she described his character the first month as fearful and easily upset, and said he was "very afraid of people and frightened by sudden noises which would not normally affect other children." Faye later said that the baby at first had a "terrible temper which he's gotten over quite nicely now." She attributes these negative characteristics to what she views as a lack of love and care, first by Teena, who she said "really didn't want him," and then by Carolyn Grayson, who she said "had too many kids to look after and couldn't provide enough time."

Morgan pored over the contact notes, carefully looking for any discrepancies in Teena's version of events, and found that the contact notes corroborated precisely what Teena Sawan had told her about her dealings with Social Services, right down to the type of envelope she had used to mail her social assistance cards in February 1992. "There had been no embellishments. Everything was consistent," Morgan said, noting that Teena did not know what the social worker's notes said, so her version could not have been tailor-made to fit them.

Teena, Donna and Dolly flew to Victoria a day before the hearing. The women who had gradually built up a telephone rapport finally met in person. Teena was expecting Jean Morgan to be someone official and "lawyerly-looking," and was surprised when a well-dressed woman no taller than herself, with a gracious manner and a warm smile, came out personally to the reception area to greet her.

Inside Morgan's office, the women reviewed the case one last time. "I think what happened to you was unconscionable," Morgan told her young client. "But it is going to be very difficult to get Jordan back because of the time that has gone by." Teena carried with her a file folder in which she had the original of the revocation letter she said she had penned February 8, 1992. Morgan looked at it and, later in the meeting, handed her young client a blank piece of paper and asked her to fold it, as if it were a letter. When she handed it to Morgan, the paper was folded exactly the same way the original revocation letter had been.

In the petition hearing, evidence was to be called by way of affidavit, rather than directly from witnesses. But following her meeting with Teena, Jean Morgan changed her mind and decided that an out-and-out trial was needed. Although she didn't like the idea of more time passing, the contents of Faye Tearoe's latest affidavit, received late in the afternoon of May 4, were shocking to the lawyer, and she wanted to cross-examine Faye. And after meeting Teena in person, she realized her client was personally impressive. She wanted the judge to listen to the young native woman.

Brian Young was also having second thoughts about proceeding by affidavit. The emotional impact of the case was lost on paper; he wanted to put Faye Tearoe on the stand. Her devotion as a mother was striking and couldn't help but sway a judge. He also wanted to cross-examine Teena Sawan about parts of her life that he suspected were being whitewashed.

The lawyers appeared in B.C. Supreme Court on the morning of May 5 and explained their desire for a trial to the presiding judge. Time was of the essence in the case, they explained, asking for a directive that the trial be heard on a "priority basis" so it wouldn't be caught in the often clogged court system. The judge agreed and the trial was set for June 14-15, almost six months after the first petition had been filed. This is relatively speedy for the civil court system, in which a year-long wait is not unusual.

Teena, Dolly LeTendre and Donna Ominayak flew back to Alberta that night. Staring out at the ocean below her as they left Victoria, Teena wished her son was in the seat beside her. But if Jean Morgan thought it was best to wait another month and have a trial, then Teena did too. The Tearoes had no qualms about the adjournment. It was more time with the little boy who had just turned seventeen months old, and who was walking, talking and a general delight. At dinner with one of Jim's brothers, with whom they visited regularly, the couple laughingly told of the boy toddling down the church aisle on Sunday, his plump arm raised high as he chortled out "Hallelujah!"

Jean Morgan immediately got to work looking into Faye Tearoe's affidavit allegations. Faye swore she had talked to RCMP Constable Robin Haney, whose name had been passed along to her by Iris Land, on Wednesday, April 28, 1993, and again two days later, and he had passed along damning comments about Teena Sawan. "He said to me that he is extremely concerned about Tina [sic] Sawan's lifestyle. He has had occasion to deal with her many times due to drug and alcohol abuse. He has also been recently involved as a result of her being assaulted by her fiance. He was advised to press charges but nothing has resulted as of this date. Although he is unable to provide me on short notice with a letter, he is willing to testify to these allegations if necessary."

Morgan was stunned. "I found it unbelievable that any RCMP officer would ever divulge anything that he had heard in any way, shape or form about another person," she said. Indeed, when sworn in under the federal RCMP Act, officers swear that they "will not disclose or make known to any person not legally entitled thereto any knowledge or information obtained by me in the course of my employment with the Royal Canadian Mounted Police."

Morgan called the officer at his home in Manning to question him about the allegations. "He was shocked those things had been said," she recalled, adding that he seemed upset and claimed, "I don't know what you're talking about."

Haney called back a day later to say that he had talked to Faye Tearoe again, and that she was going to recant that affidavit. "As for what he said about Teena, he said he did know she was epileptic and had adverse reactions to alcohol," Morgan reported. She assumed that the Tearoes would subpoena the officer for the trial.

Upset about the affidavit, Haney called Brian Young, who later sent the officer a letter confirming that he had been "misquoted" in Faye Tearoe's affidavit. Young attempted to subpoena Haney but was informed in writing by the Department of Justice, which acts as legal counsel for the RCMP, that Haney had no evidence to offer and was reluctant to attend the Victoria trial. The subpoena for Haney was cancelled.

Three weeks before the trial was slated to begin, Jim Tearoe sat at his desk and carefully wrote another letter to Teena Sawan.

May 20, 1993

Dear Tina,
I am writing to you to ask you to consent to the adoption of the child whom we have called David. Here are some reasons why we are appealing to you.

1) Much prayer was offered in Manning, Victoria and elsewhere that God's will and God's best would be done for the baby.
2) You yourself made that decision and called us to come and get him.
3) You signed him over to us to adopt as our son.
4) You wanted him to go to a Christian family with joy, happiness and stability and that has happened. We all go to church every Sunday, read the Bible and play Christian music to David. Heidi goes to Lighthouse Christian Academy School and we plan to send David there too, when he is older.

5) We have had David almost from Birth. He is now a year and a half old and has become bonded and very attached to us just as if he had been our own child.

6) We have grown to love and cherish David as if he were our own son.

7) To take him from us now would be devastating to my wife, Faye, my daughter, Heidi and to myself.

8) You are young, not even 20 years, with your life yet before you. You have every hope of marrying and having children and raising a family. We are older and have not been able to have children but have prayed for children all our married life. David and Heidi are all we can hope to have and they have brought much joy to us.

9) David always wants to be with his Daddy and waits for me to come home each day from work. He keeps watching for me through the window by the front door. He loves to do things together with us; we love him so much!

10) We have a mommy, daddy, sister and puppy dog for David to grow up with. We also can support him spiritually, socially and financially. We have been paying into a university scholarship fund for David for over a year.

11) We have told you that our home is open for you to come and visit David so that you can see for yourself his home and the love and care we are giving him.

12) We are also expecting that as David gets older, he will want to know more about his birth mother. We will tell him from the beginning that he is adopted and will not withhold any information that would help him to contact you or find out more about you as he gets older.

13) We have been praying for God's hand, protection and direction on <u>you</u> since January of 1992. <u>We</u> also care about you and your welfare.

14) A custody trial is scheduled for June 14-15. If we subpoena witnesses from Manning they would say things against you to help us win the case. We do not want to run you down, but rather want to be your friend. Please do not force us to do this.

15) Please pray that God's will and God's best would be
    done for David, for you and for us.
16) Please....let's remain friends and not run each down in a
    trial. After all, we're related now!
17) You may call us at [...], if you wish.
18) Please let us keep our son.
19) We love you, Tina, as the birth mother of our son, and
    will always be praying for you and be your friend.

With Love in Christ
Jim, Faye and Heidi Tearoe

It pained Jim to see the worried crease between his wife's
eyebrows as she squeezed David to her side while reading
him his bedtime story. Her fingers sometimes pressed so
hard on the worn pages of her Bible as she sought strength
from its words that her fingertips were almost white. Both of
their lives revolved around their children, but Faye's especially.

As the trial neared and there was no response to the letter,
Jim made a point of calling home almost every lunch hour
and talking with Faye, sometimes reading verses of scripture
over the telephone together. Often, Jim forgot to eat his
packed lunch, sitting in a brown bag on the shelf beneath a
picture of David, Heidi and Faye. Three days before the trial,
he stopped packing his lunch altogether. He believed that the
Lord wanted him and Faye to fast until the trial. It would
allow them to be weak before the Lord, so His will could be
done.

Chapter 12

◈◈ ◈◈ ◈◈

Justice Allen Melvin wheeled his Toyota Camry into the underground parking lot of the Victoria courthouse at his usual time of 8:30 a.m. on June 14. It gave him an hour and a half before court started to catch up on reading, fine-tune judgments and kibitz with the other judges over coffee.

Melvin had just settled in at his desk when trial co-ordinator Judy McFarlane buzzed him from her office on the floor below. A robbery case Melvin was set to hear had been adjourned, but she had a two-day custody matter with a "priority" designation. Though it was common knowledge that civil cases weren't Melvin's favourite—the former Crown prosecutor much preferred a criminal trial—he was available, and the case had to be heard. "Tell me which courtroom to be in," he said, jotting down the name of the case and the lawyers involved.

There are often days when all a judge knows of a case before walking into the courtroom is the name. That was fine with Melvin. "Just tell me if I have to wear red or black," he says, referring to the practice of B.C. Supreme Court justices of wearing robes trimmed in crimson when appearing before juries.

With watchful brown eyes and a thick head of grey-tinged hair, Melvin looks younger than his fifty-seven years. He is one of the most experienced justices on the B.C. Supreme Court bench, having left a successful career as a top-level prosecutor in Vancouver to take his appointment at the age of thirty-nine, making him one of the youngest judges at the time. Since, he has earned a solidly respected reputation as a fair-minded, level-headed judge, who takes pride in his judgments withstanding appeals.

Melvin's gravelly voice and rapid-fire speaking manner give an appearance of gruffness, and his gaze doesn't miss a thing. It is no secret that Melvin likes to see trials run efficiently; he does not suffer disorganization gladly. Some criticize him as being egotistical, a common trait of a successful trial lawyer, and not unusual in a business that tends to breed conceit. One often gets the impression that Melvin wishes he were on the other side of the bench; indeed, he has said that if he had it all to do over again, he would have preferred to continue practising for a few more years before becoming a judge.

He is reluctant to let bureaucracy get in the way of what he thinks is right, and he is not afraid to rock the judicial boat.

To Jim and Faye Tearoe, it seemed oddly fitting that the fight for the son they had so longed for would begin on their thirteenth wedding anniversary. After all, it was on their wedding day that they had formally joined together in their prayers for David James Tearoe.

They left their house early that morning after seeing Heidi off to school and giving repeated hugs and kisses to David, who was being looked after by Faye's parents. Heidi had just turned nine, and her birthday wish had been that the family would get to keep her little brother. She prayed that morning along with her mom and dad, and would again that night. Heidi also wanted to fast before the trial, as her mom and dad had done for three days, but Faye wasn't so keen on that idea. "Honey, that's a wonderful offer. But your dessert is down here waiting for you," Faye said as the child went up to her bedroom with Bible in hand.

The commuter traffic to Victoria from the Tearoes' home in suburban Colwood went at its usual snail's pace that morning. The name the "Colwood Crawl" was an apt one—traffic backed up for the equivalent of city blocks at the numerous stoplights on what was only a ten-mile drive into the city. Faye and Jim gazed at the long strip of car lots and fast-food restaurants that comprised Colwood's main street as they poked along. They wanted to get to the courthouse early, so they could pray in the courtroom. "As it says in the Bible, in Lamentations," Jim later explained, " 'Oh Lord, you are my lawyer, plead my case. For you have redeemed my life. You have seen the wrong they did to us. Be our judge and prove us right.' So we say to the Lord, You are our lawyer and judge. We just pray that even as you have given up this precious gift, we don't believe it was your intention to give us a gift and then take that gift back. We're just saying, Lord, we have prayed for this little man for so many years. It is the desire of our heart. We are trusting in the Lord."

Faye and Jim found the doors to courtroom B locked when they first arrived, and they sat holding hands on a padded bench in the hallway outside, waiting for Brian Young. Faye's short brown hair was curled, a light touch of lipstick brightening her lips. She wore a neat skirt and blouse; Jim wore his usual office attire, a short-sleeved dress shirt with a tie and slacks. When their lawyer came around the corner, briefcase in hand, he gave them a cheery greeting. Young was upbeat.

While the Tearoes were confident that God was on their side, Young was counting on more tangible support. In Young's view, the statute and common law were in his favour. He was planning to argue the case based on B.C. adoption law, and that put the onus on Teena Sawan to show that revoking her consent to the adoption was in the best interests of the child. There is no provision in the B.C. law for a ten-day, no-questions-asked revocation period, as there is in the Alberta legislation. And there has never been a case in

B.C. in which a birth-parent has gone to court and successfully shown that it is in the best interests of the child to be
returned.

In his briefcase was a copy of the most recent Supreme
Court of Canada case dealing with a similar situation. *Racine
v. Woods* was decided by the Supreme Court of Canada in
1983. In that case, the country's highest court found that race
and culture were important, but their import in determining
the best interests of the child decreased over time in favour
of bonding.

But perhaps the most powerful weapon Young had was
emotion. He was counting on the obvious bonding between
the Tearoes and the boy to make it virtually impossible for a
judge to separate them. Who could tear what seemed to be,
from all outward appearances, a happy child from the middle-class, two-parent home in which he had lived almost all
of his young life?

Racine v. Woods is quoted as the leading authority on the
competing interests of culture and bonding in adoption battles. At issue was who would parent a little girl named
Leticia Grace Woods, born in Portage la Prairie, Manitoba, on
September 4, 1976, to Linda Woods, a native woman, and
fathered by a native man. Woods was in the process of sepa-
rating from Lloyd Woods when the little girl was born. Linda
Woods had an alcohol problem at the time and was unable to
care for the infant, who was looked after by her brother and
then her sister, writes Justice Bertha Wilson in the Supreme
Court of Canada decision.

Leticia was apprehended by the Children's Aid Society of
central Manitoba when she was six weeks old and placed in
a foster home. A few months later, with Linda Woods' consent, the infant was made a ward of the Society for a one-
year period, and on February 11, 1977, six-month-old Leticia
was placed in the foster home of Sandra and Lorne Ransom.
Sandra left her husband a short time later, and lived with
Allan Racine, whom she subsequently married. Leticia
remained with Sandra and Allan Racine until the wardship

expired in May 1978, after a further six-month extension, and she was then returned to her biological mother, who had made no efforts to contact the child during that time.

The Racines had grown strongly attached to the girl and were invited by Linda Woods to visit. On their second visit, in May 1978, they took Leticia home with them, with Woods' consent. They believed then that Woods had surrendered her child to them on a permanent basis, and in October 1978, the Racines applied to adopt the girl. But Woods said she had told the couple they were to have Leticia "just for a while," until she came for her in a couple of weeks. She and Lloyd Woods were sometimes together, sometimes not, and she acknowledged that she was somewhat emotionally unstable at the time.

In October 1978, Linda Woods came to the Racine home and told them she was leaving Lloyd Woods for good because he was abusing her, that she was on her way to Regina and wanted her sister to have Leticia. The Racines refused to give the girl up. Woods left and made no further contact with the Racines until January 1982—more than three years later—when she launched an application for the child to be returned to her.

During the intervening years, Woods had been trying, with varying degrees of success, to rehabilitate herself. She dealt with her alcohol problem, freed herself of her association with Lloyd Woods and engaged in a program of self-improvement. But none of this was easy and periods of achievement were followed by backsliding, noted the Supreme Court of Canada judgment. It took her four years and the support of friends, relatives and her extended family at the reserve to accomplish her objectives. By this time, Leticia was six years old.

The Racines were described as a well-respected couple, active in their community and excellent parents to Leticia and their two younger children. Leticia was a well-adjusted child. She knew that the Racines were not her biological parents and that her natural mother was Linda Woods. The girl also knew that she was a native Indian.

In February 1982, while home-study reports were being
prepared by the court on both the birth-parent and the
prospective adoptive parents, Woods took matters into her
own hands. She tried to abduct Leticia and was caught. The
Racines applied for an order enjoining Woods from further
abduction attempts. Woods was granted supervised access,
and on the first visit she arranged for a reporter and photographer from the *Winnipeg Free Press* to document the meeting.
The story was given considerable prominence in the daily
newspaper, much to the upset of Leticia.

At trial, the position of the Racines was advanced by testimony that the child's best interests were met by the bonding
done with them and the security of the established home.
The birth-mother's position was bolstered by psychological
testimony indicating the importance of cultural ties, especially during adolescence. After eight days of evidence,
much of it from "expert" psychologists, County Court Judge
Ruth Krindle ruled that it was in Leticia's best interests to
remain with the Racines. Judge Krindle commented specifically that she had taken Leticia's native heritage into consideration and had concluded that the Racines were fully
sensitive to the special problems of raising a native child in a
predominantly white environment, and were well able to
cope with any identity crisis Leticia might face as a teenager.
Allan Racine was Métis, and no stranger to the hurt racial
prejudice could inflict, the judge noted, adding that he was a
model for Leticia of "how to survive as a member of a much-
maligned minority."

As well, the trial judge worried that Woods might slide
into previous bad habits, and was also concerned about the
"venom of her anti-white feelings." She asked what effect the
birth-mother's "visible hatred for all things white" would
have on the child. Although she commended Woods on her
positive lifestyle changes, Krindle also wondered whether
Woods' concern was for the child as a person or as a political
issue. The judge was extremely put off by the media incident,
saying it manifested an incredible indifference to the effect
such publicity might have on her child. She also found that

Leticia had been abandoned by Woods, as the Racines had had the child for four years without contact from the birth-mother.

The Manitoba Court of Appeal, however, overturned the adoption order, made the child a ward of the court and granted custody to the Racines, with Woods to apply for access. One of the three appeal court judges said he thought the adoption should go ahead but acceded to the majority. Justice Gordon Hall said it is not the appellate court's job to re-interpret the evidence presented to the trial judge, who has the "tremendous advantage" of seeing and hearing the parties and their witnesses. Hall said the conclusions of the trial judge were supported by the evidence, and noted that she had given particular attention to the evidence about the Racines being able to cope with the difficulties of raising a native child in a white environment.

The other two justices, Joseph O'Sullivan and Roy Matas, ruled, however, that the trial judge had erred in holding that Leticia's best interests lay with the Racines. They expressed a concern about the finality of an adoption order cutting Leticia off from both her natural mother and her native heritage and culture. The two justices disagreed with the trial judge's finding that Woods had "abandoned" her child, pointing out that she had gone to the Racine home to pick up Leticia but the Racines had refused to give the child to the mother. "In effect, Mr. and Mrs. Racine considered themselves as the equivalent of a court or a child caring agency in deciding what they though was best for the child at that time." The judges said the Racines could not say Woods had abandoned her child when they deliberately refused to return the girl.

The decision was in turn appealed to the Supreme Court of Canada, which found there was evidence to support the trial judge's finding that Leticia had been abandoned during the four-year period in which Woods had no contact with her child. The Supreme Court also noted that the Manitoba appeal court put a different interpretation on the evidence than that of the trial judge. "It is not the function of the appellate court to re-interpret the evidence," wrote Justice Bertha Wilson in the October 13, 1983, judgment. The Supreme Court of Canada found that the trial judge did not err in ruling that the best interests of the child were served by granting the adoption and emphasized that the judge had addressed the issue of the child's Indian parentage in making her decision. As well, Wilson wrote, the appeal court decision would likely result in lengthy and bitter litigation, which would not be in the best interests of Leticia. "This child should not be allowed to become a battleground—in the courts or in the media—and I believe that there is a very real risk of this if the court refuses to 'bite the bullet.' In my view, when the test to be met is the best interests of the child, the significance of cultural background and heritage as opposed to bonding abates over time. The closer the bond that develops with the prospective adoptive parents the less important the racial element becomes." The adoption was granted.

Jean Morgan's view of *Racine v. Woods* was certainly not as cut and dried as Young's, who viewed it as saying clearly that bonding superseded culture. Morgan saw it as saying that culture and race are important considerations that must be looked at in the context of the case and that their importance was secondary to bonding only with a significant period of time. Morgan also believed that the differences between *Racine v. Woods* and the Tearoe-Sawan case were significant. Leticia was almost six years old when the case was heard by the Supreme Court of Canada, and had been with the prospective adoptive parents steadily for four years. David would be eighteen months old when the trial was heard, and with the Tearoes for sixteen months. The efforts by Leticia's biological mother to gain custody came much later than the efforts by Teena Sawan to get her baby back. As well, in the *Racine* case, the adoptive father was part native, with an understanding of what that meant and a proven commitment to teaching Leticia about her culture.

Morgan also found it unfair that an adoption that could not have been completed in Alberta, due to the fact that certain

documents were not signed by Teena and the band not consulted in accordance with Alberta statute, could go through
in B.C. But her strongest trial argument, she believed, lay in
the revocation. Surely, Teena had demonstrated that she
wanted her child back within the necessary time period. The
point of the Alberta legislation was to give the birth-mother
some breathing room, not to catch her up in a technicality.

The principle of equity, defined as "fairness or natural justice," also applied, as it does in all child custody cases.
Essentially, equity means that the spirit of the law, not just
the letter of the law, must be considered. It comes down to
the biblical rule of doing unto all others as we would be done
by. In Morgan's view, equity meant this: Should the Tearoes
be able to benefit from a wrong, the wrong being, in her
view, not returning the child when Teena Sawan asked for
him? Should they be able to ignore a confused young
mother's cries because they didn't approve of her lifestyle
and because they thought she didn't try hard enough to follow the law?

When Teena walked into courtroom B just before 10:00 a.m.
on June 14, the Tearoes were already inside, sitting at the far
end of the room. Behind them sat Lynne Smith and Erin
Harris. The social workers had been subpoenaed by the
Tearoes and had a lawyer with them. Dolly, Donna and
Teena, who had flown in from Edmonton the night before,
sat in the second bench on the opposite side of the courtroom. Donna's strong physical presence shielded Teena.
Wearing a slim navy-blue blazer and white pants, with her
long black hair in a loose French braid, Donna's wide, attractive face had a straight-on gaze and her posture was perfect.
Sitting beside her, dressed in plain slacks topped with a
sweater and light cotton jacket, Teena looked even smaller
than she was. Although Teena has little money to spend on
clothes, she is always concerned about looking neat and tidy,
and her appearance was even more important to her that
day, when she felt all eyes would be on her, judging.

Young and Morgan, who knew each other from law school

and a couple of minor dealings on previous cases, chatted amiably as they set out their piles of paperwork on the long desks in front of them. The lawyers indicated to court clerk Shannon Cole-Carlos that they were ready, and she left via the side door to get the judge. Morgan straightened papers in front of her, Young readjusted the collar of his robe. Jim and Faye clasped hands, and Teena cleared her throat again.

When Morgan and Young saw Melvin walk into the courtroom, each had a distinctly different reaction to the man who would decide a child's future. Young knew then and there that the case might not be the shoo-in he had been hoping for. He had hoped for a judge with a family law background, preferably female, since he thought a woman would better understand and empathize with the issue of bonding that was the crux of his case. Instead, there was Melvin, whom Young viewed as an "old boy" who liked to flex his judicial muscles by attacking the system. Morgan was pleased. She respected Melvin's decisions and liked the way he ran his courtroom, getting right to the heart of matters.

Melvin quickly scanned the two petitions in the file before him, each one asking for the child. It seemed like a relatively standard case. The Tearoes wanted to adopt the boy, the birth-mother wanted him back. He had no inkling of what it would turn into.

Chapter 13

Brian Young's trial plan was relatively simple. The facts would come from Jim Tearoe, the heart through Faye.

With that in mind, Young made just a brief opening statement before delving directly into the case, calling Jim Tearoe to the stand.

Jim Tearoe recited the basic facts of his family, noting that he and Faye had been married thirteen years as of that day, had an adopted daughter, Heidi, and had been hoping and praying for another child. Asked what the Tearoes call the child, Jim responded: "We call him David and his second name is after myself, James. So we have called him David James."

"He's also been known as Jordan, is that correct?" Young asked, to which Jim responded vigorously, shaking his head. "Not in our home, he's not. Never. No."

Realizing this was a sensitive topic for his client, but wanting to explain to the judge that the child would be referred to by two different names in the course of the trial, Young pursued the point. "But prior to the adoption?"

"As soon as we picked him up we already had a name for him."

Morgan was on her feet, on a point she wanted to make very clear from the outset. "Objection, my Lord. The adoption hasn't been completed."

Melvin smoothed the waters, suggesting the word "placement" as a neutral alternative.

Young continued. "Prior to the placement, the child had a different given name and that was Jordan. Is that correct? Were you aware of that?"

"Yes, we were."

Jim Tearoe gave a lengthy outline of the telephone call from Teena, in which she had told them they could come and get the infant. When he talked of the child, his usually monotonous voice became excited, and his natural talkativeness emerged. "We were extremely excited. We were just delighted. And we'd always wanted a son. I guess that had been a desire of my heart. After we'd got our daughter, not that there was anything wrong with she being a daughter, but we were wanting another child and particularly we were thinking it would be nice to have one of each, a boy and a girl. And this child was a boy, and so we were quite excited and quite delighted. Also we were delighted because this child was a brand-new child rather than perhaps an older child, so we could have much more of an influence on the growing up of this child and be able to enjoy the child during those younger years."

Young asked his client if he had known that Teena was native.

"Yes, yes, we did. Because Esther Taylor had stated that the mother, as I recall, had—was one-half native. And we asked about the child, and we didn't really have very much information about the child except we understood that the father was from a—not a native. But, we weren't really sure of that. Nobody really seemed to know what—they seemed to be suggesting that the child was not native."

Jim Tearoe's comment that Teena was one-half native was the first testimony the court received about her ethnic background. It originated from a genogram signed by Lynne Smith and included in Teena's Social Services file. A white man named Bruce Scotty is named as Teena's father in that family tree. But in another Social Services document, written by Erin Harris, Teena's father is listed as Albert Auger, who is native. Teena herself has been told by her family that Albert Auger is her father, and he has identified himself as such to her. Despite Teena saying outside court that both her parents were native, she would be referred to as one-half native throughout the trial. The first reference slipped past Morgan and was never corrected on the court record.

Jim then testified about going to Teena's home in Fairview, waiting for the social workers to arrive, signing documents, having the ten-day revocation period explained, returning to Victoria, receiving the telephone call from Teena saying she wanted her child back and making the subsequent call to Alberta Social Services to ask what to do.

"[Lynne Smith] stated to us that, according to the form that had been signed, unless there was a written revocation of that consent, we should just hang tough and just stay where we were. She said there may be a letter in the mail and she would—she didn't know. But, she said in the event there's a letter in the mail, she said, you know, that may change things."

Asked what the family did after that, Jim said, "Of course we did a lot of praying." He outlined a series of telephone calls between the Victoria couple and Alberta Social Services. It was clear that the Tearoes were left with the impression that unless something was received in writing in ten days, they did not have to return the child and could proceed with the adoption, unless Teena Sawan put up a legal roadblock. Jim testified that Teena telephoned him in the spring and asked about her child's well-being. She did not ask for him back in that conversation, Jim pointed out. Shown a copy of the May 1992 letter that Teena wrote after that conversation, in which she does ask for the child back, Jim commented, "She has very beautiful handwriting."

When asked to describe the role the child has taken in his life, Jim Tearoe became visibly enthused, his voice rising.

"The sun rises and sets on him as far as we are concerned.

We think that he is very special of course. For some reason, he bonded to me personally from, pretty well from the day we got him.... He always wants to go to his daddy and he's always wanting to be in my arms.... We go on hikes.... We've taken him down to the beach.... We play music at home, and he really likes the music. He seems to have a real love of music.... He also likes to sing in our home, and he's quite a happy little man. He's a very happy little man."

Jim Tearoe read aloud anecdotes he had written down about the bonding between him and the child.

"One of them is that David waits for me to come home by the window beside the front door most days. And when he sees a car he starts calling out my name, 'Daddy, Daddy, Daddy.' Of course, I can hear that as soon as I get out of my car. And the bonding really has been, been very, very close. And it's been very exciting to have a small child that just thought so much of his dad, and so we have a very, a very, very close relationship. So, when we're sitting at the table, then David sits between myself and my wife and so we take turns feeding him and of course changing him and all of that as well. So, I spend a lot of time with him from the moment I get in the door, which is approximately four o'clock in the evening, until I put him to bed at seven o'clock; I spend that time with him."

Young asked Jim whether the Tearoes had received any birthday cards or Christmas cards from Teena Sawan, and Jim said they hadn't, commenting that this was something that "surprised him."

When Morgan rose to cross-examine Jim Tearoe at 11:35 a.m., just after the court took a twenty-minute mid-morning break, it was the first time she had talked with him. The usual examinations for discovery, during which lawyers have the opportunity to question witnesses prior to a civil trial, were waived in the interest of getting the trial on quickly. She began by exploring the Tearoes' attitude toward the boy's part-native background.

Jim turned towards Morgan in the witness box, sitting very straight, like an uneasy student facing difficult questions during an exam. His hands were resting in his lap, holding the notes from which he had earlier read.

"I just have a few questions for you, Mr. Tearoe. You've indicated that you have knowledge that Jordan is a native child. And I'm wondering what type of inquiries you've made with respect to his aboriginal background and how you intend to promote his culture?"

Jim Tearoe's answer focused on the calls he and Faye had made to Lynne Smith and others, asking for the name of the child's birth-father. Morgan stood patiently throughout what she thought was an unresponsive answer to her question. She knew from the social worker's notes that the Tearoes had been informed that Teena was a member of the Woodland Cree band, and that inquiries should have been made about the child's status. She was trying to establish that the Tearoes had knowledge of the child's aboriginal background. There seemed, to her, to be no recognition that this child was anything other than white, Anglo-Saxon because that was what he looked like.

She asked, "When I'm speaking of culture and heritage, I'm not talking about the state of his health. I'm talking about his aboriginal roots."

"Yes," Jim replied.

"What inquiries have you made in order to promote Jordan's cultural background?" asked Morgan, who always referred to the child as Jordan, just as the Tearoes and Young always referred to him as David.

"Okay. I think I have to go back and say to you that when I spoke to Dr. Hallinen, I wanted to get some information on his medical background, but also I wanted to get information on the father so that we could pursue his background.

"Now, we have been told that—I guess it's only hearsay— that the father is not native. But, other than that, I can't seem to get any information from anybody about who he is or anything else about this individual. So, I've basically run out of avenues.

"Now, the second thing is that when I spoke to Teena at the—when we were adopting David on the sixth of February of last year, I specifically asked her if she could give me as much information as she could about that father. I said, Is he tall? Is he short? What is he? And she told me that he was a very short man like herself and, other than that, that's about all she could tell me. So, I thanked her very much that she had—I said this was not an easy decision for her to make and I appreciated that—and I thanked her very much for putting her trust and her confidence in us. And I assured her that we would do the very best we could to live up to those expectations that she had, and that we would also, as I've stated earlier this morning, our house was open for her to come visit at any time and—"

Morgan interrupted him, her polite tone shaded with impatience. "That's not my question."

"May I just finish please? We anticipated that we would have had closer contacts with Teena, either by telephone or by mail, that we could follow up on that. Now, that has not happened, as you know. And so I have dealt with that through the telephone calls trying to find out through these various people more about his background and—"

Morgan broke in, and phrased her initial question again. Jim Tearoe answered questions like a wound-up toy, his flat voice going on like a tape-machine.

"Mr. Tearoe, do you then believe that the father is the only person that can give status to a child? Is that why you're concerned?"

He paused and blinked a few times quickly. "No, no. I hear what you're saying though."

"Well, I can't quite...my question then to you: You haven't contacted the band that he comes from, have you?"

Jim paused. "No, we have not."

"You've made no inquiries there?"

"No."

Having finally established that the Tearoes knew of the child's native background, Morgan went over what happened in Fairview when the Tearoes picked up the child and signed the documents, before moving on to Teena's revocation attempts.

Questioning then turned to the B.C. documents sent to Teena Sawan in the spring of 1992 by John Jordan.

"Did you tell Mr. Jordan to do up papers to send to Teena and have her sign so she would consent to the adoption so it could go through?"

Jim Tearoe said he couldn't recall specifically how it came about that the B.C. consent forms were sent to Teena Sawan to ask for her signature.

Jim Tearoe said he had not instructed his lawyer in "every specific detail...I did not instruct him really to do anything except to proceed with whatever legal matters have to be attended to go through with the adoption."

"Did you not contact a Pastor Henry Langerud, to speak with Teena to get her to sign them?" Morgan asked. Jim agreed that the pastor had been brought in because he'd been told that Teena "kept changing her mind."

The point of her question, Morgan said to Jim Tearoe, was that, despite Social Services' advice that the Tearoes could proceed with the adoption, the Tearoes were still trying to have the consents validated by having a "pastor friend" go to Teena's home.

Jim Tearoe focused on Morgan's comment that Pastor Henry was a friend. "This gentleman that you have mentioned, I have not met him personally. I only understand that he was the pastor of a church, the church that Teena was attending at the time, or at least that he knew Teena in some way, enough to be able to discuss the adoption of the child and perhaps to discuss with her what the best interests of the child would be. But, no, I have not met this gentleman."

"So, you didn't really believe the advice of Social Services then?" Morgan asked, to which Young stood and said, "I know it's cross-examination. But the difficulty I have with this line of questioning is it's trying to get this witness to admit something he has no involvement in."

But Melvin said the questioning was valid, and leaned to his right, towards the witness box, and asked Jim Tearoe, "Did you discuss the matter of further documents to be signed by the mother with the pastor in Alberta? Did you speak to him about it?"

"To be honest, sir, I do recall some discussion, but it might have been with my lawyer and my lawyer contacting this gentleman to discuss it with Teena."

"Regardless of who contacted who," Melvin continued, "did you know what the purpose of the contact was going to be?"

"It had to do with some kind of consent."

"And that it was expected that this gentleman would assist in the mother signing another consent document?" Melvin queried.

"Yes," said Jim, adding that it was his understanding the B.C. consent document "cleared the way for us to proceed with whatever had to be done here in British Columbia." He continued that he had not seen the document that was sent and that, in the end, Teena had refused to sign it.

It was clear to Morgan that the Tearoes had known there were problems with the original consent, if their lawyer, John Jordan, had continued to try to get a B.C. consent document signed. She moved her questioning to the letter Teena Sawan wrote to the Tearoes in May of 1992, having Jim Tearoe read a portion of it aloud. After doing so, he said, "So, yes, she asked for Jordan back in this letter."

"Thank you. Now—"

Tearoe interrupted. "Excuse me, could I say one thing to you on that subject? From what we understand from Alberta Social Services, notwithstanding that letter, was that on numerous occasions when they went to Teena to try to get her to sign various forms, apparently she was at one point saying yes—"

"Mr. Tearoe—"

"—the child was going to go with us and—"

"I ask the questions, and—" Morgan began.

"—other times it was going to be the other," Jim Tearoe concluded.

"Let's move on with other questions," Melvin said to Morgan.

"Yes, okay," Jim Tearoe agreed.

Next, Morgan brought up the contents of a letter written by Jim Tearoe to Teena Sawan three weeks before the trial began. "You say, 'A custody trial is scheduled for June 14th. If we subpoena witnesses from Manning, they would say things against you to help us with the case. We do not want to run you down but rather want to be your friend. Please do not force us to do this.' Now, if you believe that the consents were all valid and fine, why this letter?"

Jim Tearoe lost some of his tightly reined control. "I don't want to have to go to court. To me, as far as I'm concerned, that original letter of consent should have been sufficient. Therefore, as far as I'm concerned, I wonder why I'm even here in court today, because that original consent should have been sufficient for us to have got custody of David as our legally adopted son.

"But my counsel, and evidently you as counsel for Teena, have seen otherwise and therefore, you have seen fit that you feel you can contest that original consent, and so here we are in court today. And so what I'm saying is, for whatever reason that you see that you consider that original consent is not valid, for whatever reason, that's—"

"Mr. Tearoe—" Morgan interjected.

But he continued "—why we're here today. So, I'm saying I'd rather not have to have to do that."

Pointing to the underlined portions of the letter, Morgan suggested that the letter tries to blame Teena for what has gone on.

"This letter does not blame Teena at all. We are very appreciative that she gave us the child. But, I point out to her that it was her decision."

"Now, Mr. Tearoe, did you ever enter into any interim care agreement or interim guardian agreement with regard to the Sawan child at any time?"

Tearoe appeared baffled.

Morgan continued. "You understand that Jordan has not been adopted?"

"I believe that subsequently we were able, through the proceedings, to determine through Social Services, because they were withholding certain information from us which we couldn't understand like the—it's called I think a register of live birth or something like that, and for some reason it wasn't coming—"

Sensing another long discourse, Morgan jumped to her point. "Jordan. You have not adopted Jordan. You have no order for adoption. Jordan is not your son at law; do you understand that?"

Young rose. "That's pretty clear. That's why we're here today."

Sitting in the public gallery, Faye held her Bible tightly in her hand. Not our son? What does that mean? Of course he's our son. We've raised him for the past sixteen months.

Jim Tearoe answered, "I would say, yes, I guess. But as far as I'm concerned, there was only one thing. And that was that Teena specifically called up my wife and said, 'Come and get my baby; I am going to give him to you to adopt as your son.'"

After a brief interchange in which Jim Tearoe spoke over the next question Morgan tried to ask, the lawyer stood silent for a few seconds before saying quietly, "Mr. Tearoe, I don't want to argue with you. I just want you to answer the question. That's all I want."

"Yes."

"Do you have a custody order giving you custody of Jordan Michael Sawan?"

Jim Tearoe made a shrugging motion.

"What is that?" Morgan asked.

"I can't answer you. I have no idea. I filled out the forms that were required by Alberta Social Services, whatever those forms were for me to legally take the child and to leave. And from there I contacted my lawyer and he was to follow up for the legal adoption of Jordan."

"Mr. Tearoe—"

"And as far as the legal forms that had to be filled out or not filled out—it's up to him, and I don't know what those forms are or what those requirements are."

"Well, Mr. Tearoe, what made you believe that you had the

right to keep Jordan when you were contacted by telephone within the ten days and asked to return the child?"

"Well, I think two things: one, it was very carefully explained to Teena in my presence specifically that it was consent for adoption. And I think you need to note the words 'consent' and 'adoption' which specifically stated that, if she did not revoke them within ten days, that child would be ours and free to go ahead with the legalities of having a home-study and going through the regular routine of—"

"But she did orally revoke that consent to you."

"Yes. But—no, she did not. I beg your pardon. I—"

"You told the court that she did."

"I back that up," Jim Tearoe said. "I'm sorry, yes, she did orally revoke that but, legally, she did not because it was explained to her, and Social Services also stated in their opinion that, because they had not received a written letter revoking her consent, that in fact we could go ahead with the adoption of our son."

Morgan looked at her notes for a moment before asking, "So, your legal advice came from Social Services in Alberta with respect to your status regarding the child then?"

"I wouldn't say our legal advice, but that was—that was advice that was offered to us, was that we were free to go ahead."

Morgan asked what the Tearoes would have done if Teena Sawan had come to their doorstep February 14. "Would you have given this child up?"

"I think we would have—if she had been at—at our doorstep I think we may have—" Jim Tearoe stopped for a few seconds. "To be very honest with you, no, we would not have given him up because as far as we're concerned, it is a very serious decision that has to be made by any mother to give up her child. And we feel that she also should be considering us, and the commitment that we have made to the child as well, and that if she does not fulfil—we signed a legal document for the signing over of that child into our home and into our custody. We have committed ourselves to a lifetime of looking after that child and being the parents of that child, and it is not a light decision.

"And she had time to make up her mind for that decision. She had ten days to revoke it in writing and it was not done. Therefore, in our opinion, we could then proceed. And that's the way we look at it."

"Your concern was what you had gone through," Morgan continued. "Now, you have a young woman who is eighteen years of age changing her mind and phoning and asking for the child to be returned. There was no consideration for that, was there?"

"Oh, yes, there was. When we were in Fairview, I talked personally with Teena and talked about her life."

"No, Mr. Tearoe, I must have lost you. I was actually—"

Young stood up. "If the question is asked, he should be allowed to answer the question."

Melvin responded, "He's not answering the question put. The answer is not responsive. Put the question again. Listen to the question."

Morgan began again.

"After February the 14th."

"Yes," Jim Tearoe said, nodding.

"It's within the ten-day period?"

"Yes."

"You're not willing to give the child up. That is my understanding from you."

"We were willing to come back, but of course we don't want to. So, we phoned Alberta Social Services to ask them what we should do. We didn't say we're not going to bring the child back. We asked them, 'What should we do?' We said it would appear that the legalities of the situation are such that we do not have to at this point. And I think that you also have to consider our point of view as far as giving a child up. No, of course we don't want to give the child up, no, of course not. But, if we have to, then we will, and that's the way we felt, that if we legally had to give the child up, we would. From an empathy point of view, as far as Teena was concerned, we also knew that she had been changing her mind, at least that's what had been told to us by the social workers, that she had changed her mind on numerous occasions from—I guess from the time the child was born, whether she would adopt the child out or whether she would not.

"And after talking with Teena personally about her future and what she was wanting, she said that she was really not able to care for the child because she wanted to get her grade twelve and get some training. And so, again, we felt, well, we just pray that God's will and the best will be done for that child, as far as the upbringing of that child. But when we got that child...." Jim's voice trailed off.

The cross-examination continued for a few more minutes, mostly tidying up loose ends as to whether Jim Tearoe had been present for some telephone conversations with Social Services, or Faye was and she had simply relayed the information to him.

At 12:30 p.m., Morgan finished, just in time for the lunch break. Jim Tearoe left the witness stand and joined Faye. He was drained. As the lawyers packed up and prepared to leave the courtroom, Jim walked up to the court clerk, who was putting papers away, and asked if he could go in the back and have a private discussion with Judge Melvin.

Young inwardly groaned as he overheard Jim's request. As the court clerk shot Young a "What am I supposed to do with this guy?" look, Young came up and took his client gently by the arm, leading him away. "Jim, Jim, Jim," Young said in the patient tone he often used with his kids. "You can't be doing that. You're not allowed to talk to the judge." Young had spent a considerable period of time explaining to the Tearoes exactly what to expect in the courtroom, down to where they would sit and how they would be sworn in. He hadn't thought to warn them not to ask to talk to the judge. It wasn't something anyone usually requested.

Morgan heard the request as well. It shored up her initial impression of what Jim Tearoe thought of the court proceedings—they were a waste of his time and all it would really take was a one-on-one conversation with the judge to straighten this whole mess out.

The lunch break that day was shortened to a half hour to accommodate a meeting Melvin had scheduled for later that afternoon. Teena, Dolly and Donna grabbed a sandwich and a coffee from the CNIB stand in the courthouse lobby and ate outside in the small park behind the courthouse. Jim and Faye made a quick call home to see how David's day was going without Mom and Dad, and were told the toddler was having a great time. They sat in the deserted stairwell between the third and fourth floors, quickly eating a lunch packed by Faye that morning. They spent most of their time reading the Bible and praying.

Chapter 14

❖❖ ❖❖ ❖❖

Faye Tearoe fought off a nervous quaver in her voice as she was sworn in as a witness immediately after the lunch break. The Bible in her hand gave her a measure of comfort, as did the sight of her husband, sitting alone in the public gallery of the courtroom. When Brian Young showed her three recent photographs of David, Faye's determination became stronger than ever.

Young wanted the judge to see pictures of the tot in question, so Melvin would have a face to attach to the testimony. Snapshots showed the boy playing with a toy truck and smiling out at the camera, or sitting on Jim's knee, with Jim looking adoringly at the child. "That's our boy," Faye said, with a smile and decisive cheerfulness.

Faye recounted the family's involvement from February 6 on, and specifically Teena's February 14, 1992, phone call.

"Teena said that she'd like to have her child back," said Faye, her voice beginning to break. "And I suggested to Teena—I guess when I went into the home to meet Teena, I was concerned about where she was living and the relationship she had with the people that were there—however, I suggested to Teena that perhaps it might be a—best idea if she came out and stayed with us for a while. And I said to her that we would pay her way if she came out and carried on to go to school here, even for the six months…so that she could stay with the child and also be able to go to school and see what's happening in our home. And, and she kind of almost gave me the indication that she would maybe do that.

"And then, as soon as I hung up the phone I phoned Lynne Smith because I wanted to make sure if I should return the child, what I should do, like, whether I should do this right away or what we should do…. So I phoned Lynne and I said, 'Lynne, what would you like me to do?' And Lynne said, 'Well, by rights, you have to return that child right now.' And I said, 'Well, that would be fine,' because we were aware of that, because she had ten days in order to change her mind. And so I said to—to—to Lynne, 'Would you like us to return him right now?' and she said, well, because there was a holiday on Monday, she said it might be a better idea to wait until Monday because Teena had to go in and write a statement, a little note, a piece of paper just saying she wanted her—her child back. And so we were waiting for her to get that note in there. And she said she had to contact Teena anyway, so she would tell Teena she must get in with a piece of paper or send it by mail or whatever."

On February 19, Faye continued, Lynne Smith called her and told her that no letter had come in. "We were just kind of waiting to hear whether Teena had got the—the letter in. And so I think I phoned Lynne on March the 2nd and she said that no letter had come and as far as they were concerned, we could go ahead and proceed with adoption."

Young asked, "So what was your understanding at that point as far as the consent?"

"We were allowed to go ahead and adopt because Teena had not gone in with the letter stating that—that she wanted to have her child back."

"So, at the beginning of March 1992, it was your belief that the consent was valid?"

"Yes, absolutely," Faye answered, nodding her head. "And the papers that we had signed in front of the Alberta Social

Services we believed to be accurate and correct and therefore, we had the right to take David, and Teena had consented to do this."

Asked to recollect the events of February 6, 1992, when the Tearoes went to Teena's Fairview home, Faye's dislike of Teena's environment became apparent. "We found Teena's house and when we went in we stood by the door, Jim and Heidi and I. And we waited by the door for quite a while, twenty minutes or whatever, or half an hour maybe. And there was sort of rock music type stuff on and we were just kinda listening to that. And finally, somebody had the good sense to turn it down because my daughter wasn't quite sure what she thought of that. And then, finally, one man came out and he left, and another man and a girl, and I think another girl went in the back bedroom, or somewhere in the house." Faye went on to describe how they went in and talked with Teena before the social workers arrived.

"Did Teena say anything to you about the child's native background?" Young asked.

"Absolutely. We were delighted, as a matter of fact, to hear that he was native. As a matter of fact, he's a quarter native. And as a matter of fact, I really wanted to bring out that we have very good friends, the Craigs, that are very dear friends of ours and, as a matter of fact, Tom who was our best man at our wedding thirteen years ago is native and we still are dear friends with these people. So, I have no problems with, you know, having a native child; as a matter of fact, we're delighted about it."

Faye said she had not known of Teena's membership in the Woodland Cree band, or that the child was then a potential band member. Morgan made a note. The social worker's contact notes said the Tearoes were told that Jordan was eligible for band registration and that the band should be notified of any adoption. Faye went on to state that at the time the Tearoes picked up the child, Teena obviously knew they were white, and there was no mention of her wanting to ensure that the child's native culture was carried on.

"Really, the reason she called us was she could have

adopted the child out through the human resources but she really wanted to have a Christian family, and this is why she had gone to the trouble to find, you know, a Christian family, so that was basically what she was interested in."

Teena sat forward on her chair beside Jean, some ten feet from Faye. Morgan had asked that Teena be allowed to sit beside her, as Donna and Dolly were not allowed in the courtroom until they gave their evidence, and the lawyer had not wanted Teena to have to sit alone in the body of the court. Teena seldom looked directly at Faye during the older woman's testimony, instead focusing on her words, as she described her life with the little baby that Teena could vividly recall bringing into the world. Faye reminded Teena of a mom from an old TV show she'd seen in reruns. She wondered if Faye ever doubted that the world was a fantastic place to be in. Was everything always perfect?

As Jim did before her, Faye told of an ideal relationship with the child, and then asked if she could say something.

"If I have the right," she added. "Jim and I got married very late in life and I knew that I could never have children. And we were so delighted to have Heidi and David that— that I guess, to us, they're our life, far more than.... You know, I mean, we have a beautiful home and the Lord has provided that, but our children are our pride and joy so we, you know, David is very special to me. I mean, what can I say?"

Young's next goal was to show that bonding had occurred not only with the parents but with Heidi as well. Faye had a ready anecdote. "Oh my goodness, I'll just give you one little instance. We went for the March for Jesus the other day, on Saturday, down in Victoria. And Heidi and Jim and I all walked together, you know, carrying on. When we got to the Parliament buildings, there was a little friend that Heidi saw and she wanted to go over and see her little friend and so she disappeared. She said could she go and off she went. David was on top of Jim's back; he was in the backpack. And all of a sudden he looked around and there was no Heidi and he hollered, I tell ya', so loud, 'Heidi!!' So, I mean, they have, they're very bonded."

Faye testified at length about the family's activities together, and said that they would like to include Teena in their familial future, and perhaps travel to Manning the next summer. The Tearoes planned, Faye said, to tell David about being adopted and about his birth-mother as soon as he could understand, just as they had with Heidi.

Young wrapped up his questioning of Faye on an emotional note. "How would you feel if David was taken away from you?"

Faye's eyes teared and she answered, "Gosh, it would be like death to us. It would be very hard, but it would be extremely hard on David because David is very bonded to us. I think it would break the trust in our little man, that we've had him for a year and a half and—and he just thinks we're wonderful, you know. And I think it would just destroy something in him that would be very hard to replace."

Jean Morgan's cross-examination started off with a question about the child's native heritage.

"You have indicated that you were very delighted that young Jordan was in fact a native, an aboriginal person?"

"Absolutely," Faye responded brightly, turning in the witness box to the small woman asking her questions.

"And what efforts have you made to this point to find out about his culture and his heritage?"

"Do you know, that's a good question. But, do you know we really felt that until David is legally adopted by us, we haven't done anything at this point but, indeed, we have," Faye responded, apparently remembering something as she spoke. Her cousin, a white woman, does "beautiful art paintings that native people do," adding that this would be a "great encouragement" to David to knowing native culture.

"You say you don't want to do anything about that until he's yours; I think that's paraphrasing?"

Faye nodded. "Yes, that's right."

"But you changed his name?"

Faye nodded again. "Yes. We did that because we prayed for David James Tearoe from the time that Jim and I got married until we got him. In the car when we were coming down we all talked about it, said what would we like to do. Shall we keep Jordan's proper name or should we change it to the name that we had prayed about? And we decided—all of us took a vote and all three of us decided that we would prefer to name him David. Heidi prayed—has prayed for David for seven years."

"But he wasn't yours yet and you still thought it would be better to change his name?"

"We knew that he would be ours because Teena signed him over to us," responded Faye, her voice matter-of-fact.

"But in terms of his native culture he's not yours?"

"Oh, yes."

"But you haven't done anything to promote that because he's not yet yours; that's contradictory."

"Well, we haven't done anything to this point, but we certainly are going to look into that."

Morgan moved her questioning to the telephone call Faye Tearoe received from Teena Sawan on February 14, 1992.

"Teena said to you, 'I want Jordan back'?"

"Yes."

Faye testified as her husband had: they were told by Social Services to wait for the letter. When no letter arrived from Teena, Lynne Smith told them to proceed with the adoption.

Morgan questioned why, if they were told on February 19 that they could go ahead and adopt, their adoption petition had not been filed until December, some nine months later. Much had been made in the affidavits of Teena not doing anything about getting her child back for months; Morgan was pointing out that the Tearoes hadn't done anything either.

Young interceded to clarify that John Jordan, understanding valid consent to exist, had believed that a desk order adoption would follow, for which no petition was needed.

Morgan pointed out that no documents had been filed for a desk order, either.

The next line of questioning centred on the concern Faye had expressed earlier about Teena's home environment in Fairview. "I take it that's because there was rock music playing and there were people coming and going from the house?" Morgan asked. "You were there an hour and a half. Was the house dirty?"

"Well, there wasn't much in it so it certainly couldn't be dirty," Faye answered.

"So, it had few possessions but it wasn't dirty?"

"Um-hum."

"And what did you observe in her relationship with other people that caused you concern?"

"I—that's a good question. I guess, well, the rock music was one. The people coming and going, there was, you know—oh, I don't know. Maybe perhaps I was just concerned for Teena because I really wondered...what was actually happening here. But, as a matter of fact, again I can say, hearsay, that we heard later that there were things going on, but I just...from what I saw, I wasn't impressed."

"Teena is a young woman. She's nineteen. How old are you, Mrs. Tearoe?"

Faye thought a minute and laughed, "How old am I? Good Lord, I'm forty-eight this year."

"Rock music is not your taste, right?" Morgan asked pleasantly.

"No, classical."

"Classical. People coming and going; were they drunk? Were they throwing up? What was going on?" Morgan pressed.

"No. I guess it was just an impression, I'm sorry. I guess it was just an impression.... I wondered what kind of a situation she really was into, and it was sort of *terrifying*."

"So your concern is founded on your different lifestyle. Classical music, religion, compared to a young person's home that has few possessions?... You expressed concern, but you can't point to anything that causes you concern?"

"No, you're right."

Morgan moved on to the affidavit filed by Faye with her interpretations of what RCMP Constable Robin Haney had said in their telephone conversations about Teena Sawan.

"Is [Haney] testifying?" Morgan asked.

Faye was flustered. "He—we—we would have had to pay his way I believe it turned out and, no, he hasn't come."

"Constable Haney called you May 4th, probably about 5:00 p.m. at night, about that statement?" Morgan asked, referring to the call Haney told her he had made to Faye Tearoe to correct the statements made in the affidavit.

"Yes, he certainly did," Faye said, nodding her head. "And he went back on everything that he said. He said, you know, this was just hearsay and I had no business writing it down and he's right. I shouldn't have.... My error was in the fact that I made a statement, that is my error. But, as a matter of fact, what he told me on the telephone was exactly that. I am telling you the truth. This is what he said to me. He said that Teena had come in one morning about, whenever, before he got off work and she was all beaten up and without any shoes. And—and he—he said quite a few things that I never even made a point of. And then he said he was going to go off duty, that she should come in later on when he was back on duty so he could go home and get some rest and then he would write out the report and—"

Morgan interjected "Constable Haney said to you that he never said that she had problems with drug and alcohol abuse. Is that not true?"

"No. That's—Constable Haney told me that, that she, either she's with a crowd that has alcohol or, or no. I know he said she has alcohol problems. And he said that—"

"What you've said here is that, 'He has had occasion to deal with her many times due to drug and alcohol abuse.' That's what you said. Is that the truth?"

"Yes. This is the truth that I heard from him as far as I'm— I'm—yes, this is the truth."

Jim Tearoe stood up in the body of the courtroom, his long-fingered hands gripping the pew in front of him, and said loudly, "Your honour, may I say something please?"

Melvin shook his head and raised his hand in a stop gesture. "No, no, please. Your wife is under cross-examination. If you wish something to be brought to my attention, you speak to your own counsel about that." Young turned to his client and told him to sit down.

Faye Tearoe continued, describing the May 4 conversation during which Haney asked her to withdraw the affidavit. "He said it was just hearsay. He said I had no business writing it down, what he had told me, these personal things."

Morgan cast her mind back to the conversation she had had with Haney. "And he didn't say to you that 'I didn't tell you that she had a drug and alcohol abuse problem?'"

Faye was growing upset and fumbled for words. "I said I didn't know if I—I could withdraw. I said, well, I...what he told me was that he—she had a problem with drinking and drugs or—or—maybe just the fact that she hung around with friends that had drugs. I got the impression that she had— she drunk. I know he said that she drinks and that...that ..." Her voice trailed off.

"Didn't he say to you that she had epilepsy and that she is affected by alcohol?"

"Yes, that she only has to take a few drinks, that's what he said, and then she has epileptic fits which often—he was describing that. That's exactly right. But he said she has got a problem with drinking and, and ..."

"Did you have a conversation with him about the affidavit?"

"Yes, I certainly did. He asked me to withdraw it."

"Why?"

Faye once again admitted that she'd been wrong to use his comments in a written statement, even though she believed she was repeating them truthfully.

After a few more questions, Morgan completed her cross-examination, and Faye took her place beside Jim in the public gallery. She held tightly to her husband's hand.

Young thought the Tearoes had done relatively well on the stand. They had put across the main points he wanted—that they loved the boy dearly, that he was very bonded to their family, and that Teena Sawan had not submitted the written revocation as required by Alberta statute. Morgan had achieved her objective, too: to show that the Tearoes were well aware of Teena's revocation within the time limit and

that they believed their legal and moral right to custody of
baby David hinged on the lack of a piece of paper.

Lynne Smith and Erin Harris had spent the morning sitting
in the still court hallway. The women had taken some good-
natured teasing from colleagues about the difficulty of having to spend a couple of days in the southern B.C. summer,
instead of the northern Alberta mud. But testifying in a trial
was something few social workers enjoyed; they took oaths
of confidentiality that were strictly upheld. Erin Harris was
called into the courtroom and was accompanied by Victoria
lawyer Erin Faulkner, who had been retained by the Alberta
Department of Family and Social Services to ensure that
privileged and confidential information was not disclosed.

Young hoped to establish through the social workers that
Teena had been lackadaisical in her revocation efforts.

Harris took her seat in the witness box and began by reciting her background: she had been a child welfare worker for
one and a half years, followed by two years as an adoption
worker for northwestern Alberta, where she dealt with adoptions and new mother services. Harris had first talked with
Teena Sawan about adoption in November 1991, but she had
known Teena and her younger siblings previously in her
capacity as a child welfare worker.

Harris had several times spoken with Teena Sawan before
the birth of her child, discussing options. Their first conversation on the topic, November 28, 1991, had ended with
Teena saying she was going to keep the baby. On December
9, 1992, six days after the birth of Jordan, Harris received a
message to call Teena. On December 10, Harris received a call
"from the community" indicating that Teena was interested
in placing her baby privately for adoption. Harris called
Teena later on December 10, and they discussed private and
ward adoptions. During this, Harris said, she would have
discussed with Teena the documents that needed to be
signed, including consent by guardian to adoption, as well as
explaining the revocation requirement. She would also,
Harris said, have discussed the social and family history that

birth-mothers complete.

Young wanted to get into evidence any worries the social workers may have had about Teena Sawan's lifestyle.

"Did you have any concerns about her having the child in her care and not putting the child up for adoption?"

Harris answered his question very specifically. "At that time, I didn't have any direct involvement with Teena, besides through adoption, and so at that time I didn't have any direct concerns."

"Did you have any concerns prior to the February 6, 1992, date about her keeping the child?"

"I had heard things from other people in the office and in the community about her lifestyle that caused some concern, that she had been drinking and—" She was cut off by the judge. Harris's testimony was getting into what could be termed gossip, which wasn't admissible evidence.

Harris nodded and continued. "I know on January 13th, I had stopped by her home again to discuss adoption, because I wanted to meet with her face to face. And at that time, when I went to the home there was a lot of loud music. People were singing and there was a lot of swearing and yelling, and there were various voices. And at that time I didn't think it was very appropriate for me to go in and start talking about adoption, so I went back to the office. But through what I've heard through the community and through other—"

Melvin cut Harris off again as her evidence again veered into hearsay. Morgan made a note. On January 13, 1992, the child had not been living in the home; he was in care at Carolyn Grayson's.

For what purpose were Harris's comments, which were obviously hearsay, being offered? Melvin asked, staring down at Young, who stood with his hands on the lectern in front of him.

"What we wanted to do was be able to bring forward some evidence about the feeling of the case workers...in terms of how they dealt with this particular adoption. I mean, if they had concerns that she was not in the correct circle of friends, that would then affect how they dealt with Ms. Sawan and therefore would be evidence that would assist the court in making a determination," Young said, asking if Melvin would permit further questioning about Harris's understanding of Teena Sawan's lifestyle prior to the adoption.

"For the truth?" asked Melvin.

"Not for the truth."

"Then for what purpose?" Melvin asked again. "This is what bothers me."

"Well, then for the purpose of how it assisted this witness in how the adoption was—"

Melvin interjected. "Let's find out what this witness did specifically before we get into her perception of what may or may not be in the lifestyle."

Restricted from repeating gossip and conjecture, Harris continued by telling of her involvement with Teena's decision to give the child up for adoption. She recalled Teena calling her on December 13, three days after they had discussed Teena's options, and saying she was going to keep Jordan. Harris referred her to a social allowance worker, as she would be eligible for more financial benefits. "That was the end of my involvement in December."

Harris had no further involvement until February 12, 1992, when Teena Sawan made her first call to the Peace River Social Services office asking for her son back. "She told me that she was wanting to have Jordan back, that she loved him; he was a part of her and she wanted him returned to her care. She then told me that she had loved alcohol more than she had loved Jordan and that now she was wanting to call AADAC [Alberta Alcohol and Drug Abuse Commission] and make an appointment with an addictions counsellor. I told her she was within her rights to revoke the consent but that it needed to be in writing and within our office within a ten-day period."

Teena asked her where to send the letter, and Harris gave her the address.

Harris's next direct involvement with Teena Sawan was on

April 22, 1992, when Sawan again called, saying she wanted her son back. Young asked what Harris understood about the validity of the consent signed February 6, 1992.

"My supervisor had contacted family law in Edmonton on February 21, 1992, to ask their opinion as to how we should proceed. They indicated that even though we'd received a verbal revocation, because we had not received a revocation in writing, it was not a valid revocation and that the consent was still valid."

Young moved on to an area he thought was extremely helpful to the Tearoes' case, asking Harris about an allegation that Teena Sawan had been assaulted by Miles Schoendorfer on April 17, 1993.

Harris testified that she'd been on duty as the after-duty Social Services worker when she received a call from a Manning RCMP officer about an eighteen-year-old woman who had been choked by her common-law husband. "The officer indicated the common-law had been drinking and the RCMP had been called to the home and the common-law was placed in cells overnight, and that the woman needed a place to stay. I offered a hotel room in my capacity as after-duty worker, as well as transportation to the women's shelter. He spoke with her and she indicated that she knew someone in town who she would call. The next day I received a call from the community indicating that it had been Teena."

"And Teena had been assaulted by her common-law boyfriend?"

"Yes."

"Did she press charges to the best of your knowledge?"

"No."

Jean Morgan's cross-examination of Lynne Harris began by clarifying what the legal meaning was of the Consent by Guardian to Adoption document signed by Teena Sawan on February 6, 1992. Qualifying her response by saying that she was not giving a legal opinion, Harris said that the form puts the child in the custody of the potential adoptive parents, but the document does not give them guardianship. Often, prospective adoptive parents in Alberta obtain a private guardianship order on the child until the adoption order is finalized.

Much of Morgan's cross-examination centred on whether Alberta Social Services had followed provincial policies regarding the adoption of children who are of native descent. (Alberta is one of the few provinces to have included in their adoption legislation rules that must be followed regarding placement of native children for adoption.) Teena, as a native birth-mother living off reserve, should have been asked if she would consent to a consultation process with her band regarding the potential adoption of the child. If she consents, the social worker would then write a letter to the chief and council of the band to which the birth-mother belongs, indicating her intentions, and follow that up with a telephone call or a face-to-face visit with the band.

Harris testified that she had mentioned this process to Teena in December, when the adoptions worker was giving the young mother information on her options. However, she admitted, Teena was not specifically asked if she consented to the band being consulted at that time. Harris testified that she did not know, in December 1991, if Teena was a member of any band or not. However, Harris said she later became aware that Teena was affiliated with the Woodland Cree band. She testified she could not remember when she became aware of it, but it was after Jordan's birth.

A few days after their December 10, 1991, conversation, Teena told Harris she was going to keep her child, and there was no further talk of the band consultation process. It was not brought up again to Teena Sawan.

"So on [December] 10th when it was brought up, this issue with respect to the consultation process, this was an information process only?" Morgan asked.

"Yes."

"So, when the actual movement towards adoption was going to take place, nothing was done at that stage? Let me put it this way. You did not go to her and ask her about the consultation process?"

"No."

"So, when you said there was no consent [by Teena to consulting the band], it was really that in fact nothing was posed to her at that time?"

"I did not pose anything to her at that time."

Social workers involved in adoptions often have at least a year to carry out this consultation process, as petitions for adoptions are not usually filed for a year after the placement of the child with potential adoptive parents. Harris said she was intending to talk with Teena about the consultation process after the Tearoes had taken the child, as is standard, but Teena then changed her mind and refused to sign anything further. Morgan felt she had made her point: a necessary component for an Albert adoption had not been carried out. She moved on to Teena's February 12, 1992, call to Erin Harris.

"You received this telephone call. Did you make arrangements to go to [Fairview] to make sure that the revocation was signed?"

"There is no—there is no standard form for revocation. It takes the form of a letter from the birth-mother that is signed and dated. I did not make arrangements to go to Fairview. Teena said she would be mailing it that day. Mail between Fairview and Peace River takes one to two days."

"But there was no effort to help her revoke by your department?"

"I did not go to Fairview to meet with her, no."

Morgan phrased her question a different way. "Could you have gone to Fairview to help her revoke her consent?"

"If she'd asked me to, yes, I could have."

"So, she would have had to ask? You would never have offered?"

"It didn't come up in our conversation."

"You didn't offer it?"

"I didn't offer it."

"And she didn't request it?"

"And she didn't request it."

"And if she doesn't request it, it's not something that the

department would offer as a matter of course?"

"It's not standard practice."

Melvin spoke up. "Are you suggesting that—well, obviously I know what you're suggesting. Go ahead. Carry on with your cross-examination."

Morgan continued. "So, while your department takes care to see that certain portions of your statutory provisions are met—that is consents—the same statutory provision which required a revocation in writing, there is no care to make sure that anything in that nature is taken care of within the ten days, even if you have a client that phones and says, 'I no longer want my child adopted. I want my child back,' as did Teena?"

Harris started to answer and Young cut in. "I don't know where the question is. It seems more like argument than it does—"

"I think she understands the question," said Melvin, leaning back in his chair, his glasses in his hand, looking at Harris.

The adoption worker replied, "It's the mother's responsibility."

Exhausted, Jim and Faye drove home in the rush-hour traffic, creeping along amid the traffic jam on the Colwood strip. Both were quiet. But as they pulled into the driveway, the sight of David looking out the living-room window, his hand against the glass, a smile on his face, couldn't help but cheer them. At eighteen months, he was extremely mobile and verbal and had taken to letting out a high-pitched squeal when excited. Jim and Faye were greeted by that as they climbed out of the car and headed towards the door, where David greeted them by hugging their legs.

Faye sought solace in routine, putting a quick dinner on the table as Jim played with the toddler. Their dinner prayer was longer than usual that night.

An hour later, the doorbell rang and Teena Sawan stood at the door, with Dolly and Donna behind her. Arrangements had been made at the end of the court day, through the lawyers, for Teena to come and visit the boy.

"Come in," Jim said, taking their coats and hanging them up before leading them down the hallway. In his usual fashion, Jim talked steadily, giving his guests a chance to admire the living room. The three women politely commented on its decor, and Jim led them to the kitchen. The little boy Teena had last seen sitting on her knee with her hand supporting his back was sitting on the floor, pushing a plastic truck and making *vrooming* sounds. "Wow," she exclaimed, a smile breaking across her face. "He's so big!" The boy looked up and stared before going back to his truck. Faye stood nearby, hands clasped in front of her. It soon seemed a bit crowded in the kitchen, with all the adults clustered around a little boy oblivious to their stares, and Jim asked if they'd like to sit in the family room or outside on the patio.

It was early evening, and the sun's rays still warmed the sky as Jim unstacked the white plastic chairs and arranged them on the grass. Faye slipped a sweater and shoes onto the little boy. He wasn't shy but seemed more interested in his toys—and in chasing the dog around on the grass, making growling noises—than in the people watching him. Teena squatted down beside him and asked him about his truck.

Jim was telling them all the things the tot liked to do, such as playing harmonica and pounding out songs of his own devising on the piano. Dolly wished he would be quiet for just a minute, but resigned herself to the fact that talking seemed to calm him.

"He's beautiful," she said quietly to Teena.

"Yeah, he is, isn't he," said Teena, looking up proudly.

Faye asked Teena if she'd like to see David's room, and the rest of the house. Teena would rather have stayed where she was, but it was awkward to decline the invitation. As they walked through the house, Faye told her about each room, and about the schedule they kept the baby to, that he had two naps a day, and what time his meals were and how she prepared his food, that he was in the midst of potty-training and was doing well. Upstairs, the older woman pointed out all the changes they had made in their house for the child.

"This is our recreation room and David really loves it in here, pushing his little toys all around, you know, he just loves it." Faye showed Teena the storage area behind the louvred doors lining the far wall of the spacious room, pointing out that it gave her space for their extra bedding.

"Why is she showing me all this?" Teena wondered, nodding politely and murmuring how nice it all was. And it was nice, much nicer than the apartment Teena was living in at the time. Teena wanted to have a comfortable house too, but she didn't care that much about how much closet space she had. There was a slight air of desperation to Faye's chipper tones, Teena thought.

"This was all for David," Faye said again as they left the family room. The older woman was thrilled with Teena's comment that the home was nice. It seemed to her that Teena was relinquishing her rights then and there, an acknowledgement that her son's new home was a good one.

The group sat outside again, the rhythmic sound of a neighbour's lawn sprinkler filling in the inevitable gaps in conversation. They all did the best they could in an awkward situation.

Soon it was bedtime for the much-desired little boy and he waved goodnight to his guests as Faye packed him upstairs. Through the open window in David's room, she could hear Teena's voice, wafting up through the evening air. Faye tucked her beloved son into his crib and kissed his forehead. Teena, Dolly and Donna left a few minutes later, saying goodbye to the couple they would see again in court the next morning. It would be the last cordial visit the group would have.

Teena and Jordan, moments before she said goodbye to her son.

Teena's Fairview
home where the
Tearoes picked
up the baby on
February 6, 1992.

Kim Westad

Ray Smith, *Times-Colonist*

David reaches for his much loved harmonica while Jim and
Faye Tearoe look on.

Little David and the media in the Tearoe backyard.

Foster mother Carolyn Grayson outside her Fairview home. Grayson still thinks about the gregarious little boy whom she came to know and love as Jordan.

Kim Westad

Woodland Cree Band Chief Billy Thomas, standing along the shore of Cadotte Lake.

Kim Westad

Jean Morgan, the lawyer who represented Teena during the trial and at the B.C. Court of Appeal.

Kim Westad

Victoria lawyer Trudi Brown, Q.C. Brown took over Teena's case after the B.C. Court of Appeal decision.

Kim Westad

Ralph Cowie, stepfather to Miles Schoendorfer, outside the Manning Motor Inn. Ralph knows of Teena's past difficulties, and knew her mother, Maryann, years ago.

Kim Westad

Kim Westad

Teena and Miles in their Manning home.

Kim Westad

Teena and Miles' home in Manning.

Jim and Faye Tearoe's home in Colwood, a suburb west of Victoria.

Baby David at the Tearoe home.

John McKay, *Times-Colonist*

Teena Sawan faces the media for the first time after the B.C.
Court of Appeal decision.

B.C. Supreme Court Justice Allen Melvin. He called the Tearoe–Sawan case the most difficult of his judicial career.

Tearoe lawyer Brian Young answers questions at a press conference after the B.C. Court of Appeal decision. The Tearoes are beside him.

Teena spends time with her son after the B.C. Supreme Court decision awarding her custody.

Chapter 15

Brian Young was nothing if not media-savvy. From the time he was an articling student, Young recognized the power of the press, especially television, in forming popular opinion. He knew the Tearoe and Sawan case would be alluring to the media: it had emotion, a cute little boy, and a timely issue, adoption. Throw in the native element, Young thought, and it was a guaranteed top story.

Although Young himself was not religious, he had no negative feelings about the Tearoes' potent beliefs. Wherever they got their strength was fine with him. But he had strong advice for the couple when it came to talking to the press. He didn't want their beliefs to override what he thought could be a strong case in the court of public opinion, and there was no doubt that if the Tearoes were given free rein to talk of their faith, it would turn people off as quickly as the proverbial bucket of cold water. Whether that was fair wasn't the issue, Young thought. The general public was put off by fundamentalist religious beliefs. That was reality.

"We had lengthy discussions about whether or not God should be introduced as their lawyer," Young recalled, only half joking.

Young and Jean Morgan had estimated that the case would take two days, so two court days had been scheduled. But it became clear that it would require at least one more day. It was the usual court timing squeeze. Melvin had a continuation of preliminary matters in a grisly double-murder set for midweek, and it couldn't be postponed. The B.C. Supreme Court didn't sit in July and August, and Melvin was not going to have the custody case adjourned until the fall. So, in the way of a gesture to scheduling, day two of the trial began an hour earlier than usual.

The Tearoes' case continued with Young calling his associate John Jordan to the stand. The witness box is an unusual place for any lawyer to be, and not one they usually take to. Jordan was called to give some background concerning his involvement in the case.

The lawyer testified that on May 29, 1992, he had sent documents to Teena Sawan to sign. Jordan was aware that Teena Sawan had signed a consent in Alberta. Although he had "no question that it was valid," he still asked Teena to sign the documents required under the B.C. Adoption Act.

"Why did you send another consent form for her to sign?" Young asked.

"Well, I assumed that notwithstanding that, that I would want to get, and would have to get, a consent in the form required by the B.C. Act."

"Are you aware now that the form she signed does conform with the B.C. Act requirements?" Young asked.

"Yes."

"Yes, you are aware of that?"

"Well, I'm not sure. I would still do it the same way, even now," Jordan replied.

"Whether or not you believed the consent was valid?"

"Yes."

Jean Morgan rose to cross-examine Jordan and established that the lawyer knew from February of 1992 onwards that Teena wanted to revoke her consent. She moved on to a point that puzzled her.

"Your petition to apply for the adoption that you filed in

December of 1992 has asked to dispense with the natural mother's consent. If the consent is valid, why did you request to dispense with the consent in December?"

"I assumed that because Ms. Sawan was, I understood, attempting to revoke that consent, that it would be the best way to go about filing, and obtaining the adoption—to ask that the consent be dispensed with," Jordan replied.

Morgan noted that there had been no move for adoption by the Tearoes until Teena Sawan raised the issue of revocation of consent through a lawyer.

Young quickly got to his feet to re-examine his associate.

"In February of 1992, you spoke with the Ministry of Family and Social Services in Alberta, is that right?"

"Yes, on a number of occasions that I recall. I can't recall the exact dates."

"Did the Ministry of Family and Social Services tell you that the consent signed by Ms. Sawan was invalid?"

"No."

"Did they tell you to have any concern about its validity?"

"Not in that—not in that meeting, no."

"So, prior to December 10, 1992, from the date of the adoption which is February 6, 1992—"

Melvin corrected Young. "Placement."

"Placement," Young agreed. "The placement took place on February 6, 1992. From that date until you did receive a letter on December 10, 1992, did you hear anything from Teena Sawan or someone purporting to be her solicitor?"

Young knew the answer to that, but wanted to stress the time it took before Teena Sawan took legal steps to revoke her consent.

Jordan left the stand after just half an hour with the thought that it was far easier to be on the giving end of questions.

Young had only two more witnesses to call.

Lynne Smith took a seat in the witness box. Young adjusted the microphone in front of her and gave her a full glass of water from the pitcher put out fresh each morning by the court clerk.

A social worker with the Alberta Family and Social Services department since September 1990, Smith testified that her first involvement with Teena Sawan was on January 6, 1992.

"I visited Teena's home. I found that Jordan was well cared for. He was clean, he had lots of clothes, there was plenty of food and diapers in the house for him. I also found that Teena definitely wanted to have a placement. She said that she wanted to have time to make private arrangements for an adoption. She told me she wanted Jordan to have two parents, that she wanted him to have things that she could not give. She also said that she didn't know what Jordan wanted whenever he cried and that she felt really tired in the night."

Smith went over the event of Teena signing the one-month custody agreement that allowed the boy to be placed in foster care.

Smith testified that she had tried to reach Teena on January 16, but was unsuccessful. When Teena called her back, the social worker was out. They talked on January 17, 1992. "She told me that she had decided to keep Jordan, that she missed him, that she thought about him a lot. She also acknowledged that she was quite muddled about what she wanted. I asked her why she hadn't called me as soon as she knew she wanted Jordan back, and Teena had no answer for me. She was also asked that day what she wanted, and she said she wanted him returned to her care as soon as possible.

"We arranged for her to visit at the foster home that weekend and, because of her ambivalence about taking him back, we also discussed a little bit more about adoption and that we needed a definite decision and one she was committed to carry through, because Jordan needed to have permanent care-giving so that bonding could develop. I also felt that Teena was somewhat overwhelmed with the number of options she had and that it was hard for her to make a decision, and it was agreed that she would visit the foster home and I would contact her the next week to talk some more.

"I had further contact by telephone on the 22nd of January.

Teena was still undecided. She had been to visit Jordan and she had arrangements made to obtain a crib for Jordan. I still wondered why she wasn't ready to bring Jordan home. She said that she had been waiting for a cheque in order that she could buy him food and diapers. And at that time, I suggested that Teena had been aware that I could help her sort out these practical problems and our main objective at that point was to find a permanent placement for Jordan. Teena again was to visit Jordan. She was encouraged to visit him at the foster home direct."

"Did she visit him?" Young asked.

"I understand she did not."

"She did not?" Young said for emphasis.

"She did not. On the 29th of January, I had a further home visit with Teena. She was clear that she wanted Jordan returned. She had a commitment to him until he was eighteen. She had a crib, she was now ready for him to be returned. She'd also made arrangements through the local day-care program for Jordan to receive home-care while she went to school. She was planning to go to school the next week.

"We talked about the care of Jordan and the long hours that he would be in day-care, and I reminded Teena that she needed to be sure that she was the one who handled Jordan after school, that it wasn't her roommates, but that Teena was to be his primary care-giver."

"Did you have any other concerns about that particular point prior to that date of January 29?" Young asked.

"Prior to that date I had understood that Teena allowed other people to care for the baby. I asked her on the 29th about previous care-givers that had looked after Jordan since he was born, and she informed me that he had been in hospital for one week, that he went home with Teena and another friend and spent one other day in the care of another family. Other than that, Teena said she had cared for him herself. I asked her about her visits to Jordan at the foster home. She said that she had been twice and the second time was just a couple of days before this current visit."

During that conversation, Smith confronted Teena about the concerns she had about Teena's lifestyle. "Teena said that she was trying to put limits on her friends and she would have to learn to tell them no, you can't do this in my home."

"Did she appear committed to the child at that time?" Young asked.

"She did."

After that, Smith went on, the social worker talked to her supervisor and it was agreed that Jordan would be returned to Teena, and an arrangement in which Social Services would provide some parenting support would be agreed upon.

"I spoke to her that night and said she could collect Jordan the next day, which was the 31st of January, and she was to contact the foster mom in order to arrange another visit. I stressed the importance of her visiting that day. I thought it was important that she learn about Jordan's routine so she would be better prepared when she took him home with her. I understand since then that she did not make that visit."

Morgan objected, noting the word "understand" implied Smith did not have direct knowledge of what she had testified to. Melvin said the question should be put to whoever had direct knowledge, such as Sawan.

Young continued. "Did she pick up the child the next day?"

"She did."

It was unclear from the testimony when precisely Teena was supposed to have visited with the child before taking him home. Smith's evidence was that she talked to Teena on the night of January 30, telling her she could pick up the child the next day. Smith also said Teena was to contact the foster care mother to arrange a visit before taking him home. Apparently, both these things were to be done on the same day.

Smith's next involvement with Teena Sawan was on February 5, 1992. "I informed [Teena] that I had received calls from concerned people, and there had been some concerns about young people partying in her home, some concerns of excessive alcohol, also some concerns that Teena had been providing liquor to a minor, and at that time there was the possibility of some charges.... Teena did not address the matters that I informed her of. She rather told me that Jordan would not be staying with her and that Jordan was going for adoption."

Smith asked Teena if she would take Jordan to Carolyn Grayson's, and Teena agreed. Young asked if that was considered an apprehension.

"No it was not, it was voluntary."

"What was the purpose of that?"

"I had received phone calls that gave me some concern and I felt Jordan—it would be in his best interests that night that he was cared for in a foster home."

"You had not enough information to apprehend?"

"I didn't contact the court about apprehension," Smith replied. "I didn't need to do so. Had Teena refused to take him to the foster home, then that would be one course of action that would be open to us."

Young was trying to get some corroboration for the comment the Tearoes had told him about but which they had not testified to—namely, their contention that Smith had told them as they left Grayson's that the baby would have been apprehended had they not taken him on February 6. Young did not receive any confirmation from Smith.

"I spoke with our adoption worker and asked if she would give me some information about the sort of forms that Teena needed to sign and she said sure," Smith continued. "I called Teena back and gave her that information. I told her that the forms would have to be signed at some point, that she had thirty days in which those forms could be given to an adoption worker. I also told her if she signed that form, she had ten days in which she could change her mind, that she needed to inform us in writing of such a change. I also advised her that she should be sure to get the full legal names and address of the adoptive couple."

Smith testified that on February 6, she received a phone call. "As a result of that, I made a home visit to Teena's home." She did not say in court who the call was from or what was said, but it was the call made by Carolyn Grayson, as Jim and Teena stood in her kitchen waiting to take the baby. Smith said that she explained to Teena that the forms she had with her did not have to be signed that day, but that "she chose to sign two of them that day."

Young's next series of questions were aimed at showing that Teena Sawan had not been under pressure. Smith said Teena showed no hesitancy regarding the placement and freely and voluntarily signed the documents.

Smith then outlined Teena's second call to the Peace River Social Services revoking her consent on February 13, 1992. "I told her at that time that I was aware that she had changed her mind about Jordan's adoption and I reminded her of the need to have the notice in writing. Teena told me that she had written a letter and mailed it the previous day. Teena wasn't available to meet with me that day. She had to do some laundry and go to the bank. She wasn't available to meet with me the next day. She said she was going to Grande Prairie to visit."

Smith was not asked and did not volunteer why it was she wanted to meet with Teena Sawan. It was apparent from her evidence that Teena told her the letter had already been mailed.

"So she said to you that she was going to Grande Prairie on the 14th of February? And your office is in Grande Prairie?" Young repeated, trying to show that Teena could have made the effort to go to a Social Services office to revoke her consent in person, but his geography was confused.

"My office is in Peace River. It's in the opposite direction of Grande Prairie. I also discussed with Teena on the telephone that day the possibility of us having a further custody agreement [when Jordan was returned]. Teena thought she would agree. She agreed that there was some need at that time to address an alcohol problem and that she felt that perhaps Jordan should be in a foster home while she did that and she could visit him.

"Did you receive a letter from Teena revoking her consent?"

"I did not."

"Have you received any type of written withdrawal from Teena?"

"No."

Smith spoke with Teena again on Valentine's Day. "The 14th of February was a Friday and I asked her: When would you like to have Jordan returned? And at that time Teena said, perhaps after the weekend, Monday, because she was busy on the weekend."

"Because she was busy?" Young asked.

"She was busy on the weekend," Smith repeated.

"Did that comment surprise you?"

"It did."

"Why is that?"

"Well, I thought that if she wanted Jordan returned, she would actually be anxious for his immediate return and would make her plans accordingly."

Jim and Faye Tearoe nodded their heads as Smith testified of this. It was a comment they later interpreted as a sign from God that the child was meant to be in their home and an indication of what they viewed as Teena's lack of sincerity. At the same time, Teena jotted down a note on her piece of paper. She couldn't remember saying this. Regardless of when Teena wanted the baby returned, the ministry made the decision that he would not be moved until Teena's letter was received.

On February 19, 1992, Smith and Teena had their final conversation. Young inquired if, on that date, Teena had asked about the letter of revocation.

"She did. Teena asked if we had received the letter yet and I replied, No, we had not."

"What was her response to that?"

"She informed me that it had been mailed the previous Wednesday. I suggested she contact Canada Post in Fairview."

"Did she express any other concerns to you that the letter hadn't been received?"

"She was puzzled why it had not arrived."

"Did she tell you that she had the original of the letter in her possession?"

"She did not."

"Did she ask if there was any other way she could get the letter to you?" asked Young, who personally doubted a letter had ever been sent.

"She did not."

"Did she ask you if she could get you another copy at some point?"

"She did not."

"At that time, was there anything else you feel you could have done to assist the situation?" Young asked.

"No."

Melvin leaned forward. "There was nothing further you could do?" he repeated.

"Nothing further I could do," Smith repeated.

Young wanted Smith to state her view as to where the best interests of the child lay, but Morgan quickly objected. Smith had had no contact with Teena for more than a year, since the child was given up, and had only talked with the Tearoes on the telephone. "To compare [Teena] a year ago to today and now comment on what's in the best interests of the child is inappropriate, in my view," Morgan said. "On the telephone, you could say a person has a nice voice."

Melvin agreed with the objection, and Young went at it another way. "Have you had recent experience in the community in which Teena Sawan lives now?"

"I have not."

Smith said she had been back to Manning but had had no involvement with Teena.

"You have heard about things that have happened that have caused you to formulate an opinion in your mind, though," said Young. It was more a statement than a question.

Melvin interjected again. "You're getting into hearsay. If this witness had gone to the mother's home recently and conducted a type of investigation that's normally conducted on people, that's one thing, but to have learned by—I don't want to use the expression gossip, but you know what I mean—in a non-formal, non-structured sense, that something may or may not have occurred from someone other than Ms. Sawan is of no assistance."

Young argued that Smith should be able to testify as to what her own personal beliefs are.

"Based on what?" Melvin asked again.

"Based on her experience, her knowledge of this case and the knowledge of the community which Teena Sawan lives in, and I think that would be of assistance to the court, because what other evidence do we have of what is in the best interests—this is going to come down to the best interests of the child kind of argument—so how is this court going to ascertain what's in the best interests—?"

Melvin interrupted. "How is this person going to express an opinion as to what's in the best interests of the child without having had an opportunity to see how the child has adapted to life in the residence where the child is now?" The judge turned to Smith. "Would you normally expect to have that knowledge before you express an opinion as to what might be best for the child?"

Smith said she would not be comfortable in answering the question about the child's best interests.

"Okay, I won't ask that question," Young said. "Overall, how would you say Teena Sawan has been dealt with by your ministry?"

"I believe—" Smith started again. "In my personal contact, I believe I dealt with her with respect, that I was honest in my contact with her, and at times I said things that were rather confrontational regarding her lifestyle, but I believe that Teena concurred with me and she knew if Jordan was returned there were still child welfare concerns. I believe that I dealt with her with respect."

"Do you believe that the ministry had done everything that they were required to do?"

"I believe so."

Young went back to the ground he had tried before. "Do you have any idea what the short-term effects would be upon the child if taken away from the Tearoes?"

Morgan was quickly on her feet. "My Lord, I believe that is asking for an expert opinion."

Melvin responded. "I'll take judicial notice of the fact that if the child is moved from one place after a year or two to another place, it's bound to be disruptive."

Young looked at Smith, and asked a final question. "Would you agree with that statement?"

"I would," she answered.

Morgan began her cross-examination of Lynne Smith by emphasizing that Jordan had never been apprehended by Social Services, and that when Smith went to Teena's home, she found the baby well cared for. The lawyer moved on to questions about Smith's involvement with Teena when the teenager was deciding what to do about her child.

"Would you agree with me that she was quite a confused young woman over this whole issue?"

"I think making a decision was very difficult for her."

Morgan scanned her notes. "... You've used a number of expressions. On January 6th, you used the words that she was muddled. Then on the 22nd, she was overwhelmed with decisions and undecided what to do. Then on the 29th, you said she wanted the return of the child. So what I'm suggesting to you is that this is a person, a young person, eighteen years of age, a young person who appears to be confused about what she should be doing?"

"I believe that she told me on [January 29] that she did want him returned to her and that she was committed to that."

"So you believed she was committed to have Jordan returned to her?"

"I did."

Melvin directed a comment at Smith. "She seemed to be changing her mind from time to time. One day I got the impression adoption seems all right, and then she's not sure about it. Obviously, you're not sure what's happening either?"

"That's correct, no. At times, too, she seemed to say she wanted him returned but didn't follow through on it, and other times she did say she wanted him adopted, so there was a confusion there."

Morgan asked Smith about the February 5, 1992, phone call, in which Teena said she had settled on adoption. "At this point you have a woman that's made so many different decisions over a month. What is it that you did at that point to try and talk with her to assure yourself that in fact this was a decision that she was capable of making at that time? What efforts did you make? What do your notes disclose?"

"At that time, Teena did not wish to enter into a long discussion with me. That telephone call on the 5th of February was very much just the facts. 'He is going for adoption, I have made a decision.' I called her later in the day to ensure she would know to get the full legal names and address of the people with whom she was placing Jordan. I asked a little bit myself about how she had chosen the people, and I was informed that friends had given her the names of the Tearoes. Teena had always told us that she wanted to arrange a private placement for the child. She wanted the department to be involved as little as possible."

"If that's the case, can I ask you why at that point in time, you didn't ask her if she would consent to a consultation with the band about the adoption?" Morgan asked.

"She's now decided to adopt. I did not think to do that—at no point in my discussion with my supervisor was that suggested. My understanding at that time was that Teena was not registered, that she was also living off reserve, and there was no compulsory—there's no mandatory need for the band to be involved in a direct adoption placement for someone living off reserve."

Leafing through her copy of the Child Welfare Act, Morgan asked, "How does your ministry or department deal with the section 62 requirement of the Child Welfare Act of Alberta?"

Smith asked to see a copy and read over the section on dealing with adoptions of native children.

"I find myself unable to answer that question," Smith answered when she finished reading. "I don't know; I'm not an adoption worker."

"So...this is not something that you thought you needed to address at that time? It's not something that was in front of your mind, is that correct?" Morgan asked.

Smith then gave a somewhat confusing response, in light of her earlier testimony. "I know that I talked with Teena and I did tell her that the band should be informed about the adoption and I believed it was her responsibility to do that."

Morgan asked why in Smith's notes of the February 6, 1992, meeting with Teena, she wrote: "Tearoes aware Band needs to be informed of adoption."

"The reason I made that note was really because of a previous adoption that I was aware of in Alberta where there had been some problems, so I thought that the Tearoes needed to be aware that there was this other component to this adoption."

"What is that component, as you understand it?"

"My understanding was that Teena would—if the child was eligible for registration, Teena would have informed the band, or I also believe the department could have informed the band. That was my understanding."

Morgan asked if the social worker thought, in light of the fact that Teena had repeatedly changed her mind about what to do with her child, that the teenager had the capacity to make the decision to give up her child.

"I believed that she was seriously consenting to the adoption during that day.... I believed she wanted to have him adopted that day."

"Were you concerned about her history of waffling at all, about her real capacity to enter into an agreement?"

"I had many concerns that day. I was concerned as to how Teena had selected the adoptive parents she had chosen for her child. I had concerns she may have been coerced or encouraged, and I had concerns about how she may feel after Jordan left to be adopted. But I did believe that she felt that she was acting in Jordan's best interests when she agreed to consent to the adoption."

Morgan shifted her questioning to the phone call Smith received from Teena on February 13, 1992, one week after the consent was signed. "Did you explain to her the urgency, that the letter had to be received within the ten days?"

"I believe that that urgency was explained several times throughout the process. I believe it was explained on the 6th, the day she signed the consent, that I would have told her that if she changed her mind, she needed to let us know in writing. It wasn't enough just to call, and that it was within the ten-day period. I think I outlined to her the tenth day was the 16th, which would have been the Sunday."

"And [the phone call] was the 13th. Was there any way of meeting with her prior to the expiration of the ten days? I understand from your testimony you were calling weekly to her home?" Morgan was taking a point made earlier by Young and putting a different light on it. He had suggested that Teena could have made personal contact with a social worker and given revocation, as they were in the area at least once a week and usually more. Morgan's question pointed out that the social workers, who knew Teena wanted her child back, could also have initiated that personal contact.

"I am an investigator. I did all the work in the Fairview area. I cannot remember what my schedule was throughout that week. I know that Teena had been offered—it was felt she might want to get in contact with a counsellor and talk to people who had given children up for adoption. That was offered to her, but I didn't have any reason to see Teena again that week."

"So there was no effort made to provide Teena with any assistance to make sure that that revocation was properly done and properly brought to your office?"

"I'm sorry, I don't understand the question. I was informed on the 13th that a letter was mailed."

"Then on the 19th, I understand she phoned and asked if the letter had been received and you said not yet. It was mailed the previous Wednesday, which would have been the 12th of February. She appeared puzzled why it had not arrived. At that point in time, did you explain: Teena, you've got to come down to Peace River and you've got to get it here. This is what we have to have in our hands before it's too late?"

"My suggestion was that she contact Canada Post to see if by some way the letter was missing or had gone astray, and I also informed her that she needed to consult with a lawyer."

"It was over at that point; on the 19th, when she called, there was no hope. She had to contact a lawyer, and that position was made clear to her then?"

"I know at the time, I was also consulting with my case-work supervisor and I took some advice from that. I don't remember the exact date, but I know again that the lawyer wasn't just introduced on the 19th. The advice on how she had to revoke her consent would have been: If this is not done within the ten-day period, then it becomes a legal matter, but up to the ten days, the child is returned. It's the obligation of the couple to return the child if the consent is revoked. Outside of that, it becomes a battle."

Brian Young had just one more witness to call. He felt the case had gone well, and he told the Tearoes that as they gathered around him in the hall. "Chill out—it's going fine," he said with a smile on his way to grab a muffin and coffee before court resumed. Jim sat on the bench in the hall, and began talking with a reporter. Faye came up a few minutes later, and as Jim spoke, she took a comb out of her purse and carefully smoothed her husband's thin hair.

The Tearoes' final witness was Julie Irma Salmond, a well-spoken woman who gave effusive testimony about the Tearoes' abilities as parents. An administration officer for the Department of National Defence, Salmond has a daughter, Samantha, then ten and one-half months of age. Salmond had searched for a suitable care-giver for six months before finding Faye. "I would consider them to be, to me, model parents in that when I was looking for somebody to look after Samantha, I had an impression in my mind of what I wanted that person and the family to be like, and they have exceeded my expectations immensely."

Salmond spoke at length about the bond she had witnessed between the couple and David, as well as between David and Heidi. "To me, bonding would be where there is a shared love that is openly received and accepted and where the child lights up when it sees its mom and its father, and to me, that's very, very evident with David."

Young questioned her about the Tearoes' home, asking if it was "well kept" and if she'd had the opportunity to see David's room. She indicated that she had seen the whole house, adding that the appearance of their home was important to her "because it is indicative of the kind of family they are." She said it was "clean, orderly and had lots of toys in it."

Morgan chose not to cross-examine Julie Salmond. The lawyer never intended to suggest that the Tearoes were bad parents.

Jean Morgan opened her case without the customary statement. "I think the issues are pretty clear," she told Melvin. With that, she called her first witness, Donna Ominayak.

In her low, Cree-accented voice, Ominayak explained that she is the education co-ordinator for the Woodland Cree band and gave her educational background.

Ominayak testified that Teena had been the recipient of band funding for occasional correspondence courses since August 1991, four months before Jordan was born. In September 1992, Teena had applied for full-time funding. "At that time, we sponsored her again because she had done well with the previous correspondence courses she had taken. From then on, periodically, I would talk to Teena on the phone, just follow-up studies of how she was doing in school, and also I would talk to the institution to see how she was doing as well."

Part of her job, Ominayak explained, was monitoring attendance and performance of students. Progress reports from the schools off reserve are sent to Ominayak at her Cadotte Lake office and used in evaluating funding applications.

Asked by Morgan what type of marks Teena received, Ominayak looked at her notes, and read out, "In her basic Math 1, she received an A-plus; in her basic Math 2, she received an A-plus; for her basic Math 3, she received an A; basic Math 4, she received an A; for basic English 2, she received an A-plus; basic English 3, she received an A-plus."

"Is it possible," Morgan asked, "given Teena's recent ability and providing her marks don't drop, she would be a candidate for post-secondary education?" Ominayak agreed.

Ominayak then explained how a phone call from Teena on October 14, 1992, had made her aware of the teenager's legal dilemma, and she outlined the circuitous process she'd gone through to finally get Teena a lawyer through legal aid. With that her evidence in chief was completed.

Young wanted to make one point clear in cross-examination of the poised woman—that Teena Sawan had contact with her off and on for months before mentioning that her son had been placed for adoption.

"You had stated that you had contact with Teena Sawan in 1991?"

"That's correct."

"In August of 1991?"

"Yes."

"And you maintained continual contact with her?"

"Yes. More so in the next year."

"You would agree with me that your contact with her has been since August of 1991?"

"Yes."

"Yet it wasn't until October 14, 1992, that she told you she needed a lawyer and that she had a child; is that right? That's correct, isn't it, because that was your evidence on direct?"

"I'm not sure which question to answer," Ominayak said.

"It wasn't until October 14th, 1992, that Teena Sawan told you she'd had a child, correct?"

"No," Ominayak answered. She knew what Young was getting at, but she chose to answer his question specifically. She wasn't going to help him out if he wasn't going to ask questions correctly.

"I'm sorry, that she had the child and that the child wasn't in her care."

"Yes, in October 1992 [she said] that the child wasn't in her care."

"And it was in October of 1992—that was the first time the issue of a lawyer was raised by Teena Sawan, correct?"

"Yes."

With that, Ominayak's questioning was over.

Morgan next called Dolly LeTendre, who testified that Teena was a band member, and that, as of June of 1993, Jordan Sawan was on a waiting list to become a band member. The waiting list, which includes newborns, was to have been voted on by the band membership in September 1992, but the chief and council had been in Ottawa for a meeting, so the vote was postponed.

When she finished testifying, Dolly joined Donna in the courtroom, and Morgan called Teena Sawan to the stand. Teena rose and walked the few yards to the witness box from the chair beside her lawyer. Within a few minutes, Young realized his case was in trouble.

Chapter 16

Some judges spend as much time taking notes of evidence in court as they do watching the witnesses. Not so Justice Allen Melvin. His watchful gaze never wavers, carefully measuring witnesses and searching for the character of the person behind their spoken words. Now he turned from the Tearoes to Teena Sawan.

Teena had watched Melvin closely throughout the trial and she liked his down-to-earth manner and the fact that he seemed to be listening intently. As she was sworn in, by her full name, Cecilia Augustine Sawan, she felt more comfortable than she thought she would. "Can I call you Teena?" Morgan asked with a slight smile, helping put her client at ease.

"Yes," Teena said, leaning forward in the witness box so she was closer to the microphone.

After questioning Teena about her age, Morgan asked her about her son's father. Teena said he was Arlen Walker, who she believed was now living in Winnipeg, Manitoba.

"Did he know about the baby?"

"Yes, I believe he did."

"Did you name him on the birth certificate?"

"No, I didn't."

"When you've been asked about the father, you haven't provided much information. Is there some reason for that?"

"Yes, there is. I didn't really know him when we got together, so I've been kind of keeping that to myself; I didn't want anybody to know. The father and I were not engaged or married," replied Teena, her embarrassment evident. "It was sort of—it just happened."

Morgan wanted the court to understand Teena's background so that the teenager's rationale for wanting a private adoption instead of involving Social Services would be clear. She asked Teena where she was born.

"I was born in Cadotte Lake, Alberta."

"And you lived with your mom?"

Teena took a deep breath. She sometimes appeared flat emotionally, but when she talked about her mother or the abuse she suffered in foster care, emotions that she worked hard on keeping deep inside came to the surface. The lawyer knew it was going to be difficult for Teena to talk of those things, but it had to be done.

"I did for about four years. I believe it was four years, and then—my mom was an alcoholic and Social Services took us kids away from our mom when I was about four years old and they put us in foster homes. And me and my family were not put together; they were scattered here and there in different foster homes. They told us that we could have weekly visits, but those were narrowed down to about one a month, once every month. And then soon, they were altogether stopped and there was no explanation why they were stopped."

"So how old were you when you stopped seeing your mom?"

"I was about six years old."

Teena said she was in about ten foster homes from the age of four to eighteen.

"And were you put up for adoption?"

"Yes, I was. In about 1985 when I was twelve years old, these people had wanted to adopt me and my brother and sister, and Social Services had said okay, you can go, and we moved to Saskatchewan, and we were with these people for about nine months and—" Teena stopped, her voice was choked with tears.

Morgan suggested the court take a break. "Do you want me to get you a glass of water?" she asked Teena.

Teena nodded. "Please." She took a sip of water and after a few seconds continued. "During those nine months, I was physically and sexually abused."

"And the adoption didn't go through?"

"No."

"Did something else happen when you were there?"

"Yes. That same year, my mother died."

Morgan quickly moved on. "How would you describe your relationship with the Alberta Social Services department?"

"I would say up until I was about twelve or thirteen years old, it was really good. And then after that time, it kind of went downhill because I felt that after they put me in that home, they really were not looking after my best interests."

"So when you became pregnant and delivered your child, did your relationship with Social Services affect any of your decisions about Jordan?'

"Yes, it did. I did not want any contact between Social Services and myself regarding the adoption of my son because I felt what I had to go through in my life, I did not want them at all to have any contact with me or my son in regards to his adoption."

"So when they made recommendations to you and said things to you, how did you accept that?"

"I was—I was very upset. I did not know what to do. I didn't know who to ask about what I should do. I tried to make the best decisions that I felt possible, and I felt really influenced by them because they—I don't know, I guess I've always been influenced by people. If somebody gives me advice then I feel I should take it, and it's hard for me—it's been hard for me in the past to make decisions on what I believe instead of what other people believe is the best for me."

Morgan asked if Teena had received any counselling prior to the birth of Jordan, and if so, what kind of counselling it was.

Teena described her sessions with Gail Friesen, who had recommended adoption and given her information concerning four prospective adoptive couples. "She told me to strongly think about adopting my son. She said I had a whole life ahead of me and later on I could have children and raise them."

Teena explained that she had been a member of the Woodland Cree band before receiving her status card from Ottawa in June 1992. A person does not necessarily have to be status to be a member of a particular band, each of which sets its own membership requirements.

She also said that at no time during pre-delivery counselling had anyone talked to her about consulting with the band. "No, nobody had—they had never talked to me about consulting my band about my decision. Nobody ever spoke of my band. Nobody ever asked me if I was a member of a band, or treaty, or if I was trying to become status." Teena said she had no recollection of Lynne Smith talking with her about any consultation process available through the band, contrary to Smith's testimony.

The testimony then moved to the question of influences on Teena's decisions concerning Jordan. Morgan asked if the doctor who delivered the child, Dr. Hallinen, had said anything to Teena about Jordan.

Brian Young objected. "This would be hearsay," he said. "Dr. Hallinen isn't being called. If she wants to call Dr. Hallinen, that's fine."

"Dr. Hallinen spoke to her about the child and there were personal observations between the two of them," Morgan responded quickly.

Melvin asked Morgan where she was going with the line of questioning.

"Where I am going with it is the issue of the doctor trying to encourage her to give the child up."

Young, who had remained on his feet during Morgan's

response, followed with, "That's pretty important and I think that would be classified as hearsay."

"Well, I'm not sure I understand," Melvin said, turning towards Teena, sitting in the witness box. "Did you and the doctor discuss adoption?"

"Yes," Teena said, nodding.

"If this witness is going to say she was pressured by a doctor to adopt the child—" Young began. "... I think that's pretty crucial evidence if this witness is going to claim through this whole adoption process she was pressured."

"She can explain why she followed a certain course of conduct, such as signing the consent. She can tell me what influenced her, if anything, to sign the consent," the judge said.

Young made a last stab. "I don't think the court can hear what Dr. Hallinen said, regardless of that."

"She can tell me whether or not there was something in that interaction that influenced her," Melvin said, nodding at Morgan to continue.

"Did Dr. Hallinen ask you to leave the child in the hospital for a longer period of time?" Morgan asked, making sure the questions asked for factual answers, not speculation.

Teena told of the post-partum depression and the doctor's advice that she leave Jordan there, to give her a few days to figure out what to do. Then she went on, "When I had phoned the hospital and told them I wanted to come and get Jordan, they had expressed to me Dr. Hallinen wanted to see me before I got my son and they said she had some concerns. So I went into her office and I saw her that day and she said, 'I think it would be best if you gave the child up,' and I said, 'No, I would like to take my son home.' And she appeared to be upset with me because she figured that I should give Jordan up because I was quite young and I still had my schooling ahead of me and things like that. She appeared very upset."

But Teena did take Jordan home, and Morgan asked how the child was cared for.

"Well, Jordan was well cared for. I had a friend who was staying with me at the time because she went through my prenatal classes with me. She was my coach during my pregnancy. So when Jordan came home, there were two of us and because it was a new experience for me, we sort of took turns looking after Jordan during the night. While I slept, she would look after Jordan; when I got up she would go to sleep. We took turns so there wouldn't just be one person doing it all the time."

Teena told the court that she moved to Fairview after Christmas 1991, and that she placed Jordan in temporary care with Carolyn Grayson a short time later. To Young and the Tearoes, this seemed like the actions of an unfit mother. To Morgan, it was another indication that Teena always tried to put the interests of her child first.

"At the time of the temporary care arrangement, January 6th, 1992, as I understand it, did [Social Services] raise any child care concerns?" asked Morgan, wanting to make clear that despite what Jim and Faye Tearoe had said in affidavits, there was no indication that the Social Services department was going to apprehend Jordan.

"No, no, they didn't."

Teena said she couldn't remember how many times she visited him at Grayson's, but it was a "few times."

"Not every day?" Morgan asked. It was tactically better for her to raise this point, rather than simply have it come out on cross-examination and have it look as if she had been trying to hide something. Besides, this was not like a criminal trial, where the Crown has to present its case and the opposing side just tries to poke holes in it. Teena had to provide as much evidence about herself and what had happened in the past as was necessary for the court to come to a determination about what was best for the child.

"No, I didn't."

"Why is that?"

"Well, because I was in the process of starting to attend school. I went and registered. I was planning on attending school and I was in the process of getting a crib and things for Jordan that I needed. So I was—I'm not trying to say I was too busy to go and see him because I wasn't, but I just wanted to get some stuff ready so when he came home, I would have stuff ready for him."

Young made a note to himself for cross-examination on this point, to emphasize that the Grayson home was less than two blocks from Teena's.

Morgan asked Teena what was going on in her mind during this time, why she was unsure about what to do with her son.

"I do believe it was because I had so many people telling me yes, you should adopt and this is a good reason why you should adopt. And then I had people telling me: No, Teena, don't you adopt him, this is your son, you love him, you want him, you can be a good mother, you can learn to be a good mother, we're here to help. And I didn't know what to do because I wanted to do what was best for Jordan.... When I moved away [from Manning to Fairview], there wasn't that help any more. It kind of got rough for me for a bit, and then I started thinking maybe I should adopt Jordan; then I thought no, I loved him, and I had really bad mixed feelings."

"What ultimately led you to make the telephone call to Mr. and Mrs. Tearoe?"

"Well, I had gotten calls from Grace and Peter's foster mother, Iris Land, and she had told me of this couple that she goes to church with that know a couple who are living in B.C. who wanted to adopt. The lady gave me Tearoes' number, and I talked to her and I asked her: What are these people like? And she said: They are really good, they have a really good home, they're Christian people and very good with children.

"So then I asked her for the number and she gave me the number and then I called Tearoes. For a while there, I thought about it and I thought maybe they could give Jordan a really good home that I couldn't provide for him. So I started thinking about it and then after a couple of weeks, I decided I would call Tearoes, just get to know what kind of people they are, what their lifestyle was like, if they did go to church, what church, different things like that. I am

Pentecostal myself and I'm not really religious, but I do believe in God, and I felt it was good for Jordan to be brought up in a good Christian home."

Morgan asked Teena if she was aware that she had to make arrangements with the Department of Family Services in Alberta.

"No, I wasn't. I figured since this was a private adoption and I had heard from other people that Social Services did not have to be involved in a private adoption."

"So you didn't make contact with them?"

"No, I didn't."

"But someone called you?"

"Yes. Lynne Smith called me on the 5th. She said she had heard that I wanted to give Jordan up for adoption and she asked when the Tearoes were coming, and I said on the 6th, and she said she would come on the 6th too because there were papers I had to sign."

Morgan asked Teena if Smith had mentioned counselling at all when she reviewed the forms with her. She replied that she hadn't. Teena testified that after the Tearoes left with Jordan, she felt "really bad. I—I—I felt that I let other people make my decision for me."

"What do you mean by that?"

"Well, I just felt like I let other people influence my decision and a lot of people had told me, you know, this is the best: we're really trying to encourage you to give Jordan up for adoption, then he would have two parents that could financially and emotionally support him."

"When you say influenced you, what was the feeling you had?" Morgan asked.

"I just felt like they were making my decision for me. They told me: This is the best, Teena, you should think about the future. How are you going to buy clothes and Pampers and food? It's going to be hard for you because you're a single parent on welfare. Without an education, you can't get a job."

"So what did you decide to do?"

"I decided that yes, it was going to be tough for me and that I loved my son very much, and I knew if I wanted the best for him at that time, I didn't feel I could give it to him, so I decided that it would be the best if Jordan went up for adoption."

"After putting him up for adoption, then how did you feel?"

"I felt that no, this is not what I wanted to do in the first place, this was not your decision, and that deep down inside, I felt that I had done something terribly wrong, and I felt that I wanted to revoke my consent."

She testified about writing the letter of revocation and mailing it, separately from her social assistance cards, and then calling the Peace River office on February 12, 1992, February 13, 1992, and again the following week, and talking to Erin Harris and Lynne Smith.

"Did either of those people offer to tell you how to write that letter?"

"No, they didn't."

"After you called them and they said the letter wasn't here, did either of them, that is Lynne Smith or Erin Harris, offer to come to Fairview to see you?"

"Neither of them, no."

"Did you understand the seriousness of getting that letter in?"

"Yes."

"Did you ask them to come to Fairview?"

"No, I didn't."

"Why is that?"

"Because they didn't seem willing to help me, so I figured well, I would have to do this on my own, so I didn't bother to ask them to come down."

Melvin, who had been listening carefully, asked, "Did you ever think of sending another letter?"

"No, I didn't."

"It was never mentioned to you that you might?" he asked.

"No."

Teena told of making the third call to the office and being told she needed to get a lawyer.

"I didn't do anything at that point because I didn't know how to get in touch with a lawyer. I didn't know if there were any lawyer offices [in Fairview or Manning], I wasn't sure who to call, and at that time, I was on welfare and I couldn't afford to get a lawyer."

Morgan asked a series of questions to show that Teena Sawan had little money and no vehicle, making it difficult for her to drive to Peace River to obtain legal help or personally see the social workers.

The testimony went over the documents sent to Teena by the Tearoes' former lawyer, John Jordan. Teena said she refused to sign them because "I knew if I signed them I would be consenting to the adoption, to have the adoption finalized or something like that, so that the Tearoes could go ahead and adopt Jordan, and I didn't want that." She told Melvin of Pastor Henry visiting her, as well as her letter to the Tearoes explaining why she wanted her son back. Teena testified that she called Donna Ominayak sometime in August 1992 and there was talk of Ominayak helping Teena get a lawyer. (Ominayak had testified that it was October 14, 1992.)

As Young had done with the Tearoes, Morgan also asked about follow-up contact after Jordan was placed with the couple. Young's point had been to show Teena did not exhibit an interest in her son; Morgan's point was that contact was a two-way street in an open adoption.

"When we agreed to the adoption, the agreement was that the Tearoes would send letters and send pictures and that the communication would be open between both sides."

"And did you receive a Christmas card from them this past Christmas?"

"No, I didn't."

"When was the first communication received from them?"

"The first communication I received from Tearoes since February of last year was April 21st of this year.... They had sent a letter and they sent about eight or nine pictures of Jordan."

Teena said the first line of the letter "kind of upset me a bit because in there they said they were reluctant to send me anything because they heard that...I wanted Jordan back and they were reluctant to send me anything because they thought I would want him even more."

The letter she received a few weeks before the trial began upset her far more. "Despite the things that they said in it, it seemed like Jordan was no longer a part of my life. He was their child now, and I felt like the bad person because it was always, 'you, you, you.' You did this, you said that, you said this, you called us, and I just felt like I was no part of Jordan's life any more."

Morgan shifted to an area she knew was the backbone of the Tearoes' drive to keep the child—Teena Sawan's difficulties with alcohol.

"Now, I understand, Teena, that you have had some difficulties in the past?" Morgan opened.

"Yes."

"And are those alcohol-related?"

"Yes, they are."

"Have you done anything about that?"

"Yes. Last year when I moved back to Manning, I started living with a friend who is much older than me. She has three kids now and she doesn't drink, so I went to stay with her and I told her about my problem and she set up an appointment with me to see MITAA [an alcohol treatment program]."

"Did you follow up on that?"

"Yes. I went to see—[my worker]—she came up every two weeks to Manning and that's when I saw her. I saw her every second week for about—until about just before Christmas of last year, I quit seeing her."

"And have you had—have you been drinking?"

"Well, the last drink I had was on my birthday and that was champagne, and I had some champagne because my friends had brought me a bottle of champagne for my birthday." Teena's birthday was May 28, two weeks before the trial began.

"Have you been drinking to excess?"

"No."

"When was the last time you drank to excess?"

Teena hesitated. One drink meant excess to the Tearoes, she thought. "It was on New Year's Eve this year."

Teena was asked about her health and said she had an ulcer and a mild case of epilepsy.

"Now," asked Morgan. "Do you use drugs?"

"No, I don't."

"Have you ever used drugs?"

Teena looked at the Tearoes, staring at her, Faye's eyes and mouth downturned, Jim rigid beside her. It had quickly become apparent to Teena that this case was an exercise in labelling. If she told them about smoking marijuana when it was passed around in Fairview, she knew she would be branded a drug addict. It would be added to the roster of negatives—drunken Indian, single, uneducated welfare mother and a drug addict, too. She decided to describe her life the way she saw it—she used to drink a lot, she had calmed down considerably and didn't drink to excess any more.

She leaned forward into the microphone and answered, "No."

Morgan's questioning continued. "Did you have a motivation to quit drinking?"

"Yes."

"Could you tell the court what that is?"

"I decided to quit drinking last year after I gave up Jordan and wanted him back because I figured if I still drank and wanted him back, there was no way I would ever get him back and I knew Jordan was very, very, very important to me and he's very special to me, and at that point in time I made a decision to do everything that I could to get him back and...that meant doing anything, like leaving Fairview which I did because I had no family in Fairview and I had bad influences in Fairivew, so I left Fairview. I even started attending church with a friend of mine, and I just decided I would do everything I could to try and get Jordan back."

She answered questions about the upgrading courses she was taking, and of her plans to get her grade twelve and go on to university and study counselling.

"If you were to get Jordan back, what plans do you have?"

"Well, since I don't start school until September, I would spend as much time as I could with him until then, and the only reason why I would like to go back to school is because Jordan needs to have support, financial support, and the only way I can support him is to go to school and get an education so I can support him, and I would like to send Jordan to play-school or something where he could be around kids his own age and be able to make some friends, communicate with friends. And while I'm at school, Miles, who is my fiancé right now, his sister-in-law Carrie has a little boy that's around Jordan's age, a little bit older, and she has been willing to provide babysitting when I go to school for Jordan."

"So you've thought about this?"

"Yes."

"When you talk about going back to school to do native counselling, where would you take that?"

"After I'm done with school, I would like to go back to the reserve and hopefully get a job working on the reserve because I feel that my culture is very important to me. And because I have been denied when I was younger, having contact with the other side of my family who is native and living on the reserve, I feel that that's very important."

She said Miles would also live at the reserve, "as long as he can make sure he would be employed."

Morgan asked Teena about the social worker's report that she had been assaulted by Miles Schoendorfer. "Is that true?"

"No, it is not."

Asked to explain, Teena said, "In April, okay, there was— me and Miles were sitting at home and we were watching TV and his brother, his half-brother was staying with us for a couple of months and his friends had come over and they were carrying beer and they were drunk and they wanted to come in and I told them, I said—excuse me, let's back up. Miles was not at home. I was the only one home and Shane's friends came over and I said, 'Nobody's here but me and Shane's not here, I don't know when he'll be back,' so I asked them to leave and they wouldn't leave."

Teena said they wouldn't leave, so she did.

"Did they assault you?"

"No."

"Did they push you around?"

"Well, the one guy sort of shoved me, grabbed me and he shoved me, and then I ran."

"And you say Miles wasn't home?"

"No, he wasn't."

"Has Miles ever hurt you?"

"No, he's never. He's never, ever raised his hand to me. We get into arguments, but he's never, ever hit me."

"Now, Teena, with regard to Jordan, why is it you want him back?"

"I want him back because—first and mainly because I love him and I miss him, and I believe that he should come back to me because I have made a difference for myself and I realize that in order for Jordan to depend on me, I had to make changes in my life, and I also strongly believe that his culture should be shown to him, and he should have the chance to get to know the extended side of his family, because when I was growing up I was—like I said—I was denied access to my culture, and that is a big part of my life."

"So you weren't brought up in the Indian culture?"

"No, and I believe that is part of Jordan, his culture. And also I want to be able to share his years with him, growing up with him, and I can give him love and I can give him security, financial support."

After a few more minutes, Jean Morgan finished questioning her client. It was almost 3:00 p.m.

Chapter 17

❖ ❖ ❖

Teena, Donna and Dolly stood on the courthouse steps, where Donna smoked a cigarette. To the older Cree women, it seemed the deck was unfairly stacked, as it always was when white people faced off against natives. Neither had a lot of faith in the system and wondered how an Indian woman, one month out of her teens with a difficult background, was going to compete with an established, middle-class, white couple. But they said little about their misgivings to Teena.

Inside, Brian Young was regrouping and collecting his thoughts after the surprise of Teena Sawan on the stand. Because the lawyers had waived pre-trial examinations in the interests of getting the case heard quickly, he had never talked to the young woman and knew her only through affidavits and the comments of others. He was astonished by how well she presented herself.

When court began, Young began with what he viewed as the weakest link in Teena's case—that she hadn't sought legal advice until eight months after her baby was gone. It made no sense to him that a mother who wanted her baby back as much as Teena said she did wouldn't have been camping out on the doorsteps of the Social Services office, or the nearest law office. The lawyer didn't buy that Teena Sawan was naive. While she may not have had a lot of formal education, he viewed her as almost street-smart.

His first questions were seemingly simple. Young established that Teena had lived four and a half years in Fairview, and that she was certain there were no lawyers in the town.

"If there were, you would have contacted them?" he asked.

"Yes."

Young walked towards Teena with papers in his hand. "I am producing to you a copy of the phone book that covers the Fairview area."

There are three pages of lawyers' advertisements, right after "lawnmowers," in the phone book for the Peace River area, which includes Fairview and Manning. Some are lawyers from Edmonton and Grande Prairie advertising in the smaller communities. Young pointed out that several had 1-800 telephone numbers. Some lawyers from Peace River indicated that they had offices in Fairview and the smaller towns. There was also a display advertisement for Legal Aid, listing a Peace River office serving Fairview, Manning, Peace River, Slave Lake and Grimshaw, accompanied by a 1-800 number.

"You didn't look in the Yellow Pages when you wanted to get a lawyer, did you?" he asked.

"No."

The lawyer suggested that Teena had been "well aware that there were lawyers in Fairview."

"No, I didn't. I knew there were lawyers that came from Peace River to Fairview. I did not know of any that were in Fairview." Teena repeated what she had said earlier, about not knowing how to contact a lawyer and not having the money for one.

Young's questioning hopscotched around to several issues, a common cross-examination tactic designed to catch the witness off guard.

Young shifted to questions suggesting that Teena's life was

not stable, saying that from the time Jordan was given to the Tearoes to the time Teena contacted a lawyer, the teenager was "trying to tidy up your life, for want of a better expression?" Teena agreed.

"You were trying to get on with your life, get rid of the alcohol problem?"

"Yes, and that's one reason I moved from Fairview to Manning."

"So you realized after you had given Jordan up for adoption that you needed to tidy up your life a bit?"

"Yes, because I knew if somebody were to come into my home and did a homestudy or something, they would not allow me to have my son back because of the way that I was living at the time."

"So at the time that the child was placed with the Tearoes, you would agree with me that you probably weren't the ideal person to have custody of the child, were you?"

"No."

"And in fact, it's probably been a good thing for the child that he's been with the Tearoes; he's probably got a really good start in his year and a half of life, hasn't he?"

"For the first couple of months, yes, he probably would have had a better life living with them, but that does not mean that he wouldn't have had a good life living with me."

"Now you feel that you've gotten your life back on track, it's your turn to have the child back?"

"That's not really the way I look at it," Teena said quickly, then stopped for a few seconds to make sure she said exactly what she wanted to say. "Jordan has always meant everything to me, and if it wouldn't have been for people telling me often enough, 'You can't look after him, you're too young, you can go and have kids another time in your life when you get older, when you finish school,' I'd still have him. I had other people telling me what to do, and really my decision was to take him home to be with me because that's what I told my doctor."

"A lot of your testimony, Ms. Sawan, has been that other people have been telling you that you should have given the child up for adoption and other people did this and other people told you other things. You must agree that a lot of what has happened was done of your own free will, wasn't it?"

"Yes, it was, because I didn't have the support that—" She stopped and took a deep breath. "If my mom would have been alive, okay? What I'm trying to say is that I didn't have the support that a regular eighteen-year-old would have had from her family."

Young suggested Teena should take responsibility for her actions, and she agreed it had been up to her to contact a lawyer and to write the revocation letter.

"And when it comes down to the issue of somebody from the ministry in Alberta contacting you regarding the consent or the counselling with the band, that was something that you had to do, wasn't it?" he asked.

"It was never expressed to me or told to me by the ministry, any person, that I had to contact the band."

"But you understand now that that was not something somebody else had to do. That was your job to do, wasn't it?"

"And I am sure I would have done it if someone had asked me, 'Teena, you have to talk to the band because Jordan is a member of the band.' I did not know that."

The questioning turned to the father of the child, with Young suggesting the father could have been one of two people with whom she'd had sex near the time of conception. Melvin's pen was down and he wasn't taking any notes, often an indication that the judge doesn't think the matter at hand is relevant or has any bearing on a judgment. Since the father was not involved in the case, the question about the certainty of his identity seemed to Morgan like a ploy to paint Teena as immoral. Young also pointed out that both Jordan's father and Miles Schoendorfer were white.

"At the time that you phoned the Tearoes on February 4th, and on the actual placement of the child with the Tearoes on February 6th, you were not in any way concerned that the Tearoes were non-native or white, were you?" Young doubted the sincerity of Teena's interest in the baby's culture,

when there had been none at the time of the child's placement. He thought it was merely a timely argument.

"No, I wasn't."

"But it an issue now, isn't it?"

"It's not an issue whether they're black or white or native,
Japanese or Chinese. It doesn't matter to me what they are.
What matters to me is Jordan, and his culture. He has a right
to know his culture, he has a right to keep his culture...."

"Doesn't that bring it down to an issue of him being white
or native?"

"No, it doesn't."

"So you would be happy with the child remaining with
the Tearoes if they could give him some kind of native culture and native background?"

"Not exactly, no. I would like for him to live on the reserve
so he could be around people from his own culture."

"That's a good point," said Young, seeing an opening into
another area. He wanted to show that Teena had little involvement with native culture. "You haven't lived on a reserve for a
long time, have you? In fact, it's been a number of years, five
years ago when you were on the reserve, if not longer?"

Teena agreed.

"How are you going to feel, though, with your fiancé,
hypothetically with this child, both being white—even
though your child is one-quarter native, for all intents and
purposes he looks white—going back to the reserve? That's
just not a possibility, is it?"

"Well, there are other people living on the reserve who
aren't necessarily native, and I don't think that would be a
big problem for us to go and live on the reserve. Nobody is
going to not accept us."

"But you yourself don't have a great desire to go back to
the reserve in the first place?"

"Yes, I do. I have a great desire to, but I would like to finish my school where I started. I don't want to be jumping
from one school to another, and that's why I've decided to
stay in Manning for the rest of my schooling and then go to
the reserve."

Teena continued that if she went to university, as she would like to, that would also put off her moving to the reserve.

"So you would agree with me that your argument that you want Jordan back to go live on the reserve isn't really possible because you yourself in all likelihood won't be on the reserve for at least five years, will you?"

"No, but that doesn't mean that I would not show Jordan his culture. It doesn't mean because I wouldn't be living on the reserve for four or five years that I wouldn't take him there."

Young suggested that the Woodland Cree reserve was riddled with housing and sewage problems. Teena said when she'd lived in the area years ago there had been housing problems, but no sewage problems. He also asked her about solvent abuse on the reserve, which Teena said she knew nothing about. In any case, Teena wondered, what did other people's problems have to do with her and her ability to raise a child? Why hadn't the Tearoes been asked about drinking and gasoline-sniffing in their community?

Young went on to suggest that the fact that Teena had only visited her child a few times while he was in the care of Carolyn Grayson showed a lack of caring. Then he turned to the April 17, 1993, assault allegation, and Teena again denied that Miles had hit her. "On that night, April 17th, somebody did push you around though?" Young asked.

"Yes."

"And in fact, you had to spend the night somewhere else that night?"

"Yes."

"So every other part of what was testified to in this court to have been said by Iris Land was true; they just have the wrong perpetrator. Is that true?"

"I don't know who the guy was [that pushed me]. There was about four or five of them that came to my apartment that night, and I have no idea. I knew them all but not the person who pushed me around."

Young was stymied. He was convinced that Teena had been assaulted by Miles, but without any further evidence, there wasn't much more he could do. Meanwhile, Morgan wondered what an assault allegation had to do with the issue of parenting a child. Does every woman who is the victim of an assault deserve to have her children taken from her?

Teena agreed with Young that she'd been 100 percent certain when she'd signed the consent that she was doing the right thing at the time, and that she'd signed it freely and voluntarily.

"You didn't feel any kind of coercion from Lynne Smith?"

"I—I did feel a little bit but I didn't let it bother me." Teena said she could not recall Smith saying she would help her say no. "But it's been a year. She might have said it but I don't recall," she conceded.

"I'm going to suggest to you that after the placement took place on February 6th, 1992, and for some weeks thereafter, you were still undecided; you weren't 100 per cent sure you wanted the child back. That's correct, isn't it?"

"That's not true. I wanted him back and I did what was required of me to get him back, and to this day I have not changed my mind about wanting him back."

Later, Young questioned the authenticity of the revocation letter Sawan said she wrote February 8, 1992. He suggested that she had in fact written it "long after the actual placement of Jordan," which Teena denied. He asked if the letter had been returned to sender, and Teena admitted it had not. Young also questioned her extensively on why she hadn't made any more effort to get to the social worker's office, if she had been so certain she wanted her child returned to her.

"You didn't think to phone them and say, 'Come and see me, because I have a written revocation?'"

"No, because they told me that I was to put my revocation in writing and send it to the office. They did not say, 'If you want, we can come and pick it up for you.'"

"Do you honestly believe it was [Social Services'] job to give you assistance [in getting a lawyer]? Was it their responsibility?" Young asked.

"They seemed pretty happy and pretty fast to have me sign the adoption papers and everything. I would think they would give me some assistance in getting a lawyer."

"They didn't, and I'm suggesting to you, they didn't seem happy and fast to give you the papers. They told you, 'You don't have to sign them, you have thirty days to sign them.' You personally insisted in signing them that day."

"No, I didn't."

"You deny that?"

"I deny that. She said, 'These are the papers you have to sign.' She went through them with me so obviously she wanted me to sign them, so I signed them."

"And you felt pressured to sign them?"

"No, I didn't, but I felt that since she had gone through them with me and told me to sign them that I'd sign them."

Young asked Teena how much she could love her son if she hadn't sent him a Christmas or birthday card. "So how can this child be such a part of your life when he was part of your life for twenty-two days, and you've not sent him anything or done anything in the last eighteen months?"

"Because I carried him for nine months," Teena said, her voice rising. "And during that nine months, I was very excited. I was very happy. It was my first pregnancy and to give him up was very, very hard, and I realized that it's not what I wanted to do, and Jordan has always been special to me because that's my first and only child."

"Do you think it's fair to the Tearoes that after they've had the child for a year and a half and you've had an opportunity to get your act together, for want of a better phrase, it's fair to take the child away from them?" Young asked.

"I believe that Jordan is still my child and I have the right to have him with me—"

Young interrupted. "You agreed with me earlier that at the time of the placement in 1992, you were not the best parent to be caring for Jordan at that time; you agreed with that?"

"Yes."

"Now you're capable of looking after him, aren't you?"

"Yes. I believe that even though I did have problems when Jordan was born didn't mean that I was incapable of looking after him."

"You would agree with me your future is a little uncertain, isn't it?" Young asked.

"No, it's not uncertain. I know what I want to do and that's what I'm working towards."

"You're aware that Mr. and Mrs. Tearoe have been setting money aside for a university scholarship plan for the child?"

"Yes."

"And you're aware that they have done changes in their home?"

"Yes."

"And put in a room for him?"

"Yes."

"Would you agree with me the child is wanted by the Tearoes?"

"Yes." Teena looked up at the judge. "Could I just say something, please?" Melvin nodded. "I feel that they can give Jordan a lot more than I can financially, but just because they can support him financially and give him nice clothes, nice toys, a big home, doesn't mean that they would be better parents than I would."

Young ended his cross-examination by briefly going over her evidence of drinking. For what was an important topic in his case, there were relatively few questions.

"You went to AADAC for alcohol abuse for six months did you?"

"Yes, I did."

"Yet in December of 1992, New Year's 1992-1993, you admitted to drinking again?"

"Yes, New Year's."

"That was after AADAC, correct?"

"Yes."

"One final question. You say you love Jordan and you miss him. You would agree with me that it would be extremely difficult for him to be removed from the Tearoe family now? I mean, you've found it hard when he was removed from you; wouldn't it be harder on him? After a year and a half, it's going to be difficult for him?"

"I believe it's better now than to wait four years like I did and be taken away after four years."

Jean Morgan rose to re-examine Teena on her comments about the reserve, asking her to expand on how she felt out of place at the reserve.

"I felt out of place because I had not been allowed to have any contact with the band, with the reserve and anybody from there. It was almost like going to a new place and getting used to everybody and getting used to the people. It felt really awkward for me.... That happened to me because, I think the main reason why I was not allowed to associate with the band or my cultural roots was because of my mother, the fact of her being an alcoholic and we were taken away. We were always in the white man's culture, living in a white man's house, so that's what I grew up knowing."

"With respect to Jordan, your son, there was a suggestion by Mr. Young's questions that, really, you may never go back to the reserve; is that right?" Morgan asked.

"That's not true. I really would like to go back to the reserve but I think the reason why I wanted to go to Lac La Biche College is so that I can learn my native culture, and it would be best if I do go back to the reserve because that's when I could learn the rest of my culture.... I think the main reason that makes me want to go back to the reserve is that I really want to know the rest of my family, and family is very important to me. I have family that live off the reserve and they are very important to me, but the rest of my family live on the reserve and I haven't been able to have contact with them, and I would like to have that contact with them."

Teena stepped down from the witness box at 4:20 p.m. It had been a long afternoon, but not as bad as she had feared. Young had been aggressive but polite. Court was adjourned for the day and would resume again on Friday.

Young was concerned as he walked back to his office a block from the courthouse. He thought he had presented the points he wanted, but it had been tough cross-examining Teena. Teena denied the drug problems and physical abuse, and without hard evidence of such, he was fighting a battle with no ammunition.

Donna, Dolly and Teena changed their flight reservations again. Teena called Miles and told him she wouldn't be back until the weekend. Two days gaped open in front of the women, all of whom wanted to be home. It didn't seem a good idea to go see Jordan again. That would mean seeing the Tearoes too, and while everything so far had been very civil, there was an undercurrent of upset.

The Cree women occupied themselves by taking in a few tourist attractions, all within walking distance of their hotel. While Dolly and Donna stared at a batch of sea cucumbers at the Undersea Gardens, Teena stared into a shadowy aquarium, where an octopus was hidden somewhere in the vegetation. She waited for the creature to unfurl its tentacles and thought about how things had gone that day. She didn't know if she had done the right thing by not revealing every negative detail of her life. What if it got her into trouble? Thinking of the assault allegation upset her. She had not told everything. There had been a few people at their place that night, drinking beer. When she and Miles drank, they sometimes argued, usually about money. That night, the others had egged the argument on, and Teena had lost her temper. Then Miles had shoved her to the floor.

Teena had taken what seemed the easier road in court that afternoon. She didn't know how to explain what had happened, and she knew the incident would be judged harshly. But in her mind, she hadn't been assaulted. There were times she felt that nothing about her world would ever make sense in the Tearoes'.

Friday, June 19, dawned clear and warm, one of those summer days that have tourists agog at Victoria's picturesque beauty. Gazing out the south-facing windows on the third floor of the courthouse, Teena Sawan could see the distant Olympic Mountains melting into the ocean and sky. It was pretty, but she would have exchanged it for the Manning fields in an instant if it meant this would all be over and she could go home with Jordan. "One more day," Teena thought as she went into the courtroom and took her spot with Dolly and Donna.

B.C. social worker Greta Vanderleeden was Jean Morgan's final witness, and Young was only too glad to have her called. Through Vanderleeden, he could enter into evidence the glowing home-study she had written of the Tearoes.

Morgan's reasons for calling the social worker were two-fold. First, she wanted to show that the three-and-a-half-page, double-spaced home-study contained numerous inaccuracies about Teena Sawan that were presented as fact, ranging from the age of the baby when he was placed to when Teena had revoked her consent. Vanderleeden's report also addressed the issue of the father, saying, "I can provide the following information: no background information is known about the birth-father as the birth-mother was involved with more than one man." (Under B.C. adoption law, a birth-father is not required to give his consent to the adoption unless he has acknowledged paternity of the child by signing the registration of live birth, or he has custody or access rights by court order or agreement, or he has acknowledged paternity and has supported, maintained or cared for the child.)

But Morgan's main point in calling Vanderleeden was to show the way the much-wanted little boy was viewed by those who held much of the power in this situation. Because he looked a certain way—blond hair, light eyes—he was judged to be white.

Morgan began her examination by establishing that Vanderleeden knew Teena Sawan was native. Morgan then asked Vanderleeden why there was no mention in the home-study that the child was part native.

"Would you not agree with me that that would be something that would be important for the court to know?"

"I think so," began Vanderleeden. "From seeing the child, all I know is a blond, blue-eyed child, so there has been little thought given to the fact that yes, there is some part native."

(Although the child's eyes were always referred to as blue in pre-trial affidavits, during the trial and in press coverage, they are, in fact, hazel, leaning towards brown.)

"Is there some reason why it wasn't included?"

"No, not at all."

"Just an oversight?" Morgan asked.

"Yes."

Morgan pointed out that the home-study, which the department uses to assure itself the home is an appropriate one, involves only about six hours over six months, in scheduled visits.

In cross-examination, Young emphasized that the social worker had found the Tearoes to be loving parents, with a strong bond to the boy.

"Do you feel that in this situation that the child would suffer if it was removed from that home?"

"Yes, I think so."

"It would be detrimental to the child's well-being?" Young repeated.

"I don't think it's my—I don't think it's my role to judge that, but I think this child has a very strong bond and yes, has learned, you know, to trust and that the needs are being met on a daily basis.... It would be traumatic to interrupt at this point for any child."

Young and Morgan were finished with Vanderleeden, but Melvin wasn't. It was obvious the judge's interest was piqued, and he took the opportunity to query Vanderleeden on whether any consideration is given to cultural issues in adoption.

"Yes, they are, very much.... In ministry adoptions, first of all, we try to match if we have a child with East Indian background, we try to find adopting parents with an East Indian background. If a child is placed—like if we do the court report for the private adoptions, we very much try to look at how are adopting parents going to raise this child. Are they going to say, 'Oh, you look white so we can pretend you are white,' or are [they] going to make the child aware and proud of the cultural issues and background. And in a situation like this, the Tearoes are more than open to have ongoing contact with the child and the birth-mother to let the child know who the birth-mother is, where she lives, where she came from and make him aware, and yes, those are certainly issues that we look at and that we consider important."

Melvin asked if the ministry had tracked over time the cross-cultural impact of interracial adoptions.

"I'm not aware that the ministry has done studies like that. I hear it more often if I go to adoption conferences where there are native people who were adopted in white families and who will let you know what the impact was. But then again, you only hear the people that speak out. As a matter of fact, you know, I have an adopted child myself. I have four children, three by birth and one adopted, and one child who has—yes, a part-native background, and who has never been interested in pursuing anything of his background, no matter how hard we tried. So you won't hear from him, you hear from a few who are very outspoken. I think it's terribly important to give them the information and give them the background and let them know, but what the real impact is, whether a child really can fit in cross-culturally, I'm not aware of studies, statistics, success rates."

Morgan asked Vanderleeden a further question, pointing out that there had been no mention in the report of any ongoing contact with the birth-mother, or efforts that would be made to ensure the child knew anything of his native culture.

With that, the testimony was over. All that remained was for Young and Morgan to deliver their closing arguments. Young's argument could be encapsulated in a simple phrase: "The devil you know is better than the devil you don't." He emphasized the bonding that the Tearoes, Julie Salmond and Greta Vanderleeden attested to. This little boy knew only Jim and Faye Tearoe as his parents. He was the light of the couple's lives. It would be like death for the couple to lose the little boy who called them Mom and Dad. Jim and Faye Tearoe had provided the only home the little boy had ever known. Teena Sawan was a stranger to him. How could it possibly be in his best interests, which Young argued the test was, to remove him?

"We know what this child has in his present environment—loving parents, a sister who loves him, a stable home. We don't know what he will have with Teena Sawan." The birth-mother had not met the onus that rested on her shoulders: to prove it was in the best interests of the boy to be moved. Young cited numerous cases in which varying levels of court had ruled that bonding supercedes almost everything. He relied extensively on *Racine v. Woods*, as would Morgan.

Although Morgan talked of the importance of the child's native culture, she placed greater emphasis on the fact that Teena Sawan had made significant attempts to revoke her consent, cries that had fallen on deaf ears. Everyone involved in the prospective adoption knew Teena Sawan had changed her mind. The principles of equity were paramount. Where was the fairness in a situation in which a young mother turns for help to the system that has essentially raised her, and they do nothing but spout rules and regulations to her? The equitable response was to let the mother, who was working hard to improve her life, have her child back; let Teena Sawan take her son home.

The courtroom was silent as Melvin peered up at the clock over the door. It was 3:00 p.m. His mind was made up, and he could have given a one-line decision then and there. But he wanted Teena Sawan and Jim and Faye Tearoe to understand how he'd arrived at his decision.

"The parties involved are entitled to more than a short, snappy decision from the bench," Melvin said.

Jim and Faye held hands tightly, Faye's fingernails pressing the flesh on her husband's hand. At the opposite end of the bench, Teena was doing the same with Donna and Dolly. Each wanted to hear the decision then and there.

Melvin tapped his pen on his hand a few times. After a long pause, he asked if all the parties could attend the next morning, Saturday.

Jean Morgan excused herself and talked to Teena for a moment, as Young did with the Tearoes. They would all be there.

"11:00 a.m., tomorrow," Melvin said. The case was over.

Chapter 18

❖ ❖ ❖

Although Justice Allen Melvin has a healthy respect for his own legal intellect and trusted his instincts, he wouldn't have minded a little divine intervention in the matter of the wording of the judgment. He crumpled up another yellow sheet of paper from the pad in front of him and lobbed it towards the wastebasket. His sport of choice was sailing, not basketball, and the piles of paper around the basket bore that out. He pulled off his glasses, closed his eyes and rubbed the bridge of his nose, then went back to work, the black felt pen scratching across the paper.

Finding the words for the Solomon-like judgment was as difficult a task as he'd ever had. It wasn't like a criminal case, in which the roles were usually clear. Here, there was no villain—just two sets of people who desperately wanted to raise a little boy. He often leaned back in his leather chair, staring at the numerous pictures of his family dotted his office. On top of a stack of law books rested a picture of his only grandson.

The only resemblance to the Jerusalem tabernacle that Solomon had stood in centuries before was the enormity of the decision. After seven o'clock, his stomach growling, Melvin packed up and took the decision with him to his home in Ten Mile Point, a prestigious area of Saanich that retains a slightly rural feel despite the prevalence of half-million-dollar homes. Long after his wife Beverly had gone to bed, Melvin sat up, revising. But he never wavered on the outcome.

Lying close to the edge of the double bed at the Green Gables Hotel, sleep seemed as far away to Teena as her son. She pulled the covers tight around her for a few moments and then kicked them off. She listened to Donna's breathing and turned to stare at her in the dark.

"You're not sleeping," Donna said matter-of-factly, her voice startling Teena.

"No."

Donna tossed the covers back and padded over to her purse, on the chair by the telephone. She rummaged around and then walked back towards Teena, unclenching her hand. A small pill lay on her palm.

"Why don't you take this Gravol," she said. "It'll help you sleep."

Teena downed half the orange tablet, pulled the blankets tight over herself and talked to Donna for a while about various inane topics, anything to keep her mind off Jordan and the possibility that it might all be over tomorrow, that she might go home without her son. She didn't know what she'd do if she lost and when those thoughts came into her mind, she pushed them away. There was some comfort in knowing that she had tried as hard as she could, and that at least someone had finally listened to her. Midway through a conversation about the Chuck Norris movie they'd gone to see that night, Teena's voice drifted off and she finally fell asleep.

Jim and Faye prayed long and hard before sleep took over that night. Faye woke up a few hours later to the still of the sleeping house. She leaned over to the bedside table, picked up her glasses and carefully slid out of bed, not wanting to wake her sleeping husband. She slipped through the dark hallway to the bedrooms at the end, her daughter to the right, son to the left. Heidi often kicked off her blankets in the night, and sure enough, her feet were poking out. Faye rearranged the covers over her sleeping daughter before heading across the hall to David's room.

The little boy was sleeping soundly. Faye stood by his crib for a few moments, looking down at the tot, lying on his back with one arm up over his head. "My child," she thought. "My precious boy." Except for the first two months, she had watched him grow and develop every day of his short life, had watched with delight as he grew from an infant to an active little boy who yelled out "mom" when she walked into the room. She leaned her face towards his, felt his steady sweet breath on her cheek. After a few moments, she stole back to her own bed and lulled herself to sleep by reciting scripture.

The Victoria courthouse is barren on weekends, the usual bustle of lawyers and clients replaced by a tomblike silence. A justice of the peace is available to deal with the unfortunates arrested overnight, and a few hard-working lawyers and law students can be found in the fifth-floor library. But a Saturday court sitting is rare, and it throws a system that thrives on routine out of whack.

Jim and Faye brought Heidi with them. The nine-year-old had heard about the case throughout the week and wanted to see where it had all happened. The excited youngster sat between her mother and father in the second row of the courtroom, eagerly glancing around at the formal surroundings. She and Faye wore matching powder-blue cardigans, and the little girl's hair was short and curled, just like her mother's.

Neither the Tearoes nor Teena talked to each other that morning. They had not spoken since the visit to the Tearoes' home on the first night of the trial. The stakes were too high. They sat on opposite ends of the same bench.

Jean walked over, gave Teena a comforting smile and said the judge would be in any minute. Brian did much the same with Jim and Faye, who were each holding one of Heidi's hands. Faye pointed out to the little girl where the judge sat, trying to put on a happy face for her daughter, and noted that Jean Morgan had pressed a package of Kleenex into Teena's hand.

The tension in the courtroom was almost sickening. In moments, a child's future would be decided, and the parents who both so desperately wanted him would have to reshuffle their lives to fill the void. Someone had to lose.

The courtroom seemed an odd place for something so very personal. People come into the sterile setting of a courtroom and recreate their lives—its tangled intentions, motivations and actions while sitting in a chair in a witness box. The tools they have to convey the intricacies of human behaviour are questions that are deemed appropriate by law. Based on the narrow snapshot of reality presented in this atmosphere, which is as far from everyday life as can be imagined, futures are decided.

Little David or Jordan had no idea that his life was being decided for him by a man he had never met. Most people coming before the court have done something, some act that requires a form of judgment. The youngster had done nothing more than be loved by two diverse families.

Promptly at 11:00 a.m., court clerk Kathy Gordon gave a short tap on the door leading into the courtroom from the judge's chambers. Melvin quickly stepped into the courtroom, holding in his hand a sheaf of papers that caught Jim's eye. On those yellow pages lay a future.

Melvin set the papers in front of him and looked out at the silent courtroom over the top of his reading glasses. He wanted to get this over with.

"I appreciate the parties attending at this particular time on a Saturday," the judge began. Then, after taking a breath, he launched into the judgment that would take twenty minutes to render.

"With reference to this matter, I think it is important to deal with it expeditiously in relation to the interest of not only Mr. and Mrs. Tearoe, but Ms. Sawan and also, of course, the interest of the child, as ultimately what we are concerned with is what is perceived to be, on the basis of the evidence and submissions, in the best interest of this child.

"At the outset, I should acknowledge the nature of the proceedings, and that is basically Mr. and Mrs. Tearoe are seeking, pursuant to their amended petition to the court, that the consent of the natural mother to the adoption be dispensed with pursuant to section 8 of the Adoption Act of British Columbia and that the child be adopted as the child of the petitioner, Mr. and Mrs. Tearoe, with the appropriate changes to the Christian name of that child or given name of that child."

At this, Jim mouthed to himself, "David James Tearoe," and held his daughter's hand tighter.

"The petitioner, the natural mother of the child, seeks a number of items of relief in her petition. In short, summarizing them, she seeks a return of her child...."

"This is not a matter which I come to with any degree of confidence in the sense that one is dealing with the best interests of the child and, of course when we're speaking of that as a principle, we're speaking in terms of today and, of course, ultimately tomorrow in the broadest sense, as to what that may mean to the child throughout his childhood, adolescence and throughout the maturation process as the young boy approaches adulthood. All of these factors, of course, loom large in the decision."

Melvin paused for a few seconds and then said, "I may say at the outset, in the personal sense, I find that in the fifteen years plus that I've been involved in this type of process and adjudicating issues between parties criminally and civilly, I found this to be perhaps the most difficult of any case I've had to consider."

With that, the judge spent a few minutes reviewing the evidence and submissions that had been presented during the three days of trial.

Melvin said Teena's evidence of "waffling," of being unsure of what to do about her child, was corroborated by Lynne Smith, who had also testified to Teena's indecision prior to February 6, 1992. "On January 6, 1992, according to the witness Smith, the mother wanted placement of the child with a view to adoption. On January 12th, the mother wanted to keep the child. She was overwhelmed by her options. On January the 22nd, the mother was undecided. January 29th, the mother decided to keep the child. February 5th and 6th, obviously the decision was made to place the child for adoption. This, of course, involved Mr. and Mrs. Tearoe."

Melvin reviewed how the Tearoes had travelled to Fairview and were present when the consent was executed by Teena. "Consequently, the de facto custody, for want of a better expression, changed on that day when Mr. and Mrs. Tearoe left with the child for Victoria. What subsequently occurred leads to what I describe as the most tragic of litigation."

Melvin gave a chronology of events, including Teena's February attempts at verbal revocation, the fourth phone call to Social Services in April and the letter written by Teena to the Tearoes in May of 1992. In this letter, Melvin said, Teena "canvassed her feelings at great length. She expressed concerns in relation to the child, she expressed concerns in relation to Mr. and Mrs. Tearoe, and explained, I think as best she could, why she made the decision that she made initially to place the child for adoption, and expressing—quite clearly—that she wished the child back." Melvin reviewed the efforts made by John Jordan to have B.C. documents signed, as well as Pastor Henry Langerud's visit to the teenager.

The first issue to deal with, the judge said, was the validity of the Alberta consent and its effect on the adoption proceedings in B.C.

"There is no doubt on the evidence, and I am satisfied, that Ms. Sawan appreciated the legal effect and consequences of her execution of the consent. She may have previously been ambivalent. But on February 6, 1992, she executed the document with full knowledge of its effect. She also knew and appreciated the ten-day revocation period."

Morgan had acknowledged this in her closing address, but had also argued that because section 62.1 of the Alberta Child Welfare Act, which requires that certain inquiries be made before the adoption of a native child can be finalized, had not been complied with, the consent was not legally valid. Melvin said it was clear that the statutory provision had not been complied with, but pointed out that the legislation requires that the process be carried out before the filing of an adoption petition, not before the execution of a consent.

"The legislative process is important as it demonstrates, as in the province of Alberta, native concerns over adoption are considered of great significance and of great moment and concern. There is, not necessarily comparable, but there is a provision in the Adoption Act of British Columbia, section 13.6. It is of no applicability to the case at bar, in my view." (Section 13.6 of the B.C. Adoption Act states that where an adopted child is a status Indian, the superintendent of child services may disclose to the adoptive parents the name and location of the band of which the child is a member and may disclose, with the written agreement of the child's adoptive parents, to the band or council of which the child is a member, information in the superintendent's records identifying the adoptive parents. The word "may" is all-important in this section. It does not mean it has to be done; rather, it is discretionary.)

Morgan had argued that B.C. adoption proceedings concerning an Alberta Indian and band member, based on an Alberta consent, can't be allowed to circumvent the Alberta legislative process, which was designed to protect native children. Melvin said he could not agree, finding that a valid consent signed in Alberta was valid in B.C. He did point out, however, that had the adoption proceedings taken place in Alberta, section 62.1 of the Alberta Child Welfare Act would have had to be met. "This interpretation does circumvent the policies of the Alberta government as demonstrated by section 62.1. However, counsel have not been able to direct my attention to any statutory provision or case authority which would vitiate the Alberta consent under these circumstances."

Having established that the consent signed by Teena Sawan in Alberta was valid, Melvin turned to the issue of whether she had revoked the consent, as was her right to do under Alberta law.

Noting that only oral notice was received by the Alberta Social Services department, Melvin went on to say that there "is no doubt all parties—Ms. Sawan, the Alberta Family and Social Services and Mr. and Mrs. Tearoe—knew that Ms. Sawan orally revoked her consent and did so within the ten-day period. There is no doubt that the same parties all knew that a written revocation was necessary in the terms of the Alberta statute.... Based on the evidence and the statute, if a timely written revocation had arrived, this matter would not be before these courts, because the consent would no longer be effective and the Tearoes' obligation would be to return this child to the mother."

Melvin continued. "The statutory scheme to avoid disputes and misunderstandings requires a written consent in the first instance, and the written revocation in the event there is a change of mind in the ten-day period. And the reason for documentation such as this to be in writing is, I think, patently obvious.

"In the case at bar, the Alberta staff acted quickly to assist in obtaining the mother's consent. Ms. Smith, as I recall her evidence, was travelling in an opposite direction when she received some sort of information that the Tearoes were present at Ms. Sawan's home and the matter of adoption was being addressed. She quickly changed direction and travelled to the Sawan residence in order to facilitate.

"Those same people did nothing to assist Ms. Sawan with reference to the revocation, other than advising her of the obligation to write in the ten-day period. The question then is, can this court, when considering the equitable principles that apply regarding the best interests and welfare of infants in the context of adoption, or in any other context dealing with infants, ignore that statutory obligation, or rule that the statutory obligation is of no force or effect?"

Sitting with pen in hand and taking the odd note, Young was getting a sinking feeling that the case wasn't going in the Tearoes' favour. But he flip-flopped several times as the decision went on. There was no indication up until the last paragraph as to what Melvin's final decision was going to be.

No answer was found in the statute itself, Melvin said, and counsel did not provide him with any case authority as to the Alberta law in that respect. "In my opinion, the court can consider all of the circumstances leading up to the obtaining of the consent and the oral revocation. This evidence demonstrates, one, that Ms. Sawan was equivocal throughout regarding the adoption. She was, at one stage, overwhelmed by the options.... Secondly, based on her prior history, she was reluctant to have the child welfare staff involved.

"Thirdly, after a private placement decision was made, the Alberta officials very efficiently presented documents to Ms. Sawan on the same day when they learned of Mrs. and Mr. Tearoe being present for the purposes of the private placement.

"Fourthly, the Alberta officials and Mr. and Mrs. Tearoe all knew within the ten-day period of the oral revocation. Three-way communication occurs within the ten-day period within or between the appropriate parties. Fifthly, nothing is done when no written revocation arrives, other than the telephone advice that Ms. Sawan received.

"In my opinion, the subsequent communications between Ms. Sawan and the Alberta staff were not completely satisfactory. I recognize there is no obligation on the Alberta Family and Social Services staff to assist her in obtaining the written revocation, but as all interested persons knew of the revocation, and the Alberta staff had been prepared to act quickly to obtain the consent, one such as Ms. Sawan may have expected a more positive response to her oral advice of revocation."

Teena Sawan shredded a kleenex in her hand. This part sounded good, she thought.

Melvin disagreed with Young's argument that Teena's subsequent conduct had demonstrated a lack of sincerity in pursuing the revocation.

"The chronology demonstrates her continued concern and her continued position of wanting the child back. Her steps were not effective. But when I consider her demeanour, her

age and education and her obvious lack of sophistication, I
am not surprised that she had not moved effectively at an
earlier date. Considering the foregoing, I am satisfied that the
consent signed by this rather naive, unsophisticated eighteen-year-old was vitiated by the orally communicated revocation and should not be given any force and effect in
adoption proceedings in this province."

Young's stomach sank. Behind him, his clients were staring at the judge and trying to fathom what he was saying.
His words were like rain falling around them. The legal complexities were too much to try to comprehend.

Essentially, Melvin found that Teena Sawan's consent to
the adoption had been made invalid by her revocation
attempts. According to Alberta adoption law, Melvin could
have returned the child to Teena on those grounds. But the
judge acknowledged that the finding was "without authority," that is, this situation had never been decided before.
And had he left it there, the decision would have been open
to appeal on the grounds that his ruling on that point was
incorrect, that Alberta law did not apply in B.C. or that the
B.C. law was not applied. So Melvin turned to B.C. law and
invoked its test: was revoking the birth-mother's consent to
adoption in the best interests of the child?

Melvin spoke glowingly of Jim and Faye Tearoe's abilities
as parents. Heidi smiled at her parents as the judge said they
were "competent, caring, loving proposed adoptive parents.
I have been impressed by them.... I have no doubt as to their
suitability as adopting parents and I note the report of the
Superintendent of Family and Child Services, to the same
effect.

"With reference to Ms. Sawan, her history is less significant in the terms that I've just described Mr. and Mrs. Tearoe.
She's had problems in her life, some including alcohol. She
testifies however, as to changes she has made in her life and
plans to continue with her education, hopefully to the university level, if funding is available. Her current academic
achievements indicate that the academic ability to attain that
goal is there.

"In addition, she wishes her son to be raised in her culture and know his extended family. Her son is part Indian. The father of her son, I'm advised or I have heard from the witnesses, is Caucasian. Her ultimate hopes are to live at the Woodland Cree reserve after her schooling is completed and assist the members of that reserve. The band on the reserve speaks Cree; she does not. She has not lived on a reserve for some years and she has limited connection with the Woodland Cree reserve at the present time.

"Nevertheless, she is a status Indian and a member of the band and her son is on the waiting list to become a band member. On the evidence, it would appear that that is a process that will apparently occur at a time set by the band council, and there is no reason to expect that the child will not be accepted as a band member.

"Insofar as Ms. Sawan is concerned, her background, naivety, her lack of sophistication—despite all of those, I am impressed with her evidence and impressed with her attitude towards her child. The decision in this case would be much easier if my respect and admiration for both sets of parents, if I can use that expression, was not in existence."

"Come on, come on," Teena thought. Donna sat beside her, gazing straight ahead, her right foot crossed over her left and wiggling in a steady rhythm. Teena could feel the bench shaking. Dolly touched Teena's hand.

"Culture, the native bonding, the native connection is a factor to consider," Melvin continued. "The legislative scheme in Alberta, as I mentioned, recognizes that the band interest in the proposed adoption of Indian children, cultural or ethnic consideration and the search for roots, are being recognized and a search of roots is being sought by a variety of Canadians in all walks of life. The importance of these connections is now emphasized in Canada today. This was not so in our past."

Melvin quoted from a 1987 Alberta study, *In the Interest of Native Child Welfare Services, Recommendations from the Working Committee on Native Child Welfare.* The paper says that the consistent view from native people across Alberta is that too many native children are being removed from their families and their communities by child welfare workers. Once removed, they are frequently placed into non-native families and remain separated from their families or communities longer than other children in the child welfare system. As a result, they become estranged from their people, culture and identity.

He then went on to the case law, in particular, *Racine v. Woods*, and pointed out the significant differences between it and the Tearoe-Sawan trial. "In *Racine*, the child was seven years old at the date of the Supreme Court of Canada decision. Of course, that is not the case in this situation as this child was born in December of 1991. Consequently, the time interval and the age differences are not found in the case at bar."

Melvin also touched on several other cited cases, including one called *Birth Registration 020379*, which clearly states that the laws of equity are to be applied in matters involving custody and adoption. He quoted Justice Prowse from that case: "Thus there is little doubt that in British Columbia, under section 8 (7) of the Adoption Act, the onus is on the natural parent seeking to revoke his or her consent to adoption to show that revocation is in the best interests of the child. If the scales are balanced evenly between the natural parent and the adoptive parents, then the application to revoke must fail. However, the placing of the onus on the natural parent to set aside his or her consent to adoption does not mean that the ties of consanguinity are to be given no effect by the court in weighing the best interest of the child.... The court clearly has broad powers under its parens patriae jurisdiction to consider all factors affecting the best interest of the child, including the blood ties between natural parent and child."

Another leading custody case, *King v. Lowe*, points out that all other considerations must remain subordinate to the best interests of the child. Melvin quoted Justice William McIntyre of the Supreme Court of Canada, who wrote, "This is not to say that the question of custody will be determined by weighing the economic circumstances of the contending parties. The matter will not be determined solely on the basis of the physical comfort and material advantages that may be available in the home of one contender or the other. The welfare of the child must be decided on a consideration of these and all other relevant factors including the general psychological, spiritual and emotional welfare of the child. It must be the aim of the court, when resolving disputes between rival elements for the custody of a child, to choose the party which will best provide for the healthy growth, development and education of the child so that he will be equipped to face the problems of life as a mature adult. Parental claims must not be lightly set aside and they are entitled to serious consideration in reaching any conclusion. Where it is clear that the welfare of the child requires it, however, they must be set aside."

In determining the best interests of the child, various factors are to be considered, including the stability of the respective households and the conduct of the parties. Melvin reviewed these specific factors which included religion, "a common theme for both the mother and Mr. and Mrs. Tearoe"; siblings, "so far as Mr. and Mrs. Tearoe were concerned, there is a close relationship between the child and the daughter Heidi. The mother wishes to have a close relationship with her extended family and the child have that close relationship"; bonding, "There is the bonding that Mr. and Mrs. Tearoe have described and others have described in their relationship with the child. Compared, of course, to the mother's short interval with the child. Nevertheless this is not a child that was taken from the delivery room and delivered to the Tearoes. She had the child in her care and custody for a considerable period of time. That issue of bonding also must take into consideration the time interval between February 6 and today"; resources of the parties, "clearly is a factor which can be touched on but, in my view, it is less significant than matters of emotional and loving situation involving the child and the loving care and attention that the child may receive"; and maturity of the parties, "the plans each of the parties may have for the child and their ability to carry out those plans, the feasibility and the likelihood of those plans being achieved."

The judge continued, "And I think it's very important, in the context of this case, the native heritage, despite the fact that the mother, of course, is part Indian and the child's father, of course, is Caucasian.

"I've considered all these factors, the physical, material advantages and the psychological and emotional welfare of the child on the basis of the evidence with this sole focus—what is in the best interest of the child?"

Melvin glanced up briefly before he stepped into the heart of his decision, and his eyes met the intense stares of the Tearoes and Teena. Jean Morgan and Brian Young looked at the papers in front of them, taking quick notes.

"In my opinion, the connection between the mother and child has not been irretrievably broken as in *Racine*," said Melvin. "In the case at bar, Teena Sawan has not abandoned her child. She has sought, albeit ineffectively, to seek the return of her child and she did so within a relatively short period of time after she executed the consent."

The judge continued. "I am satisfied, in the peculiar circumstances of this case, that it is in the child's best interests to revoke [Sawan's] consent. Consequently, it will be revoked pursuant to section 8(7). The statutory provisions of section 8(8) authorizing the court to dispense with her consent have not been met; there is no foundation for it."

Jim dropped his head to his chest and Faye Tearoe stared blindly at the judge, waiting to hear the words she had prayed would never be spoken.

"Consequently, the petition for adoption is dismissed and the child will return to his mother." Rising out of his chair, he said, "We will adjourn." Without a look at the courtroom, Melvin was gone.

Dolly and Donna were in tears as they hugged the young woman between them. Teena forgot that the kleenex in her hands was in shreds and used it to dab at her nose, not knowing whether to laugh or cry.

Morgan walked back to Teena. "Thank you," Teena said as

she hugged the scratchy wool of Morgan's tailored blazer and struggled to take it all in. Now she could go home with her son.

As Melvin read the last words of the judgment, Faye gasped and stared blindly ahead, unable to believe that the worst could be happening. Heidi, unsure of what the judge's complicated words meant but understanding their impact by the look on her parents' faces, began to cry, her small face a mix of sorrow and fear. Faye sought solace in what remained of her family and wrapped her arms around the little girl, reaching to include Jim in her embrace. But Jim had turned inward. His head was in his hands, his elbows resting on his knees; he was doubled over in spiritual and emotional pain.

Young carefully gathered his papers together, giving the Tearoes a few moments to deal with their grief, before walking back to the family. Although not a physically demonstrative person, he patted Faye awkwardly on the shoulder. He told her he was sorry and that they could talk about appealing the decision. "Don't be sorry," Faye said through her tears. "Just do something to fix it!" Jim raised his head. He looked stunned.

Young walked towards the other end of the courtroom to congratulate his opponent, and overheard Morgan's husband, Dan, advising Teena to be sure to continue calling the child David for a while, so as not to confuse the boy. Teena nodded. It struck a bitter chord with Young.

Melvin had not indicated how the boy was to be given over to his biological mother, and the lawyers were unsure what was to happen next. Teena's plane left at four o'clock that afternoon, and it was already almost noon. The lawyers indicated to the clerk that they needed to consult with the judge.

Kathy Gordon found Melvin pacing around his office, hands scrunched in the pockets of his black suit pants.

"What's going on in there?" he asked abruptly, gesturing towards the courtroom. Gordon was surprised at Melvin's show of concern. He was usually much more detached. Melvin continued pacing, staring at the carpet, as she told him of Teena's hugs and the Tearoes' stunned silence. She passed on the lawyers' request. She too, had found the case difficult to deal with. The mother of two couldn't bear the thought of losing her children.

"Send them in," Melvin said, walking towards the leather chair behind his desk. Gordon walked back to the courtroom and poked her head inside the door, signalling the lawyers to come with her.

Walking towards Melvin's office, Young asked Morgan, "Why don't you give me a week? I'm going to appeal." Morgan refused. "She is entitled to her child now." If Young asked for the transfer to be postponed, she would apply for habeas corpus, which, in these circumstances, would mean giving the child over immediately. Morgan felt empathy for any couple having to give up a child they had raised for as long as the Tearoes had the boy, but that feeling was tempered by the fact that the Tearoes would never have bonded so strongly to the child had they returned him to Teena when she'd asked for him. "I do understand that even if you haven't gone about it in the right way, it's still painful. But it should never have been this way. I just have a great deal of difficulty getting past that."

Sitting in the judge's office, the trio had a brief discussion on how best to manage the transfer of the little boy. Morgan asked that the child be returned that afternoon. Waiting would not make it any easier for the Tearoes to say goodbye, she said, and Melvin agreed. Indeed, he thought a delay would make saying goodbye even more difficult for the Tearoes. There would never be a right time for the couple. The lawyers and Melvin agreed on a 3:00 p.m. transfer, giving the Tearoes three hours to say goodbye to the child they had raised as their own for the last sixteen months, and allowing Teena to catch her 4:00 p.m. flight.

After the lawyers left his office, Melvin sat alone for a while. He hoped he would never have to make another decision like this one.

Back inside the courtroom, Young stopped in front of Teena.

"I think you'll make a good mom. Good luck," he said to the surprised woman. Then he gathered his clients together and escorted them slowly out of the courtroom. Faye held Heidi tightly to her side. The group stood just outside the court-room door.

Jim released his grief and anger in a torrent of complaint. "Why do we have to pay for this girl's improprieties? She gets herself pregnant. She has a child out of wedlock and chose to give him up. Now we are being held hostage by her improprieties." His face was chalky and his voice quivered. "Does she know what we have gone through to have a child? Does she know the pain and expense of operations my wife has gone through? She doesn't abide by the rules and we have to pay! She knew what she had to do, and she didn't do it! She knew the rules! And we are paying her legal bills. Do you know how expensive this process has been? And it has cost her nothing. Absolutely nothing."

Faye pulled at her husband's arm, urging him not to talk to reporters, but he angrily shushed her and told her to leave him alone. He would talk to whomever he wished. Rejected, Faye took Heidi to the women's washroom at the end of the corridor, where she washed the child's tear-stained face and tried to calm her.

Asked by a reporter how he was going to say goodbye to the little boy who was, in Jim's eyes, his very own son, Jim Tearoe said, "She told us to come and get her child. Doesn't she remember that?... We have even considered running," he said, hands grasping his thin knees. "We'll do what we can to get our little man back. He's ours—not hers."

The Tearoes stood for a moment on the courthouse steps. The world had been transformed in that hour, in that court-room. It seemed particularly strange to do something as mundane as walk to their car, unlock the door and drive off, when the foundations of their life had been pulled loose. But that was what they did. They drove through the city, seat-belts on, baby-seat in the back, stopping at red and amber lights, heading towards home where their precious David was. They knew what they had to do.

A few minutes later, Teena Sawan was standing on the court-house steps in the same spot where Jim and Faye had been. She had stayed inside the courtroom until she was sure the couple had gone. She knew they were hurting—the sight of her would undoubtedly make them feel worse. In her characteristic, low-key style, Teena told reporters that she was "very happy at the outcome. I've waited a long time for this." She readily agreed to having a photograph of her and the child taken at the airport by a newspaper photographer but changed her mind after talking briefly with Jean Morgan. "We think it would cause more hardship for the Tearoes, and I'm sure this will already be difficult enough for them," she said. She definitely wanted the Tearoes to continue being a part of her son's life, she said that morning. "They can visit as much as they want. I'd like that, and I'll tell Jordan all about them. I don't want Jordan to forget them."

Chapter 19

The Book of Psalms is the heart of the Bible, the human
soul stripped bare before God. Faye would soon turn to it
for strength in what was the darkest moment of her life.

But the Bible was far from her mind as she frantically bundled the little boy into his car-seat, an overnight bag fitting in
snugly at his feet. David was excited to be in the car. Going
for a ride was one of his favourite activities. In the house, Jim
made sure the lights were out, the doors locked tight and the
dog Natasha outside before striding out to the car and hop-
ping in the driver's seat with a quick glance at his watch.
Two hours until Teena Sawan would arrive to take their son.
One hour until the ferry would leave Vancouver Island for
the mainland.

The Tearoes were headed for the B.C. ferry terminal,
twenty miles north of Victoria. In between prayers and con-
demnations of the judiciary and the legal aid system, Jim
watched his son in the rear-view mirror. David was staring
out the window, banging his legs against the car-seat and
occasionally letting loose with a torrent of chat.

Heidi sat in the back-seat by her little brother, listening to
her mother's prayer: "Lord, show us what to do. Show me

the road. Please protect Jim. Protect Heidi. Keep her in your care." The little girl knew that what had happened in court before had been the work of Satan, but it was all going to work out just fine. That was what her mom and dad had told her. They would all be together forever because that was God's will.

At the ferry terminal, Jim quickly parked the car in front of the ticket booth. The family stood in a tight circle on the pavement, their hands clasped and heads bowed. They were undisturbed by the jostling of people running to catch the 2:00 p.m. sailing to Tsawwassen. An announcement crackled over the ferry loudspeaker for all foot-passengers to board the *Queen of New Westminster*. Jim held David tightly to his chest, his eyes closed. "Please Lord, keep our little man safe. Protect David and Faye." As the second boarding call came, Faye gently pried David from Jim's arms and hugged her husband and daughter. "I love you, I love you," she told each, before hurrying towards the ticket booth. Midway along the long, covered walkway to the ferry, Faye looked back at what remained of her family. Jim stood with one arm tightly around Heidi, gazing forlornly towards the ferry. Faye wasn't sure when she would see them again.

She quickly brushed at tears and brightly pointed out the ship's fittings to David, who was happy to be going on the big boat. The tot seemed oblivious to Faye's distress, and she wanted to keep it that way. The two found a seat on the upper deck of the typically tourist-laden ferry. Faye wanted to be invisible and worried that someone might recognize them from the news coverage of the case. They settled in, and Faye played peek-a-boo with David for a while before he fell asleep against her chest.

At 3:00 p.m., when Faye was supposed to be handing the child she had raised for sixteen months to the woman who had given birth to him, she gazed out at the Gulf Islands. The woman for whom a parking ticket was a big deal marvelled that she was, as of that moment, in contravention of a B.C. Supreme Court order. She wondered if the police were at her home, or if they would be waiting for her when the ferry docked. She squeezed her eyes shut behind the glasses slipping down her nose in the heat.

"Please Lord, show me where you are," she pleaded. "I need to know where you are."

Outside the Tearoe house, Teena Sawan stood and pressed on the doorbell, willing someone to answer. She knew it was pointless—it was at least the tenth time she had rung or knocked—but at least the echoing chime broke the stillness.

The first few times she rang, Teena thought that perhaps the family was in the back yard and hadn't heard. By the fifth unsuccessful attempt, she knew they simply weren't there. They *had* to show up, she thought. They couldn't undo everything by simply ignoring it—could they?

A black-and-white cocker spaniel barked furiously as Teena and Donna walked around to the sliding glass door they remembered from their last visit. They squinted inside the house, cupping their cheeks with their palms to block out the tepid sunlight. Inside, the family room was in perfect order, as was the kitchen. There were no dishes out, and the counters were bare. The doors were locked tight. There was nothing to do but wait.

Teena sat sideways in the front passenger seat of Dan Tchachuk's car, her feet on the cement driveway, shoulders hunched. Jean's husband was going to drive them to the airport, but with each second, that dream was disappearing. A car-seat with the price tag still on and a Zellers bag full of clothing and toys they had recently bought were in the back. Teena stared down at her fingertips and lunch churned in her stomach. Dolly and Donna sat cross-legged on the neat lawn, picking at blades of grass. Dan leaned against the stone wall that provided a fence to the immaculately kept home. A decorative barrel was filled with potting soil, and clusters of pumpkin-orange nasturtiums bloomed, not a deadhead in sight. Rainbow-hued flower baskets hung at the side of the house, rich purple lobelia trailing down the side.

The only sounds in the peaceful neighbourhood were the usual Saturday afternoon intrusions. The buzz of a lawn-

mower sliced through the still air, and down the block a
woman washed her car. The muted shouts of kids playing at
the nearby schoolyard drifted across the rooftops.

Both Dolly and Donna offered soothing words to Teena.
"I'm sure they'll be here soon," Dolly said, trying to convince herself as much as Teena. There was no way that couple was going to hand over the boy who looked so white to a
bunch of Indians, she thought to herself. Dolly had seen
what she thought was apprehension in the Tearoes' eyes
whenever they looked at her dark skin and straight, black
hair.

Teena listened politely to the calming words, blinking
back tears and avoiding their gaze. She had gone from the
happiest she could remember being since her mother was
alive to this. Teena broke it down to its simplest form. How
did people call themselves Christian and say they believed
in God, and then ignore what the law said was right?

Jean Morgan couldn't believe her ears.

"What?" she demanded.

"They're not here," Dan repeated. He had knocked on the
front door of the house next door and asked to use their telephone. Standing in the kitchen, as the young couple who
had just arrived home unpacked their groceries, Dan kept
his voice quiet as he called Jean at home. The lawyer glanced
at her watch. It was just past 3:30 p.m. She would call Brian
Young and see if he knew what was going on. Dan said he'd
call her back in a few minutes.

Morgan caught Young as he headed out the door to take his
kids on a promised swimming trip. "Give them some time,"
he suggested.

"All right," she agreed tersely, unsure, at that point, what
else to do.

Young would say later that he wasn't "100 percent surprised" that his clients didn't show up for the transfer.

Jean Morgan fought back her feelings of frustration: they
would not do her—or Teena—any good. Then she pulled the

telephone directory from a nearby drawer and looked up the phone number for the Colwood RCMP detachment.

The little girl who lived next door to the Tearoes came out and stared. She often played with Heidi but hadn't seen her young friend that day. The next-door neighbour on the other side leaned over his balcony and idly watched as the group of people congregated at the Tearoes. He hadn't seen the family since that morning, he said, when they'd left for court, leaving the boy with people he'd assumed were the grandparents.

Dan walked next door and used the telephone again. There was still no sign of the Tearoes, he told Jean, who recommended he and Teena visit the Colwood RCMP. The lawyer had already telephoned and advised that her client might be coming down.

Dolly and Donna stayed at the Tearoes while Dan drove Teena to the RCMP station. The women kept a close watch on every car that came by. One vehicle went by twice, at a relatively slow speed, prompting them to wonder if it was a friend of the Tearoes "casing" the home to see if people were still waiting, or whether the driver was simply curious about the presence of two native women in a white suburban neighbourhood. The women tried to remember what the Tearoes' vehicle looked like, and recalled the couple driving up to the courthouse in a brown VW Rabbit. As the afternoon wore on, the women joked a bit, imagining the headline: "Three Indian women out hunting for a brown Rabbit." Dolly suggested to her friend that they set up a teepee on the Tearoes' front lawn. "Let them know we're here," she laughed.

About 4:30 p.m., Teena and Dan returned, followed a short time later by Colwood RCMP Constable Doug Stack. The eighteen-year veteran of the RCMP pulled his sizeable girth from behind the wheel of the unmarked car, walked over to Dolly and Donna and introduced himself. The women pretty much repeated what Teena had already told him, but he wrote down their comments anyway. Stack's low-key manner made him seem more like the man who came to read the hydro meter than someone investigating a crime.

The officer knocked on the Tearoe door and peered in the windows. He talked to a couple of neighbours. No sign of anything unusual. The house was locked up tight. There seemed little point in continuing the vigil outside the empty house, and at about 5:15, Stack suggested that Teena and her group might be more comfortable at her hotel. He would let Jean Morgan know as soon as he knew anything.

Dan drove them around the neighbourhood, passing by the Tearoes' a few more times, but it was clear that no one was coming back soon. As they drove back to the motel, Teena stared out the window, barely seeing the unfamiliar buildings and roads whipping by. She rolled down the window and let the wind rush in. She didn't want the others to see her crying.

Doug Stack returned to the Colwood RCMP station, a couple of miles south of the Tearoes' home, and briefly went over his notes. According to Jean Morgan, the judge had ordered James Frederick Tearoe and Faye Merelie Tearoe to return the child to Teena Sawan at 3:00 p.m. But in a conversation Stack had with Brian Young at 6:22 p.m., Young gave it somewhat different spin, according to an affidavit later sworn by Stack. Young confirmed that legal guardianship had been transferred to Sawan by Melvin but said that 3:00 p.m. was a "tentative" time for the transfer of the child. According to Stack's interpretation of what Young had told him, Melvin "tempered his direction by stating that Morgan's client should be flexible and a reasonable amount of time should be given to the Tearoes." Young advised Stack that he interpreted "reasonable amount of time" to be from one to two days. Young said he didn't think the Tearoes had fled the community and that he expected to hear from them later that night.

Stack rubbed his eyes as he sat at his desk, a lukewarm cup of coffee by his side. This was exactly the type of case police didn't like getting involved in. Family custody matters were notoriously messy. And the lack of a written court order intensified what was already an emotional cauldron, in Stack's view. Without an actual court order in his hands, and given the conflicting interpretations he had received, he was leery to do anything.

At 10:36 p.m., Stack received information from one of the Tearoes' neighbours that their brown 1980 Volkswagen Rabbit, missing from their driveway earlier that day, had now returned. Nine minutes later, Stack was knocking at the door of the Tearoe home. Jim answered and quickly stepped outside the door when Stack identified himself.

Jim Tearoe said that the child was present in the home and sleeping upstairs, Stack later swore in an affidavit. Jim also said that he and Faye had decided not to give up the boy because their lawyer had told them that if they turned over the child they would probably never see him again. "Mr. Tearoe told me they were not going to run and that they planned to appeal Mr. Justice Melvin's decision. Mr. Tearoe also told me that they had not returned home for the 3:00 p.m. exchange because they were in shock and did not know what to do," Stack later swore.

Jim Tearoe's recollection of his conversation with Doug Stack that Saturday night is somewhat different. Jim emphasized that Stack's manner was "quite pleasant." "[He] wanted to know if I or someone would be moving David out of the province and I said, 'No.' He said, 'Is he nearby?' and I said, 'Relatively speaking.' He was satisfied that my son was not out of the country, that I was not taking him out of the country, that he was fairly close, should [Stack] receive paper notice of the court order. He asked me if my son was safe, and I said 'Yes, as far as I know.'"

It was clear from this that the Tearoes believed that because the court order was not physically written up, they had some protection from it.

Stack telephoned Morgan at 11:00 p.m. and told her that Jim Tearoe and the child were at the Tearoe home. Morgan, in turn, telephoned Teena, who had spent much of the evening lying with her face to the wall in her motel room while Donna and Dolly tried to watch television.

Shortly before midnight, Teena Sawan was at the Tearoes' door. Dan, Donna and Dolly waited in the car. Teena thought if she didn't get her son that night, she might never see him again. Part of her was growing afraid of what the Tearoes might do if they had to give him back.

The carport was dark, but Teena didn't need the outside light to find the doorbell. There was no answer. "Where are you?" she thought, ringing the doorbell again. She heard steps coming towards the door and waited to see her son. But Jim's arms were empty. He stepped outside, shutting the door behind him. The two stood in the dim carport, Teena with her arms crossed in front of her, Jim with his arms slack at his sides.

"I'm here to pick up my son," she said flatly.

His voice dull, Jim replied, "No. You will not be getting your son today."

"Is my son here?"

"No, he is not."

"Do you know where he is?" Teena asked, tears of fatigue and frustration threatening to spill out.

"No. But you will not be getting your child back today. I'm sorry," Jim answered, and he went back inside the house.

Teena walked back towards the car, not believing what was happening. How could he just tell her what would and wouldn't be done? She felt so helpless she wanted to scream.

Jim heard the car back out of the driveway and idle out front for a few minutes before driving off. He stood on the other side of the door, closed his red-rimmed eyes and leaned his forehead against the cool frame. The house was still and dark.

Neither he nor Teena slept much that night, and both asked God for the same thing—that the boy return home safely.

Faye's first concern that Saturday afternoon had been getting off the ferry without anyone recognizing her and David from the news. She waited in the crush of people walking off the ferry, not making eye contact with anyone except her son, and let the others walk ahead of her. "Who do I call? Who can help me?" she wondered as she watched others being happily greeted by friends and family. The public bus was outside, and she set David down beside her as she rummaged through her purse for the right change.

Faye had to consciously tone down her normally effusive style—instead of asking the bus driver how he was, she jammed the money in and scurried to the back of the bus. As it pulled away from the curb with few people on it, Faye breathed a sigh of relief. So far so good. And one side of her had to laugh. Who would have ever thought she would be running from the law? She caught a glimpse of herself in the window reflection and smoothed her short hair. A less likely looking renegade there never was.

David pounded his hand against the window, pointing towards the ocean. Staring out at the sailboats bobbing on the water, it was hard to believe they were doing anything other than going to visit friends. But the bus shuddering to a standstill at a stop shattered the illusion. As several passengers walked on, Faye grabbed toys from the bag beside her and gave them to David, who was staring at the new people with his usual curiosity. "Please play with this toy and don't make a sound," Faye silently pleaded, adding a thank-you as the boy took the stuffed toy and shoved it in his mouth.

One passenger glanced towards the back of the bus and then walked back up to the driver, leaning forward and saying something Faye could not hear. "Oh no, please Lord, no," Faye thought. She had nightmares of the driver being told she was on the bus, telephoning the police on his radio-telephone and a throng of blue-suited officers storming the bus at the next stop, putting her in handcuffs and pulling David forever from her arms. She feared she would never see her son again, and quickly wiped the tears from under her glasses. The person at the front of the bus walked back to his seat with a transfer in his hand, sat down and pulled out a pocket book. "Thank you, Lord," Faye said.

To this day, Faye will not say exactly where she went. She has numerous friends and relatives in the Vancouver suburbs

of White Rock and Surrey, but finding a place to feel protected was exhausting for the mother and young child. At
11:30 that Saturday night, twelve hours after Justice Melvin
had decided David was no longer theirs, Faye could find no
place to feel safe, physically or spiritually. Close to midnight,
while her husband was telling Teena Sawan she would not
get her child back, Faye was running again. She had been in
one spot but didn't feel secure. Finally, she found a place to
feel safe, and she and the child rested. But she awoke Sunday
morning with a fear even more insistent than that of losing
David.

Faith had been a constant in Faye Tearoe's life for fifteen
years. The Lord was with her when she woke in the morning,
kept her company, gave her strength all day, and retired with
her at night. To be without that belief was more frightening
than anything she could imagine.

"Lord God, you have left me," she cried. "I can't stand
this. Where are you?" Faye realized then that she could live
without her son, as hard as that may be, but she could not
live without her Lord. She thought of Jesus on the cross, and
how he had stoically endured what must have been excruci-
ating pain. But now she understood that the physical suffering was nothing compared to Jesus's thought that God had
forsaken him. That was the pain that made him cry out, and
so it was for Faye. "Father, I can go right now and give Teena
back her son," she prayed. "If you want me to do this, I will
do it. Lord, what do you want me to do?"

Faye put David on the figurative altar again, telling the
Lord that the beloved child belonged to no one but Him. The
Lord let her know He was there by telling her to open the
Bible to Psalm 27.

Although Faye knew the psalm, she pulled her Bible from
her bag and pored over the words.

> The Lord is my light and my salvation; whom shall I
> fear? The Lord is the strength of my life; of whom shall I
> be afraid?
> When the wicked, even mine enemies and my foes,

came upon me to eat up my flesh, they stumbled and fell.

Though a host should encamp against me, my heart shall not fear: though war should rise against me, in this will I be confident.

One thing have I desired of the Lord, that will I seek after; that I may dwell in the house of the Lord all the days of my life, to behold the beauty of the Lord, and to inquire in his temple.

For in the time of trouble he shall hide me in his pavilion; in the secret of his tabernacle shall he hide me; he shall set me up upon a rock.

And now shall mine head be lifted up above mine enemies round about me: therefore will I offer in his tabernacle sacrifices of joy; I will sing, yea, I will sing praises unto the Lord.

Hear, O Lord, when I cry with my voice: have mercy also upon me, and answer me.

When thou saidst, Seek ye my face; my heart said unto thee, Thy face, Lord, will I seek.

Hide not Thy face far from me; put not Thy servant away in anger: Thou hast been my help; leave me not, neither forsake me, O God of my salvation.

When my father and my mother forsake me, then the Lord will take me up.

Teach me Thy way, O Lord, and lead me in a plain path, because of mine enemies.

Deliver me not over unto the will of mine enemies: for false witnesses are risen up against me, and such as breathe out cruelty.

I had fainted, unless I had believed to see the goodness of the Lord in the land of the living.

Wait on the Lord: be of good courage, and He shall strengthen thine heart: wait, I say, on the Lord.

The verse provided a lifeline for Faye Tearoe, who interpreted it as saying it was not God's will that David be returned to Teena. The Lord was telling her to be strong in her faith, and He would guide and protect her from adversaries. Faye grasped onto that psalm with her imposing will and put the terrifying doubt behind her. In her mind, Faye Tearoe was doing the right thing, for her, the child and the Lord. The court of law that governed everyone else was of little meaning to her.

At eight o'clock the next morning, Teena Sawan pressed on the doorbell for four long rings before Jim came to the door. Both looked weary. Again, Jim told Teena that David was not there, and that he did not know where his wife or child were.

"Are you refusing to return my son to me?" Teena asked, arms crossed in front of her.

"We will not be giving up the child until the appeal is heard." Jim went back into the house and shut the door.

Teena Sawan returned to the Tearoe home later that Sunday morning and their car was gone. She rang the doorbell, but no one answered, and she couldn't hear the dog barking. Noting the mid-morning time, Teena thought the Tearoes might be at church.

Teena, Donna and Dolly went to a church a block south of the Tearoe home. The jean-clad native women walked into the service, the sounds of a hymn swelling up around them as they stood at the back of the chapel. A middle-aged woman in a knee-length dress came up and asked if she could help, and Teena asked if Jim and Faye Tearoe were in the church.

"The Tearoes haven't been to this church for years," the woman answered, but they didn't trust her. After the woman stepped back into the service, Teena, Dolly and Donna walked down a short flight of stairs to the basement, where there were several small classrooms that looked appropriate for Sunday school, with brightly coloured pictures of Jesus and lambs on the wall. It might also be a sanctuary for the Tearoes.

As Teena stepped out of one of the rooms, she found herself eye to eye with the woman from upstairs.

"I told you, they are not here," the woman said, her disapproval apparent. "We're Christians here. We wouldn't lie."

Standing outside the church, there seemed little else the women could do but go back to the motel and wait.

On Sunday morning, Jim took Heidi to a friend's, who was going to drive the little girl up-island to stay with other friends. He didn't want Heidi to be around the commotion. As he returned to his empty home, Jim thought about what seemed patently obvious to him: the judge had wanted to rule in their favour but had been afraid of the "Indian issue." In Jim's view, they were fighting a political issue, and he feared the winds of social change could rip his carefully formulated family apart.

"When Faye and David left, I was so concerned they were going to be arrested," Jim later recalled. "I didn't know what would happen. I thought David would physically be taken right out of Faye's arms and that would be devastating to her, and also, David would be returned to the reserve and we might never ever see him again.... And I thought, 'Oh, I can't stand for this little boy to grow up under the adverse conditions of an Indian reservation....' He wouldn't have a good chance in life to make much of himself."

At trial, the Tearoes' underlying theme had been that Teena's talk of learning her native culture was merely a fashionable argument designed to take advantage of the interest in native issues across the country. There had been the suggestion that she never would return to the reserve. But now that she had won, her return to the reserve seemed imminent, a source of grave concern.

Jean Morgan was at her office early on Sunday, dealing with a situation that left her personally and professionally disappointed. Exacerbating this was the moral stance the Tearoes had taken throughout the trial, and for months previous. Their rationale for keeping the child after knowing Teena wanted him back was their view that the young mother had not followed the rules. The same couple who advocated a strict adherence to the law now flouted it in as blatant a fashion as Morgan could imagine. When Teena Sawan was deemed to have broken the rules, she lost her baby. When Jim and Faye Tearoe did, nothing happened.

If a piece of paper with the words Melvin had said to them in chambers was necessary to enforce what had been, in Morgan's view, an absolutely clear court order, she resolved to get one. But it was proving more difficult than she had anticipated. It was not easy to find a judge on a sunny Sunday morning in June. Morgan was angry, sad and frustrated.

She struggled to find a way to explain to Teena, that yes, Teena had won the court case, yes, she was supposed to be at home with her son now, yes, she had followed the rules, but it still wasn't working out for her. "Teena was just so law-abiding about everything. And by being law-abiding, she got nothing. That is pretty hard to take when you are a lawyer, and you promote abiding by the law."

Morgan couldn't help but wonder what would have happened had the shoe been on the other foot, if Teena had, at some point, run with the child instead of the Tearoes. What would the reaction have been then? "It's extremely difficult to ensure faith in the system after something like this," Morgan said.

Chapter 20

Unable to find a judge on Sunday, Jean Morgan spent the afternoon and evening researching and drafting a hard-hitting, unambiguous application demanding the little boy's immediate return to his birth-mother. At 9:32 p.m., she faxed the habeas corpus motion to Brian Young's office.

At 8:30 on Monday morning, Morgan telephoned the trial co-ordinator and asked that the application be heard by Justice Melvin as soon as possible. It was put on the court list to be heard an hour later.

Brian Young was definitely not looking forward to court that morning. He had already contended with an angry Jean Morgan and was about to deal with an angry Justice Melvin. Judges expect their court orders to be obeyed, and the Tearoes' actions said, in effect, that Melvin's order was worthless.

The proceedings were short and to the point. After Morgan asked for the order outlined in her paperwork, Melvin turned his gaze to Brian Young. The judge was in no mood for excuses.

Young stood to address the judge. "I can understand Ms.

Morgan's, and in particular her client's, feelings. I had no knowledge that this would happen."

"Well, there was an agreement between your clients with me that the child would be delivered to Ms. Sawan at three o'clock Saturday afternoon," Melvin said.

"I agree," Young said. "And the child was not returned."

"And the Tearoes were informed of that," Melvin said, more statement than question.

"Yes. Mr. Tearoe is in Victoria. He doesn't know where Mrs. Tearoe is with any certainty."

"I am not concerned with that." Melvin was not going to be thrown off topic. The point was, the court order had been knowingly ignored. With this in mind, Melvin granted the habeas corpus application and left no room for misinterpretation: what he had said Saturday had been a court order. As Morgan requested, Melvin ordered that the police assist in the return of the child. Then he took matters into his own hands and gave the order the force of a legal steamroller: the police were given *carte blanche* to go wherever they had to, and detain anyone necessary, to get the child back. There was no doubt Melvin meant business.

As soon as Melvin defined the order, Morgan stood and told the court that Young was aware of the child's whereabouts.

Melvin raised his eyebrows at Young. "You do know where the child is?"

Young rose slowly. "I was told yesterday by Mr. Tearoe where he believed the child was, but he has not heard from Mrs. Tearoe, and he cannot say with any certainty."

"Are you prepared to disclose that to the court?"

"No, I'm not," Young said, indicating that he thought the conversation was covered by solicitor-client privilege.

"In defiance of a court order," Melvin said pointedly.

"I can understand your Lordship's concern, but it puts me in a difficult position."

Melvin said bluntly, "I'm concerned a bit about yourself in relation to your standing as an officer of the court." Officers of the court have an ethical obligation to observe candour

and honesty in their dealings with the court and not to subvert the administration of justice. Young asked Melvin what
he should do in the situation.

"It's not a matter of my giving you legal advice, Mr.
Young," Melvin said sternly. "You have to make your own
peace in that respect, and if you don't wish to provide the
court with the information as to where the child is, that's a
decision that you make, and you live with. Insofar as my
ordering you to disclose, I will not, at this stage, order you to
disclose. The police officers will have all the authority they
need to facilitate the terms of the order, and you heard part
of the language which I used in the course of describing the
authority which is to be given to them."

Young himself, the judge implied, could be apprehended
and questioned by the police.

Although Teena Sawan's legal costs were being paid for by
legal aid, Morgan did not think the taxpayer should have to
foot the bill for the Tearoes' running and asked for costs.
Melvin agreed. He asked that the court order be typed up as
quickly as possible.

Just after eleven o'clock, Morgan had it in her hands. She
telephoned Teena with the news as a crowd of reporters
waited on the steps of the courthouse for the lawyers to comment. "I was talking with a very brave and very disappointed mother who was dealing with a great deal of stress,"
Morgan told them. "All she wants is to see her son."

Now, it was simply a matter of finding the little boy.

A half hour later, Colwood RCMP Sergeant Bruce Brown and
Constable Doug Stack drove to the Tearoe home, a certified
copy of the order in hand. When there was no answer at the
front door, the two plainclothes officers tried the sliding glass
door at the back and found it unlocked.

The empty house was in its usual pristine state. The officers saw pictures of the boy on the refrigerator door, an oversize railway cap almost obscuring his eyes but not his
toothless smile. A piece of paper with the words " 'My God
shall supply all your needs according to his riches in glory in

Jesus Christ,' Philippians, 4:19" was alongside the photographs, held up with a magnet. The officers went upstairs
to the little boy's bedroom to see if they could get a sense of
how long Faye intended to hide.

The crib was neatly made and toys lined the dresser. Brown
slid open a dresser drawer. It was filled with neatly folded T-
shirts and pants, arranged with an inch of space between each
immaculate pile. It didn't look as if much was missing.

The officers returned downstairs and found Jim's office
phone number in an address book, conveniently placed
beside the telephone in the kitchen. Brown dialled the number. Jim was a bit disconcerted at being called by police officers and likely would have been even more so had he
realized they were standing in his kitchen. Brown read Jim
the court order demanding the child's return.

"I don't want to get into trouble," Jim said, "but I'm concerned about the safety of my son if he goes back to Alberta."

Brown listened patiently and then asked, "Are you going
to tell us where the young boy is?"

"I'm not sure," Jim answered, which the officers interpreted to mean that he knew where his wife and child were.
Jim said he had a meeting with Brian Young at one-thirty
that afternoon and that there was going to be a press conference after that.

In the ten or so child abduction cases he had investigated,
it was the first time Bruce Brown, a highly respected twenty-
three-year veteran of the force, had heard of the press being
invited to become involved. He and Stack decided to attend.

Brian Young's secretary, Teresa Westhead, handed him a
thick stack of pink message slips when he walked into the
office Monday morning. "You're famous," she joked. The
messages were from reporters across Canada, all wanting to
talk to the Tearoes.

Young knew that this was a case where, as he put it,
"image is absolutely key." Public perception was vital in
cases like this, and the media was instrumental in forming it.
Handled correctly, they could be a powerful ally. While he

wasn't necessarily going to win the case in the press, it certainly wouldn't hurt to try. Judges didn't sit in a vacuum.

By one-thirty reporters had filled the seats in the boardroom at the law office of McConnan, Bion, O'Connor and Peterson. They weren't sure what to expect; most people in Jim Tearoe's situation dodge the media like a bullet. Cameramen pushed their way to the front, as they usually do in such pack situations, and radio reporters set up their microphones near two chairs at the head of the oval table. The press conference seemed a bold tactic, coming so soon after a judge of the B.C. Supreme Court had as much as suggested that Young's clients were in contempt of court.

Jim's face showed the signs of emotional wear and tear—his eyes were tired and he was unshaven. He appeared a bit taken aback when he first walked into the room and saw the crowd, but he politely nodded at the group and took his chair. Brian Young sat beside him.

Jim quickly launched into the "other evidence" they could have called at trial about Teena's background but had chosen not to. He did not say that it was unlikely it would have been admissible, or that it came from townspeople who said it was based on gossip. Both Jim and Brian indicated that they did not know specifically where Faye and David were but said the child was safe. Although Jim said he did not want to go to jail, he was unrepentant for the actions of his family.

"It's no different, really, from you being told that it was a mistake when you went to pick up your baby in the hospital and in fact, your baby had been exchanged for another baby at day one and in fact, you have the wrong baby. In other words, you had someone else's baby. So they come to you at age year and a half and say 'Sorry, this baby belongs to this couple and not you, and we're taking your son,' whom you have believed firmly from day one is your son, they are taking him or her out of your home, just like that. Just in—in the matter of a couple of hours saying, sorry, the judge has ruled that, uh, your son belongs to somebody else, we're taking him now. What would you do?" he challenged.

Jim Tearoe expressed publicly what were to become common themes in the Tearoes' view of the situation. "Once Teena Sawan signed over her child, that's it. The child is mine. She gave him to me.... Even if the mother has got her act together, that is something after the fact. I mean, once she signed over her child, she signed over her child and that's it.... I think she's being very unfair to us. We are also very concerned about his mental attitude.... That's gonna be devastating for him to go into a family, into an environment he knows nothing of. He doesn't know these people."

His voice tightly controlled throughout, Jim said his boy's "one-quarter native" ancestry should not take precedence over his other ancestry. As for Teena wanting to know her native culture, Jim pointed out that she had lived off reserve since she was a child and was raised in white foster families. He seemed to be indicating that although she was native, she had become white by osmosis and so had no valid argument on the cultural issue. If Teena had been white, Jim said, the Alberta law about adoption revocation having to be in writing within ten days would have been upheld. "She has nothing to lose. I have everything to lose," he said. It was "not natural for the child to be in a foreign place with a woman who does not know him from Adam, really." Asked if he could see the situation from the birth-mother's point of view, Jim Tearoe said shortly, "No, I cannot."

He never declined to answer a question during the twenty-minute press conference, although he often repeated the query and was slow in answering, in part weighing his response, in part fighting fatigue. When asked what his life would be like if they didn't get the child back, Jim Tearoe came close to collapse. It seemed that the possibility had not occurred to him.

Bruce Brown and Doug Stack, who had quietly slipped into the room, took notes throughout. As the press conference wound to a close, the officers waited, notebooks open. A few of the reporters wanted a photo to go with the story, and arrangements were made with Jim. That done, the officers joined Tearoe and Young around the boardroom table.

Neither Jim nor his lawyer seemed surprised to see the officers.

Jim Tearoe was read his Charter rights and standard police warnings—essentially that he had a right to a lawyer, the right to remain silent and that anything he said may be used against him. Jim's earlier telephone conversation with the officers led them to believe that he well knew where his wife and the child were, and so he was a suspect.

Asked by Brown if he knew David's whereabouts, Jim answered, "I can only guess where he is. I understand he is in Birch Bay." Brown asked if he could be more specific. "Yes. I believe he is in the Thousand Trails Campsite in or around Birch Bay." Jim said he "wasn't exactly sure" where Birch Bay was, but that it was somewhere near Blaine, Washington.

"Is that out of Canada?" Brown asked, knowing the answer but wanting to hear it from Tearoe. Jim acknowledged that it was out of Canada.

What was already an emotionally complicated situation had just become a potential legal nightmare. Canada has an extradition policy with the United States, but enacting it was a time-consuming and convoluted process. Faye Tearoe would have to be found, and a hearing held in the United States to determine if there was a prima facie case against her, before she could be ordered extradited back to Canada. But she could appeal that, and the process could go on for months. And even if Faye were extradited to Canada, the order would not apply to the child, and getting the child back was the aim at this point.

Brown and Stack went from Young's office to the Crown counsel office to discuss the case. The applicable charge would be section 283 of the Canadian Criminal Code— abduction where there is no custody order, a charge usually laid in situations where a parent, guardian or person having the lawful care or charge of a person younger than fourteen "takes, entices away, conceals, detains, receives or harbours that person in relation to whom no custody order has been made by a court anywhere in Canada, with intent to deprive a parent or guardian, or any other person who has the lawful care or charge of that person." This section is intended to force parents to seek the assistance of the courts before taking possession of a child without the consent of the other parent and is usually used in marital custody disputes. If proceeded with by indictment, the maximum punishment is ten years in jail. (There is a defence of necessity if the person who absconded with the child can prove it was necessary to protect the young person from imminent harm.) Laying such a charge requires the consent of the attorney general or counsel instructed by him or her for that purpose. Essentially, approval for such a charge has to come from someone high up in the Crown office.

The officers discussed the circumstances with a prosecutor, reviewed the Crown counsel policy on abduction and went to the B.C. Supreme Court registry to get a copy of Justice Melvin's Saturday ruling. Brown then called a lawyer at the Crown counsel policy office, who said it was premature at that point to proceed with any charge or extradition. The police and Crown decided to wait and see if Faye Tearoe and the child returned.

The ensuing media coverage was limited by the various media: subtleties don't fit into a thirty-second news item. Reporters went with quick sketches of the people involved: Teena Sawan, single, Cree, background of alcohol use, attempting to put a tough life in order and trying to take a seemingly well-adjusted, happy child back from a middle-class, married, devout and devastated couple. The Tearoes were the focus of the story—they were the ones who, at this point, stood to lose. Besides, there were voice clips and great quotes from Jim Tearoe, and nothing from Teena Sawan. It was exactly what Brian Young had been hoping for.

The main question in newsrooms and on the street seemed to be: Who *should* get the child? It was almost as if one had to be more deserving than the other to garner a prize.

When Faye disappeared with the boy, the case became national news. Young was correct that the story had all the elements of a lead news story, and the emotional parallels with a highly publicized U.S. adoption battle were glaring.

"Baby Jessica" was born on February 8, 1991, in Iowa. Two days later, her mother, Cara Clausen, signed a maternal release for adoption. Scott Seefeldt, whom Cara named as the child's father, signed away paternal rights, and the infant was placed privately with Roberta and Jan DeBoer, an Ann Arbor, Michigan, couple who had been trying to adopt for ten years. Fifteen days after her birth, the dark-haired answer to a dream was named Jessica and went to her new home with the DeBoers. In six months, she would be legally adopted.

But within days, the arrangement began to unravel. Cara revealed that Seefeldt was not the father. Cara's former boyfriend, Dan Schmidt, was, and he wanted his daughter. Cara and Dan, newly reconciled, began an arduous battle for the return of Baby Jessica—a battle that drew international attention to the struggle between those who can and can't bear children.

Tests proved Dan was indeed the child's father, and on December 27, 1991, the Iowa District Court ordered the child returned to the birth-parents. (Under Iowa law, parental rights are paramount.) But the DeBoers obtained a legal stay of the previous order while the appeals proceeded. Jessica would stay with them until all appeals were exhausted.

By the time of the Tearoe-Sawan case in June 1993, the DeBoers' battle had been well documented in the press. Two levels of the Iowa court had ruled that Jessica should be returned to her birth-parents, who had since married and were expecting another child. The DeBoers moved their campaign to the Michigan court, where children's rights are deemed more important than parental rights, and were successful. Custody was awarded to the DeBoers on the grounds that the child had clearly bonded to them. But in March, the Michigan State appeals court threw out that order, saying that Michigan had no right to ignore the Iowa rulings.

As of June 21, 1993, while Jim Tearoe was conducting his first press conference, the DeBoers and Schmidts were awaiting decision from the Michigan Supreme Court on the litigation.

The DeBoers played the case aggressively and successfully in the press. The prospective adoptive parents were commonly viewed as the victims in the scenario. The Schmidts were portrayed as the "hayseed" Iowa couple greedily trying to rip apart a happy middle-class family, and Dan Schmidt's past—he has two children from different relationships with whom he allegedly had little contact—was prominently displayed. Like the Tearoes, the DeBoers had the moral authority of the middle class.

After talking with the police, Jim Tearoe went back to his office to finish off the work day, leaving his lawyer to file several court documents. Brian Young had worked late the night before to draft an appeal of Melvin's ruling, asking that the order be stayed and the boy be returned to the Tearoes' care pending the hearing of the appeal, much as the DeBoers had successfully done in the United States. In Young's view, possession was nine-tenths of the law, and whoever had the child when the B.C. Court of Appeal heard the case would likely keep him. Family lawyers keeping an eye on the case agreed.

Along with the appeal papers was an affidavit from Jim Tearoe, focusing on the effects on the child of a separation from Jim and Faye. "I verily believe that the child will suffer irreparable harm should he be removed so suddenly from our loving home." Even a short-term removal pending the outcome of the appeal would be detrimental, Jim wrote. As well, he and his wife should have been given time to prepare themselves for the "emotional difficulty of having to give up a child that we have loved for and cared for and bonded with for the past eighteen months," and that the child should be slowly introduced to his natural mother. It was just too much, Jim Tearoe said, to expect that they should be able to give up the boy on three hours' notice.

They were valid points, and it was the first time they had been mentioned in the case. In the case of Baby Jessica, psychologists were to be involved in any transfer of the child from the DeBoers to the birth-parents. There were also plans for the birth-parents to spend time with the girl at the

DeBoers', so she could get to know the Schmidts before any move.

Young's application would be heard on Wednesday in Vancouver. There was still no sign of where Faye and the boy were, or if they were going to return.

Another affidavit was filed on Jim's behalf by Brian Young late that Monday afternoon. In it, Jim related his version of the conversation he had had with the police officers after the press conference, and it was significantly different from the officers' version. Bruce Brown, who had taken notes throughout the interview as is customary for police officers, clearly recalled Jim saying he believed his wife was at Birch Bay. Jim Tearoe maintained in the affidavit that he had told police that Faye and the child were likely near Maple Ridge, B.C., a small town northeast of Vancouver quickly growing into a city suburb. It is unclear whether the discrepancy was an indication that Jim really did not know specifically where his wife was or whether it was an attempt to make a search more difficult.

After meeting with the Crown prosecutor, Bruce Brown and Doug Stack went to the Stay and Save Motel on the highway leading to the B.C. ferry terminal. Teena sat on the edge of the bed as the officers explained that it was very likely Faye Tearoe would return soon—her husband was here, little was missing from her home and the next court date was Wednesday. Teena nodded. There wasn't much to say, and the officers left, commenting later on the young woman's patience. To Teena, there seemed little choice. It was either accept what she was told or scream at the walls. As the small woman shut the door behind them, Brown couldn't help but wonder how intimidating it must feel to be transplanted from Manning, Alberta, where she knew everybody, to Victoria, sitting in a strange motel room not knowing where or when or if her son would ever be returned.

At 10:00 a.m. on Wednesday, Brian Young and Jean Morgan appeared before an appeal court justice. It was four days since Melvin's order, and Faye Tearoe had still not returned with David. Justice Jo-Ann Prowse made herself very clear. "This court is not going to lend its assistance to anyone who, on the face of it, is in breach of a court order." The inference was obvious: no child, no court proceedings.

Although Jim Tearoe maintained that he did not know where his wife was, it didn't take long to relay Prowse's demand to her. Brian Young went outside and, on his cellular telephone, left a detailed message with Faye's parents, who, Jim later said, passed the message "down the line" to Faye. Young needed to have confirmation that Faye had returned to Victoria before he could go back into Prowse's courtroom and ask that the hearing continue. He got it at about 3:00 p.m.

The decision for Faye and David to come home had been difficult. If they obeyed, they had to give David to Teena, but the courts would then hear their appeal. If they didn't obey, Faye and David could never come home. Returning was their only legal chance of keeping the boy, and their family together.

At about 3:30 p.m. on Wednesday, while Young was back in court arguing that the child be returned to the Tearoes pending the appeal hearing, Bruce Brown and Doug Stack were on their way to the couple's home. The officers had a court order to enforce, and Brown was determined it be done in as sensitive a manner as possible. A tired-looking Faye answered the door. Brown explained why they were there and asked if he could spend some time with the little boy before they took him to the police station, where Teena Sawan would pick him up. The sergeant couldn't live with the thought of simply swooping in and scooping up the boy. He would do whatever he could to make sure the boy wasn't scared.

Faye agreed, and made two requests of her own. Jim was at work and wouldn't be home until after four o'clock. Could the officers wait until he had a chance to say goodbye to his son before taking the boy?

Faye's second request floored Brown. The media was coming, she said, and she hoped the officers wouldn't leave with

David until the cameras arrived and their separation was filmed for the news that night. She and Jim needed to get support for their case, she explained, and that was the only way to get it. She had already called the television stations and cameras were on their way.

As the little boy played with his grandparents—Faye's mother and father were there—Brown told Faye privately that while he would certainly wait until Jim got home so he could say goodbye to the boy, Brown was not going to have the situation turned into a media circus. He was not, repeat not, going to take any part in a situation where the police were pulling on one arm of the little boy as she and Jim pulled on the other. The child was not to be used, Brown told Faye, quietly but emphatically. Had he made his feelings clear? Faye assured him he had.

Brown sat on the floor in the family room and played with David for a while. The phone rang several times, mostly reporters wanting to know what was going on. "Our little man is going soon," she said. About 4:30 p.m., the tot heard the sound of a car in the drive. Jim Tearoe drove up just as a television cameraman arrived. As Jim got out of the car, greeting the cameraman, he could hear the sound of "Daddy, Daddy" from inside the house. The little boy in the OshKosh jean overalls and brightly coloured T-shirt ran pell-mell to the door to greet his dad. It was all Jim could do not to start crying then and there, but he put on a cheery face and swung the boy up into his arms. "Daddy!" the boy said, pushing a toy car towards him.

Brown and Stack stood outside in the carport to give the Tearoes privacy to say goodbye. The door to the home was left open and cameramen walked in and out. Faye told the little boy he was going out for dinner, and wouldn't that be fun? About fifteen minutes later, they came outside and walked down the driveway, with Faye and Jim on one side of the little boy and Bruce Brown on the other.

"Do you want to go for a car ride?" Brown asked the boy who squinted in the sunlight at the cameras trained on him.

"Be a big brave boy, a big, big brave boy," Faye said

brightly as she set him in the car-seat. "You'll be back in a couple of days."

"Tomorrow. You'll be back tomorrow," Jim said, standing alongside the unmarked police car.

"Amen, tomorrow," Faye repeated as she gave David a kiss. "You'll be back tomorrow, honey. You're gonna go for a car ride. I love you, sweetheart."

Jim seemed thoroughly discombobulated. "I guess he goes to the birth-mother so that's...I kind of forgot that part," Jim said. He leaned inside the car to say goodbye. "You don't really know what's going on, do you. You think all's just normal." Jim kissed the child's forehead, smoothed his hair and said, "See you later."

Faye choked back tears but put a cheery smile on her face, waving and mouthing the words "bye-bye" as the car slowly drove off. She didn't want to alarm the little boy with tears, but she couldn't hold them back any longer as she and Jim watched the car drive away. This might be the last she would ever see of the precious child she thought of as her son, the little boy she had watched take his first step, say his first word, whose hurts she had kissed better. Inside the car, David seemed unalarmed and was playing "itsy-bitsy spider" with Bruce Brown, who had climbed in the back seat beside him.

Faye turned to the cameras and said in response to a question, "We're not giving up hope. We're just believing that indeed the courts will ..." She stopped and took a deep breath. "... rule in our favour. We'll just have to believe this is only for a night." Her hand came to her face and covered her cheek as she turned blindly towards her husband. The couple clung to each other and sobbed as the police car with young David in the back seat rounded the corner and disappeared from sight. Faye's cheek pressed tightly against her husband's, their tears blending. In between gasping cries, she said out loud, "The Lord is on our side, Jim, the Lord is on our side."

The footage that night tore at hearts across Canada. At Victoria's CHEK-TV, tears rolled down film editor Dianne Sawyer's face as she attempted to meet her deadline for the 5:30 p.m. news. She had seen a lot of tough footage in her years at the job but had never been so touched by anything before. "You learn to let things just wash over you. But this is the one story I will never forget. I remember the day those pictures came in; everyone standing watching the TV screen had tears running down their face. They were handing me kleenex so I could edit the story and get it on the air." Sawyer's job is to work with the reporter, deciding which pictures are appropriate to accompany the story. But the narrative mattered very little this time. The pictures would carry it all. "Seeing someone's child taken away from them, that mother's grief.... I thought it had to go on the air. People had to see what this family was going through. It was hard not to be biased when you see pictures like this."

John Jordan, who had had virtually no dealings with the couple since handing over the file to Brian Young six months before, could barely eat his dinner. "I was devastated to see what they were going through.... I just couldn't believe this was happening," recalled Jordan. "Maybe not everyone would agree with their religious stance but they are principled people, they are honourable people." Jordan has since refused to practice adoption law. "After what I have seen in the Tearoe-Sawan case, you know, the heartache in the family.... I'm not thick-skinned enough. There is just too much heartache and heartbreak and I want to be able to sleep at night. There is enough pressure in practising law without having to worry about that."

Lex Reynolds, the president of the B.C. chapter of the Adoptive Parents Association and the father of a six-year-old adopted son, had a mixed reaction when he saw the news footage. His instinctive empathy for anyone suffering as the Tearoes demonstrated they were was tempered with a healthy dose of scepticism about intentions. "Somebody purposely made it a media event and I don't know why or how, but when that happens, I always look for intention. Somebody has a reason. It seemed to me that the Tearoes were very effective in utilizing the media...I guess I thought they were performing."

One of Reynolds' several concerns was for the privacy of

the child. "People know information about David that he
doesn't even know yet, and the public shouldn't be entitled
to that. I can't see how that is in his best interests. Everybody
is talking about doing things in the best interests of the child
and no one thinks about the privacy rights of the child. He
won't have a choice years from now, on whether he wants to
share this part of his life with a friend. It will have already
been done for him, and he had no choice in it at all."

Whatever the Tearoes' sincerity and motivation, they were
successful in making their point in the court of public opinion. The reaction was swift and harsh. Having an understanding of the facts was not a prerequisite for people to
condemn one side or the other, and it was usually Teena
Sawan on the receiving end of the denunciation. The public's
reaction to her was largely based on stereotype. She was the
epitome of every adoptive parent's nightmare: a birth-
mother taking her baby back. Wasn't adoption supposed to
be permanent? The public perception was that the adoption
had been completed—which it had not—and that Teena
Sawan had decided, suddenly and long afterwards, that she
wanted her child back. To look clearly at the issues involved
in Teena Sawan's attempts to regain her child required looking at the facts behind the emotionally charged situation. The
Tearoes' tears had to be ignored, something very difficult to
do. There were very few people who said that either parent
could provide a home, so different from each other that they
might well have been on different planets, but each acceptable in their own way. It became a matter of judgment.

The case had none of the intrigue of a high-profile murder,
no blood or guts to titillate people. But it tapped into people's
primal instincts. Parents went home at night and looked at
their children, and tried to imagine how it would feel to lose.

Courthouse personnel, used to drama, couldn't stop talking about it. Radio talk shows and newsrooms were inun-
dated with calls about the case. Said one newspaper editor,
"You know what Teena Sawan is after, don't you? A $100,000
payoff from the Tearoes. Then she'll leave the kid alone."

The case began to symbolize, in the public's mind, much

bigger concerns than either party had ever intended. It had not started out, for either Teena Sawan or for Jim and Faye Tearoe, as a political issue. They just wanted, with all their hearts, that little boy. Suddenly, Teena was fighting for all native kids that had been taken from their families and put in white homes. She had become a symbol for a changing social climate, with all the attendant fears and prejudices. The Tearoes were now speaking for the rights of adoptive parents across the nation. Some people viewed the case as pitting the validity of an adoptive family against a biological family, when this had never been the argument. No one in the case has ever suggested that an adoptive family was not a family.

Debates raged: What constitutes the best home for a child? How does someone make that decision? At what point is it harmful to remove a child from the only home and parents he or she has ever known? Was a child as strong as forged steel or as fragile as a teacup? In the Baby Jessica case, psychologists predicted dire consequences for the little girl if she were moved. Although there had been no psychological evidence called in the Tearoe-Sawan case, those predictions were carried over by the public.

Many people said they would have done exactly what Faye Tearoe did—run. Some people who agreed with Teena Sawan in principle still questioned how a mother could remove a child who already viewed certain people as Mommy and Daddy, a child who, for all obvious intents and purposes, seemed secure and adjusted. Very few asked themselves, "Would I have refused to return the baby when Teena Sawan called and asked for him back, eight days after giving him up? Would I have ignored that mother when I knew she had a legal right to his return?"

A common comment was that Melvin's decision had been politically correct, that anything native had become sacred. This was strongly believed by the Tearoes, who to this day believe that the judge was frightened of "the Indian issue," as Faye calls it. Some suggested that Teena Sawan was a pawn of the native movement, who wanted nothing more than to make political hay, implying that the "Indian band" was some malevolent force behind the case. Jean Morgan found such comments upsetting. She had heard directly from the Woodland Cree band only once in the months before and during the trial, and that was when they had informed her that they would pay for Teena's travel costs to Victoria. Morgan did talk periodically to Donna Ominayak and Dolly LeTendre. "But I never received any lectures or directions from them. The only native person I took instructions from was my client."

What seemed to draw the most anger from people was that Teena Sawan dared "use" her heritage as a native Indian to try to take something from the white world—especially a child who could conceivably be seen as white. "Why put a blond-haired, blue-eyed child on an Indian reserve? How will he fit in? Why do that to a child?" was a question heard repeatedly. The inference seemed to be that if the boy didn't look native, why make him native? One has to wonder how different the public perception and reaction would have been given a simple twist of genetics, if the baby had inherited his mother's dark brown hair, her dark eyes. Would he then have looked sufficiently native for people to say that Teena Sawan had a valid point?

If it is said that Teena Sawan "used" the fact that she is native to win the court case, could not a similar argument be made about the Tearoes? People walking into a courtroom tend to use whatever advantages they have at their disposal, and there is no doubt that Jim and Faye Tearoe employed their arsenal of middle-class values and achievements with a vengeance. All the public saw was a well-kept suburban home, a stay-at-home mom, a dad who left each morning for his white-collar job—all being ripped apart by a native.

The media's role as an image vendor was never so important. The middle-class portrait would be used against Teena Sawan for all it was worth.

Chapter 21

While the Tearoes had looked directly into the camera's lens, Teena Sawan ignored its eye as she walked out of the covered parking bay at the Colwood RCMP station, her son finally in her arms. She had little interest in the press. Jean Morgan's husband, Dan, was angry that the media wouldn't leave Teena and the child alone, and stood in between the mother and child and the cameras. In that night's news coverage, all the public saw of Teena Sawan was the side of her face, the little boy on her hip. In terms of emotional impact, the clip couldn't hold a candle to the scene of the grieving Tearoes.

As they left the police station, Teena heaved a sigh of relief. She still couldn't quite believe that Jordan was with her. It was Wednesday, June 23; Teena had slept little in the four nights since Justice Melvin's decision, wondering where her son was, and then thinking about the best way to deal with what Jordan would be going through. The Tearoes obviously loved him and he them. But she loved him too. She would make him feel cared for and wanted. She planned to introduce herself to him as Teena. She would start by being his friend and take it from there.

Teena, Jordan, Dolly and Donna said goodbye to Sergeant Bruce Brown, who had carefully watched out of the corner of his eye for signs of upset in the boy and seen none. Teena too had watched for any signs of distress—had, indeed, been expecting them—and was comforted that the boy seemed not at all upset by the strange faces.

The group went to Jean Morgan's home, where the boy chased the lawyer's rather hefty cats, laughing loudly as his feet stomped on the hardwood floors. They sat in the back yard, and after a while, the boy climbed up on Donna Ominayak's lap, grabbing at her long braid and trying to put it in his mouth. Donna called the little boy "*napiss.*" "It's Cree for little boy," Donna explained. Teena repeated the word. It was foreign to her tongue, as was the name David for the son she had thought of only as Jordan. Teena tried to call her child David but sometimes slipped and called him Jordan, hastily adding David. It came out as Jordan-David, and he still responded, so Jordan-David it became.

According to the court order, Teena had custody of her son, but how long she could keep him would depend on the ruling given by appeal court Justice Jo-Ann Prowse. Arguments were to continue before Prowse the next day, Thursday, on where the boy would remain until the Tearoes' appeal of Justice Melvin's decision was heard in two weeks. Until Prowse made her ruling, the boy was to stay with Teena, but with the proviso that he not be taken out of the court's jurisdiction, which is the province of British Columbia. Morgan had argued against this, largely on principle. Faye Tearoe had run, yet it was Teena Sawan who was being told what she could and couldn't do with the child she had legal custody of.

Teena, Dolly, Donna and Jordan went to the motel, and a crib was brought to their room. Teena settled her son in, standing by the railing, watching as he slowly drifted off. As she lay down, Teena made a list of all the items she would need. The only baby things she had were those she'd bought Saturday, before going to pick up Jordan. But Miles' sister-in-law, Carrie, who was going to babysit Jordan while Teena went to school, was going to lend her a crib, clothes and whatever else she needed when they returned to Manning.

The next morning, Teena woke early and listened. There wasn't a sound from Jordan-David. Boy, he was a good sleeper, she thought, as she looked towards the crib beside her bed. She saw the little boy sitting up, gazing at her silently. Teena stared back and smiled. After a few seconds, he reached his hand towards her. "Truck?" he said. After breakfast, the reunited pair had a pretty ordinary day, playing, napping, going to the park, all the while waiting for Morgan to call with Prowse's decision.

The second night was much the same as the first. Teena found herself at times just staring at the little boy. As she gave him a bath, she marvelled at things that later seemed silly—the length of his legs, how his shoes were real shoes, with rubber treads on the bottom that he could actually stand up and walk and run in. She felt the same wonder now as when he had come from her body. Then, she hadn't been able to believe that he actually had ten fingers and ten toes, earlobes and eyelashes. Now, his pink gums were sharp with teeth, his hands plump and wide. It was as if he had come from the womb again, at a new stage of development.

Teena tried not to think about the fact that their fate would soon be determined by another judge's decision. She tried to put the appeal out of her mind.

The high-chair sat empty beside Heidi at the dinner table. "Thank you Lord, for returning David to us," the family prayed. If they prayed long and hard enough for something, it would come to pass.

Calls flooded the home. Many were from fellow Christians, telling the family they were in their prayers. Others were from strangers who had been shocked by what they had seen on television. "People couldn't believe what we had gone through," the Tearoes said. Friends stopped by to offer their support and prayer on Thursday, the first entire day any of the family could remember spending without David. One woman told Faye she had seen a vision of the Lord riding on a chariot, plumes of fire trailing behind him. They interpreted it as a positive sign of the little boy's imminent return.

Teena and Jordan were sitting on the carpet playing on Friday morning when the phone rang. Teena ignored it and kept moving the mini-dumptruck towards her son. She could hear Donna. "Uh-hmmm, okay," Donna said. Silence. Teena glanced up. Donna didn't look unhappy. Maybe it was good news. She looked away just as Donna said, "Oh, no."

Teena abruptly got up and went into the bathroom, locking the door behind her and turning on the faucet. No, no, no. She did not want to hear this. Donna tapped on the door and asked if she was okay.

"Leave me alone." A few minutes later, Donna knocked again and said quietly that Jean wanted to talk to Teena. Teena grabbed a towel, held it over her face and inhaled deeply a few times before setting it down and walking out to the telephone.

"Teena, I'm so sorry," Jean Morgan said. She sounded as miserable as Teena felt. "The judge said she doesn't doubt for a moment that you love Jordan, but she thinks it will be the least disruptive for him to remain with the Tearoes until the appeal is heard and decided. I'm just so sorry."

Teena said through her tears that she was glad to have Morgan as her lawyer and then hung up the phone and went to the bathroom to wash her face. She didn't want her son to become upset by her tears. Teena could hear him chatting in the next room, making little sense but talking nonetheless. She went out and sat down on the floor with him again, pulling him to her lap. She wanted to cry and squeeze him as hard as she could. Instead, she made *vrooming* sounds with a plastic car on the shag rug.

Dolly and Donna packed up the clothes, diapers and toys. Dan would drive Jordan back to the Tearoes. It would be easier for everyone, Teena decided, if she and Jordan said their goodbyes at the motel, in private. Teena didn't think she could bear to hand over her son again to the Tearoes, and she was sure they didn't want to see her.

It wasn't long before Dan arrived and Jordan's things were packed in the car. Donna and Dolly hugged him and said, "We'll see you soon." Teena climbed into the back seat of the car and held Jordan to her chest. She didn't know if this might be the last she would see of her son. She wished he had been able to meet his family, that Grace and Peter could have seen their little nephew.

"Never feel alone, Jordan," she said, fingers touching his smooth face. "You'll always have me, always, whatever happens in your life."

Jordan gazed around at the three crying women. As Teena had done sixteen months before at Carolyn Grayson's, she kissed him on the temple and whispered again that she loved him. Then she settled him into the car-seat, gave him a toy and shut the door. As he waved bye-bye, Teena held one hand over her mouth and waved with the other.

Television cameras and reporters from three stations congregated at the Tearoes' on Friday morning, waiting with Faye for Justice Prowse's decision. Faye was cordial and welcoming and knew several by name, having supplied them with coffee and quotes. She sat humming in a rocking chair in the family room when the telephone rang. Jim had received the decision at work and called home. Faye lifted a triumphant fist in the air as Jim relayed Prowse's decision. "Woooooo! Isn't the Lord wonderful! Praise the Lord!" she cried.

Dan arrived within the hour. He carried the child up to the door, turning away from the television cameras, and quickly stepped inside the house. Tears glazed Faye's eyes as she held David close to her heart. The tot gazed around quietly. He had slept during the half-hour drive from the motel to the Tearoes', and was still waking up.

Jim was soon home, and David ran out to the car in his sock feet, a big smile on his face. "I guess that's okay, just this once, him going outside without shoes," Faye fretted.

"Daddy, daddy," the boy called. Jim squeezed the boy so tightly, the tot started to squirm, and Jim laughed as he set him down.

"Our little man is back. We just love our little man and he loves us," Jim told reporters inside the house as David bounced on his knee. Jim placed the boy at the piano stool and urged him to play. "I don't know why he's not playing. He just loves to," he said, as the boy put his fingers in this mouth and gazed at reporters and at the cameras pointed at him.

Getting David back into their home was the Lord's first step in righting a wrong done by Justice Melvin, the Tearoes told reporters. The pair were already praying for the B.C. Court of Appeal justices who would hear their appeal in two weeks. Jim and Faye made sense of the situation and their heartbreak this way: the Lord meant for all of this to happen so that the Tearoes would include the worldwide judiciary in their daily prayers. "The Lord knew we were strong and the Lord uses things, and I believe he wanted to change some things in the court system, and we now pray for the court system in Canada and all over the world. We pray that judges would rule justly, according to the way God wants them to judge, and this is not easy, because they could be bribed, they could be frightened of an Indian issue," Faye said. "I'm praying that...there is going to be a change in the justice system to help other people who adopt so they don't have to go through what we did. Because you know something? People that aren't Christians that had to go through this, it would be totally devastating to them. People that don't have the Lord...good Lord, they would commit hari-kari between now and then! What happens to your marriage by the time you get the child and it's all settled and the child is yours...now you go file for divorce because you don't know who is who any more! I mean, the Lord has held Jim and I together. When I'm weak, he's strong. I'll say, 'Honey, how did you ever manage to handle that? You were so clever.' And when I do something, he says, 'Honey, I'm so proud of you.' He said to me, 'I'll only say it once. Honey, I'm so proud of you that you ran with our son.'

"We don't look at things the way others in the world do," Faye said later. "We don't blame Teena. If you're going to blame someone, blame Satan. I'm sure Judge Melvin felt he should have ruled towards us but was swayed to her side by the political issue. I don't blame Judge Melvin. I would hate to be a judge, to be put in the positions they are in, and they are not God.... The Lord can lead you, but he cannot make anybody do anything. He allowed Adam to have a mind of his own, he's also allowed Judge Melvin to have a mind of his own. Even though we fasted and prayed, that man decided beforehand, but that's not for me to say."

The Lord always has a plan, Faye said, and His plan for David is that he be a pastor. "When we named David, we both prayed he would serve the Lord. We hope he is a pastor. I hope he goes back into his nation, his Indian nation, and goes and saves those people. I really do."

Asked if she thought they needed saving, Faye said, "They don't serve the God we serve, do you think?" adding quickly, "I mean, some of them do, I mean, many, many, many of them do, I'm sure."

Faye whisked David out of the outfit he was brought back in and into the bath, where he received a vigorous scrub. "He just reeked of cigarette smoke," she said. But that was the least of his troubles, in Faye's view.

"When David came back, he wouldn't look us in the eye for days. He was much less trustful. It must have been a fine time he had, I can't think they would treat him awful. But if he wanted to see Mommy and Daddy, why wouldn't they come get him? This is what hurt him. He must have got really scared. He never slept for about a week after. I'd put him down for a nap, and he was up all the time. There was no morning or afternoon nap, he was up at eleven at night."

Faye turned to prayer. "I asked the Lord to give our David peace and he slept. After I prayed, he calmed right down and slept for days." She also said that the boy had a "red rash from his neck to his privates. We don't want to blame anybody, but you kind of wonder."

Jean Morgan heard the comments on the television news. "They broke my heart, because Teena loves that little boy and would give up her life for him. I don't have any doubt about that. I saw them together and she absolutely loves that child. There was a real calmness between them.... She loves Jordan for just being Jordan, and what more could a child want, than just to be loved for who you are and not for who you may be one day, or what you may look like, or whose name you may carry?"

Teena Sawan flew back to Alberta on June 26, the day after having to return Jordan to the Tearoes. It was too expensive to continue staying in Victoria, and she had already stayed a week longer than anticipated. The B.C. Court of Appeal had agreed to an unprecedented summer sitting on July 6, but neither Jean nor Brian expected the appeal court to give its decision the same day. There was no telling how long it would take. Teena was also homesick; she wanted to be with Miles, Grace and Peter. She and Miles talked on the phone every day, and he was worried about Teena. The day she gave Jordan back to the Tearoes, she'd barely talked.

Back in Manning, Teena watched the television news at Ralph and Bea Cowie's and heard Faye Tearoe's comments about Jordan having a rash and not sleeping. Her first response was one of genuine concern. "A rash? What's wrong? Has something happened to him?" Then she realized they were intimating that she had provided inadequate care. She had bathed him several times and had seen no rash on his tiny body. Did they think she would hurt her own child?

Bea Cowie made her feelings known with a shake of her head as she walked out of the room. Ralph Cowie watched Teena out of the corner of his eye. His first impression of the Tearoes had plummeted as he watched the couple on television. "Probably the biggest disappointment was—and I should have expected it—was it just got dirtier and dirtier," he reflected. "Every time I'd hear another story about the Tearoes bad-mouthing Teena in their nice way—it was pretty upsetting. I guess that's when I started to lose respect for them. I'd been pretty impressed with them up until then, as good parents, good people. They were using the media to make themselves look good, and Teena look so bad. Why do that? Why try and destroy somebody else? How is that going to help that little boy?"

Support for the Tearoes was public and apparent. The telephone at the couple's home rang off the hook and Faye's ear grew tender from the receiver. She ended each call with a cheerful "God bless you."

"The calls we got were just amazing—amazing! Everyone agreed with what I did, when I ran with David. They said they would have done exactly the same thing!" She said there was "maybe one call out of, oh my goodness, *hundreds* who didn't agree with us having David." That phone call left Faye dizzy and she refuses to repeat what was said. A stack of letters sits by the telephone from people across Canada, supporting their case. Supporters wrote to B.C. Attorney General Colin Gabelmann asking him to intervene on the Tearoes' behalf; others wrote to Justice Melvin and to the B.C. Court of Appeal, which had yet to hear the case.

Faye watched one night of television coverage, taped by her sister-in-law, and couldn't watch any more. "You pray one thing and you see another, and it was just too hard to handle. You get too wrapped up in what the people think instead of what you think and you have to remove yourself from it."

In the legal community, the fact that no charges were laid against the Tearoes was commonly attributed to the power of a middle-class image, rather than an act of the Lord, though the Tearoes credited the latter.

The Crown counsel office reviewed the case with police and decided against charges, largely because Faye Tearoe did come back and the child was returned to his birth-mother in accordance with the court order, albeit five days late. But speculation in legal circles noted the messiness of charging Faye, who much of the public viewed as a victim of an unfeeling justice system and a birth-mother trying to rip her family apart, as important factors in the decision.

The "Crown Counsel Policy Manual" has a three-page set of guidelines for dealing with abduction of children when no custody order exists. According to the guidelines, consent to prosecute the charge will be limited to such situations in which the potential accused is a repeat offender; there is a possibility the child is in danger of harm from the abductor; there is reason to believe the person with the child is about to take that child to another country; or the whereabouts of the abducting person and child are unknown for "some extended period." The evidence to prove such must be available.

In order to lay an abduction charge, the consent of the attorney general, or counsel approved by the attorney general, must be given.

"It should be borne in mind," the policy says, "that by requiring consent, Parliament has indicated its intention that not all cases of child abduction by a parent, guardian, etc. in the absence of a custody order should constitute a criminal offence. Nevertheless, some child custody disputes in the absence of a custody order are considered crimes." It is unclear whether Faye Tearoe would have been considered, at that point in the process, a parent or legal guardian.

In addition to the criteria specifically related to abduction charges, there are several standard criteria looked at before approving any charge. They include that the charge be in the "public interest," a subjective term, and that there be a substantial likelihood of conviction. On these two grounds, it was felt that a charge was inappropriate.

The fact that Justice Melvin's order was not conveyed directly to the Tearoes in court made it difficult, in the Crown's view, to prove that Faye Tearoe had knowledge of it—a prerequisite for charges of contempt or abduction. If she had been told about it, it would have been by her lawyer, a communication that would be protected by solicitor-client privilege.

Once again, the Tearoes had put their faith in the fact that a piece of paper with official words written on it was not received. Once again, it had worked in their favour.

Whatever rationalizations the powers-that-be used for not proceeding with charges, it is abundantly clear that Faye

Tearoe knew about the initial order given in Melvin's chambers on the Saturday. Her own lawyer had acknowledged that in court the following Monday. And Jim Tearoe had said candidly in a court document that he chose to contravene the "clarified" court order, given by Melvin on the Monday following the decision: "My wife is presently on the lower Mainland and has the child with her. I recognize that this is contrary to the decision of Mr. Justice Melvin. I further recognize that this is contrary to the order of Mr. Justice Melvin pronounced on June 21, 1993." A charge of contempt of a court order does not seem far-fetched, yet it never materialized.

With the B.C. Court of Appeal hearing set for July 6, Young and Morgan were left scrambling to prepare. The lawyers had a little over two weeks to get transcripts of the trial, prepare exhibit books, documents and appeal arguments—a process that usually takes months. Brian Young ordered the trial transcript—needed to make his appeal argument—on June 25 and worked steadily after that. Morgan received Young's appeal argument and case-book authorities on Friday, July 2. She had until the Monday to read and study the transcript and prepare her response. Both barristers had to be ready to argue the appeal on Tuesday. Fellow lawyers let out a sympathetic gasp when they learned of the abbreviated time span.

As they waited for the appeal, the Tearoes had second thoughts about their lawyer. Some of that stemmed from the comments of Pastor Kelly Taylor, who had overcome an initial reluctance and gathered a few names at Jim's request and passed them along as people who may have information about Teena. When no effort was made to contact these people, Taylor questioned Young's thoroughness. The Tearoes confronted Young with this criticism, and he explained that it was very difficult to call new evidence at an appeal. An appeal is based on arguing that the trial judge erred in law, he explained to the Tearoes, who now wanted to fly Manning people down to disparage Teena at the appeal. Young reminded the couple that they had had the option of subpoenaing witnesses from Manning for the original trial but had chosen not to because of cost. At that time, the Tearoes had wanted only witnesses who could pay their own way.

Jim and Faye turned to the Lord. They had a prayer meeting. "Lord," they asked, "should we fire our lawyer?" The Lord said no. Unconvinced, they had a second meeting. Again, the Lord said no.

Young flew to Vancouver the afternoon before the appeal and checked in at the elegant Four Seasons Hotel, a block from the courthouse. He worked for a while, then went for a swim. As he did laps and tried to unwind, he went over his argument for the next day. He had several appeal grounds, but the focus was his contention that Justice Melvin had failed to adequately consider the issue of bonding between the Tearoes and the little boy, and had placed too much emphasis on native culture when Teena Sawan had not demonstrated that she was actually involved in it. After a twenty-minute swim, his head was starting to clear.

When Young got back to his room, there was an urgent message waiting for him. It was from his secretary, saying that a Dr. Daniel Bester from Manning, Alberta, had called that afternoon for Young. Young had no idea who Dr. Bester was and paid little attention to the message. He went out for sushi and a walk.

When he returned, there was another urgent message from his secretary. He was to call Dr. Bester immediately.

Within minutes, Young's earlier reflections on the case were forgotten. His entire plan for the next day changed with that call.

Chapter 22

The day of the appeal dawned grey and drizzling—typical Vancouver weather, for which Brian Young had not come prepared. He snapped open the umbrella borrowed from the hotel front desk and hustled the two blocks to the courthouse. He had been up until the early morning hours, figuring out how to deal with the information that had been passed on to him by Dr. Bester. He'd sought advice from a friend who was "high up" in the legal profession and quickly come to a conclusion: despite what Young had told the Tearoes earlier about the difficulty of calling new evidence at an appeal, he would make an application to the court to do just that. He had information about Teena Sawan that would, he thought, be of enormous interest. Even if the evidence wasn't allowed, wafting the scent of perjury in the courtroom couldn't hurt.

Television cameras waited for the Tearoes outside the main entrance to the Smithe Street courthouse. A cameraman called out to Brian, who clearly enjoyed the press attention, asking where his clients were. "Jim's on his way and Faye's at home with David," he said, swinging open the double doors into the low-ceilinged courthouse lobby. "Stick around," he thought as he walked across the lobby towards the bulletin board, "there'll be more news later."

The myriad of white sheets stapled to the cork-board near the security guard's desk mapped out the day for the seven-floor courthouse. Young was anxious to see which three judges would be hearing the appeal and quickly scanned the lists. Though he had maintained throughout the battle that the "law is on my side," he knew that much of the case was being fought on emotion. He hoped for three justices who had hearts somewhere near the surface.

Although justice is supposed to be blind, judges often take very different views on the very same set of facts. Certainly, the idea that judges are impartial judicial machines is a fallacy. Every judge brings into the courtroom his or her personal background, biases, idiosyncrasies, pet peeves, along with good and bad moods and personal leanings one way or another, warranted or not.

Young quickly spotted *Tearoe v. Sawan* on the board and the names Justice Anne Rowles, Justice Josiah Wood and Justice Patricia Proudfoot. He was thrilled. Young automatically thought women would be more sympathetic to the Tearoes' situation than men and hoped that Rowles' and Proudfoot's family law backgrounds would work in his favour. Wood's background was in criminal law, but his appeal court judgments were earning him a reputation as a liberal. Young thought his chances were good.

Morgan, too, was pleased when she checked the board a few minutes later. All three justices had reputations for being thoughtful and thorough. It was, a judge later commented, one of the most "humane" panels that could have been assembled.

Morgan stopped outside the elevator doors and popped what had to be her tenth throat lozenge since getting up that morning at 6:00 a.m. to catch the flight from Victoria to Vancouver. A cold and flu bug that would have had her flat on her back under normal circumstances had plagued her throughout the appeal preparations. She hoped the lozenges would ward off a coughing attack in the courtroom and soothe her throat enough that her already soft voice would be audible. In her hands was a copy of that morning's *Times-Colonist*, Victoria's daily newspaper. She had found a most interesting article on page A3, one she planned to show to Young.

As Morgan walked towards courtroom 60, she saw Brian Young headed her way. They exchanged hellos, and then Young said, "Your client is a liar."

"What are you talking about?" The comment came out of nowhere, and was especially surprising coming from the man who had come up to Teena Sawan at the end of the trial and said she would make a good mother.

"I'm applying to call new evidence. Her doctor phoned me and I'm going to get medical evidence," he said, dropping the legal bombshell in Morgan's lap. Morgan had no idea what he was talking about.

He told her an affidavit would be at the courthouse shortly. The information in it would show, Young said, that Teena had perjured herself and wasn't a fit mother. The lawyers had to be in court in a few minutes, and there was little time to discuss details. It seemed to Morgan like trial by ambush.

As they stood in the courtroom, waiting for the justices, Jean handed Young the newspaper, pointing to an article with the headline, "Tearoes say they might flee if birth mother wins custody." Jim Tearoe was quoted as saying the Tearoes would likely run with the boy again if they did not win at the appeal court. The comments substantiated what Jean Morgan had suspected all along. The Tearoes were governed by a court they deemed higher than the one for regular folk. It seemed like a ploy to hold the court up for ransom: "If you don't do it our way, we'll run again." Sometimes she cynically wondered what they were doing in court—the only law they followed was one of their own, and it seemed to work for them.

Young quickly scanned the article. "Great," he inwardly groaned, hoping the appeal court judges hadn't seen it. That sort of comment definitely would not look good on his

clients. His only consolation was that the article was in a
Victoria newspaper and not in one of the two Vancouver
dailies. He turned to Jim, who was sitting in the front row of
the court, and quickly and quietly gave him specific advice—
do not, repeat do NOT, talk to the press again without me
being there. The Tearoes were becoming more difficult to
control, and that would hurt their public image.

Despite Brian's preference that Jim stay at home for the
appeal, he had travelled to Vancouver on the ferry that
morning. He wanted to get into the courtroom early to pray
for the judges but had to wait until the clerk opened the
doors at a few minutes before ten o'clock. Then, Jim walked
up and looked at the judges' chairs on a raised platform at
the front of the courtroom, marvelling at the view from the
bench. He took a seat in the public gallery and quickly said a
prayer for the judiciary, adding a request that the medical
evidence Brian told him about be allowed in.

The appeal court justices walked in from a side entrance
promptly at ten o'clock and took their chairs: Justice
Proudfoot in the middle, Joe Wood to her right and Anne
Rowles to her left. Given that it was a specially convened sitting of the appeal court, the justices were more than a little
surprised when Young's first request was for an adjournment. He had new evidence he wished to call, he quickly
explained. Young knew the court was none too pleased with
his adjournment request and said, "The potential new evidence is crucial to this case in determining what is in the best
interests of the child."

Morgan stood and told the panel that she was ready to
proceed with the appeal and had just ten minutes before
received oral notice of Young's intentions.

The justices asked Young to explain the gist of the proposed new evidence, and he handed up an affidavit sworn
by Bruce McConnan, passing one to Morgan as well. It was
the first she had seen of it. In that document, McConnan—
one of the partners in the law firm for which Young
worked—said that he had spoken to Dr. Daniel Bester on the
phone that very morning, at about 9:15. McConnan outlined

their conversation, the details of which would become very important as time wore on. In the sworn court document, McConnan says:

I was advised by Dr. Bester, and do verily believe to be true, that he has been the physician to the respondent Cecilia Augustine Sawan in Manning, Alberta for the past two years.

Dr. Bester advised me, and I do verily believe to be true, he first heard of this custody application and subsequent appeal on Saturday July 3, 1993 and contacted Brian D. Young, solicitor for the appellants on Monday, July 5, 1993 by telephone during the early evening hours.

Dr. Bester advised me, and I do verily believe it to be true, he has testimony to give, and records to produce, which, in his opinion, demonstrate that it is not in the child's best interests to return to the respondent as the evidence he has to give conflicts with the testimony given by her at trial.

Dr. Bester advised me, and I do verily believe to be true, he has spoken to the Alberta College of Physicians and Surgeons concerning the possible breach of a patient to doctor relationship and he feels he cannot disclose specific evidence without court order.

I am advised by Dr. Bester, and I do verily believe to be true, he has pertinent and relevant evidence which directly relates to the competency of the respondent to care for the infant child and impacts upon the testimony she gave at trial.

Young told the justices that the doctor had telephoned him the night previous, having read about Teena Sawan's attempts to get her child back in a July 3, 1993, newspaper article. A "pang of conscience" prompted the doctor's call, Young told the court.

The judges asked Young to specify what evidence Bester could provide, but Young again said that Bester was reluctant to go into any detail without a court order, due to doctor-patient confidentiality. However, Young said, the doctor had indicated it would show that Teena had committed perjury. With a court order, Bester could divulge more.

"He has already breached that confidentiality," said Justice Joe Wood. "The court is not here to get doctors off the hook. The doctor has to deal with his own conscience and the rules of the Alberta Medical Association. That is his problem, not ours."

Jean Morgan was stunned. She couldn't believe that a doctor would call up the lawyer on the opposing side of a contentious court case involving his patient. Her gut reaction was that it was a breach of confidentiality looking for cover of a court order.

Rowles leaned forward in the high-backed chair, her face concerned as she looked at the lawyers. Proudfoot looked over her glasses at the two-page affidavit in front of her, lips pursed. Morgan asked for a fifteen-minute recess so that she could call her client and take instructions, and the justices filed out, not more than five minutes after they'd first walked in.

As Morgan walked quickly to the barristers' lounge to call Teena, she wracked her brain for any case law allowing a doctor to pass information to a lawyer. As far as she knew, the only way a doctor could release medical information about a patient was with the patient's consent, or by court order. There was clearly no court order at this point. Jean got in touch with Teena quickly and asked if she had signed any document for a Dr. Bester to release medical information about her. No, said Teena, she hadn't signed anything. What was Jean talking about? Morgan told Teena that Young was alleging that she had committed perjury. "Is there anything, anything involving alcohol?" Morgan took her oath of legal integrity extremely seriously. If there was contrary information, she would present it to the court.

Teena went over her evidence in her mind. She had been asked when she'd had her last drink and testified it had been on her birthday, two weeks before the trial. She'd been asked the last time she drank to excess and said New Year's Eve. But she hadn't been asked, and hadn't volunteered, information about the accident in February, when she had been driving her friend's vehicle and had been drinking.

All right, Morgan said, when Teena told her of it. She would have to tell the court about that. She suggested Teena go to Bester's office and look at the documents to see what he was alleging. Morgan would call her back that afternoon.

When court resumed, Morgan told of the February incident, and then focused her submission on the legalities of Young's application for new evidence. She pointed out that the mechanics of the process had not been followed: there were no documents filed and she had not been given adequate notice that such an application was going to happen. Then she moved on to what was, in her view, the substantive issue. The information from Dr. Bester, she argued, did not meet the requirements for the introduction of new evidence. An appeal is not a rehearing of the trial issues. While evidence from the lower court trial can be reviewed, the appeal court exists primarily to remedy mistakes in law or errors in interpretation of legislation made by the trial judge. For that reason, there are rules regarding the introduction of new evidence at the appeal level. For starters, it must be shown that "reasonable diligence" was used to find the evidence before the actual trial that is under appeal. If the evidence could have led the trial judge to come to a conclusion different from the one that was reached, then a new trial may be ordered.

The due diligence test for allowing in new evidence at appeal is reasonably strict for a simple reason: if it weren't, trials could go on forever, with lawyers for the losing side simply retrying their case on issues they feel they did not present adequately at trial. Such was the case now, argued Morgan. Brian Young and the Tearoes had known that alcohol use was a factor in Teena's life. That was clear from the beginning of the trial and evident in the affidavits filed months before the actual hearing. In April 1993, Young wrote to Dr. Hallinen, asking that she apprise him of any information she had that would be helpful for the Tearoes in the upcoming trial. Young received no reply from the doctor and nothing further was done. He had assumed that Hallinen was Teena Sawan's doctor, as she had delivered the baby on December 3, 1991. It would have taken little effort, Morgan suggested, to find out who Teena Sawan's regular GP had been, especially in a town of 1,200 people where there are only three doctors. He had not met the test of due diligence, she argued. As well, Young had had an opportunity to cross-examine Teena on alcohol use at trial and done so. And Teena Sawan's difficulties with alcohol had been acknowledged and taken into consideration at trial by Justice Melvin. They were not something new.

Justice Rowles interjected. "It is important to her ability to care for the child if she has an ongoing alcohol problem."

Morgan said she did not know specifically what Bester's allegations were so could not comment on their relevance, but it seemed like a "fishing expedition."

The justices were obviously troubled by Young's request. They took a break, and it extended from the usual twenty minutes to close to an hour. Although the B.C. Court of Appeal is the highest level of court in the province, in many ways, it is the least formal, at least in terms of the demeanour of the justices. They shoot questions willy-nilly at counsel, sometimes make anecdotal comments and often seem to get to the heart of the issue much more quickly than justices at lower court levels.

When they reconvened, Justice Proudfoot spoke for the three. They would order that the Alberta medical documents be disclosed, she said slowly, only because of the importance of determining the best interests of the child. But they were not, as Young had requested, going to allow all of Sawan's medical documents for the previous two years to be called. They narrowed the time frame from January 1, 1993—Teena Sawan had indicated at trial that the night previous was the last time she had drunk to excess—to June 14, 1993, the day before the trial.

Along with the court order, the judges reluctantly granted Young's request for an adjournment to July 21, to allow the lawyers time to view the new evidence. It was clear the judges wanted to deal with the matter as quickly as they could.

Spectators and the press left the courtroom with an unsettling question: Was there anything in their own medical records that, if it became public and the right slant put on it, could cause them to be labelled unfit parents?

A sick and concerned Jean Morgan flew back to Victoria, where she spent much of the remainder of the day on the telephone, trying to sort out what was going on. Teena had further news, which didn't improve Morgan's state of mind. She had been refused access to her own medical records. "They just told me I couldn't see them," said Teena, who had visited the medical clinic immediately after Morgan's call. Morgan told her young client that she would call the doctor herself, find out exactly what he had said to Brian Young and why Teena was being denied access to her own records. What did Bester think of his own patient to so easily forsake her confidence? And why did he feel his comments on the best interests of the child were so telling?

According to a 1985 policy statement of the Canadian Medical Association, and a June 11, 1992, Supreme Court of Canada decision, patients have a right to see their medical files on request. While the documents are physically owned by the physician or clinic that compiled them or had them compiled, patients have a right to medical information contained in their records. They cannot take the documents, but they can copy and look at them.

That same Supreme Court of Canada decision, *McInerney v. MacDonald*, also defines the expectations of confidentiality between a doctor and patient. Doctors and patients do not enjoy the privilege attached to the conversations between lawyer and client, which is absolute. But, the court writes, there is a fiduciary relationship—a trust and confidence— between physician and patient, and certain duties arise from that relationship. Among these are the duty of the doctor to act with utmost good faith and loyalty and to hold information received from or about a patient in confidence. When a patient releases personal information in the context of the doctor-patient relationship, writes the Supreme Court, he or she does so with the legitimate expectation that these duties will be respected. The information is to be used by the doctor for the benefit of the patient. The Canadian Medical Association's code of ethics also states that "an ethical physician will keep in confidence information derived from a patient or from a colleague regarding a patient, and divulge it only with the permission of the patient except when otherwise required by law."

Another of the basic tenets of the CMA's code of ethics is that a doctor will "protect the patient's secrets." Doctors can disclose medical information under court order, under oath or when they have written permission from their patient. While that may sound relatively clear-cut, there are a "lot of grey zones in protecting a patient's secrets, balancing it with the public good," said Bryan Ward, assistant deputy registrar of the Alberta College of Physicians and Surgeons. "Each case requires its own assessment against that standard." There are some situations in which a doctor must violate doctor-patient confidentiality. If a minor tells a doctor of physical or sexual abuse, the physician is required by law to notify child welfare officials. Under the Infants Act, suspected child abuse exempts doctors from physician-patient confidentiality. If a pilot is physically unable to fly, the aviation authorities must be advised. If someone if diagnosed with having mumps, cancers or certain sexually transmitted diseases, the Public Health Act requires that the local public health department be notified in writing.

Consensus at the medical level, Ward said, is that a doctor telephoning the opposing lawyer in a contentious court case and disclosing certain facts about a patient would appear to be a breach of confidentiality. "I understand that some legal advice would differ from my opinion on that subject, mine not being one lone voice in the wind, but rather a consensus at the medical level. [The doctor] may receive legal advice that the legal process would be better served if you were to let them know you had information that may be useful to them. Our view is that unless you can be certain there is an overriding public good, then you have an ethical duty to even keep the fact that a particular patient is a patient of yours confidential."

Dr. Bester is in his mid-forties. He graduated from the University of Natal with a B.Sc. in zoology, chemistry and microbiology in 1975 and did one year of research at the University of Pretoria before going to medical school at the University of the Witwatersrand. He graduated in 1981 with the equivalent of an M.D. After a two-year rotating internship in Klerksdorp, he went into private practice there until 1990, when he emigrated to Canada. He set up practice in Manning as a general practitioner in 1991 and has remained there since. He is one of three doctors in the community, and he has hospital privileges in general surgery, obstetrics and gynecology.

Jean Morgan called Bester the afternoon of the hearing. She wanted to know firsthand what he had said to Young since the order made by the court of appeal resulted, at least in part, from the court's reliance upon Young's representations of what Bester had told him. After she told Bester what had been attributed to him in court, the doctor seemed concerned, Morgan recalled. She suggested sending him an affidavit that would set the record straight. But although Bester indicated that he would sign such an affidavit, he would not discuss Teena Sawan with her lawyer. "I look back on it now and it's so ironic I can't quite swallow it. I couldn't understand how he felt at liberty to discuss Teena with Mr. Young and Mr. McConnan, and when his own patient's lawyer contacts him, he will not discuss matters." He also refused to discuss his office's failure to allow Teena to see her own medical files.

Morgan reminded the doctor that Teena had never given him verbal or written permission to discuss her medical file or to give medical opinions based on any of the services rendered her. At the end of their conversation, Bester told Morgan that he had a lawyer, Anthony Friend of the Calgary law firm of Bennett Jones Verchere. Friend acted for the Canadian Medical Protection Agency, an organization set up by Canadian doctors to help physicians in case of legal trouble, and Bester had called him within hours of talking with Young.

Morgan next called Anthony Friend and asked that a copy of her client's medical records be sent to her. Otherwise, she would have to wait until Young decided to pass the records along to her to see what was being alleged. Morgan was annoyed that Anthony Friend even had possession of the records: Teena Sawan had not given permission to Bester to disclose them to anybody, including his lawyer. The records had been sent to Friend immediately upon Bester retaining him. "The file is the property of Dr. Bester. He is certainly entitled to consult with his legal counsel with a matter of that nature," Friend said of Bester sending him the documents.

That evening, Morgan faxed the affidavit to Bester. She also backed up her conversation with Bester's lawyer with a faxed letter to Calgary, asking for her own copy of the medical records.

Morgan and Young walked into their respective offices the next morning, July 7, to find a faxed letter from the deputy registrar of the B.C. Court of Appeal. "What?" Young thought, reading the short and to-the-point message. The B.C. Court of Appeal had reversed their decision made twenty-four hours earlier. Justices Proudfoot, Rowles and Wood said they did not have the jurisdiction to order an Alberta doctor and hospital to produce records. A B.C. court could not impose its jurisdiction on another province. The inference was clear: if the records were in B.C., the court would then have jurisdiction. It was highly unusual for the court to simply send out a fax with a reversal of a ruling. But unusual was, by the end of the case, almost the norm.

That afternoon, Morgan called Teena and filled her in. She then faxed a copy of the court of appeal's revocation of their order for the medical records to Bester's office, and to Anthony Friend's Calgary office. She also left a phone message at Friend's office that she no longer required a copy of Teena Sawan's medical records, in light of the appeal court's change of heart.

In Morgan's view, the medical document interlude was over. The court had reversed its ruling, and she had notified Bester and his lawyer of such, and that there was no need for her client's medical records to be sent to her. To relieve some of her anger and frustration at what she considered startling actions, Morgan drafted a letter of complaint about Bester to the Alberta College of Physicians and Surgeons.

She also wrote to Brian Young, outlining her concerns about Bester's actions, or at least as they were reported by Young in court. Bester's actions would have to be dealt with by the college, she wrote.

The next day, Young fired off a response, criticizing Morgan and jumping to Bester's defence. "I do not possibly see what can result from your actions other than the intentional infliction of harm upon a doctor whose conscience said that this child could not possibly be returned to its natural mother. I should think that your concern should be with the best interests of the child and not with some vindictive motive," Young chastised. He accused Morgan of trying to "ruin" Dr. Bester.

Exactly what was said in that first conversation between Young and Bester is not known. Morgan pointed out in her letter to Young that he had told her of having "loads of information" on Teena Sawan. Young responded that he had been "paraphrasing" when he said that. After this exchange, Morgan asked that all of Young's communications with her be in writing. She wanted no room for misinterpretation.

Young made sure to send copies of his correspondence to Bester and Anthony Friend, saying "Dr. Bester's best interests need to be protected."

As a result of Young's informing him that Morgan was reporting Bester to the disciplinary body, Anthony Friend advised the doctor not to sign the affidavit sent by Morgan, pending any investigation by the College of Physicians and Surgeons.

Young embarked on a furious letter-writing campaign, faxing supportive letters about Dr. Bester to the Canadian Medical Association, the Canadian Medical Protective Agency and the Alberta College of Physicians and Surgeons, and sending copies of all the letters to Bester and his lawyer, so they would know he was in their corner.

Brian Young and Dr. Bester were, essentially, in a position of mutual back-scratching. If Bester were to be investigated by the doctor's disciplinary body for breaching confidentiality, Young was the only direct witness as to what was said in their conversation. If the new evidence was allowed and a new trial ordered, Young needed Bester to testify. It would do the lawyer no good for the doctor to be in the glue with the Alberta College of Physicians and Surgeons.

In those letters, Young says he is writing of his own volition. He writes that in their July 5, 1993, conversation, Bester "told me that he was a general practitioner for Cecilia Sawan and had concerns about her having the child live with her. He did not in any way elaborate in any detail whatsoever the type of treatment, care, diagnosis that Cecilia Sawan received.... Because of the conversation I had with Dr. Bester, I drew the conclusion that the specific evidence that the respondent, Cecilia Sawan, had given regarding her alcohol and drug abuse could be contradicted by the evidence of Dr. Bester."

If Dr. Bester had not disclosed something about what he treated Teena Sawan for during her two years as his patient, it seems Brian Young must have had an ability to read minds and medical documents over long distances, or else why would he have alluded to drug and alcohol abuse.

Bester's lawyer said in a later interview that the doctor did not breach doctor-client confidentiality. "I don't know what Mr. Young's version of the conversation was. As I understand it, in court he was certainly supportive of the view that there was no breach of confidentiality and that Dr. Bester had been careful about that. Dr. Bester's version is he didn't disclose any information in that conversation or breach any doctor-patient confidentiality. He was quite aware of his obligations. As far as I know, he didn't even disclose [that Teena Sawan was his patient]. He just said he had information concerning the case and I think at that point, the lawyer tried to get some sort of an order.... He was aware of his obligations concerning doctor-patient confidentiality before he ever made the call, so he was quite alive to the concern that he not disclose to anyone other than the patient or legal counsel any information that had arisen as a result of the doctor-patient relationship."

Apparently, Bester's lawyer had not had the benefit of reading Bruce McConnan's affidavit, in which it is clearly stated that Bester divulged at least that he was Teena Sawan's medical doctor—which some in the medical profession view as a breach—had been for two years, that he had testimony and records to produce which he obviously thought were damning and which he thought conflicted with her evidence at trial. Brian Young also writes in the supportive letters to the disciplinary bodies that Bester "told me that he was a general practitioner for Cecilia Sawan and had concerns about her having the child live with her."

Young telephoned Bester to thank him for his co-operation, then wrote to Anthony Friend to do the same. Meanwhile, the Tearoes were praying diligently that somehow the medical evidence would be admitted, and that Dr. Bester would not get in trouble.

Young's next tactic was to reapply to the court to have Teena Sawan's consent to the production of her medical documents imposed. If that was done, it wouldn't matter if the medical documents were in Alberta, and he could dodge the jurisdictional issue.

The irony of the situation would have made Morgan laugh, albeit bitterly, if she hadn't found it so upsetting. At trial, they asked that Teena Sawan's consent to the adoption be dispensed with. Now they asked that her consent to providing the court and the public with her medical records be imposed: was there anything Teena Sawan should be able to decide?

A court date of July 13 was set for that hearing, and Young notified both Bester and Friend of it.

A day before the hearing, Morgan received a faxed letter from Anthony Friend. It read:

Delivered by courier

(Copy via telecopier)
Ms. Jean A. Morgan,
Henley & Walden
Barristers & Solicitors
SIDNEY, British Columbia

Dear Madam,

I have received your letter of July 7, 1993 confirming that you act as counsel for Ms. Cecilia Augustine Sawan. As you requested on July 6, 1993, enclosed is a copy of the office chart maintained by Dr. Bester with respect to his attendances on Ms. Sawan. This chart is provided to you as the authorized representative of your patient. The chart has not, of course, been provided to Mr. Young.

By copy of this letter, I acknowledge receipt of Mr. Young's telecopied letter dated July 9, 1993 enclosing a notice of motion, returnable July 13, 1993, with supporting affidavit of Mr. Young.

Yours very truly,

A.L. Friend
cc: Mr. Brian D. Young
    (Via courier and telecopier; w/o enclosures)

Teena Sawan's medical file was en route to B.C., despite Morgan having alerted the Manning clinic that the medical documents were no longer needed; despite Morgan faxing the lawyer for Dr. Bester a copy of the B.C. Court of Appeal decision saying they could not order the documents; despite Morgan leaving a telephone message at Anthony Friend's office that she personally no longer needed the documents. And while the medical chart may not have been sent directly to Brian Young, a copy of the above letter was. Knowledge that the documents were in B.C. would make things a lot easier for Young. It gave him all the information he needed to go into court on July 13 and argue that the documents were now in the province and could therefore be ordered presented by the B.C. court. The timing seemed awfully convenient: the letter notifying that the medical documents had been sent was faxed the day before Young's scheduled court appearance to try and have the documents ordered produced.

Although Anthony Friend said he knew the court was no longer asking for the documents, he said in a later interview that he was fulfilling Morgan's request from a week earlier for the documents as Sawan's authorized representative. The lawyer said he had no record of Morgan having left a phone message that she personally did not need the documents now that the court did not require them. "I have no record of that. I checked with my secretary. She had no memory of that and Jean Morgan can say that, but there was certainly no indication of any communication like that." Friend added that he was, at all times, acting on the instructions of his client, Dr. Bester.

"It was clear to me we were caught in the middle of a hotly contested custody litigation and both Jean Morgan and Brian Young were, on a daily basis and sometimes several times a day, phoning Dr. Bester or myself, or writing letters, and I did not want to be accused of taking the side of one or the other in that dispute," Friend said later of his copying his letters to each lawyer. "This was not a standard situation at all. It was a situation where we had two combatants with swords unsheathed and I didn't want to get caught in the fray."

The records had not arrived at Morgan's office as of the morning of July 13, 1993, when Morgan and Young appeared before B.C. Court of Appeal Justice Sam Toy in Vancouver. Young asked that the medical records be disclosed and expanded his request from six months (the period deemed relevant by the first B.C. Court of Appeal decision) to two years. Morgan told the court she did not have the records in question, despite Young's suggestion that she did. Toy said there was no evidence before him that the documents were in anyone's possession, but Young could reapply to the court if that situation changed.

Morgan flew back to Victoria immediately after the hearing. There were still no medical records at her office.

That afternoon, at 2:52 p.m., Anthony Friend faxed a letter to both Morgan and Young again, confirming that a copy of the medical records had been couriered to Morgan the day before.

Morgan went home early that afternoon. She still hadn't shaken the flu bug. When she arrived at the office the next morning, Thursday, July 14, she found a fax waiting from Young, asking about the documents. Morgan's office had still not received any couriered package, and she advised him— via fax—of that fact.

Young's secretary, Teresa Westhead, phoned Friend's office at 9:45 a.m. on July 14 and was told that the medical records had been picked up by the couriers on Monday, July 12, in the early afternoon, and were to be delivered to Morgan's office by the next day. Friend's secretary put a trace on the couriered package and it showed the records hadn't been delivered because Morgan's office was in Sidney, a suburb of Victoria, making next-day delivery difficult. Friend's secretary requested that the courier company expedite the delivery and paid an extra twenty dollars. This would guarantee that Morgan receive the package by 10:30 a.m.

At 10:28 a.m. on July 14, the package from Bennett Jones Verchere was delivered to Jean Morgan's office. The documents were officially in B.C. and within the court's jurisdiction. Jean Morgan triple-checked with Teena. Had she signed any piece of paper giving permission for the records to be released to anyone? No, nothing, she had not signed a thing, Teena said. Morgan checked again with the court registry, in case the initial court order for disclosure of the records had been inadvertently entered as a valid order. It had not.

There had been no authorization from the patient or the court for Teena Sawan's records to be released to anyone, including Jean Morgan or Anthony Friend. Yet here they were.

Young scheduled a third application for the next day, July 15. Morgan had sworn an affidavit outlining what had occurred with the medical documents and did not think it appropriate that she appear on her own behalf, so Trudi Brown, Q.C., a Victoria family lawyer, appeared in her stead.

Young, concerned about his client's growing legal bill, did not go to Vancouver. Instead, he argued his points via a conference call.

Brown argued against disclosure of the documents, reiterating Morgan's earlier comments. "Surprisingly, the documents came to Morgan despite her telling them she did not need them... They came gratuitously, if I may say that," Trudi Brown somewhat sarcastically told the court.

But how the documents got into B.C., and therefore into the court's jurisdiction, did not appear to concern Justice Sam Toy. "The affidavit material satisfies me that now counsel for the respondent has in her possession amongst other things the medical records and charts of Dr. Daniel Bester that relate to the respondent from February 6, 1992 to the present time. I have not seen anything in the affidavit of the respondent's counsel that suggests that the information contained in those records and charts of Dr. Bester is not relevant to an issue to be considered, namely, the fitness of the respondent to care for the infant child, the custody which is the subject matter of this appeal."

Toy, in part, based his ruling on the mistaken belief that the initial trial had been done on what is known as an 18A basis, essentially, a trial by affidavit with no opportunity for cross-examination of witnesses. Such was not the case. But Toy, proceeding on a misconception, said because of this, Young and the Tearoes "did not know or consider the respondent's history before the hearing." This was clearly incorrect and went to the point that Morgan had argued at the first court of appeal hearing: Young had already had an opportunity to cross-examine Teena Sawan on her past.

The 145 pages of documents dating back two years and splaying out Teena Sawan's medical background arrived in a hodge-podge and covered everything from a pain in her leg after a skating fall to yeast infections to the birth of her child. Morgan looked at the papers in front of her and tidied them up as best she could. Before handing over the papers, she wanted to try and have some sense made of them by a professional. She took them to Dr. Rae Graham, a doctor who had had a family and maternity practice in Victoria since 1987 and who knew Trudi Brown. At the urgent request of Brown, Dr. Graham pored over the medical records for some twelve hours, reviewing and interpreting.

Morgan found the handling of the whole situation appalling. None of the usual rules of court had been adhered to, and the result was everyone rushing around, with little time to adequately prepare. "These records could have been obtained prior to trial, and would then have been subject to the rules of evidence." Had that happened, the side presenting the records would have had an expert—a doctor—look at them and interpret them, giving the opposing counsel a further thirty days to have another expert view the records and interpret them. As it was, Morgan was scrambling to get a medical opinion, while Young had a lawyer in his office go through the pile and pick out what seemed to her to be relevant passages.

Chapter 23

The three appeal court judges listened intently as the conflicting definitions of "the best interests of the child" were argued at the July 21 hearing. Not surprisingly, the best interests as defined by a middle-class, middle-aged devout white couple did not altogether coincide with those defined by a twenty-year-old Cree woman from a small northern Alberta town. How those differing definitions would jibe with those of three appeal court justices would have a major impact on their decision.

Brian Young argued aggressively that Teena Sawan's medical records offered "further evidence relating directly to the best interest of the child and the ability of the respondent to care for that child." He handed the judges a five-page affidavit summarizing incidents culled from the medical documents given by Dr. Bester.

Young focused on six incidents from May 29, 1992, to the day of the appeal. The first was Teena's suicide gesture on May 29, the night of her nineteenth birthday. He pointed out that she had taken pills with beer and stated "I just wanted to die." The hospital discharge summary noted Teena had "a lot of personal problems though at present she is reluctant to seek counselling for these. It is unclear whether she was in fact depressed or had a personality disorder. Discharge diagnosis: Adolescent adjustment reaction."

Young moved on to an incident on July 26, 1992, when Teena was taken unconscious to the Manning General Hospital after suffering what appeared to bystanders to be seizures. The nurse's notes quote Teena's friend Judy Waldo as saying that Teena "usually gets like this when she's drinking—had drank beer during the afternoon and vodka during evening." Dr. Bester's record says, "Intoxicated? Petit mal seizures. Aggressive, Non complaint. Combative. Drinking all day at Rodeo Vodka/Beer."

(Somehow, between the nurse's notes and the doctor's record, Waldo's comment that Teena had consumed beer in the afternoon and vodka in the evening had been translated to "drinking all day." The doctor's first comment, "intoxicated?" with a question mark, became, when entered on her chart beside the line asking for the diagnosis, simply "intoxicated"; the question mark had disappeared. And yet it remains unclear from the admitting remarks whether in fact Teena had been drunk, or had suffered an epileptic seizure, or perhaps both. Although she was diagnosed as "intoxicated" she was sedated with Valium, a drug not usually used when a patient is intoxicated unless he or she is violent. Valium is commonly used to treat epilepsy.)

Young moved on to December 19, 1992, saying that on that date, the doctor's records indicate that Teena Sawan had had a "therapeutic abortion; blighted ovum."

Morgan had to summon all her strength to restrain herself from rising and arguing on this point then and there; she would have her chance to reply at the end of Young's submissions. For one thing, Teena's pregnancy had been what doctors call non-viable, meaning it would eventually have miscarried. And the suggestion that it had been a voluntary abortion, or that it had any relevance to the case at hand, was difficult to take. She bit her tongue, but Justice Wood didn't.

Wood threw down his pen and exploded. "What has that got to do with anything? What is your purpose here—to completely destroy this woman?"

No lawyer likes getting a blast from the bench, and Young was no different. He thought, "Hey, it's not my fault she's abused substances, had an abortion and lived a rambunctious lifestyle." But he said, in the respectful tones lawyers use to judges, that he felt information pertinent to Sawan's ability to care for the child had to be before the court. He did not say specifically how this particular information illuminated Teena Sawan's abilities as a mother, putting it in the pot marked "instability."

He quickly moved on. On January 22, 1993, Young told the court, Teena was brought to the hospital after an apparent suicide attempt, in which she had been seen pointing a knife at her stomach. On January 31, 1993, Teena was involved in a motor vehicle accident in a borrowed car and was diagnosed as having a "conversion disorder. Hysteria. Patient is advised to attend a consult with a psychiatrist and undergo psychotherapeutic analysis and counselling. The patient appears to favour this course and undertakes to visit me later in the week at the clinic when such arrangements will be formalized."

On April 17, 1993, the doctor's records indicated that Teena Sawan had been physically assaulted by her boyfriend. The doctor's report noted that Teena said she had been grabbed by the neck. The nurse's record said, "Assaulted 45 minutes ago. c/o blurred vision left eye. Ankle and calf pain. Accompanied by RCMP who states left cheek had a red mark." Young said the assault reference was clearly contrary to what Teena had testified, indicating that Teena Sawan had committed perjury.

Young concluded his presentation of the affidavit by noting that Teena was presently pregnant, and that as of June 20, the gestational age was thirteen weeks.

It was in the child's best interests to know as much as possible about Teena Sawan, Young argued, asking that the medical records he had summarized be allowed into evidence at the appeal, or else a new trial ordered, so the evidence could be called directly. "I'm sorry if the information is

damaging and hurtful," Young said, still smarting from
Wood's criticism about the abortion reference. "But I have to
bring it forward. It relates to her ability to care for the child.
It is not my intention to ruin her life. The issue is the best
interest of the child. This court cannot turn a blind eye, particularly to information of the last six months."

Morgan's reply initially focused on the same objections she
had made when Young had applied two weeks before to
bring forward the medical records: the rules for calling new
evidence had not been met. "The integrity of our justice system is important, and the best interests of this child are
served when that integrity is upheld," Morgan maintained.
"My friend has come very late in the day with information
that was available to him before trial had he made the appropriate efforts."

   Morgan agreed that the best interests of the child were at
issue and argued that they could not be served by sifting
through 145 pages of medical documents, picking out isolated incidents and placing them before the court as a damning indictment of a person's capabilities. Some of the
wording on the documents was highly subjective, Morgan
pointed out, while other statements that had been put forward as fact were comments by neighbours as to what they
thought had happened and were essentially supposition. If
the justices were going to take the medical comments as evidence, the incidents should be viewed in the overall context
of Teena's life. Morgan noted that the May 1992 suicide
attempt had happened after Teena had received no response
to her emotional plea to the Tearoes, explaining why she
wanted her son back, and should be considered in that light.

   Morgan started to address Young's comments about the
"therapeutic abortion." Without hearing that it had been a D
and C, and on the presumption from Young's representations
that it had been a voluntary abortion, Justice Rowles cut her
short. "I cannot see this has any relevance whatsoever."

   As for the assumptions that Teena was drunk on several in-
stances when she was brought into the hospital, the toxicology

reports did not bear this diagnosis out, Morgan said, referring to pages of lab reports included in the documents. The only toxicology report bearing out alcohol use was the one done after the January car accident, she said. Statements about Teena having psychological disorders were never investigated by having a psychological assessment. "I suggest he is making statements, yet has no objective evidence from a doctor specializing in the area." Even if the evidence were allowed, Morgan continued, it was unlikely it would have swayed Justice Melvin's decision. The judge was well aware that Teena had alcohol difficulties and a less than ideal life, and had taken that into consideration in his judgment.

Morgan then handed forward a two-page medical-legal opinion prepared by Dr. Rae Graham, whom she had asked to review the medical documents. It read:

July 20, 1993

Ms. Jean Morgan
Henley and Walden
Sidney, B.C.
V8L 4M9

Dear Ms. Morgan,
Re: Cecilia Augustine Sawan
    DOB May 28, 1973

I confirm that I am a Doctor of Medicine, licensed continuously to practise in British Columbia since 1984. I further confirm that I undertake Family Practice and Maternity at the above address, and that I have been practising this form of medicine in Victoria continuously since 1987.

On Monday, July 19, 1993, at the urgent request of a mutual acquaintance, I met with you and reviewed the medical file which relates to Ms. Sawan.

I am perfectly confident in stating that this medical file supports the concept that Ms. Sawan has been a stressed and unhappy person in the last year to year and a half. However,

I do not feel that anything in the medical file adequately supports either a major psychiatric diagnosis or the concept that she has experienced excessive problems with drugs or alcohol.

Of the many psychiatric diagnoses that are made in this medical file, I feel that the only one that could comfortably be applied to her is adolescent adjustment reaction, which is a catch-all diagnosis that basically says this adolescent is unhappy and is having difficulties relating to recent life events. I feel this is a reasonable diagnosis for much of the behaviour outlined in the medical record.

The record begins with pre-natal care during her pregnancy, which resulted in the delivery of a live male infant on December 3, 1991. The discharge summary following the admission for delivery of this infant states unequivocally that the patient is confused and has not yet resolved in her mind whether to surrender the baby for adoption or keep the baby. It does state that she is breastfeeding him while she makes up her mind. A few days later she attended the emergency department of the same hospital in order to receive a prescription for Parlodel, a drug used to suppress lactation.

In the medical record there are repeated toxicological analyses done of blood, urine and other body secretions looking for the presence of alcohol and for substances which may be legally and illegally obtained. All the toxicological analyses were negative except on one occasion when a positive serum alcohol level of 45 mmol/L was obtained. [This was the January car accident.]

There is a question throughout the medical record of whether or not this patient had been experiencing seizures. These records observed seizure activity that is variously described as grand mal and petit mal. However, the medical file does not include a neurological consultation or an electroencephalogram, which might help to clarify whether in fact the patient was at times in a post-seizure or post-ictal state, which can cause altered levels of consciousness.

In November 1992 Ms. Sawan again became pregnant, and in the records related to that pregnancy there is no mention of substance abuse either on an on-going basis or during the pregnancy. Unfortunately, this pregnancy resulted in a blighted ovum. A blighted ovum inevitably leads to spontaneous pregnancy loss and frequently requires a D & C. There is unfortunate wording in the discharge summary of the admission for the D & C, where the discharge diagnosis is 1)therapeutic abortion, 2) blighted ovum. I would like to make clear that, in normal medical language, a therapeutic abortion means the voluntary termination of a viable pregnancy. In this case, the pregnancy was not viable, had never been viable. Most physicians would describe the procedure that was undertaken as either evacuation of non-viable products of conception or as dilatation and currettage [sic] of uterus containing a blighted ovum. The term "therapeutic abortion" would not normally be applied.

Throughout the medical record and all the numerous visits to the hospital, no evidence is available that the physicians involved were looking for either chronic alcohol or drug use....

Throughout the medical record I have found no evidence of any care, concern or counselling of Ms. Sawan about the normal grief to be expected on surrendering a baby for adoption. I feel that lack of support around the adoption may be a factor contributing to her problems, both with behaviour and substance. I also feel that her unexplored and uncounselled grief is potentially the cause of her adolescent adjustment reaction.

On the basis of careful consideration of the documents provided, I do not feel able to state unequivocally an opinion on Ms. Sawan's ability or inability to parent. Certainly, I would feel that close supervision of the infant's welfare should be undertaken should she become the custodial parent. I do not feel that there is any evidence for a major psychiatric diagnosis. However, further investigation of her neurological and psychological status may be in order.

Sincerely yours
Rae Graham MD

An incident not referred to at the appeal but included in the medical report seems telling of the way Teena Sawan was perceived at the Manning General Hospital. Miles took her to the emergency room on March 29, 1993. She had accidentally cut her wrist while chopping onions for dinner, and she thought the cut might need stitches. According to the nurse's record, Teena appeared responsive, able to walk and talk appropriately. Yet at the bottom of the out-patient form in the nurse's comments is a note saying, "Denies drinking today." There is no indication of drunkenness from any of the symptoms noted, yet she was obviously asked the question and her response noted. The wording of the comment is also interesting. It is not that Teena has not been drinking, it is that she denies drinking that day.

The judges made no immediate ruling on whether the medical evidence was admissible, instead carefully setting the medical records and Dr. Graham's letter to one side and asking the lawyers to proceed with their appeal arguments instead. That was fine with Young. Judges could say all they wanted about their ability to "disabuse their minds" of inadmissible evidence, but they are only human, and the evidence would surely leave an impression.

Young had five appeal grounds, but the main thrust was to emphasize the bonding between the child and the Tearoes. Melvin had failed to take into account evidence of bonding, Young argued, and had placed too much emphasis on Teena's native heritage.

Young painted a picture of the Tearoes as virtually a perfect family, right down to the family dog. "How is it in his best interests to remove him from his family and home, to take him away from the only mother, father and sibling he has ever known?" Teena Sawan did not meet the onus on her to show that it would be in the child's best interests to be returned to her, he argued. "There was evidence she has drinking problems, has been assaulted. How can this be in the child's best interests? There is no evidence of stability, no evidence of a husband, no evidence of what type of home she can provide." In appeal documents, Young wrote that

Teena was an "alcoholic and continues to have a drinking problem.... The respondent's home life is not stable, and her future is uncertain."

Young suggested again that Teena had committed perjury—a serious allegation to be throwing around a courtroom. It is notoriously difficult to prove, and requires that the person had both the intent to mislead the court, and the knowledge of the falsity of the statement at the time it was made. It is one of the very few criminal offences that requires corroborating evidence for a conviction. The fact that the medical records established a different interpretation of events than Teena Sawan had testified to does not necessarily mean she committed perjury.

The lawyer argued again, as he had unsuccessfully at trial, that Teena's efforts to get her child back were insincere. He said Melvin erred in saying that the twenty-two sporadic days Teena Sawan had spent with her son after his birth constituted a "considerable period of time." As for culture, Young pointed out that Teena Sawan does not know Cree and has not lived at a reserve in years. In essence, he used Teena's own evidence of feeling displaced at Little Buffalo against her. "There was no evidence before the trial judge of any type of native tie other than race. There is a difference between race and culture, and there was no evidence of her being involved in the native culture.... How can a child be shown its culture if the mother does not live in or practice that culture?" He emphasized that Teena was "one-half native," and went on to suggest that "there is no evidence that the child would receive any more native culture from Teena Sawan than from Jim and Faye Tearoe. In fact, Teena Sawan is engaged to marry a white male, and has no intention to live on the reserve in the near future. The cultural background is not significant in the respondent and therefore cannot be predicted to be significant in the child, should he be placed with the respondent."

Young said Melvin had erred in law as well. He argued that there was no legal basis for the trial judge to have vitiated the valid consent Teena gave to the adoption. "How can he vitiate what was freely and voluntarily signed?" Oral communication cannot invalidate it, Young said. If a consent is valid in another province, Young argued, it must be valid in B.C. "The effect of the trial judge's decision is to permit natural parents who have consented to an adoption in another jurisdiction to use B.C. law to revoke the consent. This cannot be the intent of this legislation."

Young quoted from a book sent to him by psychologist Barbara Fulford, who wrote to Young during the trial of the potentially devastating effects of removing David from the Tearoes. The book, *Beyond the Best Interests of the Child*, is the first of a trilogy written in the 1970s by Yale professor of law and social policy Joseph Goldstein; director of the Hampstead Child Therapy Clinic and a Yale lecturer, Anna Freud; and Yale professor of pediatrics and psychiatry Albert Solnit. The authors predict dire consequences for a young child taken from the only care-givers he or she knows. Children are vulnerable and fragile, and the change of a parent figure can cause "regression along the whole line of his affections, skills, achievements and social adaptation."

The appeal court judges listened intently as Young read several excerpts from the book. "Continuity of relationships, surroundings and environment influence a child's normal development. Physical, emotional, intellectual and moral growth does not happen without causing the child inevitable internal difficulties. The instability of all mental processes during the period of development needs to be offset by stability and uninterrupted support from external sources. Smooth growth is arrested or disrupted when upheavals and changes in the external world are added to the internal ones," Young read. The book looks at various American child custody cases and quotes a judge who said, "Harsh as it must seem to biological parents, their standing in court is no greater than that of a stranger."

A parent is the person to whom the child looks for love, caring and guidance, Young said, and in the case at hand, the child got those things from Jim and Faye Tearoe. He was growing and thriving, and learning to see the world through their eyes.

Young closed by reiterating what he had argued at the trial before Melvin, urging the court not to feel pity for Teena Sawan or the Tearoes, but to "find in favour of the child. Let him remain with the only parents he has known.... This is not an issue of white versus native culture. It is what is the best interests of the child."

That Brian Young and Jean Morgan had vastly different views of what constituted culture and race was apparent from the beginning of the case. Their views were as opposite as their clients' lives. To Young, there was "no evidence that Teena has native culture. She's native, that's the race issue...but she doesn't partake in any type of native culture, what we would know to be native culture."

Morgan saw culture as something inherent, a person's birthright. "What was at issue was whether this child has a special status in Canada. Aboriginal people are special in Canada. They have special privileges by virtue of being abo-riginal. In the past, they have suffered from that," she said later. "What we were trying to get across is that he is not just different, he is native. He could have had purple hair and skin, but by virtue of his mother, he is still native and is enti-tled to privileges associated with that. What they saw was colour of skin as determining a race and a privilege. And they are wrong."

Some basic misconceptions that originated during the trial had become erroneously and firmly embedded as truth, and they were presented as such at the appeal. Teena Sawan was described by Young as one-half native, based on the incorrect family tree in Teena's Social Services file, and being on social assistance when she was living on the educational stipend provided by the band. Other misinformation repeated at the appeal included alleged uncertainty as to the identity of David's father, with Young suggesting she "may have been sleeping with two men at the time of conception," and erro-neous descriptions of the child as being blue-eyed.

Young had the force of stereotype on his side. On paper,

the essence of a person was eclipsed by defining words. The words used to describe the Tearoes are touchstones in society—*white, middle-aged, middle-class, white-collar, homemaker, married, religious*. The words used to describe Teena are the harbingers of apprehension—*young, drinking history, Indian, unmarried, pregnant*. The appeal court was not able to see the people who stood behind the words, as Melvin had had three days to do. Teena did not translate well to paper. Her strength was in her physical presence and demeanour, and Morgan found it difficult to adequately convey her client's innate dignity and intelligence—features that had obviously impressed Melvin. Morgan was robbed of her most persuasive evidence.

Without compelling legal reason, the appeal court is not to interfere with the judgment of a trial judge, and Morgan began her argument with this in mind. The majority of Young's arguments, Morgan said, were factual findings that he simply wanted the appeal court to revisit. "Justice Melvin heard the witnesses, observed them, and clearly had the Adoption Act in his mind in making his ruling," Morgan argued. "He was well aware he was looking at the best interests of the child. He carefully examined the facts before him and was satisfied it was in the best interests of the child to revoke consent." Morgan noted that Melvin had viewed factors favourable and unfavourable to Teena Sawan and decided the case accordingly. The rules of equity are available in B.C. and Alberta law to give relief against unfairness, Morgan said, submitting that Melvin was entitled, after establishing a factual framework of unfairness, to vitiate Sawan's consent to adoption on those grounds.

Morgan referred to several cases, including two decided by Proudfoot, in which the justice had said: "The appeal court does not retry cases." She gave details of Teena Sawan's unsuccessful efforts to get her child and read aloud the letter Teena wrote the Tearoes in May 1992.

Morgan's points were, in essence, simple. Couched in the circular language that seems intrinsic to speaking in a courtroom were basic premises: How could Teena Sawan bond with a child when she asked for the child back several times within the legal length of time, and the people who had him refused to give him back? Should she be penalized because the Tearoes had had time to bond with the boy—fraudulently, in Morgan's view? The longer they had him, the better their chances of keeping him. And now that was being held against Teena Sawan.

As for Teena Sawan not knowing her culture, Morgan pointed out that Teena and Jordan were part of a frustrating cycle. "She was brought up white—not because she wanted to be. It was a government choice. She had no control. She isn't white. She's Indian. But when she goes to her Indian people, she can't speak their language. She knows she is missing something, a big part of herself, a sense of belonging. And she does not want her child to feel that." Teena Sawan was attending school, Morgan said, pregnant and engaged to be married; essentially, her life was stabilizing.

The arguments finished early in the afternoon, and the justices reserved decision; the ruling could be delivered at any time from the next day to eternity. Leaving the courtroom that afternoon, the usual guesswork began. It seemed, to courtroom observers, that Wood might rule for Teena Sawan, while Proudfoot might side with the Tearoes. Rowles seemed to be the wild card. Her tone had grown impatient with Young on occasion, yet she had also questioned Morgan several times about Teena's life. Wood and Rowles had seemed particularly troubled, but they might have simply worn their concerns on their sleeve more than Proudfoot.

The debate among reporters continued long after the appeal was over. Had Teena Sawan cleaned up her life? How relevant was it if she still had the odd drink? Did she have to live the same lifestyle, believe the same things as the Tearoes to pass muster?

There was also some navel-gazing as reporters questioned how the story had been covered. The fact that Teena Sawan was twenty years old with no job was mentioned constantly, yet the Tearoes' ages weren't. Was it "ageist" to mention that the Tearoes would be senior citizens when their son graduated

high school? What about the couple's religious zeal? Despite
Brian Young's efforts to downplay it, it was readily apparent.
But why should the Tearoes be judged harshly for their
beliefs?

How important a role did socio-economics play? While
creature comforts are supposed to have little bearing in the
judgment, those viewing the case found if difficult to ignore
the differences money makes in determining lifestyle. But
did a middle-class lifestyle as opposed to a working-class
one mean a happier, more well-adjusted child?

And at the heart of the debate was the person who, in
many ways, seemed the most forgotten in the equation. What
would happen to this child? Would he be irreparably harmed
by being moved, after one and a half years, from the only people he knew as Mom and Dad? Would his trust of the world
be permanently scarred, as some psychologists watching the
case develop predicted? Or would he, if left with the Tearoes'
suffer the persistent feeling of abandonment that many adoptive children attest to, always wondering why his mother
gave him up? How resilient were children, if moved from one
situation to another where they are loved and cherished?

There was no denying the years of abysmal treatment of
natives in Canada. Was this a case in which it was being used
as a convenient argument with no substance? Or was it a case
of systemic bias that is so ingrained, it is not even noticed any
more?

Watching the appeal arguments were Nelson Mayer and
Lizabeth Hall. Those who saw the six-foot Manitoba Cree
and the smaller woman, a member of the Nuxalkmo band
from Bella Coola, assumed they were present to show
"native support" of Teena Sawan's case. They were only par-
tially correct.

While the broader overtones—the aboriginal community's
demand for self-determination, the documented tragedy of
scores of Manitoba native children being taken from their
communities to fulfil the dreams of childless white couples—
drew their attention, it was quickly overshadowed by what

they viewed as the crux of the case.

"You put all of that aside, and you're talking about first and foremost a birth-mother who wanted to keep her child and made that point known. That's the issue. All that other stuff is a smoke-screen. The comments of 'She doesn't look native,' 'The child has blond hair.' Who cares?" said Mayer. "I saw a young woman who, to all intents and purposes, was all on her own against this huge bureaucracy which essentially parented her throughout her life, and then left her. The social workers likely decided, 'This child will be better off with someone else.' Not having her revocation in writing was their loophole, instead of providing the help she may have needed at that time."

Mayer said his attendance at the July 21 hearing wasn't a matter of "jumping on the bandwagon" simply because an aboriginal person was in trouble. "If that was the agenda, we would have packed the courtroom," said the vice-president of the United Native Nations. And it seemed to him that the "white-native" issue was something the Caucasian community seemed to be the most upset about.

Mayer, who drank a lot before swearing off alcohol in 1977 when he was released from prison, was sickened by the quest to put medical evidence forward. What relevance the past had was something he couldn't fathom. He imagined Teena Sawan wasn't the only teenager in a small northern Alberta town who had done her share of partying.

Hall had wearied of the comments about the child's "not looking native." "Those comments about being one half, or half-breed, or part native—those don't come from aboriginal people. Those come from Caucasians, trying to minimize his Indianness." There seemed to be little understanding, she continued, that the power of First Nations people comes from a belief and value system that is far different than that of the white world, not from colour of skin. As for Teena Sawan's not living at a reserve, again, it seemed to be a notion of the white world that to be native, you had to live in a certain place. "Aren't we allowed off the reserve?" Mayer asked.

Hall said there are many aboriginal people who are just learning about their culture, and that doesn't make them less Indian. "It's not what you see, it's what you believe. There's a lot of culture I don't know and I don't think anyone would say I wasn't a First Nations woman." The pressure to know every nook and cranny of native history in order to prove that you are part of it comes from the white world, Hall says.

Both Mayer and Hall had seen the difficulties faced by native people raised without a sense of cultural identity. Hall operates the Family Reunification program, and since it began (on a volunteer basis in 1989), she has seen hundreds of native people adopted to white homes as children walk through her door, asking for help in finding out who they are. Some have never felt they belonged in the white world into which they were put; others were relatively content, but still looking for something missing.

In 1992, the B.C. government banned public non-native adoptions of aboriginal children, pending a review of the adoption law. However, there is no such ban on private adoptions. Manitoba and Nova Scotia have also stopped both public and private non-native adoptions of status Indian children. Ontario follows a 1986 policy—one similar to that of several provinces—in which Children's Aid Societies have been told to first look for native homes for aboriginal children.

Hall and Mayer say they have seen some interracial adoptions work, when they are done openly and honestly, and if the native child has firsthand contact with other native people. "I'm not convinced we are capable of that right now. Standards of the middle class, which many aboriginal people do not belong to for a variety of reasons, are applied right across the board. We are told, 'You have to fit in our way, or you are not enough.' And that's what we have to fight," said Hall.

But any adoption, interracial or not, must start out with a birth-mother who is content with the decision to give up her child. "You start from a wrong place, you end up in a wrong place," Hall said.

Morgan left the hearing feeling worse than she had when she went in. She stood outside in the misty rain, waiting for a cab to take her to the airport and back home, where she would call Teena and then go to bed. On the plane back to Victoria, Morgan stared down at the Gulf Islands below and thought about the incredibly high standard being set for Teena Sawan. The Tearoes' and Young's emphasis on drinking was an easy weapon to use against Teena, Morgan thought. "Do you know how many business-people there are out there who get drunk and do stupid things? And that doesn't make it right, but you certainly don't see that being used to take their children away from them. Teena is not an angel and she has never said she is. But the standard is incredibly high for her, much higher than it would be for you or me," she said later.

In Morgan's purse was a thank-you card she and Dan had received from Teena, with a picture of Teena and Jordan. The card, which Morgan treasures, reads: "You stood by me, supported me and encouraged me through a very tough time. You believed in me when no one else did. You also taught me to believe in myself. Your friendship will always mean everything to me and your kindness will never be forgotten. Thank you. Jordan and Teena Sawan."

Only two weeks before the appeal court hearing, the Baby Jessica case finished winding through the legal labyrinth. On July 1, 1993, Michigan's highest court ruled in a six-to-one decision that Jessica be transferred to her birth-parents. The move was to take place in one month, with eight visits planned between the Schmidts and the little girl, so she could get to know her natural parents before the move. The DeBoers were marking off the days until Jessica had to go. Roberta DeBoer said it would be like walking into a black forest with Jessica and leaving her there.

Jim and Faye Tearoe refused to harbour thoughts of loss. "The Lord is our Father. God is our Daddy," Faye said. "He wouldn't do something cruel to us like that [give the boy back to Teena after all this time]. That's not the Father God's heart. If He was gonna deliver David into the hands of Teena, He would have done it by now."

Of the two, Jim had an easier time putting shadows of doubt out of his mind. "All we can do is look up to God and say, 'God, You're our lawyer, You're our judge.' And then we leave it at that. If we don't, then we start wondering, and we can't be at peace with ourselves. Many many people, all of whom support us, have said they don't know how we're so peaceful. We have been able to put our trust and confidence in the word of God, and the word of God is the will of God. And if we honour God, He'll honour us. And that's what we do, every day."

There was no indication of when a verdict would be given, so Jim and Faye tried hard to continue with life as usual. They went on their planned holiday to the B.C. interior, where they spent time with Jim's parents, and then Faye's. They attended a Tearoe family reunion, and proudly introduced David to relatives he was meeting for the first time. At one point during their holiday, Faye purchased OshKosh overalls in several larger sizes for David to grow into. "My mother said to me, 'Faye, why are you doing this? You shouldn't do this until the court ruling has come down.' I never said anything, but it crushed me. I had one of those long talks with the Lord," Faye recalled later. " 'Where are you Lord?' You have to keep the right perspective, and I thought, even my mother doesn't have the faith. But I can't expect…everyone has their own walk with the Lord."

While waiting for the appeal court decision, the Tearoes were asked what they would do if they lost; would they appeal to the Supreme Court of Canada? "We'll do what we have to because David is ours. David's our son." A few minutes later, Faye looked skyward and apologized to the Lord. "That wasn't nice to the Lord…. I know the Lord will rule in our favour. If I say He's wrong, then I've misjudged the Lord all my life."

As the appeal court and public heard about the intimate details of Teena Sawan's life, she sat in a tiny motel in

Rycroft, a small town southwest of Manning. Miles was working on a rig, and Teena had come with him for two reasons. One, she missed him when he was gone and couldn't stand to be alone now, waiting for the court to make up its mind about the rest of her life. And two, his driver's licence was still under suspension for driving while prohibited, and he needed a ride to and from the rig.

Teena's days grew monotonous. She had to drop Miles off by noon and pick him up at midnight. Days were spent in the small motel room, watching television until she thought her eyes would turn square. This pregnancy was very different from her first. She felt tired almost all of the time, and had low hemoglobin. She often lay on the bed, head propped up against the two pillows, and fanned herself with a magazine. It was hot, and the flies in the day were topped only by the bee-sized mosquitos at night. Time was whiled away filling in the blanks in her future. As always, the course Teena's life would take was being decided at the whim of others; she was so used to it by now, she barely noticed.

"People will say five years from now that I'm an alcoholic and a drinker, even if I'm not. It's just something that people place you as and you have to live with it. I realize that people have judged me and put a tag on me and I have to wear it for the rest of my life. I try not to care what people say about me. I know I've changed and I'm still changing. I'm not a perfect person, but I don't think anybody is. There have been people that have come up to me and said they've noticed a change and that makes me feel good. People come up and say they've noticed a change in Miles, that he's not the rowdy type person he was. That makes me feel good too. I used to worry all the time what people thought. But Miles says, 'So what? Let them say what they're gonna say. You know the type of person you are, you know you're back in school, you're getting good marks and there are people that really like you.'"

All the discussion of her capabilities had made Teena think about what it was that she really wanted for her kids. "I want my kids to know they are loved, and to know they can trust me, no matter what, when they have problems. You have to build a trust so that if anything happens to them, no matter how bad, they feel they can come and talk to you. Say our kids, when they're older and want to experiment with alcohol, I hope they come to us first. I'll tell them, if I hadn't gotten into drinking, I probably wouldn't have dropped out of school and probably would have stayed in a good foster home. I missed having a good home, with parents who cared and were concerned. I want to give that to my kids. I want them to know they can come to me, and I'll always be there for them."

Money will likely never be something Teena and Miles have a lot of. "Sure, money plays a role. Parents want to see their children happy, so if getting a bike makes them happy, you want to get it for them. But I'm just trying to say there are other things that are important too.... The Tearoes are thirty years older than me and they've had a lot more time to get established. I don't have a lot now, but I have a home and I can provide that for my son.

"I'm my own person.... Other people might not agree with everything I do, just like I might not agree with everything they do.... Everybody's different.... There's not just one way to bring up a child. Because Christian people always believe their way is right, it shouldn't be wrong for someone else who isn't Christian. Going to church doesn't make you a better Christian, and being a Christian doesn't necessarily make you a better person."

The weeks drifted by and surprisingly there was still no word from the appeal court. Teena and Miles moved back to Manning in August, when the rig work was done. The summer wore on. Sometimes they went swimming in the lakes around Manning. Some nights they went to the Aurora and played the lotto machines, trying to limit themselves to $25. Miles worked once in a while at the tire shop. They rented a place, a small two-bedroom brown stucco house two blocks from the adult learning centre that Teena would be attending come September. The rent was $475 a month, about $600 per month by the time they paid the utilities, phone and television bills. Teena would be paid by the band again once she started school. Savings were minimal, although Teena talked of wanting to start to set aside money each month for Jordan.

Teena always wants to do what is seen by society in general as the "right thing." It is as if she is too intensely aware of what she will be perceived to be lacking. She puts out place mats on the table when company comes. It is as if she is wary in advance of being judged and wants things to look nice to show she, too, is a "nice" person. She apologizes for having value-priced peanut butter instead of a name brand. Coffee fixings are set out on a tray, and Teena dabs her mouth with a napkin in her lap after each bite of dinner.

Teena and Miles got a dog, a fluffy black pup with two white feet, in anticipation of Jordan's return. Peter suggested Two Socks for a name, so Two Socks, or Socky, it became. Miles put up a "Beware of Dog" sign with a snarling Doberman on it. It gave him a laugh when he opened the door and the pup rushed out, jumping on people and licking faces. The couple set up their couch in the living room across from the big TV set that Miles had insisted on. Teena's certificate for high marks is in a frame by the couch, alongside two pictures of Jordan. One is of him by a swimming pool, another is of him and Heidi, a close-up smiling at the camera. It was one of the pictures sent by the Tearoes in April, when they had hoped she would drop the court case. Framed pictures of Grace, Peter, Colin, Christine and John are on the wall behind the television.

Teena's older sister Christine visited from Medicine Hat for a few days, and envied Teena her home and boyfriend. Christine's relationship with her previous boyfriend had been unhappy, and the scars of that, along with a deep-rooted sadness about her mother, came out in frequent drinking bouts. Her memories of Maryann Sawan are painful and far from Teena's idealized visions. "Why didn't she quit drinking and have a nice place for us kids to go to school and come home and stuff like that?" Christine cried, sitting at the kitchen table.

She saw Teena's anxiety over Jordan and wanted to do something to ease her sister's pain. "I wish I could take the pain from my brothers and sisters. I wish someone could do the same for me. It's hard to live in my brother's shoes, it's hard to live in my sister's shoes, because we don't know exactly where to go sometimes."

Some nights, their grandmother Annie would call collect from a pay phone. Pushing seventy and still drinking hard, Annie moves from northern Alberta to Medicine Hat and back again. She has a cackling laugh and Miles describes her as "an Indian Estelle Getty." Grace and Peter visited and Teena urged them to stay in school, not wanting them to make the same mistakes she did. Although both are members of the Woodland Cree band, neither have much interest at this point in going back to Little Buffalo or Cadotte Lake. Peter knows more about Ukrainian dancing, his hobby, than being a Cree. All Grace sees the odd time she has visited family at Little Buffalo are unattractive houses and not much to do. Their Aunt Mary wants to invite them out more, now that she has a new house. "They weren't used to how we lived," says Mary, who is extremely proud of the three-bedroom bungalow-type house she helped build.

In a small town, chance encounters with people happen with regularity. One afternoon that summer, Teena ran into Dr. Bester at Grimm's Coffee Shop. He was getting out of his vehicle as she got out of hers. The two looked at each other over the hoods of their cars and looked away. Each went in to the coffee shop. Teena sat on one side of the room, Bester on the other, worlds apart in the town of 1,200.

Chapter 24

Faye Tearoe leaned over the bathroom sink and looked a little closer in the mirror. She stared a moment, and then sighed and briskly finished brushing her hair. Well, she was almost forty-nine years old, and the last few months had definitely not been the easiest. A few grey hairs were to be expected, she supposed.

Heidi came in to brush her teeth, and Faye gave her a half-hug as she slipped past her to get David, his high-pitched chatter greeting her. "Good morning, my little man!" she said, scooping him out of his crib at the usual morning time of 6:45 and taking him back to the bathroom. He was being potty-trained, and was doing pretty well at it. Occasionally, he would yell out "Stuck!" when he wanted help getting up from the tiny potty.

The family ate breakfast together, followed by a Bible reading, and then Jim was out the door for his office and Heidi was off to Bible school. After Julie Salmond dropped little Samantha by, Faye was kept busy looking after the two children.

David and Samantha were surrounded by toys on the kitchen floor when Jim called shortly after lunch. Brian

Young had just called him, Jim said slowly. The B.C. Court of Appeal decision was going to be delivered on August 19, two days away. Tears welled up in Faye's eyes, but she was quiet on her end of the line. "Praise the Lord, Faye, praise the Lord," Jim said, shoring up his wife, who he knew was having a more difficult time than he in surrendering control. "The Lord will look after our little man." Faye agreed and hung up. She hurriedly put David and Samantha down for their afternoon nap and then went into the recreation room that doubled as her prayer room. She sat in a rocker and cried. She knew the Devil was doing his work, making her have fear and doubt, but she couldn't stop the tears. She just couldn't bear the thought of David being taken from her, especially to an environment that she thought provided little chance for a good life. That little boy had her heart. Sitting there empty-handed, she could feel his little head nestled against her neck as she read him a story and he fell asleep in her arms.

Faye grasped her Bible firmly in her hands. "Lord, talk to me! I have to hear from you today. Just tell me something." And the Lord said two words. " 'Trust me.' That's what He said to me. And I did—I continued trusting the Lord."

In an interview the day before the appeal court decision, Faye was adamant that they were going to keep David. "I just know what the decision will be. You may find that hard to understand, but I just know." The Lord meant for all of this to happen, she explained. Faye says that when Teena first asked for the boy back, she would have given him back if the Lord had given her a sign that that was the right thing to do. She said the sign was not Teena phoning and asking for him back, or her writing them in May 1992 again saying she wanted him back. The sign was not Teena refusing to sign documents their lawyer thought needed signing for the adoption to be completed. The sign was not a B.C. Supreme Court justice ruling, after a three-day trial, that the boy should be returned to his birth-mother.

"Honestly, I've given the baby to the Lord twice. It's not like I've taken him back and now he's mine! He's still the

Lord's. The Lord has all sorts of ideas in His brain and He's gonna surprise us. David's gonna be a special little man all his life. It's not like I've taken him back and claimed him for me," she says, adding, "It's just that I know he's mine. He's my child."

The afternoon before the decision, Faye called her parents. As with all the previous court proceedings, they would be there by early evening to support their daughter. Faye took out a jumbo package of frozen chicken to thaw for dinner and made a mental note to herself that Heidi had a dentist appointment the next day as well. The phone was ringing off the hook. "You watch for us on the news tomorrow night," she told one well-wisher. "We'll be on there with David." In between phone calls, Faye grabbed her curlers and set her hair. There would no doubt be a press conference the next day, and she wanted to look her best.

Jean Morgan had half joked that the minute she left town, the appeal court would give its decision. She was right.

Morgan had a summer visit with her parents planned and flew to Edmonton on August 15. Two days later, her office was notified of the impending decision. Morgan immediately called Teena, but there was no answer. She tried several times throughout the day, with no luck.

Teena and Miles were standing by the road near Dixonville, a half an hour outside Manning, waiting for Miles's sister to bring them gas for the van. The two were en route to a rig west of Dixonville when the van, borrowed from Miles's parents, had slowly chugged to a stop. It couldn't be out of gas, but that was what the gauge said. When they went outside, the tank was indeed empty; there was an obvious hole, and drops of gasoline on the pavement. By the time Carrie arrived with gas for the van's second tank, it was too late to get to the rig. They might as well go back to Manning for the night and sleep at home, instead of in the back of the van, where they had been planning to camp while at the rig to save money.

Miles was unhappy about missing a day of work, and the drive home was silent. As they walked in the door, the phone was ringing. It was Donna Ominayak, telling Teena that Jean Morgan wanted her to call ASAP—the court was going to give its decision. "Finally, finally," Teena thought as she quickly dialled the number of Jean's parents in Edmonton. The decision would be released in Victoria, Morgan told her, and she'd made arrangements for Trudi Brown to pick it up on her behalf.

Teena hung up the phone and looked at Miles. It was 4:00 p.m. on Tuesday and the decision would be released at 10:00 a.m. on Thursday. Could they make the thousand-mile trip in that time? They couldn't afford to fly, and they had only $200 between them. "Let's go for it," Miles said, and he started to load the car.

A few minutes later, Teena received a call from Adrienne Tanner, an *Edmonton Journal* reporter. Tanner had driven up to Rycroft a few weeks earlier and knocked on the motel room door. Teena thought the young reporter seemed nice, and decided to talk with her. Tanner and a photographer were going to drive out to Victoria for the decision, and the women arranged to meet in Edmonton at 6:00 the next morning to car-pool to Victoria.

The next hour was frantic as Teena raced around trying to pack up quickly. All her maternity clothes were casual— oversize T-shirts and leggings—so she went to Browns Style Shop, basically the only clothing store in Manning, and bought a magenta dirndl skirt and matching blouse. It was rare for Miles to wear anything other than jeans, and Teena had to go to his parents' house to dig out a pair of dress pants and shoes. There was no time for Miles to get his shoulder-length hair cut, but Teena made sure he packed his shaver. Within an hour they were on the road, the warm night air rushing in the open windows.

But about a half-hour north of Edmonton, the car died on a dark stretch of highway. It was past ten o'clock, and standing outside on the shoulder of the road, Teena was close to tears. They were never going to get there. She waited in the car while Miles walked the couple of miles back to a motel they had passed and called a tow truck, which took them the rest of the way into Edmonton. The tow truck driver offered to buy their car for $800. It wasn't a bad price for a 1985 LeBaron, and they took him up on his offer.

They stayed the night with Miles's brother and were up at dawn to meet with the reporter and photographer. They barely stopped until they were at the ferry terminal in Tsawwassen in time for the last sailing to Victoria. Teena and Miles slept much of the trip or sat huddled under a blanket in the back seat. By midnight on Wednesday night, they'd checked into a motel across the street from the courthouse.

It didn't seem long ago that she had last been there, Teena thought as she and Miles looked at the courthouse from their window. If they got Jordan back tomorrow, they would fly back to Edmonton with the $800 from the sale of the car and pick up a paycheque Miles had waiting. Then they'd buy a car and Teena, Miles and Jordan would all go camping, to get to know each other as a family before heading back to Manning and introducing him to the rest of his relatives. Teena shut the curtain, slipped into bed and tried unsuccessfully to sleep.

Teena and Miles were up early on August 19. A copy of the decision would be at Trudi Brown's office at 10:00 a.m. At 9:00 a.m., they were too restless to stay in the motel, so they walked around Victoria's Government Street, looking in windows. Miles talked Teena into posing for a picture at a photo shop where they dressed up in old-fashioned western gear. He thought it would take her mind off things. Miles wore a cowboy hat and sheriff's badge, while Teena was in an 1880s dress with a full skirt and bustle. A smile is pasted on her face, her eyes remote. Miles half smiles at the camera from under a ridged brow. He is self-conscious in front of a camera, even in costume.

Suddenly realizing that it was almost 10:00, they quickly dressed in their regular outfits and started back towards Brown's office. Standing at a stoplight, Teena grabbed

Miles's arm. The Tearoes stood kitty-corner from them, heading south, while Teena and Miles were heading west. If she got Jordan back, the Tearoes might still be a part of his life, Teena thought, but making polite chitchat on a streetcorner at that particular moment was something she was sure none of them felt up to. Miles blew a plume of smoke from his mouth and stared through it across the street. The Tearoes looked much older than he had expected and, to his eyes, extremely straight. He shifted in his creased dress pants, tightened his arm draped around Teena's shoulders and said, "Don't worry about it. It'll all be over soon."

The light changed, and Jim and Faye crossed in one direction, not knowing Teena and Miles were about thirty feet behind them. Faye held her purse tightly. Like Teena, she too had dressed carefully, wearing a grey-and-peach plaid skirt and peach-coloured blouse with a lace collar, tiny cultured pearl earrings and necklace. The Tearoes turned into a tall building and Teena and Miles continued up the street.

They waited in one of the offices at Horne, Coupar, a well-heeled Victoria law firm with a long history in the city. Trudi Brown talked with them briefly and then left the couple alone. It was five minutes to ten. Teena stared out the window and chewed her thumbnail. It reminded her of the original court case, when she'd stared out the courthouse window during several of the breaks. She was awfully sick of looking at the Parliament Buildings that everyone seemed to want to come to see. They just brought back bad memories. Miles tried to say calming things, and then just sat quietly and snuck a cigarette.

Two blocks away, Jim and Faye Tearoe also sat in a law office, thanking the Lord over and over again for giving them David. Young walked up to the courthouse alone to pick up the decision.

Even Young was surprised at the swarm of press milling around the appeal court registry, waiting for the decision. Although the Tearoe-Sawan case had garnered enough attention on its own, the emotionally charged handing over of

Baby Jessica to her birth-parents, just two weeks earlier, had catapulted adoption to the news forefront. The heart-wrenching picture of the two-and-a-half-year-old girl wailing as she was taken from the only parents she had ever known was splashed on front pages continent-wide. Robby DeBoer fell to the floor weeping as the little girl she'd named Jessica was returned to her birth-parents. Predictions of the irreparable harm done to the little girl by the move were ominous and guaranteed by adoption experts and psychologists.

The timing—two weeks after the appeal arguments and two weeks before the judgment was given—couldn't have been better for the Tearoes' case. The Baby Jessica case illustrated all the fears of what would happen with little David. It would seem difficult indeed, just two weeks after that seemingly traumatic event, to impose the same fate on another child.

At 10:00 a.m., Young stood at the counter in the B.C. Court of Appeal registry. In a strange protocol, appeal court decisions cannot be released until precisely that time, with the first copies going to lawyers for each side and subsequent copies available for the media. The appeal court clerks, Ron Adams and Emily Kukurudziak, were prepared. Photocopies of the decision were stacked in a pile and waiting to be picked up and paid for.

At 10:01 a.m., Young was handed a copy of the nineteen-page decision, as was a clerk from Trudi Brown's office, who hurried out the door. Young ignored the first eighteen pages and flipped to the last sentence.

The door clicking quietly shut startled Teena. She turned to see Trudi standing there, one hand on the doorknob, the other holding the decision. The few seconds of silence seemed forever to Teena, who was afraid to ask.

"I'm sorry, Teena," Brown said matter-of-factly.

"No, no, no," Teena thought as she looked blankly at Trudi, who explained that the judges thought the baby had bonded with the Tearoes and it was too disruptive to move him. In essence, the appeal court had ruled that nurture won over nature. "I'll let you have a chance to read it and then we can talk about it," Brown said, shutting the door behind her.

Teena held the decision on her knees and Miles leaned forward and awkwardly hugged her. He glanced at the papers on Teena's lap, but they made little sense to him. He saw Jean Morgan's name as being the lawyer for the respondent, so that must be Teena. He assumed an appellant was the person who didn't like the first decision. He sat back and let Teena read. She could explain to him what it all meant.

The decision was written by Justice Proudfoot, with Justices Wood and Rowles agreeing. Often, contentious court of appeal decisions are "split," with a dissenting judgment by one of the judges. The relative brevity of the decision was also a surprise. Decisions on much less significant matters with less complicated facts are often much longer. Essentially, the appeal court ruled that the Alberta law giving a birth-mother ten days to revoke her consent had no application in B.C. because the petition for adoption had been filed in B.C., as well as Teena Sawan's counter-petition for his return. Therefore, Teena's revocation attempts were a moot point, in their view. B.C. law applied, they said, and that required that they determine only what was in the best interests of the child. The justices ruled that "common sense" dictated that it would not be in the child's best interests to be removed from a stable home to one that he had never really known. There was no evidence of bonding between Teena Sawan and her son, they said, while there was evidence of bonding between the Tearoes and the boy.

The justices refused to allow the medical evidence. "Much of the evidence was irrelevant and hence inadmissible in any event. I am of the view that the evidence in question does not meet the tests established for the admission of fresh evidence; specifically, that the evidence could not reasonably be expected to affect the outcome of the appeal," read the judgment.

The decision set out the facts of the case in simplified form and reviewed the trial judge's comments about the Tearoes, who were described as "competent, caring, loving proposed adoptive parents." The justices reviewed Teena's life as well, noting that she has had problems in her life, including alcohol, for which she has sought treatment. "Ms. Sawan's mother is native; her father, non-native. Ms. Sawan stated that she wishes to raise her son in her native culture. Recently, she has gained status as a member of the Woodland Cree Band. She has not lived on the reserve for approximately six years. There is evidence that she has an extended family living on the reserve and off the reserve. There is little, if any, evidence of any contact by her with members of her family. Ms. Sawan testified that she planned to return to the band but was uncertain as to when. The Woodland Cree band members speak Cree. She concedes she would have difficulties living on the reserve because she does not know the language. However, the evidence is that there are facilities to assist her in learning Cree.

"Ms. Sawan's future plans are not settled. She wants to complete her education. At present, she is financially supported by social assistance and the Band. Ms. Sawan testified that she has a fiance, who is not a native Indian, and that they plan to marry in July of 1994. Ms. Sawan anticipates that her fiance, who works in the oil fields in northern Alberta, will live on the reserve with her and her child. Ms. Sawan's fiance was not called as a witness.

"At the time of the trial the child was eighteen months old. It can be readily concluded from all the evidence presented that he is a healthy, happy, well-cared for child. He is one-quarter native Indian. As just noted, his mother has placed his name on the list to become a member of the Woodland Cree native Indian band. From the time of the child's birth to February 6, 1992, the child had been in his mother's care, in total for 22 days. The child has been with the appellants continuously since February 6, 1992."

The appeal court agreed with Justice Melvin's finding that Teena had freely and voluntarily signed the consent, that she knew the ramifications of the consent, both legally and emotionally and knew that if she wanted to revoke it, it had to be done in writing within ten days of signing. The appeal court also agreed with Melvin's finding that, according to the law, if a consent is valid in one province, it is valid in another, by reason of section 9 of the B.C. Adoption Act.

"Notwithstanding his conclusion that the consent had been validly executed in Alberta, the trial judge went on to hold that the court, on the basis of equitable principle, could vitiate the written consent by giving effect to the mother's oral revocation. The trial judge stated that if he was wrong in that approach, section 8(7) of the B.C. Adoption Act [the best interests of the child] governed the question of revocation of the consent. Applying section 8(7), he concluded that revocation of the consent the mother had given was in the best interests of the child, with the result that he dismissed the Tearoes' adoption petition and ordered the child returned to the mother."

But, Proudfoot continued: "The trial judge was in error when he took the approach that the orally-communicated revocation vitiated the consent."

Under B.C. law, which the appeal court was applying, there are no safeguards for birth-mothers who may change their mind about giving up their child. The law is that no person who has given their consent to adoption, other than the child to be adopted, may revoke the consent unless it is shown to the court's satisfaction that the revocation is in the best interests of the child.

Therefore, the only test was whether it was in the best interests of the child to be returned to the birth-mother. Melvin had foreseen this and had applied that test, ruling that the child's best interests were indeed served by returning him to his birth-mother. The appeal court justices had applied the same highly subjective test and come up with the opposite conclusion.

The appeal court looked at the same cases that Melvin had considered and arrived at the opposite conclusion. In his decision, Melvin had quoted the No. 030279 B.C. Registration case, as did the B.C. Court of Appeal. The appeal court also quoted from a 1985 Supreme Court of Canada case, *King v.*

Low, in which a twenty-four-year-old woman became pregnant out of wedlock. Fearing her family's judgment, she did not let them know of her pregnancy and gave up the child in a private adoption to friends, so she could still have some contact with the boy. Once the child was born, the woman felt surges of love she had never anticipated and had second thoughts. Thinking the boy could have a better life with the adoptive parents, and fearing her own family's disapproval, she decided to go through with the adoption. But instead of coming to accept the loss of her child, the mother became depressed and longed for her baby. Three months after giving the baby up, she asked for him back. To her surprise, her parents—whom she eventually told—were supportive of her and welcomed the boy as their grandchild. The prospective adoptive parents refused to give him up, and the birthmother began legal actions to revoke her consent to the adoption. The case made its way to the Supreme Court of Canada, which upheld a lower court decision that the adoption go through. That case further clarified how the courts were to define the best interests of the child.

The appeal court cited *Racine v. Woods*, as had Melvin, who had made a point of differentiating the Tearoe-Sawan circumstances, writing, "In my opinion, the connection between the mother and the child has not been irretrievably broken as in Racine." Melvin noted that Teena and her son had been together for a "considerable period of time."

It was on that sentence that the appeal court based their decision to overturn Melvin's decision. To overturn a lower court decision, the appeal court must find a mistake, some Achilles heel, in the first decision.

Wrote Justice Proudfoot: "This child was with his mother, in total, for twenty-two days. The child has been with the Tearoes for over sixteen months when this matter went to trial. On the evidence, the trial judge's conclusion that the child was with his mother for a 'considerable period of time' is plainly in error.

"The trial judge's conclusion that 'the connection between the mother and the child has not been irretrievably broken' is not supported by the evidence. There is no evidence from which to conclude either that a bond between the mother and child had ever been established in the period during which the child was with her, or that if any such bond had been established, it was likely still remaining at the time of trial. Indeed, the evidence establishes beyond doubt that the only mother and father this child knows are Faye and James Tearoe.

"The welfare of the child is the paramount concern. This child presently lives in a loving, stable, comfortable environment, with a family that has looked after all his needs for virtually all his life. By all accounts, the child is thriving. To end that relationship would destroy the family bonds that have been established between the child and the adoptive parents.

"Although she offered no specific plans for the future, it is quite possible that Ms. Sawan could also provide a loving environment in which the child could thrive if he were returned to her. But in the absence of any evidence from which it could reasonably be inferred that there ever was, or now remains, any bond between natural mother and child, or that such a bond could now successfully be established, it is impossible to conclude that the best interests of the child require the consent to adoption to be set aside.

"Furthermore, common sense dictates that to disrupt the child from his present environment, and to put him through the uncertainty associated with an attempt to establish a bond with his natural mother, would cause him considerable trauma. In the absence of evidence from which it could reasonably be inferred that such trauma would be both minimal and fleeting in nature, it is impossible to conclude that the best interests of the child would now be met by setting aside the consent to adoption.

"As in the Racine case, the cultural background and heritage must give way in the circumstances of this case. A difficult choice must be made. The child's best interests must come first. The respondent has not discharged the onus which section 8(7) places on her. It is not in the best interests of this child to revoke Ms. Sawan's consent to adoption.

"The child will remain with James and Faye Tearoe.... The child will assume the name David James Tearoe."

In nineteen pages, a child's life had been decided by three people who had never seen him and whom he would never know.

Teena's tears fell onto the paper in her lap. According to this, Jordan Michael Sawan no longer existed. These judges said she had no bond with her son. How could they know what she felt? She could remember clearly her body swollen with him, his body pushing and tearing through hers as she gave birth. But mostly she remembered loving the wrinkled little baby who was placed in her arms, and her amazement that something so perfect came from her. She also remembered the bewilderment and frustration she felt weeks later when he refused to stop crying, when his gummy mouth stretched open in wailing cries and she felt that she could never do anything right. She knew how hard it had been to make the decision about what to do for her son.

Trudi Brown talked briefly with the reporters packed into Horne, Coupar's tiny conference room and told them that Teena was too upset at that point to talk to them. Perhaps later in the day.

Teena stayed in Trudi's office until the press had cleared out, and then left with Miles and Dan. One cameraman and reporter, who had been waiting in the hallway, got on the elevator with Teena. Dan told the reporter to leave. He refused, saying it was a public elevator. Miles was on the verge of taking a swing and Teena held onto his arm. Eventually, the reporter left, and the trio made their way to a restaurant, where they picked at their lunches.

A few blocks away, signs directed the media to a conference room at Young's office, where rows of chairs were assembled in front of a long table. The Tearoes came down a few minutes later.

Brian Young had begun to detect a shift in public support as the Tearoes' deep-rooted religious beliefs had become

more and more apparent, but he told his clients after the
good news that they could talk as much as they wanted
about God's role in all of this. It seemed safe to let them give
free rein to their faith, which he knew some might view as
fanaticism, now that the case was all over.

The couple started the press conference by publicly thanking Young, who sat several feet to their left. The Tearoes were
jubilant, holding hands and blinking back tears. "We're just
praising God. We're on top of the world!" Jim said. "We want
to praise our heavenly father for answering our prayers, and
the prayers of the people. I think it can quite readily be seen
that God's hand is moved by the prayers of His people.
People from all over the province have been supportive, even
non-Christians."

For the first time, the couple faced pointed questions from
reporters about how they reconciled their Christian beliefs
with the fact that the birth-mother was in pain. The Tearoes
did not at first appear to understand the question, and when
it was rephrased, they still did not answer it directly. Jim said
that the appeal court decision was the right one legally and
morally, in his view, and put forward the comment he attributed to Lynne Smith, which had never been confirmed. "The
human resources lady said to us, 'Jim and Faye, we are so
glad you have come, because if you had not come, we would
have started proceedings to find a new home for David
because of reports we have been getting about parties and
loud music and smoking.' So we felt Teena had a lot of clean-
ing up to do, not that we are judging her."

The Tearoes emphasized that they wanted Teena to be part
of their extended family and visit as much as she wanted.
"Teena has continually been in our prayers," said Faye.
"Teena is a very big part of our life. Our home is open to
Teena anytime she wants. And we will be going to Manning
soon, to meet with the people who prayed for us. My heart
goes out to Teena. It must be very hard on her." Both said they
"absolutely" wanted Teena to play a big part in David's life.

Reporters were faced with the unusual situation of running out of questions before the subjects stopped talking. The

cameramen were packing up and leaving as Jim and Faye continued to talk. Some were heading to the Tearoes' home, where the couple had said media were welcome to meet with David.

An hour later at their home, David held onto Jim's hand as the cameras clicked and didn't seem taken aback by the strangers milling about his back yard. Indeed, the little boy had become as used to people in his house carrying cameras, microphones and notebooks as any nineteen-month-old could be. "We just think this little guy is a gift from God and we want to put all the torture and terror behind us," Jim said, eyes on the boy. "We just want to hug David and love him up."

Jim urged him to play the piano and harmonica, and his eyes rarely left the child. Reporters leaving the house later had a mixed bag of comments, ranging from the Tearoes' apparent love of the child to a remark that Jim seemed "fixated" on the child. "I hope he never disappoints them," said one.

A family law practice seldom requires lawyers to hold press conferences. After August 19, Trudi Brown wasn't that keen on having another. It wasn't that the lawyer was shy—she had never been called that. But the staff at Horne, Coupar were a bit put off by the demanding group of reporters who cruised in that afternoon to meet Teena Sawan. A Toronto reporter who couldn't get a flight out on time had asked the receptionist to put the telephone receiver in the press conference so she could hear it that way. The receptionist obliged, stringing the phone line across the floor. A few female staff found some intrusive camera-people staking out the women's bathroom, hoping to catch Teena Sawan entering or leaving.

Few reporters had seen Teena Sawan in person; they knew her only through the image they had gleaned from the Tearoes' comments and the coverage of the case. The poised woman who walked in and spoke articulately, if dispassionately, about the decision surprised several. Her hair was neatly curled, her face clear and pretty, and she looked younger than twenty. There was no sign of her earlier upset. She had dealt with that in private.

She looked directly into the cameras, Trudi Brown by her side. Asked about her reaction to the decision, Teena said, "I was very disappointed. I was very hurt. I didn't think the outcome would be the way it was. I want to keep contact with my son. I love him very much and I miss him and I wish things could have been different."

She said there were "several things about the decision that really upset me. What upset me most was their comments about the bonding issue. According to what was written, they said there was a lack of bonding with my son. I feel that is false, because I do feel I have bonded with him through pregnancy and after his birth. I carried him for nine months. Even after his birth, I felt a special bonding of a mother and child after the birth. But there's nothing I can do about it right now." Teena questioned how she was supposed to bond with her son when the Tearoes wouldn't give the child back when she asked for him.

It was a nasty Catch-22, Brown said. She added that it was important to clarify two prevalent public misconceptions. "Teena Sawan is not a birth-mother who came out of the woodwork after two years," she said. "She has tried to get her son back since a few days after he left." Brown's second point was that the boy had never been legally adopted by the Tearoes, a fact that seemed to get lost in the emotion of the case.

Teena said she disliked the emphasis put on the boy's colouring by the Tearoes. "It was always said that Jordan is white, with blond hair and fair skin and blue eyes. I think that played a big role in it, and to me, that shouldn't have. He is native. I don't think the colour of his skin and hair should make a difference."

Asked if she has received support, Teena said, "People have called and said they know it's difficult for me. I thank them. That kind of support makes me feel better, like a better person, and what I am doing is not wrong."

She had made no decision yet about appealing the case further. She wanted to talk to Jean Morgan first. For the time being, she simply hoped that she could be part of her son's life, and even come to know him as a friend. "The Tearoes have never once said that I can't have contact with Jordan, with my son."

Chapter 25

There is no legal definition of "open adoption." It is up to the people involved to set the parameters of the agreement, and its success depends on good will and a figurative handshake. The number of adoptions defined as open—where the birth-parent has some level of knowledge or even involvement with the child's well-being—is increasing. Only two percent of women under twenty-five with unplanned pregnancies gave their babies up for adoption in 1992. During the 1980s, the abortion rate for young women fell to thirty-eight percent from forty-nine percent. The number keeping their children rose from forty percent to sixty percent as social supports increased and social stigma declined. A birth-mother may feel more comfortable with giving her child for adoption with the knowledge that she can keep up to date on his or her development via pictures, or even be part of the extended family, as some have arranged. Many sociologists see it as the wave of the future in adoptions, a way for birth-parents to give up their children without the fear of losing track of them forever.

But open adoption is not for everyone. For some adoptive parents, it undermines the idea of permanency. However, a study done by University of Minnesota researchers Hal Grotevant and Ruth McRoy found that after a year or so birth-mothers "were quite happy to withdraw, so much so that the adoptive parents were unready," said Kerry Daly in a May 1994 interview with the *Victoria Times-Colonist*. Daly, co-author of the exhaustive 1993 National Adoption Study for Health and Welfare Canada, said children are quite able to distinguish and manage the two distinct maternal roles.

One of the recommendations of former Alberta children's advocate Bernd Walter, in his extensive study of the Alberta child welfare system, *In Need of Protection: Children and Youth in Alberta*, is for increased openness in adoption. A guarantee of closed adoption in this day and age is preposterous and unrealistic, he said, but he added that there should be some safeguards for protecting the parties from unexpected intrusion by others in open arrangements, and access to counselling on a voluntary basis must be made available to all parties.

Open adoption is a gentleman's agreement of sorts, dependent on the well-intentioned words of people who all want part of a child's heart.

Twenty-four hours after extending a public invitation to Teena Sawan to be part of their family, and saying they wanted the young woman to be part of their and David's life, the Tearoes were saying something different. Faye Tearoe said in an interview the day after the appeal court decision that the Lord would tell them when it was time for Teena to visit, but it likely wouldn't be for some time.

"You put yourself in our position!" Faye said. "If anything, we would have full right to indeed even have hard feelings against her because we're the ones who are in debt here. But we feel the Lord is gonna meet our needs. So we certainly aren't blaming her for that, but at the same time, this has been a real battle and we both need time to breathe. At this point in time, we need a little space between us. I think we've all had enough of this whole situation. I guess we have an open adoption and that means Teena is welcome here any time.... How can I put it? I think at this point in time we've got to cool it. We've gone through a real battle here. But we really don't hold Teena responsible. We feel she was put up to it."

The Tearoes suggested that their Christian spirit allowed them to forgive the young woman their pain. In fact, Jim said, daily prayer for Teena helped them feel "love" for the birth-mother.

"We did have an open adoption, although many people have said we should close the door and never see her again and basically tell her to go jump in the lake.... Suddenly, you do care about her and realize from a spiritual point of view that really, this isn't something from her. It's something from the enemy. The enemy just tries to get in there and bring about turmoil in what has been a very good situation for us and for David too," said Jim. "This is Satan's work.... Teena can have children, probably as many as she reasonably wishes, and we have no opportunity or chance for that."

As for going to Manning—something Faye had told the press they planned to do soon—that too was out of the question a day later. "We wouldn't mind going someday, but I sure won't tell you it will be next year. It costs money and boy, at this point in time, we're gonna pay our debts off," she said.

Money was a worry to the couple. They often mentioned the "Tearoe Trust Fund" (an account set up by friends who solicited donations to help pay the couple's legal bill), which bank the fund was at and how there was not as much in there as they would like. "But praise the Lord, He's going to supply all our needs according to His wishes and glory, so I'm not even gonna look at that. I just know the Lord will pay it," Faye said. "If you look at it not in the Lord's eye, but in a regular eye, Teena has no love in her heart for us. She got her lawyer's fees all paid for. This hasn't cost her anything.... We haven't done anything to hurt her...and yet she has proceeded with this and she didn't do anything for ten months! And again, I just have to think people put her up to this. We do not blame Teena. We do not blame her."

The Tearoes were working on selling their life story and that of their son to a television company. They were quite excited about the prospect of a movie being made, especially since they hoped it would pay at least $10,000.

The couple had grown used to attention from the media and the public, but Faye's parents were a bit taken aback. Once their grandson was settled in, they went home and left Faye and Jim to deal with a 4:00 a.m. television interview, scheduled to accommodate eastern television schedules, and interviews throughout the day. Jim said they were just happy to have survived the "torture and terror" and prayed that other adoptive families would not have to suffer their pain. They hoped their case had shed light on a situation so it would never happen to anyone else. In their interpretation, they had won a big victory for adoptive parents nationwide. (It is unclear what exactly the victory was, in that the case law in Canada, as their lawyer had argued, was already very much on side of adoptive parents keeping children in the face of a biological parent wanting the child's return.)

Both relate anecdotes of being recognized on the street and at the grocery store, little David banging his legs against the shopping cart to get going as people told them they believed the Tearoes were the right ones to keep the child.

While the Tearoes were celebrating, Teena and Miles were getting off the plane at Edmonton Municipal Airport. They were able to get on stand-by out of Victoria the night of the decision. Teena was exhausted, emotionally and physically, and the two couldn't afford to stay any longer in Victoria. The $800 they had got for the car went for the hotel and plane fare. Teena also wanted to talk to Jean, who was still in Edmonton, about what she should do about appealing the decision further.

There were several excellent appeal grounds, Morgan thought, but it was Teena's decision. The young woman was feeling battered. Morgan, for her part, was angered and numbed by the court of appeal result. "They talk about this child as one-quarter native. First, I don't know where they got this from. Teena's mother was status, as was her father. Defining the child by quarters and halves—it is like they were talking about an animal. It is the lack of recognition for the special place native people hold in our society that I found shocking. It was ignored—absolutely ignored." The appeal court had also made themselves expert witnesses in their assessment of what long-term effects removing David from the home could have, thought Morgan. Most upsetting personally was Teena saying quietly to her, "I never thought it would end this way." There were times when it was easy to forget Teena's youth. Despite all of her experiences, she still had a trust that things would work out, that the system that had let her down so many times would right itself.

The only option was to apply for leave to appeal to the Supreme Court of Canada. They had thirty days in which to decide.

The division of blood into halves and quarters was one of the most positive things about the appeal court decision in Jim Tearoe's view. Jim emphasized that the child was "80 percent Scandinavian." At all court levels, the Tearoes maintained that they did not know who the father was, so it is not clear how they could so definitively state the child's ethnic origins. When the child's native background is brought up, Jim says they have "no problem with Teena being half native. We're not ashamed of that at all. She's half native and we're quite happy with that too. It just makes David one quarter native."

Told after the appeal case by a reporter that Teena had said her father is also native, making her wholly native instead of the half that they often talk about, Jim was aghast. "*What?* That's not what was said at the trial." Jim said he would need documentation of that to be sure.

At one point after the decision, Faye commented that it was fortunate David was light-complexioned. "We really are not against natives. We had hoped we could have a native child that was, like, dark. But if [David] had been dark, dear Lord, we'd have lost him long ago. The Lord sure had His hand in that." She laughed. "I guess we just liked the looks of the [native] children. They're so beautiful, with their big brown eyes and lovely coloured skin."

The fact that David looked as if he could be Jim and Faye's natural child was a "bonus," Jim said later. "When we applied for Heidi, we put down we would take a full-blooded native person. There was no race, culture we said no to. It's not a prerequisite. But I think there's something nice when…many people have said that Heidi looks like our natural child, and they have said that about David as well. That's just a bonus. I think that, if for instance, you had a negro, a person of negro background who was very very dark, and with us being very very white, I think it would be one of those things where, every time you see the child, even though you know that child is your son or daughter, I think the cultural background would perhaps ..." Jim struggles to explain. "It would be there. You would just be aware that this child has come from a different cultural background than yourself. I'm not saying that's bad and it's not, but the dream, I think that we all have, is to have children of our own loins. And of course, with that is the assumption that they would look like you. This is really the closest that God can do, if we don't have children of our own loins, is to have children who look like us."

The concept of racism in the world is one Jim Tearoe has turned his mind to. "I try to analyze that and say, why do we have these feelings as a society. I think the one [group of people] that comes to mind most readily and perhaps has been picked on more than any is East Indians. I actually know some East Indians who are very fine people. I think because they are different, not so much in terms of the way they look, but in terms of how they act and react—I think that's where you realize that people from different ethnic backgrounds think so differently. Their values in life are so different you really can't agree with them. Then their values threaten to change the value system that we in this society know. I think that's where we as a society then dislike these people, for the values they are bringing in," he said.

"From a spiritual point of view," he continued, "I do have

a problem with other cultures because I feel they potentially can bring in different religions, which we believe are false religions, which then take away from the quality of life as we know it in Canada. And Canada, contrary to what some people may realize or admit, was founded on Christian principles. In fact, right in the Parliament buildings, it gives the scriptural reference."

Asked if native beliefs subvert Christian principles, Jim says, "I think it's like any ethnic background. There are some very, very fine...it's not the people. It's the cultural background they've been brought up in, you see, that's the problem. Sometimes they are raised very non-Christian and not what we would consider to be norms in our society as far as cultural standards, and so that's the thing that we as a culture, as well as we the Tearoes, are concerned about."

Jim and Faye dismiss comments that they cannot show the part-native child his Cree heritage. They will introduce David to his native heritage, just as they have told Heidi she is of German descent, they said. "He already wears moccasins," Jim says. "Then there's the display at the Royal British Columbia Museum on the second floor. There's all sorts of native things down here. We'll be letting him know, the big canoes and the totem poles and that sort of thing, so he'll understand that these were made by native people and he's got a part of that in him." (The displays at the Royal British Columbia Museum are of the West Coast bands, which have nothing in common with the northern Cree.)

Faye adds that Jim's interest in canoeing is surely a native interest. Said Jim, "More than anything, we want to emphasize that he's Canadian and he's a Tearoe."

Justice Allen Melvin returned from a five-week trip to England just after the appeal court decision was given. The public furor took him by surprise. At the time of his decision, he had known it was emotional for the people involved, but he hadn't foreseen the public reaction. When he checked in at his office, he was startled to find several letters addressed to him personally about the case. Most were critical of his decision, although there were a couple in favour of it.

Justice Melvin never had any second thoughts about his decision. It is not his nature ("I'm not a 'what-if' kind of person," he says), but more importantly, he believed he had made the right decision in the circumstances. As for comments that it was the ham-fisted effort of an old boy trying to prove he could be politically correct, Melvin harrumphs. "Have you ever known me to be politically correct?"

Determining the best interests of a child is not something any judge relishes, Melvin commented. "You just hope that you can find something in the evidence that justifies the conclusion that the best interests are on one side or the other side. You have to find it in the evidence. You can't just be arbitrary. Is a home with a colour TV set or two colour TV sets necessarily better? We want our own children, or our grandchildren, as the case may be, to grow up in a home that has all the financial benefits or material benefits that may be available in our society. But is it necessarily in the best interest of the child to be exposed to that, and not to the natural parent? If it is, maybe the state should investigate all families and decide if it is in the best interest of any child to be with his or her parent. That value judgment can be made in relation to any family, can't it?"

Melvin, who grew up in a typically middle-class home, acknowledges that the best interests of the child is a subjective judgment that each person may approach carrying his or her own baggage. "I think you have to be aware of that potential bias, and I think that you could probably call it a bias. You have to say, 'Okay, I have to look at this with that in mind and I have to decide what I think is correct on the evidence.' You have to try and cut the emotional. Not look at it coldly, I don't mean that, but analytically, I suppose."

Teena Sawan's revocation attempts were crucial to his decision that it was in the child's best interests to return to her and played a far more important role in his decision than culture. "If she had come out of the blue a couple of weeks before the hearing, having not had the revocation conversations and not having had any prior communications, and demanded the child back, I think we have a different case. A completely different case."

As for the "native issue," Melvin said, "There is no doubt that it was argued, and there is some comment in my judgment about heritage. But on the primary issues of revocation of consent, it doesn't matter what particular race she could have been."

Jim Tearoe often wonders about what made Melvin do what he did. "Well, I wonder what Judge Melvin thinks about this," he said with a smile after the appeal court reversed the lower court decision. "I'd be very curious to know."

But for the money worries, the Tearoes decided to put the chaos of the past months behind them. They were quite confident that Teena Sawan would not appeal her case any higher. Even if she did, the appeal court judgment solidified their faith that the Lord had worked His will once, and would do so again.

Dr. Bester, too, was resting relatively easy. As of August, there had been no word from the Alberta College of Physicians and Surgeons.

The Tearoes thought the Lord was looking after everyone.

Arlen Walker wasn't much for reading, but his grandfather's favourite magazine, a right-leaning news magazine, was on the coffee table when Arlen flopped down on the couch. The sixteen-year-old was back for a visit with his dad and grandfather in the summer of 1993, on the farm outside of Fairview. Arlen had been at a group home in Winnipeg for almost a year before that.

News travelled fast in Fairview, and he had soon heard about Teena Sawan being in a big court case. He then heard through the rumour mill that he was named as the father and, at first, he hadn't believed it. But when he opened the magazine and saw an article inside—accompanied by a photograph of the tow-headed tot—he thought he might be. The little boy had bright blond hair, just like his. Arlen's ancestry was Scottish and English, and he had a short, strong build.

Teena was a girl he'd been with a few times, and he thought she was "nice, and a neat housekeeper," but little beyond that. As for the court case, he had no desire to get involved.

At sixteen, Arlen thought of himself as too young to be a dad. But maybe if he was ever through Victoria, he'd look that family up and say hi to the boy.

A framed needlepoint sampler, a gift from a grateful client, sits on the credenza in Trudi Brown's office, underneath a wall filled with diplomas. "Tough times never last—tough women do," it reads.

When someone is going through a divorce or intricate family law matter, Trudi Brown is often recommended as being the best. She is a confident and accomplished lawyer, with a formidable reputation in the legal community.

Asked by a reporter at the press conference how to spell her last name, she quipped, "Brown, no E, with a QC at the end," referring to the Queen's Counsel designation given her in 1987. She has spent the majority of her twenty-year career practising family law, after a few years in the Crown Counsel office and a brief stint doing criminal defence work. "Family stuff started flooding in the door and I found that a lot more satisfying than acting for little punks on their fiftieth break and enter." She is active in the educational side of the legal community, appointed to a litany of boards and committees, including being a bencher on the B.C. Law Society, where she sits on boards determining competency and disciplinary panels for the profession.

Since Brown had quadruple her legal experience, Morgan asked her if she would take over the case should Teena decide to appeal to the Supreme Court of Canada. It would be a first for Brown, who usually advised litigious clients to get on with their lives rather than getting tied up forever in legal arguments. But this case was different. Brown thought the issues that it raised had to be heard. She would be happy to do it, she told Morgan, if and when the occasion arose.

Eight days after the appeal court ruling, Teena made her

decision. "When I got the decision, all I could think was 'Why, why, why?' I read it and I still didn't know why." She had determined a cut-off point after which she thought her son would be too old to be removed from the Tearoes—two and a half. That conclusion was arrived at by gut instinct, from having watched other kids and her own memories of being taken from her mother at the age of four. In September 1993, her son was four months shy of his second birthday. She wanted to appeal.

"I didn't want to give up, not now. Not only because of my own sake, that I believe Jordan should be with me, but because I did what was right.... They told me I had ten days and I phoned and I revoked and I wrote a letter. I phoned the Tearoes. I did everything they asked me to and nothing ever came of it. I wasn't trying to say, by appealing, that 'Hey, I'm native and I deserve the right to have my child with me and I don't want him growing up in a white home.' It wasn't that at all. I'm not racist. I don't think natives are any better than white people, or Japanese or whatever. That's not why I did it. I did it because I love my son, I wanted him back and in order to have him back, this is what I had to do. And I did what I was supposed to."

If the Supreme Court agreed to hear the case, Brown would ask that it be heard on an expedited basis, which meant probably by the early spring.

The Tearoes were livid when they heard of Teena's intentions. "It's very selfish and silly for Teena to do this," Jim said. "This is not in my son's best interests in any way." It was one of those times when they found it difficult to be charitable towards the young woman they felt was destroying their long-prayed-for family, finally glued together by the courts.

Although Brian Young felt for his clients, there was a part of him that was doing professional cartwheels. The Supreme Court of Canada was "The Show," the major league for lawyers. To be thirty-two years old and have a case, a winning case, he hoped, in the Supreme Court of Canada—it was the kind of thing Young liked to think about before falling to sleep at night.

The Tearoes came into the office to discuss the chances of the case actually being heard. The court hears only selected cases, those in which there is believed to be an error in law with national implications. Personally, Young thought the "native issue" would make this case impossible for the Supreme Court to ignore.

Jim sat rigidly in Young's office, talking about money. The couple carefully budgeted Jim's salary of some $50,000 per year plus benefits, along with Faye's earnings from babysitting, to cover their family needs. They were in the process of obtaining a line of credit at the bank to pay the remainder of their bill, which totalled nearly $25,000. The Tearoes did not like owing money and had promptly paid the first part of the bill with their savings. Their home which had almost doubled in value since they bought it in 1988 with a down payment borrowed from Faye's parents, had been remortgaged when they did the extensive renovations upon receiving David. Collecting money was a part of his job that Young despised but one of the pressures of being an associate in a firm, where worth is often determined by monthly billings. He went out on a bit of a limb: if the Supreme Court agreed to hear the case, he wouldn't charge for his time. They would have to pay only for the disbursements, the photocopying and the ancillary fees involved in filing. He didn't think his bosses would like it but he felt compelled to offer. He knew the Tearoes were stretched financially. His Good Samaritan turn went unnoticed, however; the Tearoes hadn't considered that if the case went further, there would be an additional bill.

The Tearoes weren't the only ones with money problems. Teena Sawan, now back at school in Manning, taking grade twelve courses, had applied to legal aid for funding of the appeal. She had been turned down. According to a September 10, 1993, letter written to Jean Morgan, "Generally the committee agreed that this case raises very important questions which should, at some point, be addressed by the Supreme Court of Canada. On the whole, however, the Committee was of the view that on the facts of this case it is unlikely that the Supreme Court of Canada will rule in Ms. Sawan's favour on appeal. Accordingly, I must advise that the Legal Services Society is not prepared to support Ms. Sawan's appeal to the Supreme Court of Canada in this matter."

The letter was forwarded to Trudi Brown, who appealed the decision. The appeal too was turned down.

Going to the Supreme Court of Canada was a costly proposition. Stacks of documents had to be filed, and the photocopying bill alone would be in the thousands of dollars. Brown was prepared to forgo her usual $225-an-hour rate and take the $80 an hour that legal aid would have provided. She advised her associate, Carol Boire, who did much of the research on the appeal, to keep working on the appeal documents. They hoped funding would fall from somewhere.

Brown passed along to Teena several letters and phone messages that had come in from birth-mothers who were supportive of Teena's case. Unlike the letters sent to the Tearoes, which provided names, telephone numbers, occupations and sometimes donations, most of Teena's letters were signed with only a first name, as if there were some stigma to having been a birth-mother who did not or could not keep her child.

Lex Reynolds carefully watched the Tearoe-Sawan case, and the concern he'd had from the beginning spiralled with the appeal court decision.

The thirty-eight-year-old father was one of the last people one would expect to be personally opposed to the appeal court decision. Reynolds had adopted his six-year-old son three years earlier. But the lawyer was concerned with the process by which the adoption had gone forward, and he was recommending that the B.C. Adoptive Parents Association (APA), of which he was president, apply for intervenor status if the further appeal was heard by the

Supreme Court of Canada. "How do you make sure the current knowledge is before the court when they are making decisions of this type of magnitude?" he asked. "... This case cried out for experts. And maybe there weren't the resources to do that. There is a role for us at the APA to make sure up-to-date information about adoption issues is presented."

Reynolds advocates that issues particular to adoptive families be looked at by the court in adoption cases. One of those very real issues is the fact that "by the very nature of being adopted, that child is going to experience a loss.... At some point, David will have to grieve, and in all likelihood, he will feel a sense of abandonment, and that has to be dealt with by being acknowledged as a valid feeling and a valid issue."

Adoptive families are not second-class to their biological counterparts, but they do have different issues to deal with, he said. Society and socialization are geared towards people having biological families, so the issues that are inherent in adoptive families are not addressed.

He subscribes to the theory generated by the "grandfather of adoption studies," David Kirk, who wrote the landmark book *Shared Fate*, published in 1964, as well as *Adopted Kinship*. Kirk pioneered the decline of the "equivalency doctrine"—a doctrine that sought to pretend that adoptive families were identical to biological families. "The nature of your relationship with your adopted child is different than being formed by being part of a biological family, and it is important to mark that out," Reynolds said. "Just as it is important from the time the child is young to lay the foundation for them to understand or connect with the fact that there is another set of people who have a relationship to them, a biological one, and that is okay. They are safe where they are."

Reynolds questioned the absolute weight the appeal court put on the child's bonding with the Tearoes. He disagreed that because David was attached to the Tearoes meant he could not be attached to Teena Sawan. "There is no question that moving him will be immediately traumatic. But if you believe in adoption, that can be worked with and dealt with. Because he has spent time with the Tearoes doesn't mean that he can't go back to his biological mother and develop healthily."

He said the appeal court based its decision on bonding, when there was no evidence of bonding called by the Tearoes. The home-study done by Social Services essentially checks out the surface. "Does the boy say 'Hi Mommy and Daddy?' Does he look healthy, do they keep their house clean?... I'm sorry, that's not strong enough evidence in the circumstances to say that this child is irrevocably bonded and attached to these people. And that is part of what the court made its decision on.... I think they were distracted by the presentation."

The B.C. Court of Appeal decision seemed to say that it didn't matter how you received the child, as long as there was perceived bonding, a premise with which Reynolds disagreed. Adoption has to be built on trust. "People need to trust that adoptions are being done properly, that everything is done willingly and openly. That is in the best interest of everybody in the circumstances. It is situations like this, that aren't based in trust or where something has gone wrong, that create fear and mistrust in the process."

In his view, Teena Sawan did not consent to the adoption. "I know that technically she did, but she did everything possible to revoke. What happened in this case underscores the need for resources being put to use properly. Why didn't Social Services go to her, and find out what her issues were at that moment in time?"

The comments of the boy "not looking native" were disturbing. "I don't care if he looks white, he is part native, and that is part of who he is and that has to be acknowledged. To say, 'You look white,' is starting off from a place of denying the part of him that isn't white. That is not to say that the white part isn't important, but of equal importance is acknowledging the fact that he is mixed race. It is naming things for what they are.... He may get the impression that a part of him is bad."

There should be support and help for the thousands of couples dealing with infertility, he suggested. The report on reproductive technology said there may be as many as 30,000 couples in B.C. with infertility issues, and medical intervention may be successful in 10 percent. "It is really very sad. And there isn't a lot of understanding in our society in a general way for these types of issues. The value that is placed on having children and having babies is very high. Our society is geared toward that as a mark of normalcy."

Reynolds feels it is David's right—not Teena's, not the Tearoes'—to have some connection to his biological roots in the future, should the decision stand. "Adults have to move to the side and look at this child and say, 'We are going to get along in a respectful way for this child, and that is treating the birth-mother with respect,' and vice versa."

The appeal argument had to be filed by November 1. The Tearoes held their breath. Although Jim thought he blocked worry out, his body was telling him something different. A persistent rash had shown up on his face and refused to leave. Faye, too, tried to replace worry with prayer, and for the most part, it worked. But there were times, usually at night, when she couldn't help but cry.

On the morning of November 1, Carol Boire couriered the eleven-page argument to an Ottawa law firm, to be filed with the Supreme Court of Canada by 3:00 p.m. that day.

There was no money, but Trudi Brown hoped that if the Supreme Court decided to hear the case, legal aid would have a change of heart. The $30 filing fee was insignificant. The lawyer had already spent about $12,000 in billable time on the appeal, without receiving a cent. She would file the appeal and see what happened.

Chapter 26

Justice and law are often worlds apart. But it was the law that Trudi Brown had to focus on in her bid to have the Supreme Court of Canada hear the appeal. With luck, the two would coincide.

Lawyers agree that it is often easier to speak for a client on a case when you feel strongly, and Brown certainly did. "I think Teena has been very badly dealt with by the system, and there are issues that need to be looked at by our society as a whole." She considers the medical records "such a blatant example of racial discrimination that I was absolutely horrified. You know it's out there and you sort of talk about people discriminating against natives, but until you see medical records where someone comes in with a cut finger and on the top of the medical records there is the comment, 'Denies drinking today'; when you see comments in there that she had a blighted ovum and had a D and C, and it is called a therapeutic abortion; when you see notations where she is brought into the hospital unconscious and they say 'intoxicated,' and toxicology reports that find nothing but an aspirin in her system and there is no one doing follow-ups—you have to say this is pretty despicable."

Some lawyers suggested that the Supreme Court of Canada would hear the case simply because Teena Sawan was native. Brown replied that there would have been no case if she weren't native. "Let me tell you, if she had been white and called Alberta Social Services three or four times, and they didn't receive a letter, they probably would have phoned her and said, 'Hey, we didn't receive your letter.' Common decency would say when you are expecting a letter and it doesn't show up, you don't cross your fingers and hope you don't see it. That's what makes me angry—this could all have been avoided if Social Services had just done their job a little better, if they hadn't treated this woman so cavalierly. I think the native issue in this case is a small issue. It's a big issue in that I don't think anything in this case would have happened if she hadn't been native, but I don't think it's the main issue we've got at appeal. We've got several points that are all important."

Working evidence of social injustice into appeal grounds is never an easy task. Brown and Carol Boire had to hang their hats on errors in law in the B.C. Court of Appeal judgment, and they found six.

The competing interests of native heritage and bonding created an easily recognizable ground, and one that could conceivably catch the attention of the Supreme Court. Recognition and protection of native heritage is of national importance, the lawyers argued, and the B.C. Court of Appeal erred in finding that bonding outweighed native heritage in the circumstances of the case. The principle of *Racine v. Woods*, Brown argued, as Morgan had at trial, is that cultural heritage is initially most significant, its importance lessening to bonding only with the significant passage of time. That time had not been of such length in the Tearoe-Sawan case as to make the importance of culture secondary. The appeal court's ruling was tantamount to an absolute disregard of the importance of native ancestry. Their finding that there was no evidence of Teena's native heritage disregarded Teena's own evidence, as well as evidence from Donna Ominayak and Dolly LeTendre, outlining her evolving connection to the band, Brown suggested. The court ignored Teena's evidence that culture was important to her and that she had been denied it as a result of growing up in white foster homes. How was Teena Sawan to prove she had a connection to her background when it had been denied her by the white social structure? She is denied it, and then penalized later, by another white social structure, for not having it.

Second, and related to the first ground, was the appeal court's application of *Racine v. Woods*. Did the court err in law by relying on the Supreme Court of Canada's decision in that case as authority for their finding that the importance of native ancestry would be secondary to bonding in circumstances where the child was as young as David/Jordan was? Melvin applied *Racine v. Woods* one way, the appeal court another. "It is of national importance to the protection of not only native culture, but all racial groups, that the Supreme Court of Canada set down the proper interpretation of the Racine case," Brown wrote.

The Racine case was so different from the Tearoe-Sawan case that it is questionable whether it should even have been applied at all, especially when the ages of the children involved was so different, Brown argued. In applying it, the B.C. Court of Appeal did not take into consideration, or even acknowledge, these differences. The appeal court's application of Racine was a misapplication of the principles enunciated by the Supreme Court of Canada, Brown said.

The differences between Racine and the Tearoe-Sawan case are broad, not only factually, but also in the evidence called at trial. In Racine, home-studies were done of both parents, and experts in child bonding were called. Psychological evidence on the effect of moving the child and the effect of growing up native in white society was also presented. The position of the adoptive parents was advanced by testimony that the child's best interests were met by the bonding and security of the established home. The birth-mother's position was bolstered by psychological testimony which indicated the importance of cultural ties, especially during adolescence.

The B.C. Court of Appeal based much of its decision on what they called "common sense," saying it would dictate that moving the child who had been with the Tearoes eighteen months would be too disruptive. The appeal court erred in making this conclusion without expert evidence, Brown said. Can the determination of custody in the context of adoption be based solely on bonding where there is no expert evidence on bonding? Given that the Supreme Court of Canada stated in Racine that cultural heritage is initially the most significant factor, prevailing over bonding in determining the best interests of the child, Brown submitted that the Tearoes needed to demonstrate by expert evidence that the removal of the child from their home would have worse repercussions than denying him his cultural heritage.

As for Teena's revocation of consent, Brown found grounds in law for the possibility that the appeal court had erred. She also had strong moral and ethical arguments as to why it was wrong for Teena's efforts to have been ignored, but they did not qualify as grounds for appeal to the Supreme Court.

There is a conflict of laws when it comes to adoption legislation: each province sets its own legislation, and there is no uniformity. That caught Teena Sawan, and would potentially catch others, in a dangerous Catch-22. The baby was born in Alberta, and Teena Sawan was advised that under Alberta legislation, she had ten days to revoke her consent. However, the child was taken to B.C. and the adoption petition filed in B.C., where there is no revocation period. The appeal court said that B.C. adoption law applied. Everything Teena Sawan had been advised of was moot, because once the child was in B.C., the Alberta law no longer applied. Teena Sawan thought she was acting under the protection of a certain statute, only to find out, at the appeal court level, that she did not have any of those protections at all. In light of the marked differences in provincial adoption laws, the Supreme Court of Canada must lay down a uniform test to be applied by the courts *vis à vis* the revocation of consent, Brown said. As it stands, the legislation under which the consent to adoption is given is not necessarily the same legislation governing the revocation of consent.

Another appeal ground relating to revocation had to do with the length of time the appeal court cited in determining the best interests of the child. The court should have looked at the length of time between Teena giving up her son and the date on which she revoked her consent, Brown said, not the length of time between her giving him up and the actual trial. "At the time [Teena] revoked her consent, it was in the child's best interests that he be returned to his biological mother. The [Tearoes] should not benefit from their refusal to return the child to the applicant," Brown wrote.

One of the strongest appeal grounds was the least emotional. It is a firmly entrenched tenet in law that an appeal court is not to merely substitute its own opinion for that of the trial judge. The appeal court has to show that what the trial judge decided is wrong in law, not simply contrary to what they might have ruled had they been sitting on the case. In overturning Melvin's decision, the appeal court had hung its hat on Melvin's finding that Teena had bonded with the child for a "considerable period of time." Melvin had found that the tie between mother and child had not been "irretrievably broken," as it had been in Racine. As well, Melvin acknowledged that there would be "disruption" in the child's life if he were returned to his birth-mother. So, Brown argued, Melvin had taken into consideration the very things that the appeal court said were in error. The role of the appellate court is to defer to the trial judge, because of the advantages conferred upon the judge in examining and assessing the parties firsthand. Such an advantage is particularly significant where the court's determination rests upon what is in the best interests of the child. Justice Melvin had three days of trial to observe the parties. The appeal court had nothing but paper figures. The appeal court's decision clearly reflected a disregard for the trial judge's role, the lawyer charged.

Reflecting on the appeal petition, Brown felt she had a good case. "They stepped over the boundaries of what an appeal court can do, with very good intentions," Brown said later. "They tried to simplify it down to a best interests argument, and on the way missed a lot of very important factors, such as the revocation period, the number of times Teena tried to get her baby back and the reaction of Social Services and the Tearoes. They didn't look at the actual evidence.... What Melvin saw obviously convinced him that there were reasons to revoke the consent given. The court of appeal reversed that without seeing the parties. They reversed his discretionary opinion, which is the wrong thing for the court of appeal to do."

Brian Young saw himself in the driver's seat: the way to win an appeal, according to legal lore, is to be a respondent. He was a bit surprised by Brown's appeal grounds; he thought she would have emphasized native rights far more than she did.

In his response to Brown's application, Young argued that the "true issue" on the application is whether the case raises questions of such public importance that it be heard by the Supreme Court of Canada. "It is submitted that this case is not of such public importance and is not a case of important issues of law, or of mixed law and fact.... Further, the questions raised are not of such a nature and significance, either legally or socially, that the court ought to grant leave to appeal."

Essentially, Young said everything the appeal court had decided was right, and that Melvin was wrong. On the point of calling expert evidence, it is "within the common experience of the court to recognize bonding as a significant issue," Young said. The onus was on Teena to show that it was in the best interests of the child to revoke her consent. He said the Tearoes should not be blamed for bonding with the child when Teena did not get a lawyer for ten months.

"The issue in this case does not create a contemporary or social issue," Young writes. "Although this has been an emotional matter, the outcome is clearly supported in law at all levels across Canada.... At the time of the placement, the native heritage issue was not significant, or ever a factor to the applicant. The applicant picked the respondents herself and made all of the arrangements herself. She cannot now make the native issue the deciding factor in this case. The facts of this case do not require a revisiting of the law such as discussed in *Racine v. Woods*."

Young once again noted that Teena Sawan had a white boyfriend and did not live at the reserve.

By mid-November, all of the documents were filed. Now it was time to wait. The decision on whether the Supreme Court would hear the appeal could come at any time, and the guesswork began immediately. "By Christmas," Young thought. "We should hear by Christmas." If the Supreme Court was going to hear the appeal, they would give an answer quickly, some lawyers speculated. Oh no, it was the opposite, argued others. Lawyers might have done better to pull out the Ouija board. The Supreme Court of Canada has a heap of cases to pick and choose through, and some cynics suggest the decision on which cases will be heard is dependent on a political and social agenda.

The Supreme Court could dismiss the leave request, which meant the appeal court ruling stood, or agree to hear the appeal. If it heard the appeal, the court could uphold the lower court ruling, dismiss it and institute another, or order a new trial. The latter seemed unlikely. Time was of the essence, and a new trial could take months.

Trudi Brown's battle was in getting the Supreme Court to actually hear the appeal. Once there, she thought, there was a very good chance Teena Sawan would get her son back.

Brown wondered if they would have the nerve to hear it.

As it had been all along, time was on the Tearoes' side. The little boy's upcoming second birthday was important in more ways than the obvious. There was something much more solid about saying the little boy was two years old instead of so many months.

Teena, too, thought about the little boy's birthday. One

afternoon near the end of November, she stood looking at cards at the Manning pharmacy. At her feet were a toy truck, building blocks, scotch tape and wrapping paper. The gift was easy; it was the card that proved difficult. The protocol of how to sign the birthday card escaped her. She wanted to sign it, "To Jordan, love Mom," but his name was now David, and he knew Faye as Mom. She wanted him to know she was thinking of him, but would the Tearoes give him the card if it was signed that way? She could sign it "Love Teena." Would he remember who Teena was? She mulled it over as she read the cards with pictures of boys and puppies on the front. In the end, she left without buying one, rationalizing that David couldn't yet read anyway. She'd count on the Tearoes to find a way to explain to him who the gift was from. It would be fine with her if they told her it was from his friend Teena.

The plastic truck and blocks were sent to Trudi Brown's office and were promptly couriered the two blocks to Brian Young's office with a request that he acknowledge receipt of the package and forward it to the Tearoes.

The hard feelings wrought by the case came to the surface when Teena made plans to make a mid-December visit to the two-year-old. Teena and Miles were to drive down before Christmas, when Miles had time off work. Arrangements were made through the lawyers. Brian Young urged the Tearoes to agree to a visit, advising them in a strongly worded letter that it was the right thing to do in the circumstances. There was no doubt that refusing access would look bad, and Trudi Brown would have no qualms about going to court to ask for visitation if that was required.

Young advised Brown that there would be "no problem" with visiting and that Brown should let them know the dates Teena would be in town. But that soon changed. Within days of the first letter, Young wrote again to say that the Tearoes would permit Teena only one visit, at their home, the time to be set by them. There "must have been some misunderstanding," he wrote. Jim Tearoe said later that Faye was having a difficult time with the prospect of the visit.

Teena and Miles resolved to drive the thousand miles even for the single visit, until her doctor—no longer Dr. Bester—got word of the plans. Teena was just over eight months pregnant, and the doctor didn't think it a good idea to drive such a distance. The visit was called off.

Jim and Faye made a point of having a festive Christmas. There would be no gloom and doom to put a damper on their little man's second Christmas in his home. David was the centre of attention at the family celebration, and at age two, was sometimes as interested in the boxes as the gifts inside. Jim and Faye bought him a little set of plastic tools, because David liked to watch his dad work with his, and lots of books—the tot was fascinated with them. The couple talked brightly of what they would get him the next Christmas, and the one after that.

Teena did not send a Christmas gift; there wasn't money for that, and, given his December birthday, she thought of the previous gifts as combination Christmas-birthday presents. But the lack of a specific Christmas present did not go unnoticed by the Tearoes.

Miles was working on a rig west of Manning and couldn't get home for Christmas. Ralph and Bea Cowie invited Teena over, and she spent much of the day sitting on the couch. The baby was due in a little over a week, and she felt as big as a house. That night, lying alone in bed, she felt the contractions she still remembered from Jordan's birth. Everyone said you forgot the pain of childbirth as soon as it was over, and she had, but the memory sure came back in a hurry.

Miles's sister-in-law Carrie Schoendorfer picked Teena up and took her to the hospital, where they called Miles and told him the labour had started. He'd try and leave right away, he said. The labour continued all of Boxing Day. Carrie stayed with Teena, walking up and down the hall with her until Miles arrived and the labour intensified. After several hours of what seemed, to Teena, like very hard labour, the baby arrived, the same birth-weight as his half-brother Jordan.

That was where the similarities ended. Jordan Michael had had light hair, soft as duck down, at birth; Jared Miles's, was a cap of thick ebony.

On February 6, 1994, the Tearoes celebrated two years of David being with them by going to church, followed by a visit with Jim's brother and his family. It was a typical family Sunday. In some ways, it didn't seem that long ago that they had received the child who completed their family. Jim and Faye could each still clearly remember driving down the snow-covered Fairview street with the precious bundle in the back seat. At other moments, it seemed a lifetime ago. "We told everybody that is has been two years now that we've had him," Jim recalled. "Two years that we've had the pleasure of being with our little man, almost his entire life."

The waiting seemed to go on forever. Teena often found her mind drifting as she rubbed cream on Jared's skin, thinking about when Jordan would be back with her, and their future. "Donna Ominayak tells me I'm really smart, and that maybe we could go to university together. She said the band needs a lawyer, so maybe I could to go school and come back and be that with the band. I want to be something. It'll be hard, to have my kids and go to school, but Donna says I can do it." She also thought of taking a college course to become an addictions counsellor and believed that her background would help her help kids who want to travel the same path she did. Thoughts of returning to the Woodland Cree reserve were down the road, after she figured out what to do with her career. Teena found great strength in the fact that people told her she could be whatever she set her mind to. Internal doubts about herself and feelings of worthlessness were difficult things to fight.

Teena's world is reality-based, and as the second anniversary of Jordan's departure came and went, she couldn't help but think about how she would deal with it if the Supreme Court of Canada decided not to hear her case. She had to believe that she did the best she could.

Chapter 27

The lawyers received two days' notice of the Supreme Court of Canada decision. It would be given at 10:00 a.m., Ottawa time, on February 10, 1994, two years and four days after Jim and Faye Tearoe first left Fairview and drove into the slate-grey sky, the infant in the back seat. Trudi Brown was out of the country so her legal assistant, Marion Dodds, arranged for Jean Morgan to telephone Teena Sawan with the ruling. It seemed fitting that the lawyer who had walked much of the way through the process with Teena Sawan would be with her at the end.

Teena barely slept the night before the decision. Some of the night was spent up with Jared, who had an ear infection that made him fuss. The rest was Teena's nerves.

A province away, Faye too found sleep difficult. A television reporter and cameraman had spent some of the evening with the family, focusing on David as he played with big sister Heidi. The footage would accompany the story for the morning. Either way, it would be poignant—if the Tearoes won, it would show a family together; if they lost the boy, it would be their last time together as a family.

A curled fax message was waiting for Dodds when she

arrived at the office on the morning of February 10. In three words, it was all over: Dismissed with costs.

When the phone rang, Teena was sitting at her formica-topped dining-room table, Jared nestled in her lap. She let it ring a few times, not sure that she wanted to hear the answer. She had grown afraid of the final decision, in case it didn't go the way she hoped. As soon as she heard Morgan's voice, she knew it hadn't.

"I have some bad news, Teena," Morgan said. "I'm sorry, but they're not going to hear the appeal."

Teena was silent a few seconds and then asked why. Morgan told her they hadn't offered any reasons.

Teena hung up and sat with Jared, who already weighed twelve pounds at six weeks of age. He made nursing motions with his mouth. She held him to her breast and cried.

Teena went to school that day, dropping Jared off at Carrie Schoendorfer's on the way. It was easier to fall into routine than fall to pieces. At the break, she grabbed her coat and stood outside on the school steps, the icy metal bar biting into her back as she leaned against it. She stared at the frozen tire tracks in the parking lot, and wondered why. Two classmates asked about the decision. It had been on the news that morning. "That's too bad," they said, butting out their cigarettes in the snow and leaving after Teena didn't respond.

That evening, she watched the television news and saw a newsclip of the Tearoes and her son. Teena couldn't help but feel proud when she looked at his face. He was beautiful. A few minutes later, Miles called from the rig and tried as best he could to comfort her over the telephone. "I don't know how to make it go away," Teena told him. "I don't know how to let it go. And I have to. It's over. It's just over."

A cameraman pulled into the Tearoe driveway before seven o'clock that morning, balancing a take-out coffee in one gloved hand and a camera in the other. Arrangements had been made with the Tearoes to catch their reaction to the Supreme Court of Canada decision on tape. A legal process had created the Tearoe family—would another take it away?

The Tearoes sat in their family room, a camera trained on their faces. Heidi sat in between her mom and dad on the couch, hands clasped in her lap, looking slightly self-conscious. She wore a scarlet sweater and matching ribbon in her pretty, carefully brushed hair. David stood between his father's knees, banging his hands and playing at eating a cracker. Jim was confident the decision would go their way; he looked serene and almost happy, even before the announcement was made. There was no room for doubt in his mind. Faye's eyes were troubled as she watched and waited. She had cried herself to sleep the night before.

The day called for reporters in Ottawa to file reports of the Supreme Court of Canada decision immediately upon its release and have it to the Victoria CHEK newsroom via the wire service in time for their morning newsbreak. Like the rest of the country, Jim and Faye would find out about the decision on the news, before their lawyer arrived at his office to get the paperwork.

As television anchor Lee MacKenzie said, "Good morning," all eyes fixed on the screen. At 7:23 a.m., the words they had been waiting for came. "A long and emotional legal battle for custody of a small boy has come to an end. Formal custody of the child is awarded to Jim and Faye Tearoe. The tug-of-war went all the way to the Supreme Court of Canada, and only a few minutes ago, that court decided it will not hear an appeal by birth-mother Teena Sawan."

"Hallelujah!" Jim cried out, a beaming smile breaking over his face. "Dear, that's it, that's it. It's finally over," he said, turning towards Faye, who clapped her hands. "Thank you Lord. Praise the Lord," she said quietly, leaning forward to touch the cheek of the little boy who was busy jamming a cracker into his mouth. "Did you hear that David?" Jim said. "The fight's over now. This is your home. This is your home now." He tousled the tot's hair and pulled him to his lap in a hug, the boy's moccasined feet in the air.

"To me this is a victory, not only for us but for other potential people who want to adopt children as well, because it really upholds the lower court decision and it says we agree with that. They did not support, again, Judge Melvin's decision," Jim said, getting a last dig in at the trial judge. "That's a big victory for people wanting to adopt children."

David has grown used to the cameras, and the people operating them, some of whom were on a first name basis with his parents. He gazed straight at the camera and smiled as it zeroed in on him. "Pictures?" he said.

"I wasn't the least bit nervous," recalled Jim. "I had absolute faith. It was just a matter of getting it over with and hearing it with my own ears. In some ways, it was anticlimactic for us, even though you just never know these things. We would have been extremely surprised if it had gone any differently. Now I think we can say not only in our own minds, but in the minds of the judiciary, it is over. It's just a feeling of relief, and now I just have to deal with the bills and raise our family.

"We have been concerned about financial implications. That's been the harder of the two. Not so much losing David, or the court decision ruling against, but rather, 'How are we going to pay for all this?'"

Jim also said he had "concerns about the way the system works, where somebody can go right to the very top, right to Ottawa with appeals trying to get a child back."

Reporters asked the Tearoes if they had sympathy for Teena Sawan's pain. They said they did, thanking her for her trust in giving them her child. Jim added, "We don't dislike her. We don't think that she was really looking after the best interest of David, particularly in the latter aspects. We think this was just a lot of foolishness, but apart from that, we can forgive her for the turmoil, for the anxiety and for the high costs that we've had to incur."

A few minutes after the decision, Jim Tearoe kissed his family goodbye and went off to work.

Faye dealt with the media, who were scheduled for half-hour intervals throughout the morning. Faye said it was just coincidence that David wore a handknit Cowichan Indian sweater, a hand-me-down from his big sister.

"We're just overjoyed. We've gone through so much stress. You've no idea the stress that Jim and I have gone through. Finally, we can get on with our life now," Faye said.

The Tearoes were again taking marriage counselling, as they had just before receiving David. Jim was trying to cope with financial pressures, whereas Faye was still working through the emotional upheaval the case had wrought. She hadn't been able to discuss her distress with many people, including her husband. She was looking forward to her life getting back to normal—"if I can remember what that is!"— now that the case was completely over.

The little boy at the heart of this uproar didn't seem outwardly troubled. But one television report noted that the night before the decision was rendered, David too seemed to be "feeling the stress." The on-air report never went into what this was, but the reporter later said that the cameraman had witnessed a scene while packing up his gear to leave. David had begun shaking and crying, and Faye and Jim gathered around him, asking the Lord to rid their son of the devil. It is sometimes necessary, says Jim, to invoke the Lord's name to dismiss Satan. "If Satan is telling David, or us, lies, then we just rebuke him in the name of Jesus and tell him to pick up his weapons and flee, for he has no authority over us because we are children of God."

Why the Supreme Court of Canada refused to hear the Tearoe-Sawan case was the subject of much conjecture. The same day they refused to hear Teena's appeal, they agreed to hear a potpourri of other cases, including one handled by a lawyer from Brian Young's firm, in which a woman infected with the HIV virus through artificial insemination had successfully sued the doctor for neglect, a decision later overturned by the B.C. Court of Appeal. The law firm of McConnan, Bion, O'Connor and Peterson was walking on air that day, with two big victories.

Brian Young maintained that the decision reaffirmed that the best interests of the child were paramount, and showed the court was "not buying into the politically correct theme that legal academics are trying to bring into it," a dismissive comment which steered away from the heart of Melvin's decision—the revocation. Armchair analysts suggested that the Supreme Court was cutting down on the number of cases it heard, and that the case did not fit in with its philosophy. (Neither Young nor Brown knew at that point that the Supreme Court had heard a case with a far different set of facts but with the central issue of best interests of the child on December 7, 1993, and had reserved decision. Later, Brown would surmise that this had a lot to do with why they did not hear Teena Sawan's case. "They already had their 'best interests' case.")

Had the court heard the case, they would have had to face head-on the issue of what to do with the little boy. "I can't really accuse the Supreme Court of copping out," Brown commented, leaving a long pause, "but [this decision] may have been an easier way for them of dealing with the issue."

In the *Vancouver Sun*, guest editorials both supported and opposed the decision. Doreen Stobbe, a mother of biological and adopted children, wrote of adopting a native infant who was left by his young mother in a cold, deserted house on a northern reserve. She wrote: "He is a contributing member of society today not because he can be called native or white. It is because he was given opportunities and advantages to grow and develop into all he could be. He didn't have to use up all his energies just learning how to survive. He was taught self-esteem, given enduring values and encouraged to believe all things are possible. There is nothing racist about a court system, in the case of David Tearoe, deciding that the consistent nurturing care of two committed people offers the best chance for David as well as the native community.... I'm sure that Faye Tearoe and I both thank the women who gave birth to our sons. They could have chosen abortion, and our lives are made richer because they didn't. All those summers ago I was entrusted with a responsibility to raise up a man from this needy little boy. I was given a job to do that the Indian community could not do."

Millie Strom gave up a child when she was fifteen, and wrote of the pressures facing a young, single mother in a society telling her she should give the child up. She also wrote: "Adoption is only a palliative measure against infertility. The adoptive couple have the pleasure of raising someone else's child. But many adoptive parents live in fear of the birth-mother returning, or fear of a future reunion in a closed adoption setting. There are many factors that lead to unplanned pregnancy, but for young pregnant women, there are only three choices: adoption, abortion or single motherhood. Health and Welfare Canada reports that during the 1980s, the percentage of pregnant single women under 25 who chose adoption decreased from 5 percent to 2.2 percent. Those who chose abortion decreased by about 11 percent. The report concludes 14 percent more women chose to become single parents. Increasingly, we cannot look to adoption to answer the nationwide problem of infertility.

"The large majority of infertile people would prefer to have their 'own' babies. Infertility is the first problem. Adoption is a second choice. Greater priority must be given to funding research into the prevention and treatment of infertility. But coming to grips with the problems behind infertility would be a monumental undertaking. It is easier to manufacture acquiescence from young anxious women who face a crisis."

Native groups said it was another decision to subjugate aboriginal rights. Tom Lalonde, of the Louis Riel Metis Association, was quoted the day after the decision. "It's a blatantly racist decision. I think it shows the insensitivity of the court system to aboriginal people in general.... Every child we lose weakens our nation." Florence Hackett, speaking for the Indian Homemakers' Association of B.C., said the courts are particularly racist towards native women: "They don't want to hear the voices of native mothers. We must have a beautiful two-bedroom house with new paint, wall-to-wall carpeting and wonderful curtains. When we don't, they take away our children."

Nelson Mayer shook his head at the notion that little

David would learn about being Cree by seeing displays of the West Coast Indians at the museum. "We all look the same, right?"

Jean Morgan was booked solid in court the rest of the day of the decision, followed by appointments in her office until after six. She was glad to be busy—it helped fend off the wash of sadness at the result of a case she felt had been a legal and ethical tragedy.

Two years after telling the Alberta Department of Family and Social Services that she wanted her son back, Teena Sawan still didn't have him. Her voice had been ignored, and her chances of ever raising that little boy were gone. Morgan hoped Teena Sawan could deal with the sadness of losing her child again. The lawyer had to wonder how much the Tearoes would ever let Teena see her son. "I really hope that the Tearoes see their way to allow Teena to be a part of that little boy's life. I think it is important for her, but it is especially important for him.... I guess I'm hoping that they do the Christian thing."

Faye Tearoe rests easier now. There are still times she wakes in the middle of the night and slips down the hallway to the children's rooms, where life's most precious gifts sleep. She looks in at Heidi, and then stands in the doorway across the hall. The glow from the nightlight in David's room outlines the silk of his cheek and she watches him until she remembers to go back to bed.

Jim sleeps peacefully, and the stubborn facial rash has faded. He often chats to David during his lunchtime telephone calls home. Jim is delighted when, at the end of some talks, the little boy says, "I miss you, Daddy." Before he goes to sleep at night, the tot gives his parents a kiss and has learned to say "I love you."

The little boy at the centre of it all has grown several inches, his baby fat distributing itself on a sturdy body. His wispy hair has turned a deep butter-yellow and is styled in a little boy cut. He can chat up a storm, especially about the different kinds of trucks he likes. Seeing him, it is difficult not to think of the choices already made on his behalf between two lives so different as to be virtually incomparable. He has no idea of the adult dreams he has fulfilled.

Little David will be told all about the fight for him, say the Tearoes. They will explain to him from a young age that he is adopted and what that means, just as they did with Heidi, who was told that her mom was not able to care for her the way she wanted to.

"We'll explain Teena was eighteen, and didn't have a husband at the time she gave him up and was still going to school.... She was a single mother," Jim said. "Secondly, that she was going to school and trying to get her grade twelve. And so she didn't have time to give David the type of quality of life she wanted to give him and she wanted him to have parents as well, and Christian parents. So she did what she thought was best for David, after going through a lot of agonizing. I think it would be honest to say that, in fact, really, the bottom line is she probably didn't want to give him up, but she just felt it was better for him to be in a family environment."

As for explaining why they kept him, when it was clear Teena wanted him back, Jim says, "We'll just have to tell him that at the time, she was having a lot of difficulties in her own personal life and she had given him to us and once we got him we were very reluctant to give him back for two reasons. One, because we were concerned about his safety, his well being. And secondly, from a legal point of view. If we gave him back, his health would be in serious jeopardy because of the lifestyle that Teena was living at that time. We felt he was ours according to the Alberta and B.C. laws. He was ours."

Teena wants to be as big a part of her son's life as the Tearoes and finances will allow, and she is optimistic that the couple will let her see him. She plans to visit her first-born son again before his third birthday. When she does, she will call him David.

One day, when he's old enough, she hopes to give him a scrapbook she has made. In it are mementoes, such as his birth announcement in the *Manning Banner-Post*, a little booklet that was a health record of shots he had received, newspaper articles about the court case and letters of support Teena received from strangers. There are photographs of Teena and her family, and individual pictures of the boy's biological aunts and uncles. Accompanying each is a short biography.

Of Christine, Teena writes, "Christine Amanda Sawan, born May 29, 1967, in Manning. Christine had a baby boy but lost him to adoption. She had another daughter in 1990. My sister Christine, like brother Colin, had a rough childhood. She moved away at 15. I don't know much about her because she moved away years ago and communication has broken down between us."

Beside a picture of a dark man with a wide smile and long black hair, Teena has written: "Colin Noah Sawan. June 29, 1969, in Manning. Your Uncle Colin has a daughter, Chanelle Anne Sawan, born June 30, 1991. Your uncle enjoys sports but unfortunately dropped out of school at the age of 14. He is a member of the Woodland Cree band. He had a rough childhood which led him to the type of life he leads today. Although most of your aunts and uncles have trouble with alcohol, you must remember that each is their own person, and learn to accept them for who they are. Your uncle was excited when he found out I was pregnant with you. He was unable to ever see you because I moved to Manning. Even through all of this, he still cared about you."

"John Henry Sawan, Born September 10, 1975. Not sure where. He has been a foster child from the age of two."

"Grace Sawan. Born March 8, 1978. Your Auntie Grace is in Grade 10 and enjoys sports, and wants to become a dental hygienist. Your Auntie Grace and I have a special relationship, and trust each other with our deepest secrets. She was at the hospital 15 minutes after you were born and then rushed to school to tell everyone you were born."

"Peter Michael Sawan, born August 30, 1979. He is your uncle and is presently living with his foster parents Ellis and

Iris Land. Your uncle is attending Grade 9 at Paul Rowe High School. He enjoys drawing, Ukrainian dancing, crafts and building things with his Lego. The day you were born, he stayed and watched you the whole day at the hospital. He was very excited you were born and was already talking about how he would take you fishing, sledding and teach you to ride a bike. When I brought you home from the hospital, your Uncle Peter came to see you almost every day. You were a very loved nephew from your uncle."

A letter from Teena to her son closes the booklet. It reads:

You, my son, were born at Manning General Hospital on December 3, 1991. Your birth name is Jordan Michael Sawan. You were named for your uncle Peter Michael Sawan. You weighed six pounds, eight ounces. You were 51 centimetres long and were born at 8:15 a.m. You were a very healthy beautiful baby boy. I am Cecilia Augustine Sawan. I am your natural mother and gave birth to you when I was 18 years old. I was born into a full blood Cree family and later on in life, received my status as a treaty Indian. I was born at Cadotte Lake, Alberta on May 28, 1973. You and I are now both members of the Woodland Cree band. My mother, who was full blood Cree, is named Maryann Clara Sawan and stayed in Manning. She tried to raise six children, but eventually, we were all put in separate foster homes at very young ages. She was born June 1, 1950. She later died in 1985 in a car accident. My mother never married but her last boyfriend was Bluford Gardiner, who lived in Manning. He later died from a heart attack. My father, also full-blooded Cree, is named Albert John Auger. He is a member of the Big Stone Cree near Wabasca, Alberta. Besides these details, I know nothing else of my father. I met him for the first time when I was 17 years old. It was the first and last time I saw him.

I am presently living with and am engaged to Miles Schoendorfer from Manning, Alberta. We have been together 14 months and have been engaged for seven of those. We are also expecting a child of our own to be born in January of

1994. Miles was born January 2, 1969 and works as a floor-hand. When I met Miles, I told him about you because I wanted to hide nothing from him. I didn't know how he would react. I thought he would leave me. I guessed for the worst, but that's what I've grown to love about Miles. He is very understanding and very caring. He wants us back together as mother and son and said he would do anything to help. When we got engaged, he told me he wanted to adopt you as his very own, even though he never met or saw you. He wanted to be the father you might never have had. He loves you as his own and always will. When I went to court, Miles came with me for support. We were also hoping to bring you home with us. We together fought for something that is dear to both of us. I didn't fight for you because I wanted to rip you out of the home you were in. I asked for you back one week after you were gone. I have continued to fight since then.

Jordan, my son, I know some of the things you are about to read will hurt you. My intentions are not to hurt you, but I want to be honest and open with you, to share everything with you. I wanted to hide some things from you but I couldn't. You need to know the whole truth, including the bad. I have refused to mention anything about your father only because he didn't care to know who you were or even that you were born. I love you very much, my son. I hope that as you get older, you will be able to understand what has happened.

Love, Mom

Afterword

❖ ❖ ❖

Teena Sawan's lawyers describe what happened as an injustice, in a legal, ethical and moral sense. The Tearoes' lawyer calls it the best possible outcome given the circumstances. The Tearoes say the Lord wants them to parent this child. Teena Sawan says she loves the boy with all her heart. The one thing they all agree on is that it should never happen again to anyone.

Many would say this case should never have come to the courtroom. Had it been dealt with properly by the system, it never would have. But the handling of the case—by Social Services, the court and the public—exposed dangerous weaknesses, and allowed the future of a baby boy to be determined in as public a way as can be imagined.

The systems that are in place to look out for people, especially those with little power in society, should have worked. They didn't. The reasons for that have their beginning decades ago and show that the subtle forces motivating our institutions—our treatment of Canada's native people, our social services agencies, our provincial adoption legislation— haven't changed as much as we like to think they have.

That Teena Sawan is a Cree Indian is integral to understanding this case. As a native person in Canadian society, Teena Sawan has been treated, and her actions interpreted, against a backdrop of decades of paternalism. As her ancestors were before her, she was judged by the white, middle-class world and found wanting.

Years ago, in the northern Alberta interior where Teena's ancestors come from, the Indian registrar, a white civil servant, went in and defined who was an Indian and who wasn't. The registrar did this, history books say, in an arbitrary manner. Some of it was based on the way a person looked or acted, or what the individual registrar's personal definition of an "Indian" was. And so it was, sixty years later, with Teena Sawan. Because she did not live a life that the white world could categorize as Indian, her claim to native culture was given no credence. That her emerging view of culture meant to her a place where she felt accepted, as much as it did learning to dry moose meat or the significance of a tea dance, was acceptable to native people but not to the white world. In the judgment of the white, middle-class system, she was native enough to embody the negative stereotypes attached to being Indian—some of which she admits she lived up to with a vengeance—but she was not "native enough" to be able to put forward in court the idea that she wanted her son to learn the culture that she too was slowly discovering, the culture that she had been denied. Her upbringing was a subtle, 1980s version of what happened in the residential schools; the Cree was bled from her until she became, for all intents and purposes, a white girl.

Cultural issues allowed people to put blinders on. They could dismiss the case as "politically correct" without looking at the facts that were independent of ethnicity—specifically, that everyone knew Teena Sawan wanted her child back within the ten-day time limit. Faith was put in the fact that a slip of paper was not received. That is at the heart of this case.

Power, as defined by culture and socio-economics, played an important role in the Tearoe-Sawan case. Social Services controlled Teena Sawan's life for years. When she tried to exercise some authority by asking for her son's return, she was unsuccessful. In the court system, she had to try to justify why she didn't know her native culture—a culture that had been denied her by the white institutions that looked over her. And the lack of bonding between Teena and her son—a direct result of her child not being returned to her— was used against her. What one power system took away, another penalized her for not having. She did not even have the power to control her own medical records; they too were laid out for the public, by her own doctor.

She was made powerless, in part, because she is native, but perhaps more by the socio-economic class she was in, which may, ironically, be another way of saying the same thing.

A hearing by the Supreme Court of Canada might have gone a long way towards addressing these issues. Half the battle of change is focusing the public spotlight on the problem. Certainly it is not the Supreme Court's duty to right all wrongs done by society, but if justice is not there to protect the rights of those who have no power, who is it there for? By dismissing the appeal, approval is sent to the system that fouled this situation, and a tacit rubber-stamping of attitudes that permeated the case takes place. A dismissal of the appeal is, in effect, approval for it to happen again.

There is no doubt that the Alberta Department of Family and Social Services followed the rule book in dealing with Teena Sawan's revocation. They did nothing more or less than they had to do, as defined by the legislation. But given that the teenager had changed her mind numerous times, it would seem imperative from a moral or ethical standpoint to make some effort to ensure that she was certain.

"To insist on the fact they did not receive [the revocation] in writing is unconscionable," commented former Alberta children's advocate Bernd Walter, now B.C.'s deputy minister of social services. "Knowing the history of child welfare in this country, and in that province, I couldn't in good conscience believe that it was free from cultural issues."

There is no denying that Teena Sawan was well known in a negative way to Social Services. Did that have an effect? If so, would knowledge of Teena Sawan's lifestyle and past give them the moral or ethical justification to simply ignore the cries of a troubled young woman and turn the rule book in her face? Did they simply think it was Teena Sawan flip-flopping again, and she'd just go away?

The argument has been made that Teena Sawan could have "tried harder" to get her son back. But how hard would she have had to try before being deemed good enough to have the child returned? And by whose standards was she being judged? The Tearoes place great importance on a comment that was never corroborated or testified to. They maintain that Lynne Smith told them that, had they not taken the baby on February 6, 1992, he would have been apprehended the next day. If this comment is true, why, only five days before, had the department agreed that the baby go home with Teena, ostensibly for good? Even if the comment were true, it is not up to either Social Services or the Tearoes to play God, as tempting as that might have been in the circumstances. It is not up to them to short-circuit the rules by intimating, "This child was going to be apprehended at some point anyway, so we might as well take him now."

Alberta Social Services have been quiet throughout this case, and their role has been forgotten by many. The Tearoes were left to fight a battle not entirely of their own making. They certainly could have acted on their own, returning the child even when Social Services said they did not have to, but that might be asking the impossible of a couple who believed they had just had fifteen years of prayer answered.

Social Services' inaction wasn't approved of by all of the social workers in the Peace River office, one of whom spoke on condition of anonymity. This social worker suggested that the reason for no direct action being taken to clarify Teena's revocation likely had much to do with Teena's history with the system. "Whatever background you have on somebody is going to impact how you deal with them or interact with them..... Intent to me means a lot more than did she or did she not deliver a registered letter, a chunk of paper to a Social Services office, or whatever the hell it is that they wanted. Efforts should have been made at that time to direct the child back.... The system has let her down. Probably the same result would have come about had it been about 75 percent of the social workers employed. There may be a few more that are a bit more centred upon the people involved, but a lot like to follow the rules of the game, which is how we survive in the system today. There are department lines and there are people lines, and you keep your job if you follow the department lines."

It is a sentiment with which Bernd Walter, who wrote a scathing indictment of the Alberta Department of Family and Social Services, strongly agrees. His 321-page report, *In Need of Protection: Children and Youth in Alberta*, was released in August 1993. The result of eighteen months of study and consultation, the report found the child welfare system "fundamentally flawed." His recommendations for change received worldwide praise. However, changes implemented by the Alberta government ignored his detailed recommendations, and Canada's first child advocate resigned from his post in November 1993. "Everybody can only compromise so much. The point has come where the denial is so deep, the access so limited, obviously I can't help the children of this province. No one is listening," Walter said when resigning.

In the report, he writes of a social services system defined by a defensive, punitive culture that regards even constructive criticism as a threat and affront to its authority. Frontline workers working under "management by fear" are more attuned to jumping the hoops needed to satisfy senior management than looking after client needs. The reason, Walter said, is money. "People are being directed, because of the economic situation and the budget direction in Alberta, to basically keep people from the door and do just the minimum possible."

Asked what should have been done when Teena Sawan phoned with verbal revocation, Walter said, "It sounds to me like they should have treated her like a human being who had some rights—moral, legal and legislative rights—and acted as the keepers and enforcers of that piece of legislation to actualize those rights rather than taking this, 'Let's stay strictly within the bounds' standpoint. This is not just from her point of view, but from the rights of the child. Why do anything that could expose a child to a period of instability of litigation, tussling and wrangling? Let us do what is most likely to come out with a good result, a just result and one that does not risk traumatizing the child."

Upon hearing of Teena Sawan's vacillating, a social worker should have gone to her and talked to her, or asked her to come in, or offered some help. Or better yet, a non-partisan official could have talked to Teena, a representative of the children's advocate office, perhaps.

Certainly, Social Services are an easy target. But they wield an incredible amount of power over people's lives, so shouldn't their actions be held up for inspection? "The atmosphere created for the social worker and the constraints they're under in a business that is highly tricky, highly fluid and very very complex is difficult," Walter commented. "You're dealing with human relationships that are changing minute by minute. And they get so little support. Although they wield this enormous legal power, they are so downtrodden by the system they work in, you almost have to expect them to wield the one area of power they have. So they wield it on the person beneath them, the foster parent, the child or the client. I think it would be something that is very present in hierarchial or even certain racial types of systems where you have the status group above, depressing the ones below because they themselves are so disempowered and oppressed from above, so it translates all the way down the line to ultimately the child."

Further complicating the Tearoe-Sawan case is the fact that each province has its own adoption law. In B.C., there is the Adoption Act. In Alberta, adoption is dealt with under the Child Welfare Act. Every province, from B.C. to Newfoundland, sets its own rules on what constitutes consent, what defines revocation. "Adoption is a highly value-laden and emotional topic," noted Walter. "It is perhaps not surprising that adoption policy and practice are shaped as much by values as they are by research." People who want to adopt often search far and wide for children, so adopting a child from one province to another is not uncommon, but it presents a risk to birth-parent and adoptive parent, and mostly, to the child.

The birth-mother giving up the child should know in advance of giving away her child what her options are, if any. It is also important for adoptive parents to know which rules they are playing by. No adoptive parent takes the responsibility of a new child lightly. There should be some safety measure in place for interjurisdictional cases. If a uniformity of adoption law is not possible, then there should at least be resources so that those advising birth-mothers and adoptive parents can also advise of the law in the province to which the child is going. Informed choice is essential.

At present, counselling in adoption cases is left to the whim of government agencies. But building counselling requirements into adoption legislation from the front end could be a preventative measure. All of the options should be spelled out to a birth-mother, and also to prospective adoptive parents, who are usually on an emotional roller-coaster.

At the heart of this case is a muddy phrase with a meaning so subjective as to be meaningless—"the best interests of the child." Its interpretation depends on who is viewing the facts.

"It's a shell game," Walter said. "It's a very subjective, value-laden, imprecise term that calls for long-term predictive judgment which I don't think we have the tools to make."

Case law tries to define this phrase, and judges down the line take these nebulous guidelines and wrestle them into their own view of the world. But the process by which these standards have come to be in place and how they are interpreted is troubling. Who sets the case law standard of "best interests of the child"? White, middle-class judges. Who interprets the standard? Usually white, always middle-class judges. Of what socio-economic level are prospective adoptive parents? Middle class, and they are usually white. Who are, generally, the people giving children for adoption? Young women who may be white but are rarely middle class. They are usually single, alone, with little money or resources. Inherent in this is a form of classism. What does it say about our society that we automatically assume middle class, with all its trappings, is best?

A more in-depth psychological study of the Tearoes and Teena Sawan would have been helpful for the court. How do judges determine what kind of parent someone will be based on their presentation in the sterile atmosphere of the court? How anyone can determine a person's fitness as a parent is difficult to understand, but surely a study of some type would have been of help, and something beyond the cursory home-study done of the Tearoes by B.C. Social Services. The higher the case went in the court hierarchy, the farther removed it became from the people involved. Melvin, at least, had the benefit of direct observation. The appeal court had paper figurines created by the view of the respective lawyers.

Looking only at superficial evidence of bonding when it comes to determining the best interests of the child is not enough, said Lex Reynolds, Victoria lawyer and president of the B.C. Association of Adoptive Parents. If the B.C. Court of Appeal was going to base its decision on the bonding issue, they needed more evidence of it. "I think the court of appeal was distracted by the presentation. They looked at 'Who is better?' I don't think that they looked at what is going to be necessary for this child to have the healthiest possible adjustment given what has happened to him."

By focusing exclusively on bonding and ignoring the revocation aspect of the case, the appeal court raised a very troubling ethical question: Does it not matter *how* you obtain a child? In its decision, the appeal court did not take this into consideration; they just looked at the result, to define the child's best interests. What happens in this extreme scenario: a young child goes missing. She is found, years later, seemingly happy with another family. Would bonding take precedence? Would she stay with her "new family," no matter what they did to obtain her?

Adoptions have to be completely above board, with a willing birth-mother, if they are to be successful, Reynolds says. "The issue of practice is very important. Adoption has to be built on a fundamental trust and adoptees, birth-parents, and adoptive parents need to know that everything is done willingly.... From a larger public policy perspective, that is important for the trust between the parties who are going to have future adoptions."

Walter added that the "most vocal advocates I've heard about this case and its injustice have been adoptive parents. That's been the surprise. They were concerned that this kind of process mars and discredits the entire adoption process."

And one has to ask whether the interests of the child, as opposed to any of the parents, are properly represented in court. It has been suggested that David should have had his own lawyer, looking out for his specific interests. A child advocate could have ensured that the best information available from a child's perspective about adoption was presented, and perhaps have even found some way to settle the case before it came to court. The child had everyone wanting him, but no one speaking for him. Indeed, it is something that, eleven years later, Sandra Racine still wishes had been done for Leticia, the little girl at the heart of the *Racine v. Woods* case. Sandra Racine said having a separate lawyer for Leticia was suggested during their three-year travail through all levels of court, but never done. She regrets it to this day.

The thirty-seven-year-old nurse laughs bitterly that her family's struggles have become nothing more than textbook law. She finds it difficult to comprehend the logic of applying the legal principle culled from her family's difficulties to those of other families years later. "But that's the legal system, I guess," says the mother, who is told that *Racine v. Woods* is "probably used every day in some court in Canada."

Despite all the lofty legal principles of what was in Leticia's "best interests," the judges had no way of predicting life, Sandra Racine said.

In 1983, the Supreme Court of Canada decided that it was in six-year-old Leticia's best interests that she be adopted by Sandra and Allan Racine, who had raised the Ojibway girl since she was an infant.

Growing up native in white communities was sometimes tough, says Leticia, who remembers being called "nigger" in elementary school. But her adoptive parents always told her about her birth-mother and her family, and that she would someday know them.

At thirteen, Leticia began running away and getting into criminal trouble. She says some of it was "typical adolescence stuff." A bigger factor was Sandra and Allan Racine's divorce, which Leticia found extremely difficult. She remembers, too, waiting for her birth-mother to contact her when she turned thirteen, and nothing happening.

"It wasn't lack of love or abuse or anything that made me do the things I did. I think it was confusion and frustration about who I am, a bit of wondering where I belong. With the family break-up—they were my world, and I didn't know where I was any more."

The Racines voluntarily put Leticia into foster care at age thirteen, and she made contact with Linda Woods when she was fifteen. Leticia jumped in with both feet, wanting to move in with her birth-mother. "I thought she could make everything right. But Linda had her own problems and I had mine and it went terrible."

Leticia met with her birth-mother several more times and tried living with her. "I was heavily into drugs, she was stressed out, I was rebellious. I stole a car and ran away from her, too."

Leticia ended up in juvenile custody, which ironically gave her something she now finds invaluable. It was there that she learned much about native culture. "Native spirituality has helped me a lot. It's me. I understand it, I can relate to it. I feel comfortable with myself when I'm with it."

Sandra Racine said it was difficult for her, being white, to offer "the true understanding of Leticia's native culture and heritage. It's hard for me to offer those opportunities because I don't have an understanding of them. She has tried really hard to pull on her native culture. But up until now, it hasn't been the answer either. She is still looking for answers."

That the case became a "native-white" issue angered Sandra Racine then, and today. "It was politics, from start to finish. The press turned it into a big fight between the natives and the whites, and so did the courts. People were lost in the issue."

In the summer of 1994, seventeen-year-old Leticia was anxiously waiting to get into a rehabilitation centre for juveniles, to help her deal with cocaine addiction. She hopes to rebuild her relationship with the Racines and with her birth-mother.

Sandra Racine knows that some would interpret what happened with Leticia as inevitable. At trial, psychologists for Linda Woods predicted tough times for the little girl in adolescence as she searched for her identity, having grown up native in a white world. But whether it would have been better for Leticia to be with her birth-mother is the question no one knows the answer to. Perhaps the most realistic statement is Leticia's: "Problems happen everywhere you go. I don't know if life would have been any different."

Sandra Racine said her daughter should one day write a story about her experiences. "I think she's waiting until there's a happy ending."

Are interracial adoptions generally successful? The results of a study conducted by a University of Calgary social work professor and published in 1993 are not encouraging. Christopher Bagley studied thirty-seven randomly selected native teenagers adopted by non-native families. All of the teens had full or part native ancestry and were of native appearance. He also studied a group of twenty inter-country adopted children, aged thirteen through seventeen, as well as a control group of native children living with birth-families from which authorities had removed another child.

He concluded that native adoptions into white homes are significantly more likely than any other parenting situations to involve problems and difficulties, and a fifth of the native adoptees had, by the age of fifteen, separated from their adoptive parents. A follow-up of the adoptees two years later indicated that nearly half of the native adoptees, and none of the inter-country adopted group, had separated from parents because of behavioural or emotional problems or parent-child conflict, Bagley wrote.

"Overall, the native adoptees had significantly poorer self-esteem, and were also more than three times as likely than any other group to have problems of serious suicidal ideas or acts of deliberate self-harm. In contrast, the non-adopted native adolescents had adjustment profiles that were not significantly different from those of non-adopted whites."

Native adoptees are usually brought up with a consciousness of themselves as white, he wrote, but increasingly find themselves subject to the stereotyping and rejection experienced by the average native adolescent in urban Canada.

Bagley concluded, "The majority of adoptions of native children by white parents in our survey had experienced difficulties, often profound. It should be added that attempts by some of these white parents to give the child a sense of identity as a native person were not particularly successful—native adolescents with profound identity problems were equally divided in our sample between parents who had ignored identity issues, and those who had tried to emphasize native identity. We draw from these results the conclusion that the extreme marginalization of native people in Canada means that there is little possibility for a native child to adapt successfully in a white family. The few real 'successes' in native-white adoptions in our series occurred in children with mixed ancestry, who were able to pass themselves off as white." He recommended that native children not be adopted outside their communities.

Bagley's report is not without its critics. Elspeth Ross, information co-ordinator for the Adoption Council of Canada and an adoptive mother of three native children, said in an April 1994 interview with *The Globe and Mail* that adoptees' lives are more complex than studies indicate. She said some of the subjects in Bagley's study suffered from fetal alcohol syndrome, which caused behavioural and learning difficulties not related to adoption. And, she said in the interview, the effects of abuse and unresolved questions can be issues for all adoptees, not just native children.

Where David Tearoe fits is open to argument. The Tearoes say that he is "one-quarter native" and emphasize his light colouring, the subtext being that because he does not "look native" he won't be subject to the same problems. Native groups, however, say colour of skin does not determine a child's ethnicity and that to "pass himself off as white" is denying a part of oneself, which cannot be healthy. Evidence on the effect of growing up native or part native in a white world might have been helpful to the court. As it was, the only evidence presented on that subject was the emphasis on David's appearance.

Predicting human behaviour is beyond the realm of science, perhaps even art, and children often seem to confound the predictive powers of the experts. One theory perpetuated throughout the Tearoe-Sawan case was that this little boy could only ever really love one set of people as parents. There was no evidence called as to what the effects are on a child who goes from one loving home to another. Can the child emotionally survive, or even thrive, if love is replaced with love? "It's a question of how it's done," said Walter, who is writing a book trying to define best interests of the child. "The process is as important as the decision. There could be ways of reintroducing that child to life with his birth-mother that could have been done with a minimum of negative impact on the child."

It is a comment with which psychologist Lucy Biven, appointed by the Michigan courts to oversee Baby Jessica's transfer, agrees. The maintenance of a child's emotional health depends on a transitional period where they are allowed to form a close bond with the biological parents before leaving the custodial home. This was done, in the DeBoer-Schmidt case, in six two-hour visits over three weeks, but it could have been done in about ten days, Biven said.

Biven did not know anyone involved in the case until she was appointed to oversee the transfer. Initially, she felt strongly—as psychologists did nationwide—that Jessica would have short- and long-term trauma. But what she witnessed astonished her and flew in the face of generally accepted psychoanalytical thought.

"At no time did she regress. At no time was there an interruption in her maturation. At no time was there any indication that this progress was a brittle imitation of health. To be sure, she missed the DeBoers and she suffered ill effects of the upsetting events surrounding the transfer itself [primarily the media and the upset of the adults], but she never suffered in the ways that theories predicted that she would," said Biven, who has kept in contact with the little girl and the Schmidts. "Now, is it OK to separate a child from her parents? Is there no price to be paid? No. But I am heartened by her adjustment and attachment."

Jessica was at the upper end of the age at which such a transfer can be done—she was two and a half years old. The age of twenty months is not too late for such a transfer, Biven said, if the transition is handled correctly, and the child feels loved and secure in their new home. "We may have a very specific attachment to our children, but they are too immature to know us as well. The passion of their attachment to us is based on their need, not on our characters. So while it is heartbreaking for us as parents to realize that we can be replaced, it is very fortunate for children that they are able to love again."

The DeBoers were devastated at the loss of the girl and campaigned aggressively throughout the court process on the grounds that it was in the child's best interests to stay with them. The DeBoer Committee for Children's Rights has 51 chapters and 2,000 members in 38 states, publishes a newsletter, sponsors a 1-800 number and organizes marches to protest what they view as unjust custody rulings.

Who is really arguing for the rights of the child? Is advocating the child's rights simply a more palatable way for prospective adoptive parents to see their familial dreams fulfilled?

"Adoptive groups all call themselves advocates for children, but they are very clearly, no matter how well motivated and how strongly they feel about doing the right thing by kids, they are really also advocates for concepts like adoption and for themselves," commented Walter. "So their advocacy and their position is not without its 'conflicts of interest.'"

The question often asked over the course of the trial and afterward was: who *should* get the child? The wording of the question is revealing. It wasn't, "Where would the best place be?" but who *should* get him, as if he were a prize going to the most deserving player. And perhaps in some ways he was.

Said Brian Young after the case was over, "In the end, the only people who have done well in this case are the partners in this law firm. Jean Morgan was on legal aid, Trudi Brown didn't get a dime out of it, Teena Sawan doesn't have her child, the Tearoes spent a lot of money and went through a lot of emotional turmoil. Who has won this one?"

One hopes that the acrimony and bitterness of the court case will not spill over to that little boy's development. Will he be happier living a life in a middle-class suburban home, rather than in a small northern Alberta town or on a new reserve? What constitutes a good home? One hopes that he can, in time, have the richness of knowing both his adoptive and biological parents, that he can love and appreciate both for the different things they offer.

In this case, hearts were broken and they never should have been. This child should never have gone through such a crisis, nor should Teena Sawan or the Tearoes. The questions should never have had to be asked.

The case illustrates a breakdown in the system. And when there is a breakdown, it is usually those who can least afford it who pay, and not necessarily financially. Teena Sawan's chances are gone, over now with the Supreme Court of Canada's decision. But it's not over for the next teenager who has misgivings about giving up her child, or for the couple who receive that child. How loud will her voice have to be to be heard? If nowhere in the system is there acknowledgment that something has to be changed, that something went wrong, she might as well scream into the hushed prairie sky.

426

Copyright Acknowledgments